MW00451274

EYE ROLLS & AWE

A NATIONAL PARK ROAD TRIP WITH TEENS

Merry Brennan

Copyright 2020 Merry Brennan
All rights reserved
ISBN: 978-0-9888478-9-7

Cover: A wild burro in South Dakota, photo by Ciarán Brennan
Design assist by Grass Creative (www.grasscreative.com)

In Gratitude

I can't imagine my life, or my country, without our public lands. I applaud everyone whose foresight, passion and commitment gave us these sanctuaries.

Regrettably, though, the story of the U.S. National Parks is like all human history: woven with sorrow. Yosemite, for example, was "discovered" in the mid-1800s when an army battalion attacked an Indian village. A military doctor named the breathtaking California valley for what he believed to be the title of the expelled tribe. Yosemite actually translates as "they are killers." In the east, the government "relocated" rural families from their mountain homes to make way for Shenandoah and the Great Smokies. While this book doesn't delve into the darker side of our national parks, we must never discount the numerous records of displacements and senseless bloodshed.

Yet, we all are immeasurably richer for the preservation of our natural gems. I celebrate all who continue to ensure that these places – which belong to every U.S. citizen – don't become elite private resorts, goldmines for logging and energy industries, or blacktopped strip malls.

On a more personal note, I want to thank my writing pals, Freda Karpf and Pat Heaney, who spurred me on when I felt like calling it quits, helped improve my book, and brought great joy and community into my life during the process. I also owe appreciation to several other colleagues and friends who took time to read early drafts. You know who you are. Your feedback and enthusiasm fueled my motivation.

Finally, of course, is my family. Writing this book allowed me to relive our adventure, warts and all. It also confirmed the impact of our travels on the fantastic adults my three children have become and has deepened the bonds we share. My tribe has rooted for me ever since I mentioned starting the manuscript. They are thrilled to see this published, even if their portrayals at times might embarrass them.

Tom, Ciarán, Aislínn and Sean: thank you! I love you bigger than words.

Contents

Point Lookout, Mesa Verde

INTRODUCTION
WEAVING FAMILY HISTORY

“ *We don't see things as they are, we see them as we are.* ”

Anaïs Nin

When we first got serious about a family road trip to national parks, a few friends called us crazy. Cooped up in a car or campsite with a trio of teens? At the mercy of their adolescent moods? For a whole summer? After I mentioned we were ditching devices, or at least keeping use to a minimum, they were positive we'd lost our marbles. Other pals, though, thought the idea was pretty cool. They just couldn't imagine how we'd pull it off.

This book is for both camps. Without a doubt, planning this kind of togetherness can be daunting. Right off the bat are the two big T's: time and tech. We're harried and distracted; our kids are over-scheduled and constantly connected (just not to us.) Even without these prevailing parameters, we can't ignore the age-old H: hormones. Theirs *and* ours.

Yet I'm not exaggerating when I say carving out an adventure with teens is not only doable, it is transformational: for our kids, for us and for our national treasures.

Decades of research and plain old common sense prove that family travel builds bonds and molds memories. Recent evidence takes the value of shared time to a whole new level. Multiple studies done in the last few years link strong parent-teen relationships to offspring with better social, emotional and academic skills. When we're involved in our kids' lives, even if they bristle at our butting in, they're not only more likely to do well, they're far less inclined to engage in risky behaviors or consider suicide.

Add natural environs to the mix and the benefits are off the charts for us all. The healing power of flora and fauna is now known to make us happier, healthier and more creative. Given the data, it's not a stretch to conclude that sharing experiences with our teens in the great outdoors is clearly a Big Deal. (*See the appendices for more on this research.*)

These outings are also crucial for the future of our public lands. We often forget that our country's 400-plus national parks, monuments and other domains belong to every single American citizen. Today's teens will be tomorrow's guardians. They will protect what they care about most.

Imagine our impact when we help ignite their love affair with nature? No

1

video game or action movie can substitute for the magnificent mystery of exploding geysers, the exhilaration of scaling a mountain or the crazy fun of riding roller-coaster rapids. From Mesa Verde's cliff dwellings to Glacier's mind-boggling ice, our family was continually awed, amused and truly alive. We had snowball fights in July. Soaked in natural hot springs. Celebrated our son's 16th birthday under a full moon. Caves, peaks and remarkable sunsets brought us nearer to nature; hours on the road and around a campfire brought us closer to each other.

For six weeks, across 7,000 miles and through 20 national parks and monuments, we laughed, pouted and learned about each other. Were there sibling spats? Many. Spousal quarrels? Sure. Was it an adjustment to live in small spaces, wear the same clothes and not be able to switch on the TV? Of course. But our bubble of togetherness was precious. With few other diversions, conversation became commonplace. In the see-saw that is adolescence, we witnessed charming moments of childlike relish and impressive displays of maturity.

Now bona fide adults, my progeny agree that our national park odyssey was not an incredible trip, but *the* incredible trip of our shared lives – and one that deeply shaped their individual growth. I personally see it in their continuing enjoyment of outdoor adventure, their advocacy for natural spaces and, most important, their friendship and care with each other. In a million little ways our summer road trip is woven into the fabric of who we are as a family. And I know it will bond our children long after I am gone. I can hear them at summer barbecues or Thanksgiving dinners laughing at my highway freak-out during Ciarán's driving practice or their dad's singing *Bohemian Rhapsody* to scare the bears.

It is my hope that our journey might inspire other families to foster togetherness in the often-independent adolescent years and stir people of all ages to cherish our incredible natural treasures. I realize not everyone desires, or can take, this kind of extended vacation. That's why I pass along *Travel Tips* to help bridge turbulent teen waters even on shorter, easier get-aways. I also include *At-a-Glance* info on the 20 national parks and monuments we visited, as well as ecological, scientific and historical tidbits in numerous boxes.

At its core, this is a story of family, of foibles, of relationship with one another and our remarkable country. Enjoy the ride!

[NOTE: While we chose and love our kids' names, we know they can be tricky to pronounce from written form. Here's a cheat sheet: Ciarán = key + ron; Aislínn = Ash + leen; Sean = Shawn]

Bright Angel Trail, Grand Canyon

Milk from Chickens
by Margaret Hasse

The day my son declared with hammerhead certainty
that milk comes from chickens was the day
I yanked him out of the city
and drove west to farm and prairie land.

Like a nail pried from hard wood, he complained
from the backseat, missing electronic games and TV.
Near the South Dakota border, he saluted
a MacDonald's as we flew by.

In my country, always summer,
it is never too late to find freedom,
to open a screen door to an entire day spent outside,
not missing anything.

I wanted my boy to take a turn lifting barb wire
to slip under and into open fields
keeping an eagle eye out for the crazy bull.
I wanted him to hold a bottle for a lamb

to feel the fierceness of animal hunger,
the suck of an animal mouth.
He needed to sleep out in nights encoded
with urgent messages of fireflies,

to see the bright planets in alignment overhead,
to stand on the graves of his grandparents,
dead so many years before he was born,
and to trace the names etched on granite pillows,
hard as the last sleep.
How else to plant in him the long root of prairie grass,
help him reach water in drought,
know who his family is?

© Margaret Hasse, *Milk and Tides*, Nodin Press, 2008
(used with permission from the poet)

Old Faithful, Yellowstone

Prologue:
THE CRAZY PLAN

" *If future generations are to remember us with gratitude rather than contempt, we must leave them something more than the miracles of technology. We must leave them a glimpse of the world as it was in the beginning, not just after we got through with it.* *"*

President Lyndon B. Johnson

Yellowstone River, Montana

"*Ewwwww!* Sean!" Aislínn leaned as far away from her brother as she could, not easy in the back seat of our SUV. "Did you let one out?"

In milliseconds we all noticed.

"Seaaaaan!" My husband, Tom, doubled down on the accusation.

"I didn't *do* anything," our youngest defended himself.

"Haha. Buffalo scare the crap out of you?" His brother teased, referring to the huge herd of American Bison we just encountered in Yellowstone National Park. He opened his window.

Instead of dissipating, the stench increased. Tom and I realized simultaneously and shouted, "*Close it,* Ciarán!"

Too late. We were nearing Yellowstone's Mud Volcano mecca. If we thought Old Faithful was the be-all in the park's alien landscape, we hadn't yet witnessed the hissing, gurgling, eerie muck of the marvelous mud pots.

Sulfur, the villain behind stinky eggs and intestinal gas, also sculpted this other-worldly wonder. Like flesh-eating bacteria, it fed on the wet earth, creating reeking cauldrons of silica and clay.

By the time we parked and began a half-mile boardwalk loop through the sloshing and belching, we stopped whining about the odor and started wowing over the scenery.

The kids ran to the edge of Dragon's Mouth Spring, a small cave where boiling water rolled in and out like a flashing tongue. Sean retrieved a stick from his pocket, tossed it in and laughed as it moved back and forth beneath him, periodically lost in rhythmic hiccups of steam.

Ciarán raised both arms toward the mist, inclined his neck forward and in his best Voldemort voice snakily snarled, "No essscape onccce you're trapped in thissss."

We all cracked up.

"Who would'a thought mud could be so cool!" Aislínn.

Cool indeed! What a sensory carnival of plopping, crackling sounds; fantastical, rippling shapes; wickedly foul scents; and delightful surprises of color. Some mud pools swirled with pinks, reds and purples, courtesy of iron oxides and related minerals. Others shimmered blue, green and gold, like earthbound aurora borealis', thanks to acid in the mucky water.

"Pretty amazing." Tom chuckled and pointed. "But I'd really hate to get stuck in *that* slime."

One huge bull lay wallowing near the path. Apparently buffalo liked the glop because it deterred biting flies and helped shed their fur. Without warning, my oldest pushed his sister off the low boardwalk toward the dusty snoozer.

"You *kidding* me?!?" I quickly pulled her back.

"Whaaat? He's not even awake." Ciarán shrugged.

I glared at him. All three of my teens burst out laughing.

I huffed away, amusing them even more. But then I turned and smiled. How could I stay annoyed? My trio of teens was having a blast in this strange, breathtaking land. Wasn't that exactly what I hoped for when my daughter and I dreamed up the trip all those months ago?

Blizzard brainstorm

"Mo-om," giggled Aislínn. "It's like a zit attack."

She was right. We could never visit even a tenth of the places we marked with red dots on our gigantic map.

We started that morning after learning school had been canceled for snow. With the blizzard too stormy to venture outdoors, my boys, 12 and 15, hunkered down in some alien PlayStation journey. But my 14-year-old daughter and I decided to concoct a *real* trip. What if we shoved a tent into the trunk of my car, left our Jersey Shore home and stopped at as many national parks as we could?

"Just the *two* of us!" Aislínn side-eyed her brothers. "For the *whole* summer."

"That would be amazing." I was thrilled that my middle child decided to hang out with me, let alone imagine a vacation together. Lately, she preferred hibernating in her bedroom with a book.

I dug out a gigantic old U.S. map. Aislínn found a blank school binder and promptly magic-markered *Cross Country Trip*. Yes, a little far-fetched. But inventing a warm-weather adventure sure seemed like an awesome way to pass a wintry day. Plus, ever since a family get-away to Acadia National Park in Maine years before, we often imagined visiting other national parks.

As I scrolled online for info, she took notes. We oohed. We laughed. We searched some more.

"Yesssss! I want to go to the caves… here… and the hot springs… here … and the canyon … here." She leaned across the map on our living room floor and stuck red dots on parks in Kentucky, Arkansas and Colorado.

"Wait. What about the Everglades? Look how beautiful!" I showed her images on my screen of large reptilian snouts emerging in mangrove-filled waters. I handed her another tiny circle to place on Florida's tip.

She thumbed it on the paper. "In a while, crocodile!"

"You dope." Her younger brother, Sean, looked up from his controller. "There's no crocs in Florida. It's gators."

"OK." She shrugged. "See ya later, alligator!"

In between their galactic battles, the boys had been snorting at us all morning. They figured this idea would soon go the way of the dozen terra cotta planters we ditched after painting just four. Or the purple cloth that remained by the sewing machine long after Aislínn outgrew the dress it was supposed to become. Until she was a teenager and took to retreating behind her closed door, our mother-daughter M.O. used to be over-the-top enthusiasm that soon vanished with her attention.

Only this time it didn't fade.

For weeks when she got home from school, we plunged in and plumped up our plan. My daughter's girly handwriting filled pages with stops for which we ordered what she called "the trip tickers." We could have just downloaded these AAA (Automobile Association of America) TripTiks® of tailor-made maps and tips. But we wanted the free printed versions.

When we were just entertaining ourselves on that snowy Thursday, the research was just plain fun. In the days that followed, I continued to play along with this fantasy trip, relishing shared time with my increasingly distant girl. Like my boys, I, too, waited for her to get bored. But each new trip ticker that arrived in our mailbox fueled her gusto.

About three weeks in, with notes and maps spread on the kitchen table, something shifted in me. I looked across at Aislínn's round, eager face. She definitely had a good head on her shoulders. From short trips we'd taken together to places like Busch Gardens, I knew she was a smart co-pilot and

---

TRAVEL TIP: Planning Support

Dozens of free sites and apps can help you plan your adventure. A good one is TripIt (www. tripit.com), which organizes your master itinerary so you have all the information you need at your fingertips. If you're a member of AAA, you have access to hundreds of free maps, guidebooks and tailored TripTiks®. While we went for hard copies, all AAA resources are available online and through the AAA app.

terrific traveling companion. And I *did* want to see those parks.

I smiled and raised my eyebrows. "Y'know, Bean. I think we really could do this."

As if she had been waiting for this moment, she jumped up from her chair and ran to my side to reassure me. "We can, mom. I *know* we can."

I stood and offered a high five. She met my clap then put her arms around my shoulders. At 14, she already was a couple of inches taller than my 5-foot, 3-inch frame. I leaned in and hugged her back, excitement spiraling between us. Our adventure suddenly turned real.

With the newfound intention, however, our pile of information became pure overload. How did we even start when our public lands included 62 national parks and more than 80 national monuments? Not to mention a bunch of other official "national" places like wildlife refuges, forests, seashores and scenic rivers? The choices were flabbergasting.

The conservationist in me beamed with domestic pride. My inner planning diva, not so much. So we did what any pair of clueless geeks would do. We cannonballed in and followed links to more links, with my teen taking notes in her decorated trip binder.

This was probably not a good idea. Our destination dreams grew with every gorgeous photo and fascinating factoid. We definitely couldn't miss Mammoth Cave, the longest underground system in the world. Or Death Valley, with the most extreme elevations of any park in the continental U.S. And who could skip Crater Lake, the country's deepest?

By the time we were done arranging our red dots on the lower 48, the optics were hilarious.

The map definitely had acne. We already figured we wanted at least two days in each park to hike and explore. At that rate, we'd need years to zigzag to all these places.

We had to get a grip!

Carving an itinerary

Like surgeons during liposuction, we studied the marks on our map and sculpted a fairly oval route from our New Jersey home. We'd cross the southern states to California, head up the Pacific coast, then return through the northern states.

> **NATIONAL TREASURES**
>
> The U.S. is home to an amazing 419 national parks, monuments and protected
> lands that make up the National Park Service system, created on August 25, 1916,
> when President Woodrow Wilson signed the Organic Act:
>
> *"to conserve the scenery and the natural and historic objects and the wild life
> therein and to provide for the enjoyment of the same in such manner and by such
> means as will leave them unimpaired for the enjoyment of future generations."*

How bittersweet to pull off dots that fell outside this initial guideline. When we realized we still had too much planned, it was torture to weed even further. We comforted ourselves by vowing to visit the "discarded" parks one day. Our extreme culling left us with nearly three dozen destinations, still tight for the 10 weeks we allotted. True to the research doyens we were, we took deep breaths and dove further into our pool of information.

We looked up each finalist in Fodor's and Frommer's most recent national park guidebooks. Then we devoured Frommer's *Family Vacations in the National Parks* by Charles Wohlforth. While these are available as e-reads, I loved hunkering down in my comfy chair to dog-ear, highlight and compare attractions and facilities.

We even tailored our map to give us a better visual: green dots for parks, pink dots for monuments and yellow for other enticing lures. Then we started to make the tough choices. To tell you the truth, it came down to eeny-meeny-miny-moe; we eliminated Mt. Rainier and opted for Crater Lake. We bypassed Zion so we could see the dwellings at Mesa Verde.

Hotel respite

Along with narrowing the parks itinerary, we had to find places to stay in between, since some destinations were just too far to reach in a day. AAA's state guidebooks were an easy way to learn about areas we'd be passing through and determine our stop-overs.

Because I'd still have to work, we already decided to stay in cheap hotels on travel nights instead of camping. As a freelance writer with a regular newsletter gig, I needed to conduct online interviews and upload articles on time. Hotels (marked with blue dots on our map) would be my safety net.

TRAVEL TIP: Online Connection

It may seem like wireless and cellular service are everywhere in the U.S. today. Not so. In many valleys, mountaintop lodges and other remote areas, service is spotty at best. If you are telecommuting on your adventure, or a social media junkie, double check that you're staying in a place where connection will be a sure thing.

All the while, my sons snarked and teased. They remained certain that things would go south. One afternoon after Aislínn and I had pretty much mapped things out and were estimating costs on a calculator, Ciarán walked past, wrapping his hands around his neck with gagging sound effects. Right behind him Sean burst into laughter. My daughter shot them the evil eye and a wayward finger.

That night, ready to show our itinerary to her dad, Aislínn cleared the dishes and spread the dotted map. The boys left to do homework. While I explained logistics, she breathlessly interjected trivia about each stop. At last, I looked at my husband, my eyes searching his.

"Don't worry." He smiled broadly. "This sounds great! We'll be fine here. Maybe a little too much take-out. But you guys will have a…"

"Heeeeeeeeeey." Surprised, we turned. Ciarán leaned against the kitchen doorway. "Y'know… that trip sounds, uh, pretty sweet."

"Yeah it *does*, doesn't it?" Aislínn smirked. "What do *you* care?"

"Yeah. Um. Well maybe, uh…" He pulled Sean next to him and ran the words together like an oncoming train. "We-thought-maybe-we-could -come-too."

"Yeah," squeaked Sean.

Everything stopped for a beat. My sons had mocked us so much, it never occurred to me they might be interested. I automatically assumed they'd stay home with their dad. But now they wanted to come? Might we *all* go? Really?

The five of us started chirping at once like crickets at dusk. I sought out my daughter's eyes and lifted my brows questioningly. She nodded.

Expanding the troupe

After a blink of sadness at ditching our *Thelma and Louise* vision of speeding down an open highway, just the two of us, Aislínn and I were thrilled.

When the confetti settled we got busy again, this time with Tom's help. We didn't have to start from scratch, but it did mean some major re-thinking.

Like many teachers in our shore town, Tom worked summers at the beach front. He was able to trade and squeeze every inch of his schedule to come up with six weeks. We had planned 10. So right off the bat, we again had to hatchet our stops. My daughter visibly slumped. But Tom's fresh eyes on our color-coded map ignited another idea.

Dramatically drawing air circles over the left portion of the county, he pointed out that a majority of the national parks are in the American west. Building his case as if he were a seasoned attorney instead of an elementary school band director, he pressed on.

"It'll take weeks," he noted, "just to hit four of the destinations east of the Mississippi. And we'd have to spend lots of boring days driving between them."

"Soooooo, why not fly out to, say, here or here." He zoomed his finger down, touching Colorado and Arizona. "Do a big loop where we hit as many parks as we can in six weeks, then fly back home?"

It's a go!

Aislínn took a little longer to come around than me; she had a hard time giving up Mammoth Cave in Kentucky. But once she did, we fired up again. A few short searches later, I found the best airfares were to Denver. We selected our dates and I booked five round-trip flights.

"WHOOOOO-EEEEEEE." Tom whooped at the top of his lungs, an act usually reserved for Yankee games and youth soccer. The boys ran in from whatever they were doing to join in the noise-making. I happy-danced around the living room. After all our reading and dreaming and making

---

TRAVEL TIP: You Can Get Away!

Like many folks, Tom and I had work, bills to pay and kids committed to sports leagues, music lessons and Junior Lifeguards. Plus, I was a councilwoman on our borough's governing body, which meant I attended several meetings a week. The trick? If you want to travel, there are ways to make it happen. Ask your boss and co-workers (or fellow council people), call the kid's coaches, check websites for home rentals and pet sitters. More than anything else – just put it out there. Verbally spread the word about your trip. I can't tell you how it works, but I've seen it happen again and again: when you express your dreams and needs, solutions often present themselves.

---

lists, that magical mouse click meant we were really truly going!

It also meant we had to hustle into even higher gear. We spread the trusty map again, this time guided by start and end dates. Figuring on two or three nights in each park, we methodically moved our dots into a do-able itinerary with a great mix of national treasures and awesome cities.

By sticking to the west, we actually could include a few parks that got tossed during our earlier slashing. We had a 7,000-mile route. Now, we just had to firm up the specifics.

A dog's tale

We divvied up a to-do list covering everything from booking to barking. Yes, barking as in our dog, my single biggest worry once this became a family trip.

Scout was a big, goofy, neurotic mess of a yellow Lab. He'd had three owners before age two and came to us with a few, let's just say, issues. He didn't listen. He lunged to lick anyone who walked through our front door. But mostly, he craved food. When we weren't looking he regularly broke into our locked refrigerator and devoured whole turkeys, lasagnas and gallons of ice cream. Bolted cabinets did nothing to keep him out of the kitchen garbage. Even a crate couldn't stop our Houdini of hound dogs. Of course we tried whisperers, boot camps, bear-strength pens. Nothing worked. But we loved Scout. And he loved us. As long as we were around. What would happen if we left for a summer?

My first thought was to take him with us. A quick search revealed that most parks on our itinerary didn't allow pets in campsites. Plus it would be pretty tough keeping a 100-pound pooch happy during thousands of miles of driving. (It would be hard enough with my human offspring.)

Boarding Scout also seemed out of the question. Beyond the expense, he'd bark himself (and everyone else) crazy and then bend through steel to escape.

TRAVEL TIP: Pets and Parks

In general, pets are permitted in national parks as long as they're restrained. Some parks, however, don't let pets (other than therapy animals) in certain buildings, campgrounds and trails. Be sure to check each of your destinations for its rules.

Universe provides

At the same time I obsessed over Scout, I had this brainstorm: with everyone coming, we could rent our house to help pay for the trip. We live a few blocks from the beach in a popular Jersey Shore town, so why not?

Tom voiced several reasons against this idea. In no particular order, he didn't want strangers around his stuff, he worried about liability, and he was sure something would get broken. I promised to vet potential tenants, lock our favorite possessions in the attic and seek advice from others in our town who leased their homes each summer. He begrudgingly agreed.

I took photos and listed our home on a couple of sites. I also spread the word verbally. Lots of bites started coming in about the rental, but the dog dilemma? A dead end.

That's when the universe answered. While chatting with the owner of my favorite shop in town, I shared our problem. She perked up.

"Y'know, my in-laws just lost their German shepherd and are really sad. Maybe they'll want to stay in your house and watch Scout. They'd get to see my kids a lot more, plus it'd be nice for them to get away from Brooklyn for the summer." She reached for her phone.

I listened, astonished, as she kept supplying them with more details and getting an eager response. She could have tipped me over with a dandelion. I kept my fingers crossed until our initial meet and greet later that week.

The introduction led to love at first sight, for all of us. Scout wagged so hard he knocked our lamp over. Cathie and Tony just laughed. They brushed away our warnings about his high-spirited pranks and constant need for attention. Within an hour they not only offered to stay at our house, but insisted on paying us despite our protests. The dog-sitting alone, we argued, was worth its weight in relief. We finally conceded to taking half of what we would have gotten in full rental fees.

I began to cry with gratitude. Little could we imagine that Scout would be a different dog when we returned. But more about that later.

Nailing it down

While I handled plans for the home front, Tom took on the heavy lifting for transportation and reservations. Even with all the background info we collected, this was not as seamless as anticipated.

> ### *TRAVEL TIP: Helpful Hints*
> *We learned a few things the hard way:*
> - **There's no one-stop shopping for park stays.**
> *The National Park Service is making great strides with www.recreation.gov, which theoretically lets you build a trip and links you to reservation services at each park. The system works best for single park visits; booking multiple destinations can take more work. You may be directed to various third-party vendors.*
> - **Do your homework before you book.**
> *Some parks – especially popular ones – have more sleeping options than a small city. Luxury lodges. Condo-like cottages. Bare-bones cabins. And, of course, camping. The rates vary widely, from less than $30/night for a campsite to more than $500/night for a deluxe private-bath room with a view. Be aware that a lodge or cabin in Glacier may be quite different than a lodge or cabin in the Cascades. It pays to be a Google geek when it comes to a good night's sleep. We based our campsite reservations on a few druthers: Good view? Not too far (or too close) to bathrooms? Cooking allowed? Near hiking trails? Our choices were part educated guess, part luck.*
> - **Popular parks sell out fast.**
> *Many parks have a "first-come, first-served" policy for accommodations, meaning you don't need a reservation. Don't take that chance, unless you're traveling off-the-beaten-path or off-season. Most parks let you book six months in advance; a few offer a 13-month window. Some stellar places, like Phantom Ranch at the bottom of Grand Canyon, fill the day reservations open. It was March when we reserved campsites for July and August, and were already too late for the Grand Canyon. (We opted for a basic lodge instead.) If you're traveling during peak season and have your heart set on particular lodging, be sure to book early.*

It took a combination of online booking and direct phone calls to finally nail down our national park stays. Tom made hotel reservations for our in-between nights the same way. Using Aislínn's notes and some additional online searching, he compared possibilities near the cities and towns we'd pass through and picked what he thought would work best. Our primary consideration was cost. We did wind up switching one motel, but mostly we landed in charming, inexpensive gems. As a treat, Tom also got tickets for two major league baseball games. Once we had mapped out our route, adding in these perks was easy.

Trip "bible"

Even though it's simple to organize documents online, which we did,

Tom also printed our reservations and stored them chronologically in a binder, along with maps and directions for each leg of the trip. Then I created a calendar outline for the front. This simple cover sheet listed our itinerary, travel times and basic reservation details like addresses and confirmation numbers.

Yes, perhaps overly thorough, but we constantly referred to this makeshift trip bible, especially in places without cell service. Plus it was a quick way for the kids to be involved and see where we were going each day.

SUN	MON	TUE
27 Cranbrook, BC 5 hours St. Mary's Campgrd Conf# 2-2103386 $69	28 Glacier MT	29 Glacier MT
Glacier MT 3 Yellowstone WY	Glacier MT 4 Yellowstone WY 2 hrs Carter Mt. Motel $92 – Lynn (hus NJ) 1701 Central Ave. 307-587-4295 Conf Fran286589	Glacier MT 5 Cody WY 3.5 hrs Alamo Motel – 113.30 1326 N Main St. (307) 672-2455 E921770221BRE-379.

Wheel predicament

It took some consideration to decide what to drive those 7,000 miles on our circular route from Denver. We checked rental options for RVs, trailers and all kinds of SUVs. Then we weighed the pros and cons.

An RV had the highest rental cost but would certainly cut down on hotel stays. All the parks on our list offered trailer campsites, yet maneuvering in cities would be harder (picture parking on the hills of San Francisco.)

A motor home would certainly feel more like, well, a home for all that time on the road. And it would give the kids more space while we were in transit. Still, some highlights on our bucket list could only be accessed on roads that prohibited RVs and trailers.

The choice was difficult, but we finally opted for an SUV. We wound up renting a Chevy Suburban. For us, seeing those remote "no RVs allowed" places won out.

TRAVEL TIP: Share Your Itinerary

Common sense, sure. Yet there are far too many awful tales of people on the home front not being able to contact traveling pals and relatives in an emergency. Cell phones and social media don't always ensure connection. Leave an electronic or print copy of your itinerary with at least one family member or friend.

Gas pains

When Aislínn and I first dreamed up this adventure, gas was barely two dollars a gallon. The next month it crept to three dollars and I shuddered at the thought of heading cross-country in my small hatchback. By the time we were ready to book a 12-miles-per-gallon Chevy Suburban, fuel closed in on four bucks.

We almost ditched the dream entirely. No kidding. Tom and I sat at the kitchen table, staring at the math.

"I don't know." I gritted my teeth. "You're not working your full summer. And I can't do as much from the road."

The cash from our house-sitters would help cover our mortgage, but we still had other bills.

"Now we're talking fifteen hundred more in gas," I lamented.

Tom nodded. "Yeah. It's a tough one."

We went back and forth for the next hour, crunching numbers, trying to cut costs. Cheaper hotels? Different SUV? Nothing seemed realistic.

Then Tom, who couldn't leave a convenience store without a Snickers bar or diet Dr. Pepper, suggested, "How 'bout we make a rule that we don't buy any snacks anywhere?"

I practically spit out my mouthful of tea. "Yeah. *Great* idea."

He laughed, his blue eyes sparkling. "Mer. We're pulling at straws here. This is a once-in-a-lifetime family adventure. You know we gotta go."

The corners of my mouth slipped upwards. "Yep."

"No matter what," decreed Tom. "It's only money."

He ripped our calculation sheet into little pieces and threw them in the air. "I think we should call it the *We Don't Care What Gas Costs* trip."

And that's exactly what we did, marking the name front and center on our trip binder. Good thing, too, because by the time we got to northern California, we paid well over five dollars a gallon.

Bum slide

Five weeks before leaving, we nearly got sidelined by another curve ball. Aislínn slid into third base during a nail-biter of a softball game. She was safe, but could barely get up. The foot-first dash jammed her ankle so badly that the doctor said she had to stay off it for weeks.

"How many weeks?" I told him about our trip. "Will she be able to hike?"
"Probably." The doctor shrugged. "Kids heal quickly."

For the next few days, Tom and I again debated whether to cancel. Aislínn, hobbling in her air boot, insisted we still go. After two weeks she purposely walked without the brace, doing her best to hide a grimace. By the end of school she thankfully felt better. The ankle, though, remained a thorn – and Aislínn's go-to excuse – the entire vacation.

Packing prowess

We started pulling things together three weeks out from departure day. Guided by Fodor's and Frommer's books, we came up with our own list of what to bring. We even followed a suggestion to ship some camping items ahead of time so they'd be waiting for us at our first hotel. This made it possible to fit everything else in our checked luggage without any added fees or concerns.

Since we'd be doing laundry as we traveled, we limited our clothing to what we'd need for a week (give or take): seven pairs of underwear and socks, one pants, two shorts, four t-shirts, a long-sleeved shirt and our sleepwear of choice. We also brought rain gear, a warm fleece, hiking boots, sneakers and a hat. Aislínn and I each packed regular and sports bras and sandals. We could have shared personal care products, like a big toothpaste or shampoo, but we opted to each bring travel sizes. This definitely prevented squabbles.

Other important packables included our 35 mm camera, our first-aid kit and books on the kids' summer reading list.

TRAVEL TIP: Consider Shipping

If your journey includes flying, double check your airline's baggage limitations. We shipped a box of heavier, more solid equipment (stove, coffee pot, pans) to our Denver hotel. Everything else went into our checked luggage, letting us stay within our one-item-per-person limit without paying overage fees, which would have been far more than the cost of shipping the box. Our family of five used three soft-sided suitcases, stuffing our sleeping bags, tarps, and clothes. We also filled one hard-sided cooler and one milk crate with camping supplies wrapped in towels. We secured the tops of both with duct tape. The cooler would be our "refrigerator" throughout the trip, and the crate would store our paper goods and cooking tools. They went through the baggage check just fine.

Banishing tech (and angst)

One thing we didn't let the kids bring? Any devices except their phones and iPods. Plus, we told them we'd be limiting online time; that we'd *all* be switching to airplane mode for most of the trip.

Crazy, I know. But we wanted our children to stare out the window at our great country, not at screens. With their excitement so high about the trip, my trio barely griped about our anti-tech rules, at least not then.

As the blast-off got closer, though, anxiety sabotaged my anticipation. It didn't help that a couple of close friends kept telling me I was nuts to take three teens away for the summer. (Okay, Sean was 12; not numerically a teen, but he sure thought he was, and even government data classifies adolescents as 12 to 19 years.)

One gal pal uttered the words "camping trip" like an infectious disease. The other suggested Disney. They double-teamed me about the volatile emotions of adolescents. Their nay-saying did a number on my head.

At night I tossed and turned. What if the kids *were* miserable without their devices and friends? How would they sit in a back seat for hours when they fought over who was in the middle on a 10-minute drive? What if their hormones erupted more often than Old Faithful?

For days, the doubts danced around like gnats at dusk. Mostly, I swatted them away.

TRAVEL TIP: Ixnay on the Internet-tay

Trust me on this one. Set limits on device use – especially your own. Minimize online connections and you'll definitely maximize natural ones. Perhaps, set a little downtime each day to binge, and then turn everything off except your camera. (Service is spotty in many parks, so this also avoids the frustration of trying to post live pix and videos.) We had our share of device battles. But all three of my children will vouch for the fact that our decree made a huge difference. Their presence and focus heightened greatly without electronic distractions.

Peanut poker in Yellowstone

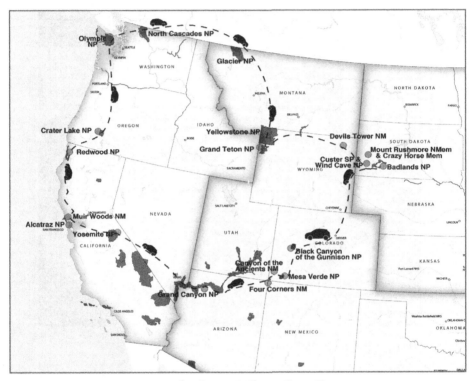

Our *We Don't Care What Gas Costs* Adventure:

- ★ 7,000 miles
- ★ 10 states
- ★ 20 national treasures
- ★ Countless memories

THE ADVENTURE

" *Nature's peace will flow into you as sunshine flows into trees. The winds will blow their own freshness into you, and the storms their energy, while cares will drop off like autumn leaves.* "

John Muir, the Father of our National Parks

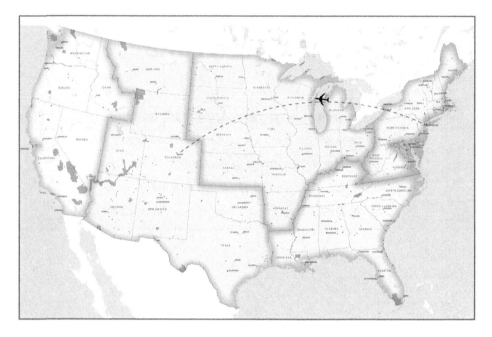

New Jersey to Denver, CO

Chapter 1
We're Off!

Any last day of school would've revved up my kids. Add the anticipation of a colossal adventure and our house was like a convention of eels. Their energy could have powered a small planet.

Of course, each child displayed their enthusiasm differently. Our firstborn, Ciarán, became highly animated whenever he got excited. Okay. Whenever he was awake. By the time we got to Newark Airport, he was off the charts. He dub-stepped across the terminal, making chipmunk cheeks with gulps of soda, wiggling and poking without a care. His antics kept his two siblings, and many other waiting travelers, entertained.

I could understand his animation. I felt like twirling myself. My family hadn't flown since my youngest was in a stroller and now my kids were teens. Here we were, about to leave for the summer on a journey that would take us through 10 states to 20 national parks and monuments. Who wouldn't be excited?

But once my trio got seated on our Boeing 737 in a row across from me and their dad, my daughter no longer appreciated her brother's conduct. Before we even reached the end of the runway, Aislínn issued a loud, "Cut it *out*, Ciarán."

Tom and I could ignore the dynamics of our brood. But heads turned. So my husband quickly unbuckled his seatbelt and switched with her. The boys quieted for a few minutes, until Ciarán snuck a jab to Sean's ribs. My youngest giggled and retaliated with a sideways kick. Soon they were in full tussle across their shared armrest.

"Knock it off," hissed Tom. They shot straight up, backs stiff, eyes forward, hands in laps. Sean tried to hold his breath behind tight lips to complete the rigid pose, but spit it out in a big *pppppppptttt*. Ciarán laughed and landed a stealth prod. He got a quick shoulder bash in return.

Tom desperately looked across at me. I shrugged and mouthed, "They're just nervous." Thankfully they soon hunkered down for the in-flight movie.

On the ground in Denver, they amped up again. My husband no sooner loaded our last piece of luggage on an overstuffed cart when Ciarán leapt onto its rear bar and pushed off like on a skateboard. The top bag tumbled off the mountain and landed on the floor with a thwump.

The giggling boys picked it up and attempted to balance it again, snorting even harder when it slid. Tom grabbed the suitcase and shoved it at Ciarán.

"Now carry it."

"And *you* help me push," he ordered Sean.

They steered the wobbling mass to the car rental counter, making faces at each other. When the rep pointed to sliding glass doors and said, "Across the lot to space 46. Keys are in the car," the boys took off.

"WHERE DO YOU THINK YOU'RE GOING?" Tom glared after them. They sheepishly returned to help with the cart. But as soon as Ciarán spied the golden Chevy Suburban, he rushed ahead, dropped the suitcase and swung open the back door. He swan dove in, arms wide.

We had researched several options for our road trip, but finally decided that a large SUV would give us room while still allowing us to travel to places that prohibited RV's.

"It's like a couch!" Ciarán bounced onto his backside and sprawled across the seat.

Aislínn scrambled to the opposite door, sinking into the tan upholstery. "Oh my god, it is!"

And thus our ride was christened. For the rest of the trip, we simply called it "The Couch."

Sean joined them, forced into the middle by his older sister. Like pups marking turf, they jostled to lay claim to seat pockets and floor space. Hands frantically unloaded books, headphones and other treasures from their backpacks.

I leaned into Aislínn's window and saw her pull out four thick paperbacks from AAA. "You brought the guidebooks? I thought we were just going to use the notebook."

I was carrying the "trip bible" binder we created for our reservations, maps and notes about each planned stop.

"Never know if we'll need 'em," she sing-songed.

"Didn't that make your backpack heavy?"

She shrugged and continued pulling things out. Three novels from her summer reading list. A fat vampire trilogy. Crossword puzzles. Binoculars. Pens.

It was like watching a magician. I laughed. "How much do you have in there?"

"I dunno." She looked up, smiled, then carried on her excavation.

I walked around and climbed into the front to do my own nesting. I found perfect cubbies for our trip binder, my tea mug, tissues, pocketbook. Then I turned my attention to programming the Sirius XM.

We knew better than to help load the cargo. Tom was a self-proclaimed spatial relations expert. He hated being challenged, assisted or even watched. So we gave him wide berth with the baggage and had a ball settling in.

TRAVEL TIP: Food Figuring

If camping, purchase your staples and non-perishables (paper goods, condiments, pasta, cereal, biodegradable detergent, s'mores fixins, etc.) in cities or large towns. Most national parks and smaller burgs have markets, but they're more expensive with less selection. Always grab a lot of ice to ensure your refrigerator (aka your cooler) stays chilled.

Stocking up

At our Denver motel, the manager directed Tom to a back room that had the packages we pre-mailed to save on baggage costs. Shipping our camp stove, coffee pot, pans and a few other heavier items turned out to be much cheaper than paying to fly them. It's not that I thought they wouldn't be there, but I let out a sigh of relief when I actually saw the boxes.

Tom ripped open the cardboard and finished arranging The Couch. Then we found a local supermarket. The kids immediately scrambled, searching for treats. They located Tom and me in the canned goods aisle and dumped their stash in our cart.

"Whaaaa?" I took in the mound of chips, chocolate, candy, cookies, crackers and soda cans. I shook my head. "No way."

Tom puppy-dog smiled at me. "Well, we could use *some* snacks."

"Oh, really." I put my hands on my hips. "This from the man who suggested saving money by eliminating his daily fix of Snickers bars?"

"Well…" He grabbed my hand.

"Told ya." Sean elbowed his sister. They certainly knew their dad's sweet tooth.

"I mean it." I pulled my palm away. "We are not getting all this crap."

"Mo-om. C'mon. We're on va-ca-tion!" Aislínn stared me down.

"Yeah. It's supposed to be *fun*." Ciarán shoved the cart.

I frowned.

Tom put his arm around my shoulders. "How 'bout everyone picks two things. That should be good for a while."

I exhaled loudly. "Okay. Just two and put the rest away. I'm grabbing the plates and napkins."

When I returned, I eyeballed the wagon. Half the pile was gone, but it still looked like more than we bargained for. I glowered at Tom.

He grinned sheepishly. "Well maybe I added a coupla things, too."

This first big shopping stop netted us the non-perishables for our trip. We'd restock meats, milk and other fresh food along the way. Our plan was

---

TRAVEL TIP: Altitude Adjustment

If you're traveling from lower elevations, take simple precautions to avoid altitude sickness when arriving in places above 5,000 feet. The higher it is, the thinner and dryer the air becomes. That means your heart has to work harder because there's less oxygen, you dehydrate easier because there's less moisture and you burn easier because sun rays are stronger. To adjust to higher altitudes:

- *give yourself a day or two to relax before getting active or increasing elevation.*
- *drink plenty of water before and during your trip.*
- *always use sunscreen.*

Even if you think you're acclimated, check in with your group on steep ascents. Symptoms include headache, fatigue and nausea; in some circumstances, altitude illness can be life threatening. If unsure, return to lower elevations where symptoms should subside quickly.

---

to keep things simple with the same camping meals for the duration: cereal or eggs for breakfast; sandwiches or leftovers for lunch; grilled cheese, hot dogs, chicken, chili or pasta for dinner. And, of course, s'mores.

We also picked up five cheap canvas camp chairs that would get a lot of use before we gave them away after our last campfire.

Mile High victory

With the prep all done, we were ready for some major league baseball. For years, Tom brought the kids to see the New York Yankees, so they were right at home at Coors Field. Denver's beautiful, mile-high stadium was a perfect choice to relax and acclimate from our sea-level town.

With no skin in the game, we still cheered the home team Rockies to a 4-0 win over the San Diego Padres. As the sun set beyond the open-air arena and towering lights snapped on, I leaned into Tom and looked at my crew. We were really here! My core buzzed with delight.

Mt. Rushmore

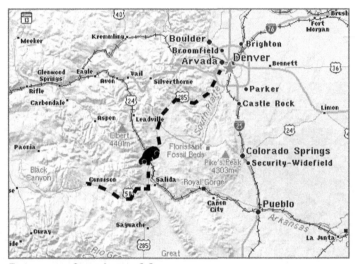

Denver to Gunnison, CO
4.5 hours

Chapter 2
Power of Chat

Early the next morning, we all exploded with eagerness. The kids raced to The Couch. I slid in front. Tom hit the gas and headed south out of Denver. The previous night's tingle mushroomed in my chest.

"We are on our way!" I clapped my hands. "Mesa Verde, here we come!"

"WOOOOO HOOOOOO HOOOOO!" Tom's holler filled the SUV. Howls erupted from the back. Our windows echoed. The cacophony must've been loud outside, too, because a passing driver gave us the hairy eyeball. We cracked up. I settled in, a smile on my face, trip bible on my lap.

In less than an hour, we were speeding past gorgeous, sprawling cattle ranches. Livestock dotted miles of lush fields under a brilliant blue sky. Tom glanced at me. "Certainly not your New Jersey farms. Looks like the Marlboro Man's gonna ride by any second."

"Sure does."

"Huh?" Sean, again stuck in the middle, popped his head forward.

"Oh that's right." Tom chuckled. "You guys are all too young."

"No we're *not*." Ciarán huffed. "We know Marlboro."

"Yeah, dad." Aislínn slapped the seat. "We're not *three*."

"I know you know the cigarette. But I'm talking the man. Dark hair, tan, rugged. Marlboro hanging from his lip like a trophy. In the commercials he'd ride out on his horse, just owning these big ranches."

He gestured widely across the windshield. "You can feel that part of history in this landscape, He was quite the cowboy. A real guy's guy."

"Hmmmm." I smiled. "Not just the guys. Got half the girls in my high school to smoke."

"Including you? You used to smoke, right ma?"

I twisted in my seat to look at Aislínn. "Yeah. But grandma did that, not the Marlboro man. She gave me a cigarette when I was 13. Told me I could smoke at home so I didn't get caught in school."

Ciarán snorted. "What? I never knew that. She let you smoke? At 13? That's craaaazy!"

"Yup." I hadn't thought about it in a while and couldn't imagine allowing my own kids to light up. But I wasn't going to throw their grandmother under the bus.

I caught my son's eye in the rearview. "Well I'm sure she just wanted to keep me out of trouble. Back then my friends were caught smoking in the bathroom all the time and kept getting detention."

I looked out the windshield and said almost to myself, "Hmmm. Funny thing was they allowed the seniors to smoke on the Senior Green."

"The what?" Sean, still leaning forward, cocked his head up at me.

"Oh, a place in front of our high school. With grass and trees and a few benches."

"And they let you *smoke* there." Ciarán shook his head. "That's insane."

"You want to hear insane? I used to work in a tiny office with no windows. People came in and were swallowed in this haze like it was a Halloween fog machine. And I barely even noticed the smoke. Now *that* was crazy."

"Wait." Aislínn squinched her face. "You smoked in your office? I thought that's not allowed."

Tom took the volley. "Not now. Can't even smoke on the beach now. But back then it wasn't a big deal anywhere. Every time I walked in the teacher's room, it was one big smogfest."

"You smoked, too, Dad?" Sean ping-ponged to Tom.

"Only for a little while. In my twenties. Quit by the time I was 30. But I did add to that teacher room cloud for a while."

I laughed. "Yeah, when I worked in the hospital, doctors and nurses always raced into the employee lounge to grab a quick puff. The place was a smog pit. No one really talked about the health impacts."

"Sad too." Tom gestured again out the windshield. "Cause I think three or four of those Marlboro Men wound up dying of lung cancer."

I nodded. "I know. Awful."

After a few moments, Ciarán piped in again. "Jeez, no wonder those old guys at Jack's kept complaining about having to smoke in the back alley." He referred to a local restaurant where he worked as a busboy. "They probably were used to smoking at the bar most of their lives."

Tom nodded. "Yep...Change is hard."

So began the first of countless conversations where our children learned

---

TRAVEL TIP: Talk, Play, Connect

Car rides and campfires offer perfect opportunities to converse. Ask questions. Share your own stories. Even the quietest or most reticent kid will enjoy hearing your tales, and, in time, may begin to reveal theirs. It's also fun to listen to radio shows together (we liked Comedy Central) or play verbal travel games like license plate alphabet or billboard numbers, where everyone in the car is on the lookout for the next letter or numeral. This often leads to lots of laughs and is yet more reason to limit electronics!

more about us, our childhoods, our generation. Before long, the kids started sharing their own anecdotes. About school. Friends. Enemies. Times they got in trouble and never told us.

A couple of days later, sitting around the campfire, Sean ratted out his brother for smoking with friends, a charge immediately denied. We didn't press the matter; we were thrilled to be weaving these verbal threads with our increasingly taciturn teens. These moments became an unexpected, priceless side effect of being cramped together for hours on end.

Wow's commence

Flying along the highway, we got our first clear view of the Rocky Mountains. Compared to our flat-as-a-ruler Jersey Shore, the sight was simply spectacular. The Couch broke out into a chorus of wow's.

Even though it was July, snow blanketed the summits, thrilling all of us. Our astonished vocals amplified as we maneuvered up and down three seemingly endless switchbacks on 11,000-foot Monarch Pass. Six Flags' roller coasters had nothing on this ride.

Atop one peak Aislínn off-handedly noted that Eskimos had dozens of words for snow. This inspired her as we careened south and the white gave way to a wealth of green.

"Kelly!" She pointed to passing bushes, then aimed at distant treetops. "Olive."

We all jumped in, conjuring up names for the verdant variety outside our windows. Emerald. Hunter. Asparagus. Mint. Apple. Um, lime. Um, um, grasshopper.

"Envy," shouted Aislínn.

We all laughed. Ciarán offered her a high five. "Good one Bean."

My heart did a little dance.

Medium well

Gorgeous scenery only went so far when stomachs started growling. As wows became whines, we had to stop. What better place for our introduction to western eats than the Gunsmoke Restaurant in Buena Vista, CO?

Ciarán's eyes popped at the glossy cattle-decorated menu. "Chicken fried steak! What the...?"

East coast ignorance, for sure, but we never heard of it. This meant our eldest, already a foodie at almost 16, had to have what turned out to be a gigantic plate of breaded beef and crispy fries with gravy.

> ### TRAVEL TIP: Know Your Eaters
>
> *Your crew may be fine with donuts for breakfast and fruit or chips for lunch. Mine needed real meals to subvert the crankies. If everyone is happier with more food, then make sure you allow time in your schedule to eat. This doesn't mean restaurants all the time. Whether you are driving, hiking or hanging in a hotel room, it's a good idea to have some cereal and sandwich fixings in your cooler. I'd like to put in a plug for healthy snacks (nuts, carrot sticks, cheese bites), but we also went through plenty of Snickers and Doritos. Keeping food on hand is especially important if you have a picky eater or someone with food restrictions.*

Tom wanted a rare burger, but there was no such thing as pink meat at the Gunsmoke.

"Not here sweetie," drawled the jean-clad, middle age waitress. "We only make 'em medium-well or well."

I giggled. In all our planning, it hadn't occurred to me that we'd find new culinary delights. Coming from a state where people flocked for pork roll and authentic bagels, I should have anticipated this gastronomic bonus.

Sean and Aislínn doubled down on the burgers, medium-well, adding bacon and cheese. Sadly, I was the most difficult eater in our clan. And not just for my policing of chips and sweets. I'd been gluten-free long before it was trendy and I didn't eat red meat. At the Gunsmoke, I had one choice: the Deluxe House Salad, a wedge of iceberg lettuce smothered with ranch dressing.

Gunnison grumps

We could've done the seven-hour run from Denver to our first campsite in Mesa Verde National Park. But that didn't include bathroom or meal stops and we thought things might get pretty dreadful if we stayed on the road too long.

So we booked a night in Gunnison, CO., a college-military town that's home to Colorado's oldest rodeo. Our earlier euphoria definitely waned, but I was determined to make the most of our stay.

"Look!" I cheerily pointed at a poster in the local pizzeria where we sat eating dinner. A free outdoor concert was happening a few blocks away at the Cowboy Park Fairgrounds.

My children acted as if I suggested swimming in tar. They reluctantly followed and immediately became mortified when Tom pulled me into a slow dance on the sidelines to a country tune from an Air Force band.

"Hey." Tom shouted loudly to them as he sent me for a twirl. "It's not as if we're two-stepping in the middle of the arena."

Our trio quickly strode away, pretending not to know us. From the corner of my eye, I saw Ciarán push Sean, then duck to avoid a return punch. Aislínn about-faced in a different direction. All three made their way back when equestrians began some jumps, apparently a preview of a show scheduled for the next day.

I smiled cheerily. "Anyone want to come see it before we leave?"

"NO!!!" Three voices rang in unison.

The emphatic verdict made it clear it was time to return to our roadside motel. While we walked, Sean complained his ear hurt. Ciarán grumbled he was bored. Aislínn announced she wanted to go home. Suddenly *I* was swimming in tar. Maybe we *should* have driven straight through to Mesa Verde. We slogged silently into the room.

No stranger to Brennan earaches, I pulled out my first aid kit and selected the remedies I knew would sooth my youngest. Then I told him to lay down with a warm rag on his ear.

Ciarán already sat moping in the middle of the double bed they were supposed to share, his music so loud we could hear it through his earbuds. Furiously texting, he paid no attention to my request that he move over. Aislínn sprawled dramatically on the blow-up twin mattress we squeezed into a corner, also busy tapping on her phone.

I could feel my pulse in my head. I took a deep breath.

Tom had turned on the TV and totally zoned into some serial drama. But I was a mess, struggling to fix our real drama, wanting everyone to be happy.

It didn't work. Sean moaned, Ciarán ignored, Aislínn snapped whenever I opened my mouth.

Finally, I gave up and slumped onto the other double bed next to Tom. But, unlike him, already snoring, I remained wide awake in a ping-pong of worry and resentment.

What if Sean's ear gets worse… What if Ciarán can't calm down… Maybe

---

TRAVEL TIP: You Are Not in Charge of Your Family's Feelings

You and everyone else will have a much better time if you do not try to fix bad moods or orchestrate happiness. Normal emotional swings will be even more evident when you are together for periods of time, especially in tight quarters. So unless there is obvious wrongdoing for which intervention or apology is necessary, butt out. Allow individuals to have psychological space to get over their grumpies.

I should have just come with Aislínn... It's only our second night. How could they be acting up already... Don't they get how lucky they are...

Around and around and around. The longer I laid there trapped in my spiral, the lower I sank. *Maybe we all should just go home.*

Yes, we hit our first moody bump. From sensory overload? Adrenaline crash? Hometown friend news? Too much rich food? Who knew? It didn't matter.

If I left things alone, our slump would have passed quickly. Sadly, my meddling made it worse. Did I learn that lesson before the next episode? No. I wished. (So did my kids.)

Colorado textures

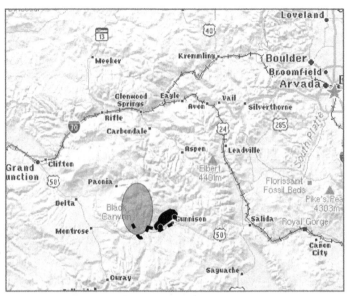

Gunnison to Black Canyon of the Gunnison, CO
1.5 hours

AT-A-GLANCE:
Black Canyon of the Gunnison National Park
Black Canyon boasts some of the roughest pinnacles, steepest cliffs and oldest rock in North America. This vertical wonder reflects more than two million years of sculpting by the forces of weather and the powerful Gunnison River. The entire canyon is 48 miles, but the park contains 14 miles of its deepest portions, with depths to 2,700 feet.

LOCATION: The park is in southwestern Colorado. The South Rim is east of Montrose, CO. The North Rim (only accessible on an unpaved road) is southwest of Crawford, CO. It takes 2-3 hours to drive from rim to rim.

OPEN: The South Rim Road is open to vehicles from early April to mid-November. In winter, it is open to Gunnison Point. The North Rim Road is closed in the winter.

COST: $25/vehicle or $20/motorcycle; reduced fees for bicyclists/pedestrians

INFO: https://www.nps.gov/blca/index.htm

Chapter 3
Black Canyon Beauty

As Little Orphan Annie predicted, the sun did come out the next day. In the sky and in The Couch. By the time we yawned ourselves awake, ate breakfast and got back on the road, there weren't any ear pains, gripes or grimaces. I'm the only one who had to force my way out of a funk.

South of Gunnison, as Tom piloted us smoothly past the peaks of Blue Mesa Recreation Area, Aislínn pointed out her window at a huge lake. "Check it out guys!"

Everyone except her dad peered to the left. The Blue Mesa Reservoir lay so flat and still that it created a perfect mirror of mountains and sky. We marveled at the Alice-in-Wonderland trickery, almost unable to distinguish between real and reflection.

"You gotta see this Tom," I urged him to slow down.

He pulled over and stared along with the rest of us. He gestured upward then at the robin-egg blue image on the lake's surface. "Is the sky really higher here, or does the water just make it look that way?"

"Yeah," whispered Sean, leaning across his sister to get a better view. "So sweet."

We certainly had waterways in our town and enjoyed our share of beautiful echoes. Yet we fell under a spell; being together on an adventure somehow heightened our power of observation and sense of thrill.

Miles later, just north of Montrose, CO, smiles surged again at the iconic brown wooden sign for our first national park: Black Canyon of the Gunnison. We didn't plan an overnight stay, but we couldn't pass up the chance for a quick exploration. I happily showed our new America the Beautiful National Parks Pass at the entry gate.

After stopping at one of many viewpoints along a seven-mile rim road, Sean and Ciarán hurried to the edge of the nearest cliff. They leaned over, hollered down, then arched back up with huge grins. As soon as I got close, I could see why. The abyss ran deep for sure, truly a Black Canyon.

Dramatic crags, like stone icicles, pierced downward through a gorge carved into Precambrian rock, the oldest on earth. We knew the Gunnison River snaked far below us, but it remained veiled by steep, shadowy walls on either side.

Although more than 1,000 feet across at the top, the opening at the bottom narrowed to just 40 feet in places. The ribbon of water running through it could only be glimpsed a few hours later in mid-day sunlight. Otherwise the depths remained eternally dark.

Aislínn and Tom wandered farther down the rim trail. They called us over to a point that seemed, impossibly, even deeper.

Tom scanned the cliff walls. "Holy moly. Like looking into the *Twilight Zone*."

We each gazed in silence, tiny human specks in this wondrous space. Even the boys stood momentarily still. Staring into 2,000-foot depths was humbling in a way that would become abundantly familiar – yet never taken for granted – over the next six weeks.

What a great family inauguration to the national parks!

TRAVEL TIP: National Parks Are a Beautiful Bargain

Of the 400-plus sites in the National Park System, about 300 are free. The rest charge entrance fees. Depending on your destination(s), a pass may be your best bet. While funding cuts and increased operating costs forced the NPS to raise fees, our public treasures remain one of America's greatest tourist bargains.

Single destination: *Prices range, so check each park individually. For instance, as of 2020, Black Canyon of the Gunnison NP cost $25 per vehicle for a seven-day pass, while Yellowstone NP was $35 per vehicle. Some parks have different rates for vehicles, motorcycles and those entering on bike/foot. Children under 16 are usually admitted free.*

Bargain Pass: *If you plan to visit a few parks in a year, take advantage of an annual pass. The America the Beautiful National Parks Pass cost $80 and gives you a year's access to all the national parks and hundreds of federal lands managed by five different government agencies.*

Military Pass: *Annual passes are free for current U.S. military members and dependents in the Army, Navy, Air Force, Marines, and Coast Guard, as well as Reserve and National Guard members.*

4th Grade Pass: *All fourth graders in the U.S. can bring their families for free to the parks for one year through the "Every Kid in a Park" Program (www.everykidinapark.com)*

Senior Pass: *If you're a U.S. citizen 62 years or older, you can get an annual pass for $20. A Lifetime Senior Pass is $80. Lifetime passes purchased before the 2017 price increase will still be honored.*

Access Pass: *A free lifetime pass is offered for U.S. citizens with permanent disabilities.*

For info on the passes see: https://www.nps.gov/planyourvisit/passes.htm

---

Black Canyon of the Gunnison

Black Canyon of the Gunnison to Mesa Verde
3.5 hours

AT-A-GLANCE:
MESA VERDE NATIONAL PARK

Seven centuries of Ancestral Pueblo peoples lived at Mesa Verde, first making their home atop the huge plateau or "green table" for hundreds of years before moving into the renowned cliff-side pueblos in the 12th century. No one is sure why the tribes left the area in the next 100 years. But Mesa Verde National Park still protects 5,000 archeological sites, including nearly 600 cliff dwellings, recognized as some of the best preserved in the country.

LOCATION: Park entrance is on Highway 160 between the towns of Mancos and Cortez, CO, and about 35 miles west of Durango, CO. Once you enter the park, the first view of a cliff dwelling is 21 miles (approximately 45 minutes) along a steep, narrow, winding road.

OPEN: daily, year-round

COST: $30/vehicle May 1 - Oct. 31; $20 rest of year; reduced fees for motorcycles, bikes/individuals

INFO: https://www.nps.gov/meve/index.htm

Chapter 4
Mesa Verde Mystery

The Rockies' geology shifted before our eyes as we continued our quest southwest. Crossing Las Platas Mountains, an arm of the mighty San Juans, we saw why people raved about winter sports in the area. After snowboarding only in the northeast, Ciarán couldn't believe the exciting elevations.

"Imagine flying down these? Soooooo dope!" He eyed the lush peaks. "We gotta come back in January!"

I laughed. "You're on. Next trip, you help plan."

Relaxing into my seat, I became entranced by the view before me. The road turned into one long optical illusion borne of scale and distance. A far-off blur of green and brown morphed into a finer natural patchwork which then became actual treetops, cliff sides, leaves and sandstone, while new blurs arose on the horizon. Macro into micro and back again; what hypnotic entertainment at 70 miles an hour!

Beyond Las Platas pass and San Juan National Forest, we finally headed down into the valley toward our destination: Mesa Verde National Park. The descent brought us eye level with the enormous flat "green table" or Mesa Verde rising above Colorado's Great Sage Plain.

"There it is!" My enthusiasm roused the backseat trio, who took turns leaning forward to get a better look. We dipped another 1,200 feet into the valley, then slowly made our way up the steep entrance into our second national park.

Everyone appreciated the cloudless sunshine, but I was particularly grateful. I'd read the tall slopes of the mesa – including the road leading up to it – consisted of something called Mancos shale. Rain turned it into a muddy, dangerous landslide.

I kept this to myself as we inched higher in low gear. Living where the land is level probably exacerbated my anxiety and I white knuckled it, imagining our SUV losing traction and slipping backwards despite the great weather.

Once in the park we easily found our reserved site in the wide open, neatly delineated areas of Morefield Campground. Tom scrutinized the terrain and extricated our tent from its skin-tight casing while the kids unloaded everything else. Organizational king to the max, my husband insisted on orchestrating the placement of sleeping bags, suitcases and air mattresses.

"Put them over there," he ordered, indicating a space on the dirt only a few feet from where the kids had originally dropped them.

"Why dad," challenged Ciarán. "We just have to move them inside when the tent's up, so who cares?"

"*I* care. When I put the tent poles together they might be in the way."

My eldest just laughed and grabbed the stack of collapsible metal. He began snapping the joints together into poles. "See? They're not in the way."

"Don't do that yet!" Tom took the 19-foot poles, held them like he was walking a tightrope and carefully placed them at the edge of our campsite. "I have to find the best spot for the tent first."

Ciarán shook his head, rolling his eyes.

After choosing the most level, rock-free location, Tom started to unfurl the nylon. Sean and Aislínn yanked at its sides to help flatten the bottom.

"No," Tom scolded. "You're making it worse. Sean, you go to that corner. Aislínn, you take the other one."

"Da-ad." Aislínn stood tall, hands on hips. "We got it. You don't have to be a drill sergeant."

"Yeah." Sean bent to pull the nylon. "Let us get the floor right first."

Tom's face flushed. Steam puffed off the sweat on his shaved head. He was about to rebut. At first I chuckled at the commotion. So did our "neighbors," a young couple in the site next to us who were enjoying the Brennan show. But I realized if I didn't do something, the ruckus would escalate into a sit-com gone wrong.

"Tom." I took his hand and smiled. "They know what they're doing, hon."

He jerked away. "Yeah, but…"

"No but. We got it. You did all the driving. Sit down and chill." I retrieved one of the new camp chairs and opened it up near the fire ring. "Hey Sean. Get your dad a Dr. Pepper."

Tom reluctantly retreated. Our spawn happily built our temporary house, crossing the poles and tucking them into the correct nylon pockets. When they were ready, I offered a fourth set of hands. We each steadied our corner and popped the poles up into a dome.

Next came the fly. What a perfect name for it. We each held onto our edges and hoisted. The cloth overshot and soared off the rounded roof like pterosaur wings. The kids collapsed in giggles. After three tries and lots of wobbling back and forth, we finally balanced and tethered it.

Unable to stay in his seat, Tom started to blow up the mattresses with a pump plugged into the SUV's amp outlet. He glared at our missteps.

I walked over and hugged him. "You really are the best at making sure things fit. Please tell us where you think the beds and bags should go?"

He smirked and pushed me. "You're such a jerk."

"Thanks."

He instructed the boys on the interior decorating; Aislínn and I arranged camp chairs and organized food. The routine soon became mindless (with Tom not allowed to touch the tent), but what a thrill to see everything set up that first day.

Card sharks

Hours of driving did take its toll on Tom. All he wanted to do was relax with a book. The rest of us felt antsy. So we started a new habit of finding the park's nearest visitor center. Intriguing exhibits made us even more eager to climb into a cliff dwelling the next day.

Under hot afternoon sunshine, we walked a bit of Prater Ridge Trail near the edge of our campground. Sweet junipers, grasses and mountain shrubs lined the arid path. The boys raced each other up a mild incline, doubling back for the water I had in my hip pack.

"Hey guys, that's all I have," I warned, handing my Nalgene bottle to Sean, "So we should head back soon."

He gulped the last of it, ignoring Ciarán's outstretched hand.

"Oops." He threw the empty at me and took off giggling, with his brother at his heels.

At camp, the two bent over, breathing heavy. Ciarán slumped into the tent and announced that all his t-shirts were dirty.

"How?" I snapped. "We've only been gone three days."

"I dunno." He emerged grinning. "Guess I changed a coupla times?"

I let out an exasperated breath and checked my watch. Plenty of time until dinner. I queried the troupe. "Who else has clothes that need to be washed?"

"Me," said Aislínn.

"Me," echoed Sean.

Tom looked up from his book. "If you're doing it anyway I have a few things."

TRAVEL TIP: Valuable Visitor Centers

Even if you've done a lot of pre-trip reading and familiarized yourself with a park's layout and offerings, stop at a visitor center early in your stay. Exhibits vary wildly depending on the park; from simple posters to high-tech animations. But you'll always find a wealth of info, up-to-date event schedules and current alerts about fire, water or weather cautions. Plus, there are often shops or, at the very least, ice cream!

TRAVEL TIP: Live a Little Dirty

Sure, there are laundry facilities in many parks and most towns. It's even fun the first couple of times to play cards while waiting. But, believe me, it's worth lowering your standards so you're not constantly sidelined. We made a rule that except for underwear, socks and totally rank t-shirts, everything had to be worn at least four times before washing.

"Okay. One load. Warm. Get your stuff," I directed.

Everyone scrambled into the tent to retrieve their dirties. I shoved it all into a big plastic bag and headed toward the laundry facilities on the far end of the huge campground. I stopped and turned. "Hey, anyone feel like seeing what else is there?" The kids followed.

There wasn't much. Just a plain building with a few washers and dryers and some vending machines outside. Aislínn pointed at a nearby picnic table.

"You wanna play?" She pulled a deck from her back pocket.

Ciarán beamed. "You have cards with you?"

She smiled. "Just in case."

"Yeah! Poker," suggested Sean.

"With what for chips, dummy," uttered Ciarán.

I looked on the ground. "Rocks and pebbles?"

"Noooooo." Sean sing-songed, staring wide-eyed at the vending machine. "How about M&Ms?"

While the wash whirred, we sat and laughed through more than an hour of high-stakes games, a pastime that continued for the next six weeks. Blackjack. Five-card stud. Spit. War. My young card sharks even taught me Texas Hold'em.

Geologic homestead

A flyer in the laundry room announced a ranger-led talk that evening at Morehead Amphitheater. After a delicious chili and rice dinner (I cooked, the boys cleaned up at designated camp faucets), the kids and I left again. Tom still just wanted to read.

We joined two dozen other campers in a small outdoor arena. Jeff, a middle-aged ranger immediately recognizable in the Park's button down shirt, tan khakis and Smokey Bear hat welcomed us.

"So," he queried. "What do you know about Mesa Verde?"

"It's OLD," shouted a little girl in yellow shorts and pigtails.

"Yep, it sure is," the ranger agreed. The rest of us smiled. "But do you want to know *how* old?"

The girl pumped her head.

"Well, let me tell you. We'll start all the way back at the dinosaurs." He spun slowly, his outstretched hand taking in the landscape. "Back then, everything you see here was under water. A great big ocean."

"But then the earth started to shift and change. The sea receded slowly, leaving thousands and thousands of feet of dark muck called Mancos shale." Jeff lifted his Stetson and rubbed his crew cut. "That Mancos is really slippery stuff. You could slide right off it!"

I elbowed Aislínn and whispered. "See. I told you." Once we'd made it up the park's steep entry road, I'd shared my fear of a mudslide.

She shushed me and looked back at the ranger, who noted that if the shale were the only thing around, the land would have washed away eons ago. But over millions of years, the retreating seashore and subsequent swamps also deposited a tougher material: sandstone.

"This whole area became a mud sandwich." The ranger held out his hands, one above the other. "Sandstone landed on the bottom and top. But the middle filled with this mucky Mancos shale mixed with some run-of-the-mill coal." He brought his hands close to his mouth and pretended to take a bite.

"Yummy, right?" He smiled at the girl in yellow.

She shook her head and leaned into her mother.

"So what do you think we called this sandwich?" No one ventured a guess. "The Mesa Verde group of rocks." He chuckled. "I know, I know. Not very creative."

"But the real question is: how did we get from a muddy sandwich to the amazing cliff dwellings that we have here?" He turned and motioned once more to the land around us.

Sean leaned forward, clearly fascinated.

The ranger smiled broadly. "The magic of moisture!"

He let the words sink in before continuing. "Rain and snow fell for millions of years on our sandwich. Sandstone is porous, so the water seeped through. And the wet drips completely washed away the muddy Mancos middle. What remained? Large open spaces with strong sandstone overhangs for roofs and hard sandstone floors underneath."

He winked at the little girl. "In other words...terrific housing potential! What really sealed the deal, though, was the prospect of food."

He said centuries of wind blowing silt onto Mesa Verde's plateau left thick, rich topsoil, ideal for growing beans. "The Ancestral Puebloans used to be nomads. But with built-in dwellings and fertile land, the cliffs became their perfect home for generations."

He went on to describe daily life and rituals of the people who lived in the cliff dwellings until the 1300's. My sons paid rapt attention to warfare of the day, especially how the high alcoves offered strategic protection from attackers below. I preferred hearing about ceremonies and communal living.

Starry night

We happily made our way back to our campsite. My young male warriors hooted and ran ahead, darting in the brush then jumping out from behind bushes to startle their sister and me.

Midway, Ciarán hurdled over a random split-log fence in the path, arms in archer mode. He sailed almost across with a loud "AYYYYY YAAAAAA!" Then his back foot caught the rail, plunging him to the ground with a thud.

I gasped. Sean convulsed in high-pitched, rapid-fire chipmunk chortles. From the time he'd been a tiny tot, my youngest son's giggling was contagious, so I found myself cracking up despite my concern.

"Heeeey, Big Foot," he choked out then doubled over again, making me laugh even harder.

"Are you ..you ...o ...o...kay," I sputtered, trying to curtail my awful snickering as I extended a hand to my eldest.

"Shut up." Ciarán glared at Sean, ignoring my offer. He rose and dusted himself off.

"Really." I bit hard on my inner lip. "Are you all right?"

"Yeah," he mumbled, eyes narrow. He swung at his little brother, who darted away. Ciarán sped after him.

"And they're off again," reported Aislínn, the most mature one there.

I finally got a hold of myself as we sauntered, watching the blue sky morph into a palette of pinks and oranges. We got back to camp with the

---

TRAVEL TIP: Caution with Campfires

Uncontrolled fires in and near national parks can be tragic. Parks post regular updates about their fire threat, based on wind, drought and other factors. Check fire regulations in each park you visit. Do not build a campfire if it is prohibited. Only build campfires in approved areas or fire grates. Many parks sell stacks of firewood, or you can often purchase wood at roadside stands before you enter.

DARK SKIES

Sunsets stir our senses. But they are only half of nature's remarkable spectacle. As gorgeous solar hues subtly fade, stars and planets peek through the darkness like fireflies at dusk. Their shimmers brighten as night deepens, gifting us with a sense of magic, a taste of solitude and a respite from our busy lives. Along with wonder and peace, dark skies offer relief from the bombardment of artificial light that scientists now know may disrupt sleep, increase stress and add to chronic disease. A host of plants, birds, insects and animals also depend on the cycles of natural darkness. Sadly, they are threatened by light pollution in nearly every place on earth. This not only makes our moments under the stars even more precious, but may compel us to protect the night. To learn more about what you can do wherever you live, visit www.darksky.org.

---

last ribbons of color fading to gray. The boys excitedly shared Puebloan trivia with Tom as he threw logs on our first fire.

We circled our canvas chairs around the blaze and gazed overhead at the beckoning show. In the growing darkness the Milky Way arced across the heavens, a chorus line of sparkling dancers.

Between s'mores, Tom and the kids searched for constellations with his astronomy app, connecting pretend dots from Orion to the Big Dipper. But I remained content to just lean back and aimlessly gaze. When I thought there couldn't possibly be any more glimmering space in, well, space, I noticed a whole new twinkling cluster. I sank deeper into my seat.

We are really doing this, I thought, feeling metaphorical layers of gauze unwrap from my limbs. Our lives brimmed with constant confinement, at home, school, the office, stores, theaters, cars. Sitting with a perfect duet of flames and night sky, surrounded by nothing but air and the people I loved most in the world, I allowed myself to expand. In a peaceful lull, I felt my whole being relax more than I had in years.

Eventually, we retired into the tent, our suitcases placed neatly at the heads of three inflated beds: two doubles and a single for Aislínn. On future nights we'd wind up ordering our offspring to take their raucous bouncing and wrestling outside. But, on this, our first eve under the stars, we all quietly fell asleep to our own ponderings – at least for a while.

In the wee hours, a crying baby in a nearby campsite woke Tom. This astonished us because he was partially deaf from childhood ear infections and years of loud rock 'n roll. On top of that, he had to pee. Aislínn and I were the ones who worried about middle-of-the-night bathroom calls; he almost never needed to go.

Not used to sleeping at ground level, he grunted himself up, pushing off the mattress for a boost. Except, air mattresses don't give a boost. The inflation immediately sank, causing him to slip back. His foot flung out over the adjacent bed, clipping Ciarán's slumbering head.

My son's startled "*Heyyyyyy*" got drowned out by Tom's trademark, "*Sh%t-god--d@mit!*"

With a final heave, he somehow hoisted himself up. But as soon as his weight left our mattress, the shifting air dumped me onto the ground. I added my own, "*Heyyyy!*"

Now everyone was wide awake, probably in the surrounding tents, too.

Tom groped for his shoes and fumbled with the zipper on the nylon tent door, all the while grumbling profanities under his breath. This set us all laughing. We snickered again when he loudly returned. At least once he laid back down, I buoyed off the floor again.

Ahhh, life in a tent!

Carved palace

After breakfast, we returned to the visitor center to book a 10 a.m. tour of the Cliff Palace, the largest dwelling in the park. Since it faced west, we'd avoid the heat of the sun by going in the shadowed morning.

At the allotted time, we waited with a group of 30 on a rock platform about an eighth of a mile from the ancient abode. From our vantage, it looked like a miniature sandcastle. People in the troupe before us were colorful dots moving around tan turrets and columns.

We soon followed our guide down more than 100 uneven sandstone steps. Until now, we'd been walking on flat land, so I worried about the ankle that Aislínn sprained just weeks before. She insisted it was fine.

Another few hundred feet along a paved path led us to the remarkable ruins.

We gathered around a large excavated circle known as a kiva, the Hopi word for "ceremonial room." After a brief talk, most of which we learned the night before, we were free to explore on our own.

Sean and Ciarán headed toward a maze of connected rooms. Aislínn and Tom wandered into a nearby storage tower. I remained at the kiva and stared for a long time into the deep, round chamber.

Of the nearly 600 cliff dwellings in Mesa Verde, most have fewer than five rooms; many are just single compartments. Cliff Palace, with 150 rooms,

ANCESTRAL PUEBLOANS

They're often called Anasazi, but please don't. In Navajo, that means "ancient enemy" or "enemy ancestor." So instead, refer to these prehistoric peoples as Ancestral or Ancient Puebloans, who lived as nomadic hunters and gatherers before figuring out how to irrigate crops. Agriculture let them move into permanent homes. Remains from their cliff houses, rock art, pottery, baskets, jewelry, clothing and "road" systems continue to ignite imaginations. Archeologists have puzzled together their culture from these artifacts, as well as other findings like plant pollen, turkey bones and coprolites (human poop). The Ancient Puebloans learned to grow and weave cotton, use a bow and arrow and send messages via smoke signals from the top of mesas and mountains. They probably traded goods as far away as Mexico and California. It's unclear why they abandoned their cliff dwellings around 1300, but two main theories are drought and over-population.

is thought to have been a major gathering and ceremonial center where about 100 people lived.

It's one thing to admire the architectural beauty and construction of the village. It's another to stand quietly on floors that carried vibrations of those who lived here more than 800 years earlier. I could picture circles of Ancestral Puebloans gathered in the kiva for healing rites, praying for rain, or offering herbal gifts for hunting prosperity. An inexplicable reverence infused my imaginings. I let it steep for a few more minutes before looking for the rest of my family.

"Over here, ma," I heard as I walked down a sandstone hallway. I turned into a large room where Ciarán squatted on a window ledge cut into the rock wall. Sean leaned against the hard sill. Aislínn snapped their picture and turned to me.

"Hey, did you see the marriage kiva?"

"No, which one's that?"

"Over there."

She led me further down the hallway into a room with another round chamber in the ground. Its middle contained a smaller, deeper hole, which I knew from the larger kiva, was the fire pit.

Aislínn pointed. "I heard the guide say this was where all the weddings probably took place. Wonder what it was like."

I studied the circular hole. "Me too."

53

"Think they sat there?" She nodded at four vertical blocks next to each other. They could very well have been seats.

"Don't know. But why four and not two?"

"Maid of honor and best man," she said matter-of-factly.

I laughed. "I think that's a more modern thing."

"Maybe not." She shrugged.

"Hmmmm, maybe."

We found Tom and the boys deep in a narrow hall that Sean contended had to be a secret passageway. "This is sooooo dope." He crouched in ninja stance. "I would 'a loved being an Indian back then."

"Yeah, right." Ciarán smirked. "And you'd be dead when you were like 30 or 35. Didn't you hear the guy last night say they had really short lifespans?"

"Oh, right." Sean giggled. "Never mind."

He stood up and we continued through the stone corridor to a "doorway" leading to the other end of the village. Tom, at 5 feet 8 inches, had to duck through the opening.

Ciarán laughed, sticking a knife into his little brother's sore spot. "Haha. You'd fit right in Sean. The ranger said the men were like 5-4. What are you, 4-11?"

"Shut up jerk. Look who's talking."

He was right. At almost 16, Ciarán still hoped for that growth spurt. Actually, Aislínn was the tallest of the three, which suddenly occurred to the boys.

"Hey Bean," yelled Ciarán. "Been bangin' your head?"

Sean laughed.

"You guys are both idiots." She tossed them a look and strode after her dad.

Our 40 minutes in the ruins flew by. When we had to leave, though, exiting the Cliff Palace turned out to be more challenging than the trip in. Our guide led everyone to a tall wooden ladder attached to the rock wall. He instructed us to climb single file.

Halfway up, Aislínn had to stop to wait for Tom, who moved too slowly ahead of her. She froze. Heights had never been her favorite, but hanging onto rungs on the side of a cliff sent her into panic mode. From my perch on the ground, I could see her shaking. Sweat broke out on her forehead.

"You got this Aislínn. Just take a deep breath," I shouted. "I'm right behind you." I started up the ladder.

Her brothers, who went first and already scaled the top, leaned over. Ciarán offered, "You want me to come get you Bean?"

She shook her head, locked in the same place, gripping tightly.

"Just bring your leg up to the next step," encouraged Tom, finally up.

She inhaled deeply and hesitantly lifted her foot to the rung. Then the next and next until she was on level ground. I rushed behind her.

"You okay?" Sean patted her back.

She nodded, then looked up and gulped. We followed her gaze. The top of the mesa remained far above. We had to climb three more 10-foot ladders, looming like appendages in the cliff wall.

Tom put a hand on her shoulder. "You can do this. I don't like it either. Just don't look down."

"I was *fine* until you slowed," she snapped, shaking his hand off. "Let me go first this time."

And she did. Without stopping, she methodically moved up the first ladder, then the next, and finally the third. I practically held my breath until she was up. The boys followed. I could hear them giving her high fives at the top. Before then, I hadn't realized just how much heights scared her. I felt a pang of guilt. But she seemed to bounce back quickly, joking with her brothers as we made our way back to The Couch.

Ancient messages

After some chips and drinks, we drove to Chapin Mesa Archaeological Museum to access the famed Petroglyph Point Trail. Beyond its promised views of Spruce and Navajo canyons, we couldn't wait to see its namesake attraction: the largest panel of ancient etchings in Mesa Verde National Park.

Tom set a steady pace on the uneven sand-and-rock path. Before long, we came upon remarkable sandstone formations, gorgeous sentries that, like cliff dwellings, had been sculpted over eons by weather and water. Darker minerals marbled the tan statues, giving them depth and nuance. Like clouds, they took the shape of heads, hearts, dragons, and whatever else we saw in them.

"It's a monkey," exclaimed Ciarán, rushing ahead to leap onto one gangly form.

I laughed. "Oh geez, it really is."

Aislínn looked further ahead. "There's a face!"

She hurried to pose next to the stunning feminine silhouette, with hair, nostrils, mouth and chin formed by gradient brown swirls in the rock.

"Wow. That looks like it should be in a museum," remarked Tom. "Like it was carved by a master."

I poked him. "I think it was."

Tom again took the lead as the trail narrowed and wound through a maze of multi-level formations. Along with igniting my imagination, I guess the rugged terrain also triggered my digestive system. Because as soon as we hoisted ourselves up and through a narrow opening, I felt my stomach rumble. I tried to hold it, but couldn't. I was just as astonished as everyone at the sound of my noisy, slow eruption.

My sons, a few feet ahead of me, stopped in their tracks and exploded in hysterics. Twenty seconds later, a young couple clambered through the same opening, clearly suppressing smiles.

"SEANNNNNN!" I shouted. "Why did you do that?!?"

"It wasn't me, mom. It was YOU," he shot back through his snorts.

I glowered at him, mortified, as the couple chuckled their way past us. "You could have covered for me," I hissed once they were out of earshot, my face crimson. But with Ciarán doubled over and Aislínn grinning from ear to ear, I broke down too.

"It wasn't that loud," I insisted through a gasping laugh.

"Oh, yes it was," declared Tom, eyes flickering with glee.

Ciarán decided to re-enact the moment, reappearing through the crevice and mouthing a noisy *pppffffffffffft*, spit flying into the air before he crumbled into a chortling ball with us hooting at the antics.

Still giggling, we fell into line behind Tom again. His pace, however, didn't cut it with the kids. Aislínn and Ciarán pushed ahead on either side of him. Just as she elbowed in front, my daughter stepped down onto a rock the wrong way.

"Ahhhhhow." She yelped and frantically lifted her ankle. She tried to take a few steps and clearly couldn't put weight on the foot.

"We're going back," I announced. We were about half a mile in and had another two-and-a-half to go.

"Nooooo. It's our first hike," she retorted. "I'm fiiiiine."

"No you're not." I looked her in the eyes. "You're not walking the rest of the trail. The description said it gets steeper and there's a few scrambles up the side of the canyon."

"Let's go." Tom started back the way we came. "You heard your mother."

She stood defiantly, arms crossed.

I gently urged, "C'mon hon. Let's get some ice and you'll be better for the next hike. We have the whole trip."

Ciarán, leaning against an arrow-shaped formation, surprised us all. "Hey, why don't you guys go with Sean. I'll make sure Aislínn gets back okay. We'll get ice at the refreshment stand and wait for you there."

"No way." I frowned. "I'm not letting you go back alone."

"Mom," Ciarán said calmly. "We're good. We definitely won't get lost; it's a solid trail. Plus, she's a Red Cross certified babysitter."

"Whaaa?" The line made me laugh out loud and softened my knee-jerk reaction. I looked at my spouse.

He nodded. "Sounds like a good plan plan to me."

I turned back to Ciarán. "You sure? We may take a while."

He smiled. "Give us some money for snacks and we'll be just great."

Aislínn, who had been silent during the exchange, murmured, "Thanks Ciarán."

And so it was that I watched them slowly retreat, Ciarán providing a strong shoulder for his sister. I turned to Tom, conflicted.

"They'll be fine, Mer. Let 'em go." He took the lead again, Sean behind him. I sighed and followed.

We wound through narrow chambers that did indeed open to sensational views of the canyon. While scrabbling up and down the terrain, we kept passing incidental sandstone shadings and cliff markings. At least twice I asked Sean, "You think these are the petroglyphs?"

All doubts vanished when we finally arrived at the ancient engravings. Beneath a huge sandstone overhang, ancestral art filled the rock face: stick figures, swirls, handprints, animals. We saw all kinds of mysterious lines clearly etched into lighter layers beneath the dark tan wall.

"Wow," I whispered, unable to say anything else.

Sean inched closer to the symbols, peering intently at each section of the huge panel.

Tom leaned in as well. "Wonder what it means."

Sean pointed excitedly. "There's a lizard and I bet that's an eagle. Can't tell on this one, but it's some kind of wild animal. And the people are maybe walking? Dunno. Pretty sweet, though."

"Hmmmm. Maybe the swirls are magic," I guessed.

"Or bad weather," interjected Tom.

"Or black holes to another dimension," quipped Sean. I smiled, wishing Ciarán and Aislínn could see this.

We admired the petroglyphs for quite a while before ascending dozens of natural rock stairs. Climbing slowly, I had another surreal hit: our feet walked the same steps used by Ancestral peoples 1,400 hundred years ago! What a mind-boggling sensation to absorb history in such a physical way.

The trail mostly hugged the canyon floor in welcome shade. When it eventually rose to the rim, a 360-degree sunny view of the arid expanse

SIPAPUS, SWIRLS & KACHINAS

Mesa Verde's largest panel of ancient etchings have evoked various guesses at its mysterious meaning. Here's what some current day Hopi say: the large squarish swirl represents "Sipapu," the place where Ancestral Puebloans emerged from the earth, thought to be by the Grand Canyon. Among the stick figures are "whipping Kachinas," spirits who guided the tribes on their journey. At various distances from the Sipapu are symbols for the Eagle Clan, Mountain Lion Clan and Horned Toad or Lizard Clan, which may indicate where they separated from the group during their migration. Or perhaps, as some suggest, they are all-powerful animal spirits who watched over the people in their travels.

greeted us. Dozens of black birds dive-bombed into barely visible cracks in the far cliff, captivating Sean and me.

"C'mon, it's getting hot. Let's go." My husband clearly wasn't as taken with the aerial acrobatics. So we finished the hike under the blazing rays and found Ciarán and Aislínn lounging comfortably at an umbrella table.

Happy 4th

After resting at the campsite, we headed out once more, this time for a late-afternoon tour of Balcony House, a smaller but still remarkable dwelling. I tried to talk Aislínn out of it when I read this one was even harder to access. It required descending a 100-foot flight of stairs into the canyon, walking along a path, then climbing back up a 32-foot ladder into the ancestral home.

She swore her ankle felt fine and was determined to rise above (literally) her height phobia. I took a deep breath and let it go.

In our much smaller group of less than a dozen, Aislínn went first as we made our way into the communal abode. Like all other Mesa Verde dwellings, Balcony House stood about 7,000-feet above sea level. Its 40 rooms had been excavated in 1910 by archaeologist Jesse Nusbaum, who went on to become one of the park's first superintendents.

Although our guide described it as mid-sized, it seemed more like another big city with multi passageways into kivas, plazas and dozens of chambers. My family and I again marveled at how it must have been for 13th century mothers and children, fathers and grandparents to live in this sandstone maze.

But our ponderings petered out as soon as it came time to leave the ruin.

We had to crawl (yes, crawl) 12 feet through an 18-inch (yes inch) tunnel. Good thing none of us were claustrophobic. Or wide (although Tom had quite the squeeze). Then we climbed 60 feet of stone steps and ladders. I use the term ladder loosely. Indents into rock-face served as handholds while iron bars passed for rungs. Aislínn definitely faced her fears, although it wasn't easy for any of us. We all giggled with nervous energy until our feet touched solid ground.

There, we explored the wide-open mesa and stopped at the visitor center one last time for ice cream before making our way back to our campsite. The sun slowly drifted behind mountains on the western horizon. Comfy in our chairs, we quietly watched the sky flame before dimming to dark.

It was the Fourth of July, the first time my children would not be at a large oceanfront fireworks display. Instead, we enjoyed an all-American hot dog dinner. Then our camping neighbors handed out sparklers. Not exactly big booms, but still fun.

We lolled around the campfire for hours, enjoying our final evening at our first national park. Stars frolicked and capered above us, the astral show even more spectacular than the night before. I didn't know if the rest of my family missed their normal seaside tradition, but I couldn't think of a better way to celebrate our country.

Point Lookout laughs

Tom always woke at the crack of dawn, no matter what. Left alone, Ciarán and Aislínn could easily sleep until noon. Sean and I landed somewhere in the middle. When my husband shook me awake at 6 a.m. and urged me to climb Point Lookout before we packed to leave, I felt conflicted. Should we force the kids to get up and deal with the blow back? Or should I just pass on the hike?

"C'mon, Mer. They're fine sleeping."

"We can't just leave them," I whispered.

"Why not? They were fine yesterday on their own. They're fine at home on their own. And they'll be fine here on their own. Stop treating them like babies. Ciarán's almost driving. And don't forget, Aislínn's a certified Red Cross Babysitter."

I smirked and got up. Sean heard us debating and decided to come along. We let the other two know; they groggily nodded and flopped back to sleep.

The Point Lookout trailhead was a short walk from our campsite, not far from the amphitheater where we listened to the ranger our first night. Funny how that seemed like such a long time ago.

> ### TRAVEL TIP: Leaving the Kids Alone
>
> *If you travel as a family for any length of time, you'll be faced with one or more children wanting to stay behind or go off on their own at a campsite, hotel or visitor center. You need to use the same reasoning you would at home. Are they normally allowed to stay alone? Are they aware of safety precautions? What are their directions for contact and assistance if something happens? What are they permitted to do (i.e., use the cooking stove, sit in the vehicle, go to the hotel restaurant or pool)? It can be empowering and healthy for teens to have some time on their own, as long as you are comfortable with their maturity, safety and contingency plans.*

We began the two-mile hike in silence. For amusement, though, Sean had to make a game of things. When he was little, he regularly dared me to skip over sidewalk cracks, count every red car on the highway and bury tiny plastic cowboys under each daffodil I planted. This time he wanted to wager about the number of switchbacks to the top of the mountain.

I grinned. "You're on."

He was a tough negotiator. We already rounded our fourth hairpin bend with him still haggling. Finally, we settled that the loser would have to do the winner's dishwashing for a week.

"Deal?" I stuck out my hand.

"Deal!" He shook.

Tom took our estimates. I said 18; Sean guessed 30.

"No way." I looked up. "Twenty at most."

"We'll see." Sean giggled, rushing ahead.

At first, Sean and I tried to keep track, calling numbers after each turn. But he got bored and offered other challenges like stepping only on rocks instead of the dirt ground, walking toe to heel to be as silent as possible, and slaloming across the trail like skiers. While we remained too busy laughing to remember the count, Tom kept silent tabs.

About an hour later, we zigzagged around our last switchback onto the peak, panting from the climb. My husband smiled broadly. "Twenty-seven!"

"What?!? You sure?" I demanded, catching my breath. "You shoulda counted out loud. It's hard…."

He cut me off. "I'm sure."

"Well," I grumbled, "he went over. Normally doesn't count if you go over."

Tom chuckled. "Don't be a sore loser, Mer."

"Yeah, ma." Sean grinned. "Don't be a sore loser."

Now it was my turn to laugh. "Good thing I didn't take your gamble to sit in front of The Couch for the rest of the trip."

"That would 'a been soooo sweet," sighed Sean. "But dishes are okay, too."

We ventured to the edge of the summit. Low green sagebrush, tall blue lupine and the delicate red petals of Indian paintbrush dotted the sandy ground. The view, at 8,700 feet, momentarily took our breaths.

In the distance, we could see both Montezuma and Mancos valleys waking up from their shadowy peaks. I closed my eyes. The wind against the cliffs sounded exactly like waves crashing on shore. Rhythmic. Soothing. I felt something on my shoulder and startled, quickly lifting my lids. It was my youngest, putting his arm around me.

We stood together like that for many minutes with the warmth of the rising sun on our backs, my heart as bright as the light spreading across the land below.

Mesa Verde Cliff Palace

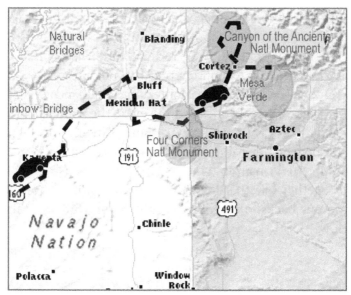

Mesa Verde through Canyon of the Ancients to Four Corners to Kayenta, AZ

5.5 hours

AT-A-GLANCE:

CANYONS OF THE ANCIENTS NATIONAL MONUMENT

Declared a National Monument in 2000, Canyon of the Ancients covers 300 square miles in southwestern Colorado. Archeologists estimate the area may contain as many as 30,000 ruins from Ancestral Puebloan and other early Native cultures. Some 6,300 ancient sites are officially recorded, more than anywhere else in North America. They include cliff dwellings, multi-story adobe structures, shrines, towers, petroglyphs, great kivas and rock paintings. The sites are accessible from various points along the Trail of the Ancients National Scenic Byway. Motorized travel is restricted to designated roads, although many are rough and unpaved. Visitors are encouraged to stop at the Anasazi Heritage Museum and Visitor Center for maps and trail conditions.

LOCATION: Anasazi Heritage Center (Canyons of the Ancients Visitor Center & Museum): 27501 Highway 184, Dolores, CO (10 miles north of Cortez)

OPEN: March - Oct. 10 a.m. - 5 p.m.; Nov. - Feb. 10 a.m. - 4 p.m.

COST: March - Oct.: $6 per person aged 18 and up; Nov. - Feb.: free

INFO: https://www.blm.gov/programs/national-conservation-lands/colorado/canyons-of-the-ancients

Chapter 5
Uncrowded History

Taking down our tent was literally a snap. The kids raced each other to unclip, extract and fold the poles, then grinned as the dome collapsed like over-leavened bread. The challenge, though, as anyone who's ever camped could attest, was fitting that gigantic square of lumpy nylon into its tiny compression bag.

My offspring bounded onto bubbles of air pockets in the deflated cloth. As soon as one crushed, others sprang up like whack-a-moles. Aislínn hop-scotched across the bumps, while Sean and Ciarán slid head-first and rolled away from each other in spins of giggles. My daughter finally suggested folding the material. So the boys stood up and each grabbed a corner.

"Mom." Aislínn waved me over. I picked up the fourth edge.

"Okay," she instructed her brothers. "One…two…three. Walk to me and mom."

The boys handed us their corners and we carefully placed the doubled over rectangle back on the ground. We took one look and cracked up. All that did was create one big igloo of air. Ciarán cannon-balled onto the lump, undoing our neat crease. Sean and Aislínn slumped down next to him on the still-bulging material. We laughed too hard to catch our breaths.

"Where's dad when you need him," my daughter gasped.

A few minutes later, returning from the restroom, he surveyed the scene. "Get off," he commanded. "You're going to rip it by laying on it."

I caught Aislínn's eye and we both swallowed our remnant chortles. Good thing he missed the vaulting and spinning!

"Patience is key," Tom said in his best teacher voice. He demonstrated how to slowly, tightly roll the nylon to remove trapped air, then methodically store all the parts in their matching sacks, skills we soon mastered.

Heading away from Mesa Verde, we could see Point Lookout towering over us. Sean excitedly tried to show his siblings where he had been just a couple of hours earlier. They completely ignored him.

We had another dose of antiquity on tap for the day. We planned to drive parts of Colorado's Trail of the Ancients National Scenic Byway to get a taste of Canyons of the Ancients National Monument.

What a mouthful. And what an adventure!

Luckily, we started at the Anasazi Heritage Museum and Visitor Center in Dolores, CO, the only manned hub in the entire Canyons of the Ancients.

MONUMENTAL DISTINCTION

Some people are thrown off by the word "monument," picturing a single carved statue or a contained marvel. In federal parlance, however, a monument is a place set aside for preservation because of its historic, scenic or scientific interest. In some cases, it covers a large geographic area. Canyons of the Ancients is one of these, protecting 176,000 acres of land dotted with historic sites that date back to 10,000 years.

The one-story brick and stone building, just yards from the picturesque McPhee Reservoir, featured "please touch" exhibits, hands-on demos and films about Native cultures in the Four Corners region.

Although we intended only a quick stop, Ciarán announced he had to use the facilities. The rest of us occupied ourselves skimming past artwork and artifacts.

Twenty minutes later Aislínn whined, "Tell dad to get him. He's doing this on purpose."

"No he's not," I insisted. Though truth was, my boys definitely dawdled on the toilet and I never really knew whether they genuinely had to go or just wanted a little control over the gang.

I distracted my daughter by dragging her into the museum's small gift shop. We each picked out a couple of postcards. More importantly, in the everything-happened-for-a-reason realm, the delay let us get maps and guides to places we never would have found on our own.

Finally, my eldest appeared beaming. Aislínn fired daggers at him. Back in The Couch, Tom tried to enter our first stop into the GPS.

"C'mon Sally," he cajoled the satellite system. "Help me out here."

I waved a Xeroxed map. "Told you. They said nav systems won't find these roads. We have to do it the old fashioned way."

We cruised along, me squinting back and forth between the road and hand-written markings on my photocopy. "WAIT, OVER THERE," I said loudly so Tom could hear me. "Back there. I think you missed the turn."

He reversed to a barely visible opening.

"I can't go down there. It's someone's driveway."

"No, look." I showed him on the diagram. "It's gotta be the road."

Off we went, over the bumpy, narrow path, tall grasses scratching our doors. We chuckled uneasily. After hitting several gullies, Tom flipped into four-wheel drive.

"You sure this is it?"

"Yeah, dad." Aislínn leaned from the back. She held one of the pamphlets we had picked up. "It says here: *Auto routes through the Monument are few; most roads are unpaved and primitive.*"

"No kidding," interrupted Tom.

She continued. "*Most archaeological sites in this 'outdoor museum' are not apparent to the untrained eye and precise locations are not publicized.*"

"Oh great." Tom tightened his grip on the wheel. The boys laughed.

Aislínn concluded, "*This a place to explore on your own.*"

"Well," I reasoned, "Lowry Pueblo's supposed to be one of the most popular so it can't be that hard to find."

"Really?" His sarcasm coincided with a quick veer into the grasses to avoid another gigantic pothole. His sons sniggered at him again.

After crawling for a long time on that rutted lane, we came to a crossroads. "Hang a right," I instructed. "It should be just over there."

"Where? I don't see a thing."

The kids peered out the windows as we crept down this second dusty dirtway. After a few minutes, Sean declared, "Over there!"

Sure enough, we could see the outline of clay-colored ruins up ahead. I let out a relieved breath.

Great exploration

After all that off-roading, Lowry Pueblo's parking area turned out to be surprisingly easy to identify, with a picnic table, basic outhouse and one handicap spot. Ours was the only vehicle there.

The emptiness felt both humbling and freeing as we made our way down a short path to a huge rectangle of decaying structure. Interpretive signs clued us in. At its 11th century peak, about 100 people lived in this Great House. Like the Balcony House we'd seen the day before, its 40 rooms and eight kivas made it a typical medium-sized home.

Although many walls no longer stood, the building once boasted three stories. Or, more accurately, two stories above ground, since the first was subterranean. When archeologists first excavated the pueblo in the 1930's, the underground chambers had been buried for centuries. The original inhabitants lived in these deep "pit-houses," but later generations started building surface rooms for their main living space.

A dirt track brought us to the half-ruined rooms. Squatting beneath a low archway to enter, Sean led the way through slim halls and openings.

"Hey look," he announced at the doorway to a large round chamber. "I found the painted kiva!"

ANCIENT ARTISTRY

When unearthing the Anasazi Great House, archeologists discovered four painted kivas. Ancestral artists had plastered thick layers on the curved kiva walls and used natural pigments to create stunning geometric designs, like those found on petroglyphs and pottery from the same period. Fairly intact when first found, the artwork unfortunately couldn't be preserved, except for a fragment on display in the Heritage Museum.

We carefully stepped into the gathering space, one of four painted kivas at Lowry. Looking closely at the faded surface, we could make out ghosts of once bright marks.

"Pret-ty cool," whispered Ciarán, almost reverently.

No one thought twice about his lowered tone. At the crowded Mesa Verde kivas, people talked, shouted, laughed. But something about being alone in this ancient sacred place compelled our softest voices.

We explored our way through the pueblo's accessible areas. I touched the red-tan bricks that, despite haphazard, irregular shapes, seemed perfectly stacked. How long, I wondered, did it take to sun dry mud into blocks and assemble them, without grout or mortar, into these remarkable living quarters?

Experts surmised residents remodeled and expanded Lowry at least half a dozen times, from its single kiva, four-room core to the 40-room Great House we stood in. What made the dwelling especially unique was that it reflected two distinct native cultures. The pueblo's early portions resembled styles seen in Chaco Canyon, 100 miles south in New Mexico. Later additions mirrored Mesa Verde architecture, indicating at least some connection between these important areas from the 12th century.

No one really knows why the entire population abandoned their home in the early 14th century. As with Mesa Verde, drought and over-population remain two popular theories.

Trickster mosaics

Once outside again, we followed another footpath past tall, fragrant sage brush to a magnificent Great Kiva. My trio sprinted to the edge of its huge masonry ring, some 50 feet in diameter. Aislínn pointed with glee to the grassy bottom, where stones and slates laid mosaic-like in the shapes of two massive figures.

"Kokopelli!"

Indeed, one of the forms did look like the prankster they knew from childhood tales about the dancing, flute-playing Native American with his fancy headdress. Actually, Kokopelli originated in ancient Anasazi Indian mythology and passed down through Hopi legends as a musical fertility deity who oversaw childbirth and agriculture. But, somehow, he also garnered cred as a trickster, which made him perfect for kid stories and, according to my daughter, for this immense kiva.

"Nah," said Tom, reading a small sign. "Says here they represent summer people and winter people, opposite cultures who alternately inhabited the site."

"Well, looks like Kokopelli to me. Bet he was the summer person." Aislínn jumped a few feet down into the circle and walked to the figure.

I joined her, gazing around the huge ring. Historians surmised that up to 100 men, many from neighboring communities, would meet here for ceremonies, political meetings and other business of the day. Back then, bold geometric artwork had covered these walls, too, and small square platforms held pillars to support a roof.

Ciarán and Sean began tightrope walking around the stone perimeter.

"This is sooooo awesome," said my eldest, now using his outdoor voice.

It truly was. When visiting other parts of the world, I often heard people taunt the United States' lack of historical heft, its 200-year infancy. I wished they could spend a little time sitting in this Great Kiva. Especially sans visitors. With sage swaying peacefully in the warm breeze, I could almost hear the ancient whispers.

Remote quadripoint

After stopping briefly at a few other small ruins, we headed to Four Corners Monument on the Navajo reservation. Sean, who finally had a turn at a window seat, took in the arid, rugged landscape.

"What do kids *do* here?"

"I know, right?" echoed Ciarán, looking out the other side.

Coming from a bustling beach town with parks, ball fields, shops and constant activity, they kept watching for signs of youth-friendly life. But aside from some boys swimming in a small pond and one worn baseball field, we didn't see much in the nearly100-mile drive.

I, too, wondered about the local residents. Did they work on the few ranches we passed? How far did they travel for school or shopping? Would they hate the congestion where we lived? Miles of ponderings became an unintentional gift as we each compared these unfamiliar environs to our own little piece of the world.

We'd heard more than 250,000 people a year drove to contort themselves

AT-A-GLANCE:
FOUR CORNERS NATIONAL MONUMENT

The Four Corners marker, originally a simple cement pad erected in 1912, was redone in 1992 in granite embedded with a bronze disk ringed with the words: "Here meet, in freedom, under God, four states." Each state's seal rests within its geographic boundary on the disk. Their flags fly above, alongside Navajo and Ute flags. The Navajo Nation owns the Monument land and offers dozens of booths where local vendors sell jewelry, native crafts, fry breads and more. The site has no running water; on-site bathrooms are primitive. Fuel, food and lodging are extremely limited within a 30-mile radius.

LOCATION: Off US Highway 160, about six miles north of Teec Nos Pos, AZ
OPEN: Open year round at 8 a.m.; closing time varies with the month
   Closed Thanksgiving Day, Christmas Day, New Year's Day
COST: $5 or $10 per person, depending on the month
INFO: https://navajonationparks.org/tribal-parks/four-corners-monument/

for a photo straddling the states at Four Corners Monument. Luckily, we encountered barely any other tourists.

As soon as we arrived, Sean raced up onto the granite platform denoting the joint borders of Utah, Colorado, New Mexico and Arizona. He promptly laid across its circular bronze marker, making sure he had an appendage in each state. We gathered around him, laughing. One of the few visitors there offered to snap a full-family shot.

Aislínn stepped around her brother's sprawled body to put each foot onto a quadrant and bent to place her hands in the other two. "How do they know this is *exactly* the border of four states? They could just be saying it."

A CIVIL SOLUTION

Four Corners Monument is the only U.S. "quadripoint" – the neat intersection of four states (Utah, Colorado, New Mexico and Arizona.) We have the Civil War to thank for this rare geographic phenomenon. Before then, the New Mexico Territory was one big area covering what's now Arizona and a piece of Nevada. But the southern half became the Confederate Territory of Arizona when Confederate sympathizers led a successful secession. New Mexico remained loyal to the Union. After the war, the government basically squared the boundaries by continuing the Utah-Colorado border all the way down to Mexico.

"Nah," replied Tom. "The government wouldn't put it on the wrong spot."

In fact, they did. Not on purpose, though. The monument was indeed carefully mapped by meridians and parallels. But survey technology of the early 1900's wasn't precise. So the *real* Four Corners is 1,807 feet, or about a third of a mile, to the west.

We stood on the platform a while, six flags swaying above us, one from each of the states, along with the Navajo and Ute banners. The tan horizon shimmered in the heat, as if the land itself was moving.

Ciarán squinted. "Ha. Never saw a mirage before. No wonder those desert dudes crawled into oblivion."

Then he hopped off toward a field of flea market booths offering local treats, from gorgeous native crafts to aromatic eats. We all followed and admired the goods. I chose a small hand-carved sandstone engraving of none other than Kokopelli. Ciarán, of course, went for Navajo fry bread burritos.

Heads filled with history and lore, we headed to Kayenta, AZ, for the night at a hotel on the Navajo reservation. After dinner, we floated in the pool as the sun sank behind the desert. Then Tom and the kids walked to an old movie theater next door while I settled in to do some work.

Lowry Pueblo and Kiva

Kayenta to Grand Canyon, AZ
3 hours

AT-A-GLANCE:
GRAND CANYON NATIONAL PARK

Often called one of the seven natural wonders of the world, the Grand Canyon is up to 18 miles wide and more than 6000 feet deep. The canyon's layers of rocks, carved by the copper-colored Colorado River, record billions of years of history. The spectacular land is managed by the National Park Service, the Hualapai Tribal Nation and the Havasupai Tribe.

LOCATION: The Park is in the northwest corner of Arizona, near Utah and Nevada. The canyon into the Colorado River divides the South Rim and North Rim.

OPEN: The South Rim is open 24 hours a day, year-round. The North Rim is open May 15 – Oct. 15 (It takes five hours to drive from the South Rim village to the North Rim village; 90% of visitors go to the South Rim.)

COST: $35 per vehicle, $30 per motorcycle, $20 per bicyclist/pedestrian, under 16 is free

INFO: https://www.nps.gov/grca/index.htm

Chapter 6
Truly Grand

At dawn, Tom and I snuck out on our sleeping lumps of kids to drive through Monument Valley. Morning light on the famous ocher terrain left us speechless. Sandstone buttes gleamed against the brilliant blue sky, a cityscape of rock and earth. I spied castles and spires, turrets and towers. Hoodoos became hobbit chimneys. I half expected cliffs to move, sure the alluvial fans at their base were really pachyderm toes.

Alone on the open road, dwarfed by these geographic wonders, we gaped and grinned. Any logical inkling about sand, wind, water and erosion evaporated as we wound across the surreal corridor known as the 17-mile Valley Drive. We let ourselves float through the delicious dreamscape.

Our return trip delivered a completely new show, the rising sun altering shapes and shadows. As if to reflect my inner awe, mother nature had chiseled one red rockface near our exit with the unmistakable curves of a huge glowing heart.

License to panic

After breakfast, I packed while Tom took Ciarán for his first drive, as in driv-*ing*. New Jersey teens got driver permits at age 16. My eldest was hitting that milestone in less than two weeks and even though he wouldn't be home to claim the actual piece of paper, we promised him some behind-the-wheel practice. The hotel parking lot and nearby empty roads seemed perfect for the task. My son practically tap danced to the Chevy, totally stoked.

When they returned, Tom announced that all went well and suggested Ciarán continue for a while. I thought it too soon for real piloting but couldn't deny my excited teen. We loaded The Couch and I climbed into the back.

Everything stayed smooth at 25 mph on vacant side roads. At the main street, however, morning traffic made my stomach tighten. Since the speed remained low, I kept my tongue. Then Ciarán approached a two-lane highway.

Tom instructed, "You just have to go faster on the ramp so you can merge into the traffic. Check your mirror and keep going."

As Ciarán turned his head to the sideview, he rotated the steering wheel in that direction too. A horn blasted. I cringed. He quickly corrected.

"You're doing fine," Tom encouraged. "Just give it some gas."

I closed my eyes, holding my breath until we were fully in the right lane. When the first 18-wheeler flew around us seconds later my husband directed,

> ## BUTTES, HOODOOS & MESAS, OH MY
>
> Breathtaking geologic formations adorn Monument Valley Navajo Tribal Park, a red sand desert on the Arizona-Utah border. Scientifically, each reflects the magnitude of the forces that shaped them in this unique Southwest landscape. Here's a shakedown:
>
> **Plateau**: large hill or mountain with a significant area on top that is fairly level. Plateaus are often cut by deep canyons.
>
> **Mesa**: medium size flat-topped hill.
>
> **Butte:** remains of what once was a mesa. Buttes can be hundreds of feet high with steep sides and narrow pointed tops or very small flat tops. If you can graze cattle and find water on top, it's a mesa, not a butte.
>
> **Hoodoo**: tall, thin spire of weathered rock, often called an earth pyramid.
>
> **Alluvial fans**: triangular-shaped indents and embossings typically seen at the base of mountains, hills or steep canyon walls, sculpted by eons of water flowing down them. They often look like elephant hooves or toes.

"You have to increase your speed, Ciarán. Push the pedal."

We lurched forward as he tried to hold the SUV steady. I white knuckled my door rest, dread rising in my gut like lava. This wasn't one of those wide super highways with wiggle room. No, it was an increasingly crowded commuter road with narrow lanes and an even slimmer dirt shoulder.

The speedometer climbed to 50...60...70 mph. I felt the tires beneath me swerve over the uneven pavement on the right edge. I gasped so sharply that Ciarán again pulled the steering wheel to the left, overcompensating us halfway into the fast lane. Cars swerved, horns blaring as they shrieked by.

My anxiety exploded. "STOPPPP!"

Tom turned and glowered at me. "Leave him alone. He's doing just fine!"

He directed Ciarán to straighten the wheel and hold it tight. Vehicles flew past, doing at least 80. Each one pounded my chest. My eyes welled.

I tried to breathe deeply. I closed my eyes once more, mouthing to myself *calm down... calm down.* Nothing worked. In rapid pants, I choked out, "He. Was never. Behind the wheel before. He. Can't go. From a parking lot to 70."

"Mer," Tom snapped. "It's more dangerous to go slow when everyone's doing more than the speed limit. Let him get used to it."

But I was in full panic mode. Every car that careened past us, every little wheel adjustment, made me jolt. Finally I sobbed, "He HAS to STOP. This is CRAZY."

Sean sat in the middle next to me, clearly torn between concern for my tears and certainty that *I* was the crazy one. Aislínn, obliviously listening to her music, barely looked up. Tom coached Ciarán onto the shoulder. Both gave me death stares as they purposely walked past my window to switch seats. My relief far outweighed my guilt. Needless to say, I didn't help any of my children learn to drive. Nor did they want me to.

With Tom behind the wheel and me still in the back, we drove through Navajo and Hopi reservations, stunned by the striking juxtaposition of shacks and broken-down trailers amid amazingly beautiful vistas.

For quite a while, Ciarán buried his head in his phone, daring me to say something. I remained contrite. Yet as hours wore on, the gorgeous sunlight on elegant tiers of vivid bentonite clay and sandstone warmed our hard surfaces, too.

That morning's colors in Monument Valley were only a tease for the Painted Desert palette around us. Hills and buttes shone with parfait layers. Luscious lavenders. Gorgeous grays. Vibrant reds, oranges and pinks.

Shifts in the earth's crust, volcanoes, earthquakes, sea waters and a host of mineral elements created this canvas over millions of years. But the incredible pigments looked, as the name proclaimed, as if they were simply brushed on. The miles of masterpiece captivated and comforted us.

Magical depths

Our wonder at the landscape swelled even more when we arrived at the Grand Canyon's South Rim and peered, for the first time, into an expanse and depth like none we had ever seen. No matter that it had started to rain. No matter people scurried away like spooked gazelles. We stood and stared, each in our own resonance with the magnificent gulf below.

My throat tightened and nostrils filled in a surprising precursor to tears, the kind that snuck up on me during a sad movie or poignant article. The big hole in the ground – so large Rhode Island could fit in it – transported me out of my minutia into a humbling universe of awe. I sniffed and wiped my eyes.

"Is mom *cry*-ing?" Ciarán grinned and looked me square in the face. "Ha! She is!"

"Shut up!" Aislínn put her arm around my waist. "This is *really* amazing."

Ciarán moved to my other side. "Only kiddin' ma. It really is."

I didn't take my gaze from the vast chasm.

Tom stood behind us. "Yeah. They used to think the Colorado River sculpted this whole baby five or six million years ago. But now they think some of it might be 70 million years old! The geologists still argue about it."

My brain couldn't grasp, or care about, numbers right then. I remained entranced by the view as I stood on the cream-colored earth of the canyon rim. White explorers had named only this top layer "Kaibab," the word they thought meant limestone. But the Paiute, one of five Native American tribes living in the park, reverently called the entire canyon Kaibab, or "mountain turned upside down."

The Hopi, another of the resident tribes, long considered it a gateway to the afterlife. The Havasupai, who made the canyon their home for the past 800 years, held deep connections to the land and water. Looking into the expanse, I yearned for their spirit of place.

Tom finally broke my spell when he grabbed my hand. "C'mon Mer. We should go check in."

The kids took off toward Yavapai Lodge. We hadn't booked in time to get a campsite, so we chose a basic motel-style room in one of the park's centrally located accommodations.

The afternoon storm cleared in time for sunset. We joined the throngs at popular Mohave Point, claimed a spot amid a few sparse trees and waited for nature's evening performance.

Subtle at first, the canyon's terraced cliffs glowed in pale yellow and pink then flared into golds and crimsons. Orchestrated by the sinking sun, these gradients paraded up the cliffside like royalty. The sky flamed in dazzling harmony, suspending us in a bath of brilliance far above and deep below.

A curtain of shadow rose from the depths, inching higher and higher until it extinguished the glowing rock and sky. Slowly, very slowly, light left the day.

Bright Angel delight

The million-plus acre park boasted many topside trails, including its most traveled 13-mile path along the South Rim. But we were determined to see the canyon walls up close and personal.

TRAVEL TIP: Don't Miss the Golden Hours

You'll be well rewarded if you follow advice long shared by professional photographers and wildlife experts: explore or view nature during the "golden hours." This means the hour after sunrise or before sunset. The lighting is superb for photographs and many wildlife feed or roam during these times. In busier places, sunrise is also your best bet to escape the crowds. As a plus, the golden hours are usually cooler during the heat of summer (although they can be a bit buggier.)

> **WALKING BACK IN HISTORY**
>
> Along with containing five different ecological zones from rim to river, the Grand Canyon also is a time machine into an ancient landscape. Scientists estimate that the top is around 270 million years old and every mile down takes you back another 150 million years.

At 5:30 a.m., we shook everyone awake to get an early start on the Bright Angel Trail. A free shuttle, part of an extensive transport system, dropped us at the trailhead.

Tom whistled. "Looks pretty deep."

Before he even got the words out, our offspring sprang down the steep, cobbled path.

"Hey, wait for us," he yelled. When we caught up, he tried to take the lead, but our tribe split around him like ants at a pebble and marched on. Aislínn's ankle seemed just fine.

"Let 'em go." I took my time on the precipitous descent.

He nodded and smiled. "If this is listed as the easiest way down, I'd hate to see the harder ones."

With each careful step, the surroundings gradually transformed before our eyes. Colors, plants, even the ground itself shifted. Indeed, we were moving through "life zones." Top to bottom, the Grand Canyon contained five of seven such sectors in North America, the ecological equivalent of traveling from Canada to Mexico. Not only that, each descending layer was chronologically older, taking us back millions of years with each mile. The wonder of it all saturated my heart.

Sheer fascination distracted me from the steady, hot hike down. Our fleet-footed trio waited for us every eighth mile or so, merrily teasing about our sluggish pace. We saw few other hikers though periodically had to step aside for mule caravans.

"I wanna try that. It'd be sweet." Ciarán nodded at a procession of riding tourists while we rested on some boulders for a water break.

"Uh-uh. Looks way scarier to me. They're all bumping side to side and hanging on for dear life…"

"*Geeez*, mom." Ciarán stabbed me with remnant disgust from the driving incident. "You're too much."

He shook his head and barreled forward. I ignored him and focused on the dozens of tassel-eared Abert's squirrels darting around our feet. Aislínn and I couldn't decide which was cuter: feathery tufts on their large pointy ears or their long fluffy tails. These small mammals built nests in the canyon's ponderosa pines and lived off cones, buds, twigs and tree sap. But scrambling for dropped trail mix was clearly a favorite pastime.

Sean laughed. "Better watch out. They're not as entertaining as they look."

His sister frowned. "What d'ya mean? They're adorable."

"Maybe, but I read that squirrels are the most dangerous creatures at Grand Canyon. Lots of people get bit each year."

"Get out'a here."

"I'm not kidding. People try to feed 'em and they go for the flesh."

Aislínn dropped another pinch of trail mix. "I don't buy it. You're saying *most* dangerous in the whole park? What about snakes. What about bears? What about mountain lions? What about tarantulas?"

"I'm telling you, there are more emergency room visits from squirrels than anything else. It said rock squirrels, not these Abert's. But you never know."

"Hmmmm. Still don't buy it."

We hoisted our daypacks and continued down the terraced levels, the rim a distant line above us. As we walked, Sean conceded that the park had more than its share of venomous creatures, including the Grand Canyon Pink Rattlesnake, found nowhere else in the world, and the Gila monster, the largest lizard native to the U.S.

"But they're more afraid of us. It's the squirrels you gotta watch out for."

Catching up to Ciarán, we all slowed in the increasing sunshine and heat. The canyon was well known for its weather differences, often gaining more than 25 degrees from rim to river.

From our vantage, we admired the rugged tiers of rock above and below, marked with countless sandstone mesas and dark openings. I stopped and nodded at one back hole.

"You know, there's around a thousand caves here. But they've only explored about a third. They found twig figurines probably used by prehistoric hunters used in religious rituals."

Ciarán hopped ahead of me. "Pretty sweet."

We continued in silence, me trying to imagine, as in Mesa Verde, the lives of those who dwelled in this arid beauty for millennia. Then Sean suddenly

---

TRAVEL TIP: Venture Off the Pavement

Up to 90 percent of visitors never leave the paved paths in national parks. You can enhance your experience by discovering more of what makes these gems so magnificent. If you're able, hike, walk or bike on trails and unpaved paths. You'll be glad you did.

RETURN OF THE CONDORS

Plentiful in dinosaur times, California condors became extinct in the wild by 1987. In fact only 27 were left on the planet when the Los Angeles Zoo helped save the beautiful birds through an innovative breeding program. Now the world population is about 500, with almost half living in captivity. Yet the species, known for its 10-foot wingspan, is not out of the woods. Hunting, power lines, lead poisoning and other hazards bring survival rates down to 50 percent, keeping the avians critically endangered.

---

halted. Our *Animal Planet* junkie pointed at two specks in the air across the canyon.

"Condors!"

His brother snorted. "No way. You can't see that far."

He took the words right out of my mouth. We should have known better. Within a minute, the soaring grace of black wings became visible.

"Wowwwww." Ciarán shaded his eyes for better vision.

Tom squinted. "Holy crap."

"How cool," agreed Aislínn.

Sean and I just gaped. The pair neared enough for us to make out bald heads and white markings on the underside of their magnificent wings. We silently followed their aerial dance until they, again, were just dark spots blending into a canyon crevice. I thought Sean would lift off in elation. I almost did, myself. What a gift to view these largest of North American land birds!

We never planned to hike the full eight miles down to the Colorado River, but we did clock a little over three. Resting before our ascent, my daughter leaned against me.

"I'd love to go all the way and stay there one day."

Along with the Park Service's much-coveted lodge, called Phantom Ranch, the canyon's base also held Supai Village, the most remote community in the lower 48 and the only place mail still arrived by pack mule. Just 208 people lived in Supai, the capital of the Havasupai Reservation.

"Me, too!" I high-fived her, promising we'd return.

Huffing up 2,200 feet in the blazing sun seemed even more challenging than the descent. I could confirm, though, the deep rewards of passing our "we can jog this" teenagers bent over in breathless, sweating slumps.

Hare and tortoise for sure.

Natural architecture

Later that afternoon, revived by a few hours rest, we shuttled to the last stop at the park's eastern end: Desert View Overlook. Along with distant views of Painted Desert and the serpentine Colorado River, the breathtaking cliff was home to the celebrated Watchtower.

Mary Jane Colter, one of few female architects of her day, designed the 70-foot building in 1932 to blend in with its surroundings. I studied the rough, unpretentious tower, noticing cracked stones and scattered petroglyphs that Colter purposely chose to mimic ancient Native American sites. But she did add her own touch by interspersing decorative pale yellow bricks in the façade.

When our turn came to tour its interior, we walked up large stone steps into a huge round room centered by a now-familiar kiva. This one boasted a wide fireplace. To avoid the crowded first level, we headed up spiral stairs along curved walls covered in artwork depicting origins of Hopi life. The architect had commissioned a Native American artist for the work.

"This is definitely dope." Ciarán examined primitive, symbolic figures on murals that wound all the way to the top landing. There, however, the illustrations ended.

The only embellishments? Eye-level openings in the convex wall. Aislínn rushed from one window to the next in the deliberately bare chamber.

"A-mazing!" She repeated the word at each portal, taking in the 360-degree panorama.

We laughed and joined her spherical exultations. In the waning sun, the canyon began its daily show, blushing in a rosy glow. From our perch in the watchtower, the deep cliffs and endless sky looked positively magical.

South Kaibab views

Hankering for another look inside the canyon, Tom and I went down again at early dawn, just the two of us. The kids preferred sleep. Although Bright Angel had been listed as the easiest descent, we were delighted to

---

PLANE SAFETY

In the 1950s, commercial airplanes would sometimes detour over the Grand Canyon to give passengers a view of the natural wonder. In 1956 two planes flying from Los Angeles to Chicago each requested permission to fly into the airspace. The planes collided directly over the canyon, leaving no survivors. As a result of the crash, the Federal Aviation Administration (FAA) was created in 1958.

THE GREAT MYSTERY

The Grand Canyon has 250-million-year-old rock layers that lie directly against rocks that are 1.2 billion years old. No one knows what happened to the hundreds of millions of years of missing layers. This is a geological phenomenon known as the "Great Unconformity" and the Grand Canyon is one of the most visible examples in the world.

find South Kaibab Trail much less strenuous. At the very least, our feet and knees agreed the path was smoother and more gently sloped.

About a half-hour in, a young couple passed us, the only other people we saw. They hustled down and became diminishing dots. Tom laughed. "Man, I guess they like to fly when they're under twenty-five."

I smiled. "Let's see 'em on the way up." We took our time strolling past compact pinyon pine trees and chuckling at the fluffy squirrels.

My thrill magnified at Ooh-Aah Point. From that aptly named lookout, the depth below, the width before and the blue sky high above were almost too much to comprehend. The only thing that seemed even remotely appropriate in that exhilarating vista was to ooh and aah. So we did.

Near Cedar Ridge resthouse, 1.5 miles down, bronze and tan ground gave way to sculptural rock. Jetty-like outcroppings glowed golden in the broadening sunlight. I scrambled up one of the largest ledges and raised my arms high, simultaneously a queen of the hill and a freckle in the deep expanse.

Then we sat for a while, leaning against the ancient sandstone. Sipping tea from my water bottle, I considered the glorious geologic terraces. The lower regions, a vertical desert, bloomed with cacti, scrub brush and other invincible shrubs. Lone flowers amazed me, single stems breaking through dusty ground, reaching for a sky even more vibrant from these depths. Awash now in an array of earthen colors, the entire canyon was fully awake.

"Our planet is so amazing." I lolled abstractedly, stretching my legs across the warm rock. "I could do this forever!"

"Well, let's just get through the next few weeks."

"Way to break a moment."

"Hey, you know me. Mr. Practical." He stood and offered me a hand. "Speaking of which, we should head back up. The sleepy heads will be rising with empty stomachs soon."

Although still tough, the 1,100-foot ascent, unlike the day before, followed the shade. We passed a few hikers on their way down, but the trail stayed delightfully empty. Not so once we reached the bustling rim. We boarded a standing-room-only shuttle to our lodge.

The kids yawned awake upon our return. After breakfast, Tom wanted to nap. The rest of us decided to wander along the South Rim Trail.

"Beat that!' Ciarán hurled a juniper berry into the canyon at one empty overlook.

The gnarly, fork-trunked conifers blanketed the area. We each grabbed a handful of their small purple fruit and took turns tossing into the void. Sean backed up and dashed in his pitching hop-skip, whipping his elbow and releasing his fingers. "Gotcha, Ciarán!"

"How can you even tell?" I snickered and cocked my arm. My berry barely made it past the cliff edge.

"You're awful, mom." Aislínn demonstrated her own flinging prowess, giving her brothers a run for their money. After a few more competitive rounds, we sat cross-legged on the ground.

"You know." Aislínn leaned her chin on hand, "These trees have been around since the before the Puebloans."

I raised my eyebrows. "Really. Junipers? How d'ya know that?"

"Read it."

"Duh." Ciarán threw a berry in her lap.

"Yeah." She lobbed it back at him. "Indians used the bark for diapers cause it's soft and absorbs a lot. And they've been eating these berries and using them for medicine forever. Still do. The Yavapai and Havasupai."

"Hava-who?" Sean giggled.

"The Native Americans who live here now, idiot."

"And they eat the berries?" Ciarán stared at the tiny round fruit cupped in his hand.

"Yep."

"Well then…" Before I could stop him, he popped a palmful into his mouth.

"Ciarán! Spit them out. You don't know if they're safe or clean or what."

He stared at me and swallowed. "You're just a germ-a-*pho*-bic."

I glared and tsked loudly. The other two chuckled.

We continued to walk the rim, hurrying through popular lookouts and leisuring in remarkably empty spots. As the siblings launched into another berry-tossing tourney at one of these, I leaned contentedly against a juniper's wizened trunk, absorbing the dazzling canyon panorama.

We had no schedule, no stress, no angst. The kids jested like best friends. My heart floated.

Berries or bug?

Initially, we'd been disappointed the campsites were full by the time we reserved. But when Ciarán got a sudden headache and stomach cramps later that afternoon, we cherished our room with a private flush toilet.

"It *wasn't* the berries," he insisted between bathroom rushes.

"Probably just a bug," agreed his dad, laying a wet cloth on his forehead. "Do you think you could sleep? It'll be the best thing for you."

Ciarán nodded miserably. I confirmed the fruit wasn't poisonous and hoped whatever caused his upset would pass quickly. We sat with him until he dozed deeply.

Then the four of us walked to Yavapai Point observation platform for our last sunset over the canyon. Tom and Aislínn claimed a spot on a bench and immediately buried their heads in their phones. I didn't argue. How could I enforce our tech rules when Tom was itchy. While they stared into their laps, Sean and I caught every second of the astounding solar show.

Luckily, or maybe because he just couldn't stand missing out on food, Ciarán joined us at Maswik Lodge for our final Grand Canyon dinner.

Grand Canyon smiles

Grand Canyon to Las Vegas, NV
7.5 hours

Chapter 7
Feeling the Heat

We bid farewell to the Canyon and hit the road early. There's just one word to describe our trip from Arizona to Las Vegas: Scorching! The Couch's temperature display climbed to 108 degrees, before 9 a.m.

The desert offered quite a change from the canyon. Nothing but brown and dry. If you gazed long enough, you could distinguish the hues of buff, beige, bran and even a light tawny. But, really, it was one big blur of brown. Not to mention, HOT!

Just to torture the kids (not really, but you'd think so the way they griped), I wanted to see the famous Route 66. Tom ignored their protests and moved into the slow lane so we could take the next exit off the highway.

"C'mon guys." He tried to catch their eyes in the rear view. "It's more than a road. It's the path of pioneers!"

The back seat groaned in unison.

"Really. It was the American dream." He broke into a rendition of the celebrated song.

"*If you ever plan to motor west…*"

"NOOOO." Ciarán hit the driver's headrest.

"*Travel my way, take the highway, that's the best,*" he belted.

"Not fair." Sean harrumphed.

"*Get your kicks on Route 66!*"

Aislínn covered her ears. "Stop it dad!"

He chuckled. "What? You don't like it? Everyone from Nat King Cole to the Rolling Stones sang it." He started again. "*Well it winds from Chicago to L.A… more than 2000 miles all the way.. Get your kicks on Route 66!*"

We rounded the exit ramp and had our first full view of the storied roadway.

"Yeah. Looks like friggin' paradise." Ciarán banged against his seat, arms crossed.

I laughed. The stretch of blacktop definitely seemed bleak. A few forsaken buildings and a strip mall stood on the left, an old gas station on the right.

"Really great," shot Aislínn.

Undeterred, Tom continued his serenade. "*Would you get hip to this timely tip… and take that California trip…*" I joined him in the reprise. "*Get your kicks on Route 66!*"

"SHUT UP," bellowed Ciarán. "It's a stupid song."

Tom gasped. "Stupid? Why, it's an all-time R&B classic."

"Well it's stupid," replied my eldest. "And so is the road. It's a dump."

I couldn't disagree. Maybe some other places between Chicago and Los Angeles might have been terrific. But the stretch we happened upon was, well, fairly dumpy. Yet, determined to get at least one photo of something that said "Route 66," I clicked a quick shot of some crappy motel thinking, you win some, you lose some.

The short detour, however, pushed our brood past the run-of-the-mill wrangling that entertained them all morning. Before we were even back on the highway, the squabbling intensified. Tom and I eyeballed each other. "Knock it off," he commanded and turned up the radio.

Within minutes, we heard Aislínn's loud, "Leave him alone, you jerk.

Sean's muffled scream immediately followed. "Get off me. Move over."

I wrenched around. Ciarán had his brother squeezed in a wrestling hold, leaning so far across the seat that his own head was nearly in his sister's lap. She whacked him on the earlobe. He released his half nelson and smacked her back. Free at last, Sean sprang forward, slamming Ciarán's arm against the back of my seat. This took all of 10 seconds.

Ciarán rose up to retaliate. I screeched. "That's *enough*. Stop it." This only interrupted him momentarily. He grabbed for Sean again. Glaring into the rearview, Tom roared. "I... SAID... KNOCK... IT... *OFF.*"

He steered the Suburban to the shoulder and slammed to a sudden stop. So did the action in the back seat. With his head glowing as red as the 114-degree dashboard display, Tom yelled. "THAT'S IT, CIARÁN."

"Whaaa? Why me? We were just foolin' around." He looked to his siblings for back-up, exaggerating his mouth into a clownish frown. They all giggled.

"ALL OF YOU." Tom barked through clenched teeth. "Move over and don't touch each other. Got it?"

When we started to roll again, Ciarán curled himself into an upside-down squat, his feet and butt in the air, his shoulders resting on the seat. His brother and sister cracked up. We sped calmly down the highway once more. When we got to Hoover Dam, I brightly offered that it might be fun to tour the historic museum.

"NO!!!" The response was swift and resounding. They wouldn't even get out to take pictures, not even Tom.

Standing on the platform by myself, I didn't blame them. Anyone who tells you "it's the humidity not the heat" hasn't been in the Nevada desert at midday. It was the hottest hot I'd ever felt.

Nonetheless, the Dam and the spectacularly high bridge across it were both stunning and impressive. Plus, rumor had it that touching the foot of

---

LUCKY TOES

The Winged Figures of the Republic Monument on the Nevada end of the Hoover Dam have been called angels, aliens, demons and more. No matter how you interpret the duo of seated mythical giants, it has long been said that touching their tootsies will bring you good fortune. The bronze figures are weathered to a green patina, but their toes have been burnished soft gold by thousands of tourist touches. The iconic pair, with their 30-foot wings, flank a 142-foot-high flag pole. The monument is surrounded by a floor tiled in the design of a celestial chart that depicts the exact position of key stars on the day President Franklin Roosevelt dedicated the Hoover Dam in 1935.

---

the giant winged statues overlooking the water brought good luck. How could I resist?

When in Vegas

Because external heat taxed our air conditioner, we kept the thermostat at 85, better than the triple-digit July outside but still pretty toasty. The kids got lost in their ear buds and I stared quietly out my window.

We raced by scenic Lake Mead, created by damming the Colorado River, then for hours through arid desert. The sight of green in the distance shocked us out of our road trances. Was it a mirage? No. Just acres of cloned tan tract houses on perfectly landscaped lots leading to downtown Las Vegas.

Mile after mile of magazine-worthy lawns in the middle of a desert made me boil even more than the blazing sun. As I grumbled, Tom reminded me that we were zooming along in a gas guzzler with the a/c on. The kids simply joked that they'd definitely wind up at the wrong door in this land of look-alike homes.

When we finally got to the Strip, the Stratosphere was a welcome sight. With a cheap nightly rate, I expected a bare-bones hotel. Instead, we walked into a handsome lobby. Just steps from the front desk loomed a huge casino area with ceiling globes that lit rows of slot machines and blackjack tables atop plush red and gold carpet. Certainly no Caesars Palace, but after more than a week of grungy living, it sure looked luxurious to us.

Despite our nylon roll-bags and dirty shorts, the clerk acted as if we were pulling Louis Vuittons. While I finished paperwork, Tom went to find a bathroom. Aislínn parked herself in a comfy chair.

When I was set with the room keys, I walked over to her. "Where're the boys."

She shrugged. "Dunno."

I sighed and sat down next to her, our dusty luggage at my feet. I heard a gruff voice from behind. "These yours, ma'am?"

I turned and saw a red-jacketed security guard ushering Sean and Ciarán. "No one under 21 allowed in the casinos, ma'am." He stiffly nodded at each boy. "You need to keep an eye on 'em."

As soon as he left, Ciarán burst into laughter, which set Sean off. I shook my head. When Tom returned, we had to pass the wide-open gaming area to get to the gilded elevator. Sean looked longingly at the one-armed bandits.

Gamblin' man?

In our surprisingly large 23rd-story room, we immediately changed into bathing suits and rushed up to a huge roof-top pool. We kicked off our flip flops and raced toward the sparkling water.

"YEOOOW!" Tom and the boys hopped like they were on burning coal. We rushed back for our footwear. We might've been champs on hot beach sand, but even our calloused heels were no match for the blistering tile floor. We joined the geeky tourists wearing sandals into the pool.

I finally learned why they call it "dry" heat: before I even got back to my chaise lounge, my suit was bone dry. An *Insanity* ride, with arms whirling over the opposite edge of the hotel roof, teased us roller-coaster loving Brennans. But it was just too hot to even consider.

Instead, we floated, played some cut-throat ping pong on outdoor tables and tried, without success, to sit on lounges for more than five minutes in the full-on 114-degree sun. One by one, we dodged back to the air-conditioned room. Eventually, we all showered and dressed (in our nicest shorts) for the hotel's buffet dinner.

My food-loving family hit the proverbial jackpot. Their eyes widened at the sight of dozens of stations positioned around a banquet hall the size of a football field. Tables held roasts, fillets, pastas, soups, burgers. Other stations boasted crepes, tacos, Chinese stir fry. Not to mention dozens of parfaits, pies, cakes and cookies.

As soon as we forked over the inexpensive per-person, the kids took off like horses from the gate. After who knows how many courses he gorged on, suffice it to say Tom went into a food coma. He stumbled back to the room and promptly passed out. After their third dessert, my offspring talked me into wandering around the hotel.

We couldn't walk anywhere without passing slots. Sean eyed the flashy machines like a puppy near beef jerky. I pulled him ahead, looking for a non-betting locale. We came to a food court but, for once, that was a non-starter. Marching onward through yet another bank of bandits, Sean begged. "Maaaa. Can't I just try one? "Pleeeeease?"

Ciarán and Aislínn cracked up. At first slightly alarmed, I thought, what the heck? We'd gone to boardwalk arcades since he was little and we'd been playing M&M poker all week. He beamed as I headed toward a gleaming row, digging in my pocket for some dollar bills. Before we even touched the electronic display, a red jacket appeared out of nowhere like a stealth drone. Different voice, same message. "No one under 21 allowed to play, ma'am."

"But *I* was going to play."

"Doesn't matter, ma'am," he retorted gruffly. "No children allowed by the machines, even to watch."

That ma'am thing really started to irk me. And why did they put the slots everywhere if they were going to be like the Gestapo with kids? Yet I couldn't help but wonder what would happen when Sean actually turned 21.

With nothing else to do, we returned to the room where we peered out the window onto Sunset Strip's spectacle of lights. Pretty striking, we all agreed. I personally preferred the starry sky over Mesa Verde.

Winged Figures of the Republic at Hoover Dam

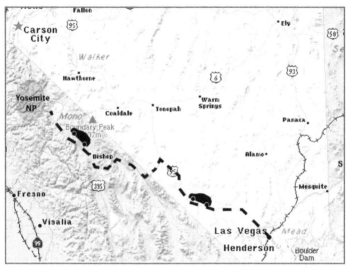

Las Vegas to Yosemite, CA
9 hours

AT-A-GLANCE:
YOSEMITE NATIONAL PARK
Famous for its giant sequoia trees, breathtaking waterfalls and granite cliffs of El Capital and Half Dome, Yosemite is a shrine to the High Sierras. First protected in1864, the park comprises nearly 1,200 square miles that also boast beautiful meadows, vast wildlife and much more.
  LOCATION: The Park is in Sierra Nevada of California, centered 200-300 miles from Reno, NV; Los Angeles, CA; San Francisco, CA; and Sacramento, CA.
  OPEN: Yosemite is open all year, but from approximately Nov. - May some areas are inaccessible by car due to snow.
  COST: $35 per vehicle, $30 per motorcycle, $15 per bicyclist/pedestrian, under 16 is free
  INFO:https://www.nps.gov/yose/index.htm

Chapter 8
Ansel's Palette

Although we aimed for no more than five hours of road time throughout the trip, the distance from Grand Canyon to Yosemite National Park forced our two longest rides. We'd already clocked more than seven hours on the first leg. The remaining route to the park would be another nine. That's why Tom wanted everyone up and out by 5 a.m. Remarkably, we dragged ourselves into The Couch only a little after that, with minimal griping.

Tom practically cheered, not because of our promptness. No, he was super psyched for his morning coffee. The previous night, he lit up brighter than the flashing neon when he saw online that Vegas had a Dunkin' Donuts. He missed his daily DD brew. He barely tolerated the Starbucks, 7-Eleven and boutique brands we came across so far. If he had realized how hard it would be to find out west, he would've packed some.

"Dunkin'... here I come," he announced as we pulled away from the Stratosphere in pre-dawn darkness.

The rest of us hunkered down to go back to sleep. In minutes, he slammed the steering wheel, shouting a few choice words. So much for snoozing. Sally Satellite, it appeared, led us to an old auto garage. Tom checked the address again.

"Noooooo. This is it," he insisted, banging the dashboard.

"Oh well," I dismissed. "Must've closed. We should get going."

Certain the location he'd read was just a misprint – that there *had* to be a Dunkin' around – he thrust the SUV into drive and began a block-by-block search. I didn't know which was worse: the backseat gripes about getting up early or Tom's mounting disappointment. Maybe, as the commercials chanted, America ran on Dunkin' but apparently not in Vegas.

Eight streets later, Sean announced that he had to go. Of course. We all groaned. But it got Tom to surrender his manic quest and pull into the next 7-Eleven. We sat waiting for my youngest. Tom grimaced at his cup 'a joe. The sun peeked above the horizon as we rolled out of Vegas a little after 6.

Hills have eyes

Peace filled our first hours across the Mojave Desert, with the kids dozing and me lulled by the monotonous topography. We zoomed past tan and brown flatness, tan and brown mounds, tan and brown crags. Even the periodic greenery appeared coated in tan and brown. It didn't help that the air seemed to literally wiggle in the triple-digit temperature.

I lolled, deep in mental wanderings, when Ciarán, finally fully awake, exclaimed, "Hey! It looks like *The Hills Have Eyes*!"

His siblings rustled to attention.

"It does!" Sean scanned the landscape.

Sun beat down from a cloudless sky, creating shadows on the undulating tans. Minutes later my youngest furiously tapped the window, pointing at a dusty embankment. "Look. Look. Over there. Dad! Slow down! I think I saw something."

Ciarán snorted. "Right Sean."

"No. I swear. I'm not kidding." His pitch rose with every word.

"Well then why would I slow down," snarked Tom. "So it can get us?"

"Probably a squirrel or a chipmunk," I offered.

"NO." Sean undid his seatbelt and rotated quickly to look out the back window. "I swear. It was something. Really big. I'm *not* kidding. It was moving." He strained his eyes across the terrain.

We all snickered… uneasily. Nothing like letting a cult horror plot about a family on vacation driving through the west get under our skins. We knew better. There weren't any nuclear zombies around.

Yet a sliver of apprehension spread through our psyches like hives. Tom tightened his grip on the wheel. All three kids intensified the search.

"I wish another car would pass so we aren't alone here," I mumbled.

No one said anything for a long time. We just remained on edge. Who knew what we were waiting for. Careening tire punctures? A shattering windshield? A barbaric carjacking? Three pairs of backseat eyes continued to examine the hills.

"Aaaaaaaaaa…stop already," Tom cried at last.

We tried to laugh it off, but the heebie-jeebies held on for a while. Chalk it up to hours of desert, little sleep and, for Tom, bad coffee.

We visibly relaxed at the sight of the eastern Sierras. I would have said we breathed easier, but actually we were distressed to see, and smell, a hazy veil shrouding the beautiful horizon before us.

Through the gossip chain that bonds park travelers, we already heard that forest fires had erupted near Yosemite. Knowing and seeing, though, were very different.

Aislínn gasped as we headed toward the smoke. "Oh my god! That's awful."

"Sure is." Tom shook his head. "The mountains look like huge, eerie ghosts."

White Wolf seclusion

When making our reservations back in March, all 10 campgrounds in Yosemite had been booked. So we opted for a campsite in the national forest next door, although next door was pretty relative in a 1,200-square mile park.

We knew through the grapevine there might be last minute cancellations inside. But we'd already driven nine hours. It would take at least another 60 minutes to the nearest park entrance to even check. If no site was available, we'd have to schlep all the way back.

This was the perfect set-up for a Brennan debate. One thing about a family of five, we never had a tie. And it was quite the power trip for whoever cast the winning vote.

The boys just wanted out of their seats. But I coveted a campsite in the park. My husband sided with me. Two-two. That left Aislínn as ultimate decider.

Tom, like any descendant of die-hard Irish orators, laid on the logic. "C'mon Aislínn. We might waste a little time now. But we're already on the road. And we'll get to see some great parts of the park on the way." He stared into her eyes as if to telepathically convince her. "Plus, if we get a site, we'll save hours going back and forth tomorrow. It's definitely worth a shot."

Ciarán hit back with his own brand of persuasion. "Hey, Bean. I'll take your turn making dinner tonight if we stop now."

Tom got a little firmer. "*I'm* the one who's done most of the driving. And if *I'm* willing to go an extra few miles, you shouldn't complain."

Sean turned to his sister. "I'll sit in the middle again on the next long drive."

Ciarán targeted another sweet spot. "And I promise I won't give you a hard time anymore about being tall."

Seeing she was about to cave, I began to implore her. "Y'know, Bean…"

But Tom cut me off. "No deals."

Everybody knew what was coming.

"We are going," he declared.

"Da-ad! Not fair!" Ciarán punched the front seat and hurled angrily against his own.

Sean followed suit.

Aislínn glared. "You can't do that. It's *my* say."

"Well guess what? I can and I am." He stared ahead and drove past the forest campsite.

TRAVEL TIP: Quirky GPS in Yosemite

While Yosemite offers shuttles to popular destinations, many people prefer driving. Just realize that this park, like many others, is known for GPS inaccuracies. If you choose to drive, make sure you have a map. Then, when there's a conflict between what your GPS instructs and what the map or road sign indicates, ignore the GPS.

"Not fair," Ciarán spit. His sister and brother echoed the sentiment.

They were right. It wasn't. So much for democracy. But I was thrilled to at least try for a campsite in the park and prayed we'd get one. Everyone remained pretty quiet for that long hour into Yosemite.

Perhaps it was the forest fires. Or a weekday lull. Or my fateful foot rub of the Winged Creatures at Hoover Dam. Luck smiled on us. Not only were sites available, we had our choice, including the popular Yosemite Valley campground, which Tom heartily endorsed.

But the boys argued for White Wolf campsite, a more remote locale on the mountainside. A big selling point was its 8,000-foot (meaning colder) elevation; they were sick of the heat. Plus they just wanted to disagree with their dad's preference.

I looked at Aislínn. She just shrugged, still annoyed. With Tom about to interject, I smiled at him then handed over the cash for a White Wolf site.

Dragonfly Lake

Our ears popped as we drove up the slender roadway. We easily found our spot amid an outcropping of beautiful boulders. The kids couldn't get out of The Couch fast enough. They king-of-the-hilled it to the top of a huge rock, where Ciarán lifted his brother horizontally in triumph. Aislínn claimed her own rounded peak, arms high in a victory pose.

Eventually, she and her dad walked to a small nearby camp store for supplies while the boys and I easily set up the tent. With the air definitely cooler and the teens noticeably happier, we all took off on a late-afternoon stroll to Lake Luken. All seemed right with the world on the serene tree-lined trail.

About a mile in, a large mound of scat sat smack in the middle of the path. Sean squatted, gleefully bobbing his head.

"You sure?"

"Yeah, mom. Definitely. And it's pretty fresh." He'd been yearning to see a bear and could hardly contain his excitement at the telltale pile of waste.

Tom, on the other hand, bristled. As an elementary school band teacher, he perfected the art of piercing claps and stern commands. He smacked his hands together and shouted, "STAY A-WAYYYYY. STAY A-WAYYYYY."

We laughed, assuming he was just spoofing the tip about making noise in case of black bear encounters. He wasn't. We quickly discovered that the thought of meeting anything in the Ursus family petrified him. For the next mile and a half, he chanted every few minutes, just in case. His children begged him to stop, but he remained undeterred.

We saw nary a bear. At the lake, however, thousands – maybe even tens of thousands – of iridescent blue dragonflies flitted and sparkled around us like flakes in a snow globe.

The boys and I tiptoed onto a dead tree trunk protruding over the water's edge. We sat, removed our shoes and dangled our toes in the soothing liquid. I gazed at the sunlight that angled on the lake's surface in a shimmering ballet with the graceful dragonflies.

When one briefly perched on my thigh, her delicate elongated thorax glistened like a sapphire. The intricate lace of her momentarily still wings seemed almost miraculous. I didn't realize I exhaled in elation until the boys giggled at me. Ciarán stood and tried to shake the log. I darted back to solid land.

At the campsite, we ate a hearty grilled cheese dinner made by my daughter. Tom, still on bear alert, went into drill sergeant mode to make sure we cleaned up every scrap. He stored our food, toothpaste and anything with a scent in a nearby bear locker.

Ranger dreams

Once excused from crumb detail, Sean and I walked to White Wolf's small amphitheater. The evening's presentation couldn't have featured a more perfect topic: bears. Before the talk started, Sean animatedly announced our afternoon discovery.

"Yes!" Ranger Sue responded with matching enthusiasm. "We've had quite a bit of activity up here in the last few weeks."

Judging by their alarm, several other visitors were clearly in Tom's faction when it came to the large animals. But my son and I beamed.

"So," Sue began after formally welcoming everyone. "What color are black bears?"

"Duh. Black," said a boy in the audience.

"Nope." Sean knew differently. "Some are brown, some are black, some are other colors, too."

Sue smiled. "You're right. Although called black bears, few are really black. Most are blackish brown, cinnamon. Some are even light blond."

TRAVEL TIP: Bear Necessities

First and foremost, bear attacks are rare. Bears would rather not meet humans. But encountering a bear is serious business, so make sure you follow rules. Every national park in bear territory (whether brown, black or grizzly) offers information, tips and warnings about camping and hiking to minimize problems. Bears are always looking for food. Heed advice for disposing trash, cooking food and storing anything with a scent (including toothpaste, candles, snacks, gum). Never bring any of these into your tent. If bear-proof storage containers and garbage receptacles are available, use them. If not, hang your food and trash from a high tree limb (check online for instructions.) If you see signs of a black or brown bear (scat, tracks, clawed tree trunks, trampled vegetation), make loud noises to warn the bear of your presence. If you see a bear in the distance, take a wide berth or go back the way you came. If you come upon a black or brown bear, do not run. Make a lot of noise, clap, sing, shout and back away slowly. Raise your arms to make yourself and your group appear as large as possible. Some people carry bear bells and/or bear spray (made of capsaicin, the active ingredient in chili peppers), however this spray is off limits in several parks, including Yosemite.

She explained that the park's wildlife managers worked hard to protect bears in Yosemite from their biggest threat: people.

"Once they got a taste of our hot dogs, candy, chips, forget about it. We humans totally messed up their natural foraging habits." She bent and lifted a leafy branch with a cluster of berries hanging from it. "We're trying to get the bears back to eating their own diet, not ours."

Sue looked around the smattering of people on a semicircle of benches. "I'll tell you a little more about these marvelous mammals. But first I'm going to ask, does anyone here have a dog?"

Several hands, including ours, raised.

"Did you know your dog's sense of smell is 100 times better than yours?"

Heads nodded.

"Well guess what? That's nothing compared to bears. Bears can detect smells at least a thousand times better than humans. In fact, we believe they have the best sense of smell of any animal on the planet!"

Sean leaned forward, smiling.

"So do you think this excellent smell makes up for poor eyesight? We always hear that bears don't see that well, right?"

"Right," offered one man to our left.

"False! Contrary to myth, their vision is at least as good as ours. Plus, they have this special reflective membrane on the back of their eyes that give them excellent night vision. So watch out!"

Some nervous snickers ensued.

"Only kidding." The ranger grinned. "Bears want your food but they don't want anything to do with *you*. Their ears are good, too. About twice as sensitive as humans. That's why they often hear us and get out of the way before we ever notice them."

Sean slumped. "But do you think we'll get to see one?"

Several folks chuckled.

"Maybe… if you're lucky." Sue winked. She finished up with tips about camping and hiking safely in bear territory.

Afterward, when everyone else left the circle, I chatted with the young ranger and learned she left a cushy Silicon Valley tech job the year before to move to Yosemite with her husband and five-year-old. She never looked back. In Mesa Verde, the ranger had been a science teacher who spent summers living in the park with his family. A hiking guide I met in Grand Canyon was a retired engineer.

"Y'know," I said as Sean and I ambled back to the campsite, flashlights in hand. "I'd love to be a ranger one day."

"You *should*, mom!"

Shimmery dragonflies fluttered in my heart.

Spectacular Vernal Fall

The boys were right about White Wolf. We reclined on our mattresses in t-shirts and comfortably fell asleep, not a drip of sweat. Good thing, because it would have frozen.

We woke shivering, our breaths visible in the early dawn light. "Got your wish," I mumbled.

"We didn't ask for winter," squeaked Sean. "It's tooooo cold."

As usual, early-bird Tom already had risen and left the tent. The rest of us lay curled in balls, reluctant to move from under the sleeping bags we pulled on top of ourselves for blankets.

"Hope dad's making a fire," whispered Aislínn, as if the exertion of speaking louder would steal energy needed for warmth.

But instead of crackling wood, I heard something else. A purring engine. I draped my sleeping bag like a robe and unzipped our door to peek out.

"Oh my god." I laughed. "He's sitting in The Couch!"

We all scurried like jackrabbits into the vehicle, where the heat roared full blast and the outdoor temp read 29 degrees.

"J..j..just p-p-picture 120 in the d-d-desert yesterday. Shoulda b-b-b-brought my gloves," joked Tom. In a few minutes, he ventured out to muster up a blaze.

After defrosting, I shut the engine. We hurried to dress and hunkered around the flames in our fleeces. Slowly, the sun warmed the morning. We carried on and got ourselves down to the valley where it was at least 20 degrees balmier.

The lower we went, however, the worse the smoke became. We could have been driving into morning fog, except for the acrid smell.

"Glad we didn't camp down here." Aislínn pinched her nostrils.

"Yeah, I'd rather be cold than fumigated," agreed Sean.

"You mean polluted," corrected Ciarán. "Fumigate is when you disinfect."

"Whatever." Sean giggled. "Just happy we didn't sleep in stinkyville."

I laughed. "Actually, I think the word is asphyxiated. And I'm sure they keep tight tabs on air quality. They're not going to let people stay here if it's dangerous. You wouldn't even notice it after a while anyway."

"That's okay. I'm still glad," said Sean, getting in the last word.

Even a fire-induced shroud could not diminish Yosemite Valley's grandeur. Stark granite peaks towered gloriously above as we parked in Curry Village. In contrast to White Wolf's quiet, secluded environs, the valley bustled like a small city. People of all ages wandered its shops, restaurants and Happy Isles Nature Center. But nowhere appeared more jam-packed than our destination: the Mist Trail to Vernal Fall Footbridge.

Smell now forgotten, we joined the hoards hoofing it up the mile-long climb. We expected the popular trail to be busy, especially because it was paved. But not in our wildest imaginations could we have pictured the variety of visitors on this unmistakably steep quest.

When it came to hiking footwear, Tom could be ridiculous. His warnings to the kids about proper boot-tying should have been written into a sitcom. Yet even I, who regularly trekked in hiking sandals, was troubled by the flip flops, loafers and, kid you not, heels, making their way up the angled black-top. Normally, I loved to see folks appreciating nature, no matter what. But not after passing more than a few wheezing, huffing, limping tourists who clearly were used to elevators and sofas.

We started placing bets. The blonde in the t-strap pumps? Twisted ankle for sure. The couple holding onto to each other, drenched in sweat? At least one case of heat exhaustion. The guy in a suit and tie with stiff oxfords? Definitely blisters. Yes, mean. We couldn't help it.

Looking up, though, I could understand why they kept plodding ahead. Who wouldn't want to get close enough to see the stunning, tempestuous Vernal Fall crashing into the Merced River?

Thankfully (and smartly) most of the ill-outfitted and infirm turned around at the first overlook after admiring the remarkable view. Still, dozens had their eyes on the prize at the top of the cascade. We wound up on a long, sluggish line mounting 600-plus precipitous rock steps adjacent to the waterfall.

Used to keeping a fairly brisk pace, or at least a steadily moving one, we each grimaced. But there was no getting around parents helping five-year-olds and nervous novices making their way up the challenging half-mile of unwieldy granite stairs.

Things slowed down even more where waterfall spray slickened the surface. My antsy boys whined and tried to harumpf ahead without success. I didn't mind the crawl. The more leisurely we moved, the more I could admire the sparkling droplets. Thousands of tiny rainbows danced in the mist like fairy dust over the falls.

Besides, the few zealous hikers seemed far more troublesome than the slowpokes. Aislínn got sideswiped on a narrow landing by a young man rushing past with a huge backpack. Tom had to grab her arm to keep her from tumbling.

Regardless of the masses, the climb was worth it. A jaw-dropping panorama of Yosemite Valley rewarded us atop Vernal Fall. Leaning over brought a bird's eye view of water surging down 1,000 feet. We could feel its thunderous power.

Tom whistled slowly, the sound swallowed by the water. "What a pounding!"

"Mannnnn. Wish I could soar over this like a hawk," declared Sean.

"Yeah," added Aislínn, worshipfully. "Sooooo cool."

"You got that right, Bean." Ciarán draped his arm around her.

Leave it to me to burst the moment when I asked everyone to turn around and pose for a photo with the falls as background. The snarls in the shot said it all. Some things were meant to be savored, not captured.

We found an empty boulder to sit on, not an easy task. I pulled out our trail mix and oranges. I barely opened the baggies when one of Yosemite's famous beggar squirrels scurried within inches of my feet. In seconds, bushy tails surrounded us.

"Worse than the gulls on our beach." Aislínn grimaced. "Guess they're everywhere out west."

"Nah," observed Sean. "Pretty sure these are different than the Aberts in Grand Canyon. I think these are Gray Squirrels." He tossed some seeds that got tackled faster than a Super Bowl quarterback. "They're all pretty cute."

"No they're not." Tom swung his foot. "HEYYYYY, GET OUTA HERE."

The scroungers barely noticed. Stellar Jays joined in the fun. The peculiar blue and black birds scrambled among the squirrels to dash for crumbs.

"SCAT," shouted Tom, lashing out with his hands.

The begging crew must've thought he was handing out treats. All their cousins flew to join the party. Jays swirled around us like something out of Alfred Hitchcock's 1960's thriller, *The Birds*. The squirrels, with their own reinforcements on hand, got more daring. Tom continued shouting. Sean jumped up and down, waving his arms and legs, giggling. Nearby tourists got a kick out of the unexpected entertainment.

The fur-and-feather menagerie was winning. Our only solution? We took our snacks and skedaddled.

Bohemian Rhapsody

Most people returned the way they came, which, with the slippery rocks and throngs of people, was about as appealing to us as laying in a pit of spiders.

Luckily – or as I believed, another gift from the universe – we happened to meet an off-duty ranger. He suggested another option. If we went a little higher, we'd come to the Muir Trail, a longer but much less popular route. No debate needed, we hurried upward.

Little did we know the path would provide some of the most stunning vistas in Yosemite: Half Dome, El Capitan, Nevada Falls. Few other hikers passed as we navigated switchback after switchback, stopping at periodic clearings to rehydrate while absorbing the magnificent landscape.

Our mouths opened wide at every sweeping view. Giant sequoias adorned with brilliant moss dappled the horizon. Gorgeous red, purple and yellow wildflowers shone against the powerful, exquisite granite cliffs.

My breathing slowed as I took in images I knew from my cherished Ansel Adams calendar, his dramatic black and white photos now before me in their astonishing beauty. From the top of my head, cooled by elevation breezes, to the bottom of my soles, rooted to stone beneath me, I felt somehow connected to the man who made Yosemite his favorite playground and, in doing so, championed all of our national parks.

It was nirvana. Or at least until Sean innocently recounted tidbits we'd learned the night before, including the 300 to 500 bears living in Yosemite highlands, i.e., where we were. Tom panicked.

He instantly began his repertoire. Clap. Clap. "STAY AWAY." Clap. Clap. "STAY AWAY."

"C'mon dad," yelled Ciarán. "That's really annoying."

"Yeah. Stop!" Aislínn tried to grab his hand mid-slap. "We're fine."

"Tom." I took his arm. "We're definitely making too much noise on our own. No bear will come near us. Really."

Not only were our footsteps and voices pretty noisy, we had an additional source of sound. Probably from too many raisins and nuts. Or maybe the altitude. Who knew. But after my Mesa Verde embarrassment, we had even more reason to be thankful for the empty trail. As if on cue, Ciarán released a loud one and grinned. "No worries, Dad. That'll scare 'em away."

Four of us hooted. Tom scowled and marched ahead, resuming his hand thwack and deep-throated, "STAY AWAY!"

"Pleeeeeeeease stop it," moaned Aislínn. I sighed. We walked in silence, waiting for the next outburst.

Instead, we heard melodic tenor.

"Is this the real life?... Is this just fan-ta-sy?" His singing got louder. *"Caught in a landslide...no escape from re-al-ity..."*

Was he channeling his inner Freddie Mercury? At the second verse the boys joined in. By the middle of the song, we all belted out, *"scara-mouch, scara-mouch... will you do the fan-dan-go?"*

We happily sang our way down the mountain. Or, more accurately, my family happily sang their way down. Fortunately, the kids inherited their dad's talent. My vocal skills? Meh. I never remembered words and often strayed from melodies. So I piped in with a random (but boisterous) *scara-mouch* and *Galileo* and left the rest to my jolly tribe.

From that morning forward, Queen's *Bohemian Rhapsody* became our go-to bear deterrent. Within the week, Tom and our trio perfected four-part harmonies as we hiked. To this day, they can break out in a flawless rendition.

Crystal Lake Tenaya

All that walking and singing made us hungry. We ordered way too much during our cafeteria-style lunch in Curry Village. But, as I said, the Brennans could eat. We didn't have a scrap left over.

Bellies bursting, we drove back up past our campground through a lovely stretch of the park to Lake Tenaya. The alpine waterway was delightfully secluded, not another person in sight.

Why, we wondered, did the majority of people flock to the same places in national parks instead of exploring the wealth of uncrowded beauty? We felt lucky to have found this gem. Though anyone reading a guidebook could have discovered it, too.

My ocean-reared kids stripped out of their sweaty clothes, shimmied into bathing suits behind makeshift towel curtains and raced into the dark blue water, swimming fifty yards out. Tom plodded behind them. I followed but stopped short as soon as my feet submerged. I couldn't feel my toes.

"C'mon, mom." Sean waved. "It's great."

"No, it's not. It's freeeeeezing." I backed out.

"Well what d'ya think?" Tom laughed, pointing at the white peaks around us. "The lake's fed by snowmelt. That's why it's so clear."

"You'll get used to it," assured Aislínn. "You just have to get in fast."

I steeled myself and tip-toed forward. I thought my legs might fall off. I held my breath, dunked to wash off the hiking grime then hightailed it back to the narrow beach ignoring my family's taunts. I spread my towel and laid on my stomach, grateful for the sun's heat. At 5:30 p.m., its rays formed a golden highway on the placid lake.

Cheek to the ground, I was nearly eye-to-eye with tiny quartz crystals sparkling among the sand grains, minuscule princess gems. I peered over them, across the shimmering water, beyond the splashing Brennans, through lodgepole pines lined up on the far shore like crows on a wire. My focus landed on magnificent granite domes.

I knew firsthand from our morning hike the rugged, unforgiving terrain on those immense mountains. Up close, they reigned as foreboding guardians over the rest of the earth. Yet from my prone view on the peaceful beach, they appeared gentler, smaller, like beautiful, curvaceous adornments.

Eventually, the others joined me. We rested atop our towels, just us, five tiny beings in this wondrous wilderness. On my back, I relished brightness on the inside of my closed lids, filling me with warmth from far more than the sun.

Huggable creatures

After a hot dog dinner and meticulous bear clean-up, I again walked to the amphitheater for the ranger program, this time with both boys. That night's topic? *Huggable Creatures of Yosemite.*

A different ranger, a young man, started a campfire in the center of the circle then asked the small gathering which creatures we found offensive.

"My brother," Sean shouted, to immediate laughter. Ciarán's love tap on his sibling's arm brought more chuckles.

We settled down and listened as Ranger Josh talked about the diverse wildlife in Yosemite. "Of course we all hear about the bears," he began. "Bear this. Bear that. And I appreciate bears. But we have so much more."

I liked him immediately; he reminded me of an older Sean. I couldn't help but picture my wildlife-loving youngest as a ranger. What if we could do it together! I kept this to myself. I didn't even have to imagine his eye roll.

Josh said the wide range of elevations and climates within Yosemite drew hundreds of awesome species, including, to my boys' delight, diverse birds of prey. Falcons. Eagles. Owls. Hawks. If we stopped on our hikes and listened closely, he teased, we would hear feathered inhabitants defining their territory or attracting a mate.

He also encouraged us to keep our eyes peeled for endangered red-legged California frogs, yellow-legged Sierra Nevada frogs and handsome (not!) Yosemite toads. From mule deer to marmots, the park teemed with visible mammals, as well as some reclusive residents, like mountain lions.

Walking back to the campsite, Sean lamented leaving the next day. He wanted to come across more creatures than the deer, squirrels and blue jays we'd seen so far. Because of its reputation for crowds, we'd only planned two nights. But the wonder and possibility of the Yosemite wilds definitely whet our appetites for a return visit.

Angry burrito

During a nightcap of s'mores around a blazing fire, the boys and their dad cracked each other up with bad bathroom references to squeezing out the perfectly "browned, squishy" toasted marshmallows between their graham crackers. Then we all washed up in the well-kept restroom facilities.

Ready for the cold this time, we layered in sweatpants and long shirts before snuggling into our sleeping bags. It was the first time we actually went *in* the bags.

After one-too-many thrashings in his sleep in Mesa Verde, we'd relegated Sean to the single mattress on our right. Aislínn and Ciarán claimed the double on our left. As soon as my daughter shimmied in and zipped all the way up, she tried to turn from her back onto her side – no easy task in the mummy-style bags we purchased especially for the trip.

"I feel like a caterpillar," she squeaked, maneuvering in little bounces á la Mexican jumping bean. She popped her torso up, landed, squirmed and repeated.

Tom and I smirked at her spastic progress.

"Hey. You're right," we heard from the other side. "I'm a burrito!"

Confined in his form-fitting bag, Sean rolled side-to-side. "Do it like this, Bean. It'll get you over."

He picked up so much thrust that he wobbled himself right into the gap between our airbeds. He rotated furiously for a full minute to get back up. No luck. He lay stuck on the ground.

"You dope." Ciarán sat up, laughing harder each time his brother plopped into the gap.

Sean barreled again, almost making it up onto his mattress before sliding down into a heap of snorting giggles. We all hooted. He caught his breath and hurled himself once more, only to land in the crevice. Tom and Ciarán yelped with hilarity. My eyes watered.

Aislínn re-attempted her twisting. Our attention ping-ponged between them. Sean wriggled feverishly; Aislínn writhed without success. Back and forth they volleyed, fueled by our hysterical cheers. Thank goodness the campsites were spread out.

Sean slumped in a lump on the ground, panting. Ciarán egged him on. "C'mon you leeetle leg burrito!!! Use your leeeetle legs."

He couldn't have pushed a more sensitive button with his short sibling. In a single burst, Sean arched up like a serpent and somehow launched himself onto our mattress. Giggles reignited, he spun over us like a steamroller until he was on top of his brother.

We tried to tell them to knock it off, but our words collapsed in bursts of spittle. Tom whooped at the boys' armless wrestling in their sleeping bags, their own snickers muffled in nylon. I doubled over from the sight.

Then seemingly out of nowhere, Aislínn rose up in her sack, ambushing them from the right. She landed full force across both brothers.

"And they're pinned," she announced gleefully.

Stunned, the boys conceded.

"Good one, Bean!" Ciarán pulled his arm out of his bag to give her a high five.

"Yeah." Sean added his palm.

They had to unzip to get back to their places. I soon heard Sean's snores on my left and heavy breathing on the other side. But I stayed awake for quite a while. My sons always got physical with each other. But the last time all three fooled around with such absolute abandon? Years and years. As the saying went, priceless!

Smokey farewell

Our departure from Yosemite felt bittersweet. The park definitely lived up to its reputation as one of the country's most beautiful. We might not have seen a lot of wildlife, but the land itself teemed with energy and splendor. We were blown away by the entire valley, the views, the vast terrain.

Although we left in a different direction than our arrival, smoke again thickened as we descended from White Wolf campground. Encroaching flames near the park's western border forced a detour. In the distance, we observed fully-suited firefighters battling the blazes. No one said a word. A few miles outside the exit, we passed a make-shift camp with acres of tents that housed these heroic men and women.

Yosemite hike

Yosemite to San Francisco, CA
6.5 hours

AT-A-GLANCE:
ALCATRAZ ISLAND NATIONAL RECREATION AREA

Nicknamed "the Rock," Alcatraz Island is part of the Golden Gate National Recreation Area. It offers an intimate look at the site of the infamous federal penitentiary. Excellent self-guided audio tours are available. Additionally, the grounds, preserved as a nature sanctuary, boast a wealth of gardens, tide pools, bird colonies and spectacular bay views.

LOCATION: Alcatraz Island lies 1.5 miles off the coast of San Francisco. A ferry, located at Piers 31-33 (cross streets of Embarcadero & Bay Street) will take you to the island. Just remember to make your reservation early since it often sells out a week or more in advance. The walk from the boat dock to the cellblock is equivalent to a 13-story building, but there is also a tram.

OPEN: Open year-round. Alcatraz Island is only closed on Thanksgiving, Christmas and New Year's Day. Certain island areas may be off limits because of nesting seabirds.

COST: There are a number of Alcatraz tours available, ranging in price from $20 to over $65, with family packages available. The tickets are all inclusive, covering the ferry transportation and the cell-house audio tour.

For information on schedules, prices, and to purchase tickets in advance visit the Alcatraz Cruises website (http://www.alcatrazcruises.com/)

INFO: https://www.nps.gov/alca/index.htm

Chapter 9
San Fran Friskies

California Highway 120 zigzagged out of Yosemite much the same as the mountain roads in many parks. In fact, it reminded me of northwest New Jersey. That is, until we came to a stretch with more hairpin bends than an accordion, connected by short stretches that seemed to go straight up.

In amusement park form, we thrust sideways to offset the serpentine turns then pitched backwards against our seats on the verticals. Sean perfected the art of puking out his back window. Gross. But funny. Had to hand it to a kid who could hurl then giggle.

Thankfully the route settled into the even spaces of the San Joaquin valley, a serene quilt of farms and gently rolling landscape. I could hardly contain my glee when I spotted a bona fide wind farm, its rows of blades spinning like giant pinwheels on the hillside. After two minutes, my kids let me know they didn't need to hear any more about the virtues of alternative energy. I shut up. But the sculptural vista thrilled my eco heart.

Approaching the Bay Bridge into San Francisco, we merged onto good old U.S. 80, the same U.S. 80 that we regularly traveled on the other side of the country by New York's George Washington Bridge.

Tom nodded appreciatively. "That's pretty cool when you think about it."

Our offspring couldn't care less about his enthusiasm, either. Unfortunately the highway's bumper-to-bumper traffic mimicked the east, too.

Wharf wanderings

We lugged suitcases to the second-story room of our inexpensive but decent motel near touristy Fisherman's Wharf. Sean definitely needed a shower, regardless of his spewing prowess. Tom stayed with him while I took the other antsy siblings for a walk.

"Isn't that just goooorgeous?" I pointed to the Golden Gate Bridge, expecting them to share my delight at the iconic art deco span arching in orange glory across the sparkling San Francisco Bay.

"Yeah, mom." Aislínn shrugged with the gusto of cement. Ciarán wove ahead on the crowded pier. I sighed. My daughter and I followed silently along the waterfront until we came to Ghirardelli Square.

"Now you're talkin'!" Ciarán pumped his fist. Brother and sister rushed into the famous chocolatier. I had to smile. Few things in life broke through the obnoxious teen façade like a candy store. I watched my two adolescents light up like seven-year-olds at the shelves of sweets. I told them I'd spring for one treat each; they'd have to use their own cash for anything else. Then I went to search out the caramel section for Tom and Sean.

Chinatown duel

Back at the motel, with everyone fully sugared up, we left and found a city bus to Chinatown, the oldest such section in North America. We passed through its Dragon Gate into a wonderful new world.

Colors and shapes kaleidoscoped around us. Red lanterns swayed under bright awnings. Dead sea creatures, round eyes staring, hung like laundry over wooden tables stacked with a rainbow of mysterious vegetables and fruits. Trinkets and woven goods crammed wide doorways. Our focus darted everywhere as we moved slowly amid crowds on the small streets.

Like eagles in a teeming forest, the boys lasered through this visual cacophony until their attention feasted on their desire: a basket filled with carved wooden warrior swords.

Just as their arms extended for the grasp, Tom barked, "Don't even *think* about it. You are *not* bringing these on the rest of our trip."

Obedient as always, Ciarán removed one from its casing and swung it in the air. His brother did the same.

"I'll buy it with my own money." Ciarán struck forward in a deep lunge.

"I said *no*!" A ruddy flush flew up Tom's neck to the top of his head.

"But they're not even sharp." Ciarán jabbed an end into his brother, who promptly giggled and stuck him back. Within a mini-second, they were

---

PASSING THROUGH DRAGONS

Are they guarding or welcoming? Depends on who you ask. Either way, the fanciful creatures at the entrance to San Francisco's Chinatown adorn the only authentic Chinatown Gate in North America. Seems fitting, since it is the oldest Chinatown in the country. Like its ceremonial counterparts in China, the two-tiered pagoda-style Dragon Gate has three passageways: two small side ones for common folks and a large center entrance for dignitaries. Also called Gateway Arch, this oft-photographed icon with its green-tiled roof is adorned with sculpted fish and dragons and flanked by two large lions meant to thwart evil spirits. It was built according to the ancient Chinese principles of feng shui, which dictate that a city's grandest structure must face south. A wooden plaque hanging from the central archway declares: *"All under heaven is for the good of the people."*

TRAVEL TIP: Getting Around in Cities

Since traffic can be tough and parking is usually at a premium in larger cities, it's often a good idea to leave your car at your hotel lot and take advantage of transportation alternatives. Some hotels offer shuttles to popular attractions, so check that first. Taxis or services like Uber and Lyft are good options, but can add up. We found local mass transit (bus, subway) to be an inexpensive, interesting way to get around a city. Routes and fares are easy to look up. Plus, you often meet more people and see areas that you'd otherwise miss.

---

jousting. Sean accidentally backed into one of the tourists trying to walk around us. Tom exploded.

"SEE! That's what I mean. Put them back. Riiiiight nowwww!" He watched them return the faux blades and strode away with a gruff, "C'mon."

The boys sulked after him.

One thing about Chinatown: the shops were far from unique. Over the next several blocks, we saw the same souvenirs again and again. With each passing display of swords, my boys' dejection grew. Sean frowned. Ciarán simmered. My mom guilt kicked in, perhaps compensating for not letting them have toy weapons growing up. (Yes, I was *that* mom.)

At the next shop with fake carved handles, I said loudly, "Wow, look. More swords. They *are* pretty cool. I don't know, Tom. I think they'll be all right."

Underhanded, for sure. Tom could either dig in and cause a bigger ruckus. Or he could let it go. The boys didn't wait to find out. They dove for the pleather sheaths and did a victory swagger. I paid, avoiding my husband's scowl. Then I hurried off to help Aislínn pick out beaded bracelets and miniature Buddhas.

Unsuspecting gourmands

We strolled down jam-packed Grant Street, peering into intriguing side alleys. Chinatown had five times the population of any other part of San Francisco. Locals, in traditional garments, added to the bustle as they animatedly chatted in Cantonese. The exotic atmosphere enchanted me.

Eventually, Tom softened and we walked hand-in-hand. The boys knew better than to press their luck and kept their swords at their sides. Evening blossomed with the light of dozens of street lanterns.

Since we were going to be in a campsite when Ciarán actually turned 16 the following week, we planned to treat our foodie while we were in the

TRAVEL TIP: Kids and Their Spending Money

When our children were little, we would "pay" (okay, bribe) them for their good behavior on road trips: 25 cents for each 15 minutes that they sat peacefully without annoying anyone. An egg timer rang and we'd tally another quarter. On a 10-hour drive, say, to Maine, they'd each usually net enough for a nice souvenir. Of course, they outgrew this enticement. So for our national parks odyssey, we needed another strategy. A camping chore chart was too much work and buying them anything they wanted was too indulgent. We decided on a weekly allowance. It's smart to figure out your money method before you go, so everyone knows what to expect. Just be prepared for your kids' different financial personalities. In my tribe, Ciarán was the spender; money flew out of his pocket, usually for food. Sean liked to save, carefully planning the few purchases he made, but also holding onto cash to take home. Aislínn landed somewhere in between, buying things she liked and setting a little aside for the next stop. On the trip, they used the allowance for souvenirs, activities and treats that we wouldn't fund. It worked pretty well, and became quite entertaining when a broke Ciarán tried to bargain with his siblings for a loan.

city. The first restaurant on my recommended list had an hour wait. Not a good idea with stomachs already rumbling. We had enough drama for the day, even if all was good now.

We checked a few other eateries before deciding on House of China. Through its ornate red and yellow door, we were led upstairs to a large round table in the rear. Along with menus, the waiter brought a few bowls of fried noodles. Four pairs of hands emptied the crunchy snacks before he even came back with a pitcher of water.

"Sorry." I smiled sweetly. "Haven't eaten in a while."

He nodded with a slight bow, then circled the table to fill our glasses. Another waiter appeared with more noodles. I shot my children a wordless warning. "Look at your menus," I instructed evenly.

Familiar with our take-out back east, we each ordered an appetizer and entrée. Who knew? An immense Lazy Susan on the table's center soon overflowed with huge steaming bowls. Hot and sour soup. Egg flower soup. Sesame noodles. Pot stickers. Dumplings. These were just the appetizers.

"Oh my god!" Tom turned it slowly and we helped ourselves to a little of each. We barely dented the first course when enormous plates of spicy fish, Szechuan beef, pork chow mein, rice noodles and shrimp got crammed onto the spinning dispensary. The kids laughed out loud at the sight.

"Best. Birthday Dinner. Ever!" Ciarán piled his plate.

"Gonna have a landslide there," jibed his sister.

"Nah. I'm on it." He gleefully thrust a loaded chopstick into his mouth.

Every few minutes our server brought more rice, more sauce, more noodles. Like a magician with trick containers, he deftly shuffled the platters to make room. We kept digging in, barreling through as much as we could humanly consume. Yet the rotating centerpiece still held a lot of food.

"The waiter should've told us to just share a couple of things," I huffed, so full I could hardly breathe.

"They're having too much fun watching us." Tom, spooning yet another helping onto his plate, nodded toward the trio of servers, who, indeed, stood smirking in our direction.

"Bigger the bill, bigger tip for them," mumbled Ciarán, mouth mid-chew. He'd gotten a serving job at a boardwalk restaurant and loved receiving gratuities.

I don't know where they put it, but my family kept shoveling. Every once in a while, they'd push away and moan. But then they'd dive back in. Finally, when most of the platters were shockingly empty, the waiter cleared the Lazy Susan and asked about dessert.

Tom dramatically leaned back and spread his hands on an exaggerated belly. "I couldn't eat another thing," he wisecracked, invoking Monty Python's famous exploding Mr. Creosote.

The kids repeated the line, vying to out-do each other's British accent, cracking up mid-sentence. People at neighboring tables joined in our amusement. The main waiter stood placidly. I had to give him credit. Tip or no, he stayed pretty patient with silly tourists.

Unbelievably, my totally stuffed family did want something to top off the meal. They split a couple of small tarts. By the time we rolled out of the restaurant, we officially groaned in unison. We planned to walk it off a little, but the idea was short-lived.

A few blocks away, Ciarán announced he needed to go back to the motel, stat. No elaboration needed, we rushed for the nearest bus stop. However, when I went to look up the schedule, I realized I left my pocketbook at the restaurant. I'd hung the small pouch over my seat and totally forgotten it.

"Maaa-ooooom." Ciarán snarled, grabbing his stomach and bending over. "Why do you *always* do that!?!"

It was true. I had a history of absent-mindedness. And I felt awful. Why didn't we just look for a public restroom? I'm not sure. All I thought to do was run, full speed, to retrieve my bag.

I rushed into the restaurant, where our waiter met me with my purse. I dashed back and thankfully the bus was just pulling up. We made it to the motel quickly and my eldest sprinted in.

With all that food, let's just say the bathroom remained popular for quite a while. We rock-paper-scissored for access. After losing twice, Sean gave up and hurried down to the lobby.

Oh, the digestive dilemmas of family trips!

Benny pleasures

Our tiny Jersey Shore hometown turns into a major vacation destination every summer. For generations, we locals called the tourists "Bennies." No one really knows where it came from but folklore attributed the snarky label to our visitors' origins in **B**rooklyn-**E**lizabeth-**N**ewark-**N**ew **Y**ork or those who came via Philadelphia's "Ben" Franklin Bridge. We had no idea if San Franciscans had a name for their guests, but from the moment we woke the next day, we became quintessential Bennies.

First, we jumped on a cable car at Fisherman's Wharf and roller coastered along its tracks to Union Square. The boys lit up with each rise and dive on the city's celebrated hills. Aislínn got excited about the four-story Barnes and Noble at the end of the line. We couldn't deny our book-lover a browse. Then we moseyed around the famous square, where enormous artsy hearts adorned each corner. Tom and I compared them before choosing the northwest sculpture for our photo op. I hoped it reflected good feng shui.

On a return streetcar, we hopped off at the top of Lombard Street. With dozens of other sightseers (and a few brave drivers), we sauntered down this "crookedest" road in the world. Multi-million dollar homes and lush landscapes fronted the steep, snaking blacktop.

At a border of manicured shrubs, Sean lurched into them, expecting to be enveloped by cushy leaves. The branches barely budged. Giggling, he tilted in again with a little more force. He practically bounced off. Chuckling, I looked closely.

Sure enough, thick woven topiary wires bolstered the bushes. Pretty cool, I thought, wondering how I might copy this to protect my own greenery from

---

HEARTS in SAN FRANCISCO

San Fran's General Hospital launched a special fundraiser in 2004 inspired by Tony Bennett's hit song, *I Left My Heart in San Francisco*. Every year, selected artists paint gigantic heart sculptures that are installed around the city, including on the corners of Union Square. The hearts are auctioned off annually, with proceeds benefiting the hospital.

---

being trampled by our beach-goers. I could only imagine what the upscale Lombard residents thought of their daily trespassers.

We hadn't eaten for at least three whole hours, so we found a nice café for lunch then headed back to the Wharf. After years of mocking our Bennies in jest, it turned out to be quite fun to play tourist. We went in every shop, admired public art, watched sailboats on the bay and threw dollars into the hats of street performers. Our favorites were The Silver Men, shimmering head to toe in skin-tight lamé as they mimed to a hip hop soundtrack. Aislínn and I even sat for a mother-daughter caricature portrait while the boys, surprise, surprise, had ice cream.

Mysteries of the Rock

Next, we queued up at Pier 33 for a 3:30 p.m. boat excursion to Alcatraz Island. The boys got pretty stoked seeing the faces of gangster Al "Scarface" Capone, murderer Robert "Birdman" Stroud and other notorious inmates staring from posters.

After the gangplank steadied, we quickly found seats on the ferry's top deck. The 15-minute ride across San Francisco Bay offered spectacular views of the receding city in the afternoon sunshine. Beacons of light shot off skyscrapers as the Golden Gate glowed blood orange.

In front of us, the small bump of an island grew larger and larger until we could make out a white building abutted by a towering lighthouse. Sean, on a bench with his dad a couple of rows back, came over and elbowed me.

"Hey," he whispered, "I just heard some guy say that Alcatraz is supposed to be one of the most haunted places in America."

"Really?" I leaned in. Many people might brush something like that off, but we Brennans were always game for the supernatural. "What'd he say?"

"I dunno. Just that lots of spirits hang out there."

"Hmmmm." I eyed the horizon. From a distance, the island could've been a high-end private resort with flourishing grounds. But any impression of posh exclusivity faded quickly once we neared the jagged outcropping of "the Rock," Alcatraz' apropos nickname.

Pulling up to the dock, we took in the austere cement façades, barred windows and, most telling, a huge white weathered sign. Black capital letters declared "UNITED STATES PENITENTIARY."

While waiting to disembark, ever-observant Sean noticed a pigeon resting on a fan dormer above the sign. He pointed at the lone avian. "Look!"

That's all it took to get us going. The dormer seemed suspiciously like a bird house. Could the Birdman's spirit still be here? Were the descendants of the pigeons he raised flying around Alcatraz? Were they haunted, too?

As the kids bantered about Birdman, I moved my attention to graffiti sprawled across the dingy concrete wall behind the penitentiary sign. Faded red spray paint proclaimed, "INDIANS WELCOME."

Once on shore, I asked a park ranger about the incongruous message. I learned that in 1969, six years after the prison closed, a group of Native Americans claimed the island on behalf of the "Indians of All Tribes." Mostly young and urban, the protesters wanted to build a university and museum. Citing an old treaty that called for retired or abandoned federal land to be returned to the Native people, they started what was called "the Occupation of Alcatraz." For more than a year-and-a-half, the peaceful demonstrators refused to leave, until the U.S. government finally forced them to.

The ranger emphasized the word "forced." I cringed. He said the failed campaign did, fortunately, lead to some changes in national policy on Native American rights. I inhaled slowly and looked up from the boat landing to the buildings above. Who knew how many stories a single piece of land held? If only those rocks could talk.

Tom and the kids had walked ahead on the inclined pavement to the prison. I caught up and shared my new info.

Sean raised his eyebrow. "Hey. I wonder if that means some of the ghosts here are natives."

"Could be." I sighed. "Pretty grim."

Cellular confinement

Once inside the imposing 600-cell structure, we each shivered, and not just from the cool air bouncing off its reinforced concrete walls. A riveting audio tour plus a little imagination propelled us back in time through the rest of Alcatraz' dark, disturbing history.

It was one thing to think conceptually about incarceration. It was totally another to observe rows of cells, stacked floor by floor like container trucks and picture human beings living in bleak spaces smaller than my bathroom.

Although the boat had been full, the immense building swallowed us. We barely saw anyone else as we slowly explored on our self-guided tour, our footsteps echoing eerily off the cement floors. The boys hammed it up, striding into the one "display" cell. But when the bars slammed shut, they quickly pushed them open.

Remnants of convicts seemed particularly wrenching – impressive pencil drawings on chipped walls in one cell, stacks of books and letters on a tiny shelf in another. These personal artifacts were hard to reconcile with the horrific stories broadcast through our headphones, some by past inmates and guards.

We heard gory details about gangsters, cold-blooded murderers, prison riots and unyielding wardens. Take Alvin "Creepy Karpis" Karpowicz, the FBI's first Public Enemy No. 1, who spent a quarter century locked up in Alcatraz, more than any other prisoner. Or brothers Clarence and John Anglin, whose bodies were never found after their 1962 escape from the Rock. And, of course, Alphonse Gabriel Capone, whose seven year reign as Chicago's crime boss ended at the tender age of 33 when he was convicted of tax evasion. We also found out that despite his "Birdman of Alcatraz" nickname, Robert Stroud was not permitted to raise any winged creatures during his 17 years there, as he had while locked up the 30 previous years in Leavenworth, Kansas. I nudged Sean.

"Yeah. Guess the pigeon was just a regular bird," he said, clearly disappointed.

Once outside the prison again, I found myself gulping breaths of fresh air. My family didn't even laugh at me. We strolled around the island, the kids excitedly recapturing highlights of the audio tour.

I took in the handsome grounds, dotted with pre-civil war buildings that for decades housed prison staff and their kin. Bright cultivated patches of flowers and greenery brought welcome color against gray stone. Far below, hundreds of sea birds hovered over rocky shores, picking at fertile tide pools.

The island was, indeed, beautiful. But even on our relaxing ferry back to Fisherman's Wharf, I couldn't dismiss images of those cold, tiny cells that

---

STRATEGIC ISLAND

Mapped in 1775 as La Isla de los Alcatraces, or Island of the Pelicans, Alcatraz was first used by the U.S. Army for a harbor fortress. By the 1850's, thought, top brass figured that the isolated scrap of land was perfect to house military prisoners. Even if inmates escaped, the bay's frigid waters would make it impossible to survive. Eighty years later, in 1934, the U.S. Justice Department took over and the former Army prison became a federal maximum-security penitentiary, housing the country's worst criminals, too dangerous or too difficult to be handled elsewhere. It became the "prison system's prison," where sparse conditions and few privileges – not to mention other tactics – taught disruptive inmates to follow rules. Those who learned to behave got transferred to less severe lock-ups to finish their sentences.

remained home to nearly 1,600 inmates before the prison closed in 1963.

Seal of approval

Sea lions and a Pacific Ocean sunset seemed the perfect antidote for our prison blues. Years earlier, I'd seen the adorable mammals lazing off San Fran's northwest corner on Seal Rocks, also famous for its sunsets. After a lifetime of eastern sun rises, it would have been awesome for my family to see our closest star dive *into* the ocean.

We made a pit stop at our motel and quickly got ready for the short ride. But in our 20 minutes inside, the city's trademark fog wisped onto the horizon like a wintry breath. Soon it would infiltrate the entire bay.

"Guess we aren't going anywhere." Tom shrugged. "By the time we get there, we'd be walking in vapor."

Instead we roamed aimlessly along the Wharf again. To our great surprise and delight, we found our sea lions anyway. Five lounged like prima donnas on wooden floats by Pier 39. With long whiskers and dark saucer eyes, they fawned over each other like puppies. Flippers draped, noses nuzzled, blubber wiggled.

"Think they're doing it on purpose," whispered Sean.

"You mean porpoise?" Tom smirked.

"Duh. … No I mean it looks like they're used to this gig."

I nodded. They sure did seem to be enjoying their growing circle of fans. A hefty female lavishly rolled over and let loose with an explosive bark. The crowd returned a chorus of claps and laughs. Two pups began to wrestle.

Tom snorted. "Must happen with all siblings."

"Yeah, but at least their dad doesn't yell at them," Ciarán retorted.

"How do you know?" Tom pointed at a large male starting to yap.

"Haha. So funny."

We relished the antics for nearly an hour. The fog literally rolled onto the pier, covering us with fine beads of moisture. The sun, in a surreal dive behind the mist, sank into the dark water.

At a nearby courtyard, we found a magic troupe staging a free show. Claiming a spot among the crowd, we enjoyed every trick, twist, juggle and dare. Our spontaneous good karma continued at Bubba Gump Shrimp Company, where we landed a coveted window table.

But the tenor quickly shifted when we asked for a children's menu for Sean. In other restaurants along the way, he'd ordered his favorite chicken fingers and French fries, and I'd been glad for the kid-meal cost savings.

"I am *not* getting anything off this." He slammed the colorful paper on the table and grabbed his brother's large laminated menu.

Ciarán mimicked in a high pitch, "I'm NOT getting anything off this." He pulled his menu back. "Yes you are, you leetle one."

Sean shot out of his seat. "Shut up!"

I stood next to my youngest and tried to put my arm around his shoulders. He shimmied away.

"I'm sorry Sean. I thought you liked chicken fingers..."

"I *don't*. Well I do, but he's always getting the most expensive thing and you make me get the kid's crap. It's not fair."

Ciarán chimed in again. "Not fa-ir."

"Quiet Ciarán!" I gently urged Sean to sit again. "You're right. I'm really sorry. You order whatever you want." I handed him my menu.

Amazingly, as we ate, the fog lifted to reveal a stunning night sky with a great view of the sparkling bay. From here, Alcatraz again looked like an exquisite destination. Inside, our ice cream sundaes seemed to wash down any remaining antagonism.

Alcatraz Island

San Francisco to the Redwoods, CA
7.5 hours

AT-A-GLANCE:
Muir Woods National Monument
Muir Woods, named for conservationist John Muir, became a National Monument in 1908 to protect its old growth coastal redwoods and the abundance of plant and animal life they foster. The tallest of all living things, redwoods reach heights above 350 feet and have an average lifespan of 600-800 years, with some standing more than 1,200 years. They are vital to carbon, nutrient and water cycles in this primeval forest, which is also part of the Golden Gate National Recreation Area,
    LOCATION: Muir Woods is 11 miles north of San Francisco in Mill Valley, CA.
    OPEN: Open year-round, 8 a.m. to sunset.
    COST: $15 per person, ages 15 and under are free. (Parking/shuttle additional.)
    INFO:https://www.nps.gov/muwo/index.htm

Chapter 10
Tree-mendous

When I opened my laptop at dawn to get work done while my brood slept, my mood plunged faster than a downed rocket. Disjointed pixels filled the screen. Nothing I clicked made them go away.

The day before, Tom purchased some state-of-the-art device he thought would improve my camera speed. Hundreds of daily photos were choking the Canon EOS. I just wanted a few sim cards or a cheap external drive to offload the pics. But my gadget guru saw this pricey gizmo in an electronics shop on the Wharf and insisted it would be better. I gave up arguing. As I blissfully fell asleep, he happily installed or destalled or whatever on my computer. I didn't quite get what it was supposed to do.

But I knew it shouldn't make my Macbook look like an after-hours 1950's television set. I anxiously beckoned my husband. Mouth wide in surprise, he frantically rebooted and fidgeted until my regular home screen appeared. I let out a sigh of relief. Tom shook his head.

"Looks like it didn't take," he muttered through gritted teeth. "I don't know why. They all seemed to be going through when I went to bed."

"What do you mean it didn't take?" Tightness edged into my confusion.

"The photos... they didn't transfer... sorry." His curt tone sounded anything but apologetic.

"Then give me the camera. I'll get a couple of sim cards like I wanted in the first place." I tersely extended my arm.

He stiffened and said too quickly, "Can't. Everything's erased."

It took a moment to sink in. Blood rushed to my head.

"*Erased*?" I paced across the room, trying to comprehend. I turned and glared, my breast heaving. "*HOW?!?*"

He stared back defensively. "I figured everything was good. I emptied the memory so it would all be ready to go."

We'd taken more than 800 photos. From Black Canyon of the Gunnison. Mesa Verde. Canyon of the Ancients. Grand Canyon. Yosemite. Chinatown. Alcatraz. All the miles of landscape in between. The reality hit me. Everything was gone. Totally lost. All we had were a few instamatic shots.

I attempted to swallow my fury. It was like squeezing toothpaste back into the tube. At that moment, I was not a good role model for my children, now wide awake. Neither was Tom, asserting it wasn't his fault. We yelled, we screamed, I cried. Then I slammed out the door, barely able to see.

I'd previously arranged to have breakfast with an old friend who moved to San Francisco from New Jersey years earlier. Instead of happily catching up, I battled knots in my stomach. All the petty annoyances at Tom over the past weeks oozed and dripped like the syrup on Alicia's pancakes. My feeble attempts to chew some omelet only added to my abdominal constriction.

Hours later, back in the room, I saw the kids doing what they always did when their dad and I clashed over something that didn't involve them: act as if nothing happened. Aislínn sat reading; the boys watched TV.

When I brusquely side-stepped Tom to get to the closet, my sage 14-year-old looked up from her book and advised, "just get over it, ma." I stopped myself from scowling at her, too.

After strained packing, we hit the road again for a three-day trek to our next national park: Crater Lake in Oregon. Approaching the Golden Gate Bridge, I curtly said I wanted to show the kids one of my favorite spots, the Presidio, a former fort turned beautiful national recreation area.

"There it is dad, up ahead," Ciarán announced from the rear.

But instead of veering off at the designated exit, Tom proceeded over the bridge.

I snapped my head at him. "What are you doing? That was the turn-off."
"Where?"

"The one you just passed. The one that said in big letters: PRESIDIO." I frowned out my window at the beautiful greenery below us.

"Well Sally said to go straight."

"I know," I hissed, my voice rising. "But *we* were saying to turn. Can't you ever listen to *us* instead of the GPS?"

"Mom, let it go." My daughter's voice stopped mine.

Anger pulsed in my temples like war drums. I took slow breaths until the pounding subsided. I didn't care about Tom, but knew it wasn't fair to the kids if I fumed. Tom made no effort to turn around and I had 'to let it go.'

Muir Woods magic

The twisty roads leading north into the valley did little to calm my nerves or stomach. Thankfully, the sight of redwood groves at Muir Woods provided a balm. From afar, the giant trees merged with the sky, their crowns mingling with the clouds.

As we parked and began walking manicured trails, I felt like a mere dot under the imposing evergreens, the tallest living organisms in the world.

The ancient conifers – some nearly five times older than our country

> **NATURAL HEALING**
>
> Scientific research is finding what many of us have long known: forests, waterways and other natural settings may be more effective than medication in healing anger, anxiety and depression. Recent studies verify that a walk in the park can lower blood pressure, stabilize heart rate variability and calm stress hormones. At a time when public lands are threatened and most of us have less time to enjoy them, our national treasures may be just what we need to improve our health and happiness.

itself – radiated strength and serenity. Their massive trunks and graceful branches seemed to extend a message of peace. Each step into the grove washed away my evil spirits. How could I dwell on my petty drama in the midst of these majestic guardians?

We each experienced our own form of connection to these keepers of the earth. At one point Ciarán stopped short in front of an immense trunk.

"Do you feel it, mom? Right here." He pounded his chest. I knew just what he meant. We stood wordlessly gazing up into the thick, yet delicate, canopy.

Then, in the about-face that is teenage boys, he snatched my arms in one of his grappling moves and lifted me off my feet until I was horizontal in his arms. Back in Yosemite, he'd spontaneously done the same to Sean, launching a series of photos with that pose in every stop since.

I smiled. All those other pictures might be gone. But what better place to start the ritual again than in mystical Muir Woods?

Foggy Mt. Tam

Much mellower, we drove out of the valley toward Mount Tamalpais. That's Mt. Tam to fans of Percy Jackson, the half human, half god son of Poseidon who starred in Rick Riordan's bestselling young adult books. Nothing like YA cult fiction to ignite enthusiasm. Mt. Tam was the secret evil fortress of Kronos, King of the Titans. My kids couldn't wait to hike to the top.

We wound through chaparral, tall grasses, oaks and, of course, redwoods on our climb. Although only 2,700 feet in elevation, the mountain seemed much higher. On a sunny day, folks said you could see beyond San Francisco Bay to the Farallon Islands 25 miles at sea. Sometimes you could even spy the Sierra Nevada more than 150 miles away.

Once again, though, we were foiled by the Bay area weather sandwich: fog in the morning, mid-day clearing, fog in the afternoon. By the time we ascended Mt. Tam, mist obscured the Golden Gate Bridge and draped over the mountain treetops in an eerie cascade, like a demigod entranceway for sure. This would've been incredibly cool if the sudden rumbling we heard was some supernatural underground activity. Miserably, it came from me.

Musical relief

The early morning agita might have left my mind, but it stayed alive and kicking in my gut. As we stood gazing into the thickening shroud on the summit, I knew I was in trouble. My afternoon serenity couldn't reverse remnant rage and road woozies. Without even acknowledging the kids' laughter, I hightailed it down to the nearest port a-john.

Despite my years of outdoor travel, few things grossed me out more than the rank metal bathrooms. I'm not talking garden variety revulsion. My porta-potty phobia threw me into irrational crisis.

Luckily, as I reached the lone outhouse, the motion seemed to trigger a biological sedative. For a fleeting moment, I believed I was okay. I truly thought I wouldn't have to enter the dreaded container, that I could wait until we got all the way down to a real restroom. My whole body relaxed.

Then an intestinal tremor hit with such force that I had to take action. Immediately. I frantically looked around. The trail was too exposed to find privacy outdoors, which I would have much preferred.

Tearing up, I started to hyperventilate. I reached for the green door. Wretchedly, I took a huge breath, the deepest I could possibly inhale, and rushed in, sweat glistening on my forehead. I begged myself to grow up and calm down.

Within seconds, I heard sniggering, followed by a gurgled, "Hey, ma. You alive?"

The boys had followed me. I panicked. If I answered, I'd have to let out the air in my swimmer's lungs. My plan had been to make it out before inhaling again. So I just offered a short, tight-lipped, "mm-hmmmm," which set them off even more.

Their trill giggles did me in. I burst out in a cheek-popping spit of air, then screamed, "Gooooooo awayyyyyyy. You. Made. Me. Breathe."

Kronos must've been rolling his eyes beneath us. When I emerged, gray-faced, my sons vibrated with glee.

"You should see yourself, ma." My eldest put his arm around me. I shook him away. They couldn't stop laughing. Through their chuckles, they began:

If you're climbing up Mt. Tam,
And your stomach's on the lam …
Di-a-rrhea!
Di-a-rrhea!

When you gotta go the most
Doesn't matter if it's gross
Di-a-rrhea!
Di-a-rrhea!

Yep. The good old diarrhea ditty, aka *Butt Mud, Poo Goo* and *Montezuma's Revenge*. No kidding. Look it up and you'll find plenty of "official" verses, like the artful:

When you're climbing up a ladder,
and something starts to splatter...

or:

When you're riding in a Chevy
and you feel something heavy.

You get the idea. But the creative Brennan boys tailored lyrics to meet my particular needs. They continued to serenade as we hiked back to the top.

When you feel something spotty
Gotta use the porta-potty
Di-a-rrhea! (Cha Cha Cha)
Di-a-rrhea! (Cha Cha Cha)

They turned and wiggled their rears.

"Enough!" I snorted, finally giving in to their hilarity.

At the peak, we were astonished to see – or not see – anything. The fog moved in so quickly that it probably would have swallowed Tom and Aislínn if my bathroom break took any longer.

My husband came over and tentatively put his arm around me. "You okay?"

I stiffened, an automatic response to our earlier battles. But then I looked at him and leaned in.

"Yeah, she's fine now." Ciarán made the loudest raspberry he could. "She's all good now." Tom cracked up.

"Leave me alone." I pushed him, although I was smiling. I walked over to my daughter, who, unphased by her brothers' juvenile antics, stood taking in the transcendent non-panorama.

"Pretty cool, isn't it?" I asked softly.

She nodded and put her arm around my waist.

Garberville rest

The boys got a kick out of pointing out the culprit potty on our way down to The Couch. Once there, my family munched on sandwiches we'd prepped earlier. I opted for a banana. Then we set off on an uneventful four-hour ride through Sonoma Valley to Garberville, CA.

Tom cranked up the radio and sang, accompanied in spurts by various support vocals while we passed stunning grape vineyards and fruit orchards lush with rows seemingly groomed by meticulous beauticians. Further north, the landscape morphed into dry hillsides. At one point we thought we were approaching a carnival. But we soon recognized the familiar tents and canopies of heroic firefighters.

In Garberville, we quickly settled into a cozy roadside motel. We'd gotten good at pulling out what we needed for the night and automatically choosing our spots in the room. Aislínn claimed the cot; the boys took a double bed. Tom immediately laid down for a nap on the other queen. The kids switched on the TV and I set up my laptop to work, barely acknowledging our morning fracas.

We found a nice little eatery that to everyone's delight offered pizza *and* burritos. I, personally, was thrilled for the chicken soup. My belly hadn't quite settled yet, but my psyche filled with gratitude.

In the morning, Tom took our dirty clothes to a laundromat in town.

AT-A-GLANCE:
REDWOOD NATIONAL PARK

Although known for its conifer giants, Redwood National Park also protects a broader ecosystem: miles of native Pacific coastline, rivers, prairies and oak forests. The stunning preserve is co-managed by the National Park Service and California State Parks.

LOCATION: Roughly 50 miles long, Redwood National and State Parks are located in northernmost coastal California, from near the Oregon border in the north to near Orick, CA in the south. Five information centers are located along this north-south corridor, including the Park headquarters in Cresent City, CA.

OPEN: Redwood is open all year; the visitor centers and campgrounds operate seasonally.

COST: The park is free to visit.

INFO: https://www.nps.gov/redw/index.htm

After I uploaded my last file, Aislínn and I strolled around the small, artsy shops in Garberville. I craved a heart-to-heart with my daughter, but knew better than to push.

On the sidewalk in between stores, I casually asked, "You doing okay?"

She side-eyed me. "Yeah. *I'm* fine. I'm not the one who went crazy."

I sighed. "You're right. I'm sorry. I..."

She cut me off. "It's all good, ma. People have their moods. We're all human."

We walked in silence, me flipping between wanting to defend myself or dig deeper into *her* perspective of the trip so far. I did neither. I just followed her into the next shop, where we fawned over some handmade candles.

Shortly after noon, The Couch rolled again, embarking on one of the most extraordinary drives of our trip.

Lifted by giants

There's a reason old U.S. Highway 101 is called "Avenue of the Giants." The enormous conifers in Muir Woods seemed miniature compared to the living skyscrapers that welcomed us. No words, no radio, no earbuds disturbed our awed hush as we rolled into the astonishing sanctuary, the Suburban a tiny Matchbox under the towering trees.

A pull-off beckoned us, the only travelers in sight. Exiting slowly, we bent our necks back to spy the distant canopy. Then we approached a huge trunk, where we stretched arms and grabbed hands to encircle it.

"C'mon, leetle ones," commanded Ciarán. He instructed us to let go of our grips and touch only fingertips to cover more circumference. We still barely made it half way around.

Giggling, Sean stood next to a fallen tree, which even on its side stood

---

REMARKABLE REDWOODS

Some are taller than the Statue of Liberty, wider than a greyhound bus and 10 times older than America itself. The redwoods of Northern California are the largest living things on earth! Measuring up to 20 feet in diameter, many grow higher than 300 feet. In fact, the tallest tree in the world is a coast redwood named Hyperion (yes, more Greek mythology.) It stood 379.7 feet when it was discovered in 2006 in a remote area of Redwood National Park. These majestic sentinels are also among the oldest on earth; some live for more than 2000 years. The species itself, *Sequoia sempervirens*, has graced the planet for more than 240 million years!

a couple of heads taller. Multi-tanned rings visible in a clean break on the downed trunk reflected years and decades and centuries. How tiny and young we were. We all took deep breaths under these incredible lungs of the planet.

"I bet this is what astronauts feel when they look down on the amazing earth." My youngest had dropped to the ground on his back in a stand of the gargantuan timber and stared skyward. "Only we're looking *up* to an amazing world. That's so sweet."

"You're not kidding." Ciarán joined him, sliding his arms and legs to make an angel in the soft pine needles that blanketed the ground.

"Yep," agreed Aislínn, copying her brothers. "I think this is my favorite so far."

My spirit did a double flip.

Tight squeeze

The meandering 40-mile drive through the redwoods wove past small towns that capitalized on their renowned residents. Every few miles we'd see another wood-carving studio, gift shop or forest-themed restaurant. None caught our fancy until the Shrine Drive-Thru Tree in Myers Flat, CA.

"It'll be a hoot." Tom pulled into the entry, marked by a life-sized redwood bear that was carved with a chainsaw.

"Really?" I asked the long-time Shrine owner as I handed him our ten bucks. "How in the world did they get all that detail?" He shrugged, smiled and pointed us to a short dirt road on which his famous tree stood.

We inched our vehicle toward the ancient trunk. The "drive through" was a large split on the tree's bottom creating an upside-down "v."

It seemed far too narrow to me. "Maybe they made this before SUV's. I really don't think we'll fit."

"Mom." Ciarán hissed, clearly still disgusted at any vehicle-related concerns I might utter.

"Don't worry, we're fine," assured Tom. "Everyone has a pickup here." But he did reach out to fold in his side-view mirror. I did the same.

The owner, probably used to skittish Easterners, waved us on from behind and shouted, "PLENTY of room!"

Tom crawled ahead, edging the nose of our Suburban into the opening. The optics seemed even more unnerving eye-to-eye with tree bark. I winced.

"Shhhhhsh!" Tom warned.

"I didn't say anything," I retorted.

"Quit gasping," shot Ciarán.

DRIVE-THRU DISPUTE

It was a classic case of conservation vs. commercialism. Environmentalists weren't happy that Redwood entrepreneurs tunneled through the base of select trunks so they could charge visitors for the unique 30-foot ride through a wooden giant. The tourism proponents, however, said you have to understand trees to realize the drive-throughs don't cause harm. Below their bark lies a thin cambium layer, where tree growth takes place. Inside that is the sapwood, which is like a pipeline that sends water from the root system. The heartwood at the tree's center is inactive. The businesspeople claimed that as long as the bark, cambium and sapwood layers were healthy, then a redwood would continue to grow even if its heartwood was hollowed out as a vehicular tunnel. No go, said the courts, which outlawed the practice. So now there are three remaining drive-through trees that are carefully preserved. These legendary tourist magnets, all in California, are: the Shrine Drive-Thru Tree in Myers Flat, the Chandelier Drive-Thru Tree in Leggett, and the Tour-Thru Tree at the northern end of Redwood territory near Klamath.

Tom rolled some more. I clinched, waiting for unmistakable scraping on metal. Sean giggled nervously. The wheels continued to creep until we were all the way in, wood on both sides. From the interior, I was relieved to see we actually did have leeway.

"We got this now." Tom grinned. "We're over half way."

He pressed the gas more freely and we cruised out the other side. Tom lifted his arms to high five whoever responded from the back and let rip a loud, "YOOOOOWWWWWW WEEEEEEEEE."

Everyone cracked up. No doubt the owner laughed too, but not *with* us. We pulled away from the famed tree, a tourist ploy, for sure, but certainly fun. The Shrine Tree park also boasted a Drive-On Tree, a fallen giant with a partially paved ramp, but we passed on that. We also skipped an intricately carved tree house and walk-through stump that would have been a blast for younger kids.

We did, however, enjoy the redwood factoids posted around the property. Plus, I loved the gift shop's beautiful creations, some ceiling high with mind boggling delicacy. Aislínn and I strolled over to a gorgeous redwood wishing well, scrawled notes on an attached pad and tossed them in. Neither of us divulged our desires.

> ## BIOMASSIVE MARVELS
>
> The coast redwood, which grows in a thin strip of land along the Pacific northwest, is one of three sequoia tree species. Unlike many other trees, these giants do not rely on a single deep taproot. Instead, they have a shallow root system that spreads out for hundreds of feet from their trunks, entwining with the roots of neighboring trees to add stability to the whole grove. These forests have an abundant undergrowth, including many types of ferns. But the greatest biodiversity is sky high, between the interwoven branches where hanging gardens thrive under the redwood canopy. In fact, there is more biomass per square foot in a typical redwood forest than in any other area on the globe, including Amazon's rain forests. This dramatic environment hasn't escaped Hollywood: the redwoods provided lush scenery in *Star Wars* and *Jurassic Park*. Unfortunately, redwoods make a wonderful construction wood. An estimated 96% of original redwood forests have been logged and deforestation continues. Thankfully, most remaining groves are preserved in national and state parks.

Here's looking at you, kid!

Even the most spectacular stimuli on our adventure eventually gave way to yawns. Biology was to blame. Science has shown that after a while brains adapt to extreme sensory input and send it into the storage crate with other normal, familiar stuff.

Not so with the redwoods. They never lost their magic as we continued our journey north. When the path veered toward the coast, we noticed distinct changes. Sunlight diminished as if on a fader switch. Moisture – critical to the giants' survival (and also awesome for movie backdrops) – thickened with every mile.

Just south of the Redwood National Park boundary, my kids got their first ever glimpse of the Pacific. No one had to say a thing; Tom turned into the next pull-off. Our wheels barely stopped when Sean jumped out and ran to the cliff overlooking the ocean. He scanned the horizon below, pointing excitedly.

"Look! Pelicans!" He moved his finger. "Look! Loons!"

Neither seabird were common in New Jersey. He raced down a steep trail to the beach, his sister and brother on his tail. Tom grabbed our binoculars from the glove compartment and followed.

We happily waded our east coast feet into the west coast sea, marking the milestone with a collective whoop. Back on dry sand, Sean directed his index finger again, this time at a brown head bobbing in shallow surf 20 feet off shore. "Wow. It's a seal!"

He tip-toed to the water's edge. Instead of scurrying, big eyes returned his stare. The pup paddled a few yards south and turned as if to invite Sean to follow.

For the next minute, the two paralleled each other, my son catching up every time his new friend swam and beckoned with a glance. The rest of us watched, amazed, until the young seal turned out to sea. Sean glowed.

Voluminous vocabulary

A familiar brown federal sign let us know when we entered Redwood National Park. Free to all visitors, it didn't have the marked boundaries or pay stations we saw at other parks.

The further north we ventured, the forest grew, incredibly, even more powerful and inspiring. At one point, we pulled over to gawk at impossibly tall trees. We thought we'd already seen the loftiest. Yet these pierced the heavens. We got out and walked to their base.

The land under our feet stopped, yet the immense trunks still loomed ahead. We were on a cliff! We peered down through barely illuminated spaces between the trees and made out more of their trunks far below.

Hundreds of feet above, the lush canopy arched over us with its graceful, intertwined branches. Random openings in the leaves allowed muted rays of light that also revealed hanging plants, snaking vines and lavish ferns.

We stood speechless until Aislínn vocalized our awe. "I've never seen anything so cool. I feel like I'm standing in a living cave."

Back on the narrow road, our voices kindled. We tried to outdo each other in describing the most spectacular inhabitant in each passing grove.

"That one's eeee-normous," shouted Ciarán, arm darting out his window.

"No. This one's totally *mas*-sive," countered Aislínn, directing us to her side.

"Over there! It's gar-*gan*-tuan," chimed Sean, leaning across his brother to get a better view.

"Titanic," added Tom, pointing through the windshield.

Vast. Gigantic. Mammoth. Colossal. The word-loving Brennans ran out of synonyms as we, in our mushrooming joy, rolled up old Highway 101.

Burl-dacious

As if their height and breadth didn't mesmerize enough, many of the trees boasted another magnetizing allure: hefty burls bulging from trunks into magnificent 3-D sculptures. As with clouds and sandstone formations, these abstract appendages carried shapes and stories galore. We laughed and deciphered imaginary images in dozens of bodacious burls, some as big as The Couch.

Views from ocean-side bluffs grew increasingly dramatic as we wound our way up the rough, often unpaved, coastal drive inside Redwood National Park. Stopping on another small dirt cut-away, we stared at the arresting, stark landscape fashioned by weather, woods and water.

Stunning lines of quartz infused the granite cliffs we stood on. Driftwood decorated the sand below as if arranged by an artist. Dense air vapor tinted everything gray. Despite the calendar saying deep July, the temperature read below 50 degrees. It had been in the 80s in Muir Woods.

"Brrrrr. This is certainly different." Tom, who usually relished cool over heat, said he was ready to call it a day.

Flip-flop foibles

Since we booked based on price, our hotels became a crap shoot. Several definitely Photoshopped their web pics; a couple were downright dingy. As long we had a passable bathroom, two double beds and wi-fi for my work, all was fine.

Every once in a while, though, we hit the jackpot, like the Lighthouse Inn in Crescent City, CA. The kids and I got the keys and entered a huge room with three queen beds, unheard of in our budget accommodations.

Massive trees *and* massive zzzz's? The siblings went wild. Literally. They bounded like high-jumpers onto the trio of oversized mattresses and sprang back and forth, laughing out loud. None of us noticed Tom enter with our suitcase.

"*Heyyyy.*" He slammed out bag down. "Knock it off! What d'ya think you're doing!!!"

Ciarán trampolined into a somersault. The other two giggled. I sighed.

Still in the doorway, Tom hissed, "Go. Get. Your. Bags."

They each launched across the duvets in one more glorious leap before dismounting and chuckling out the door under their father's glare, which he then turned toward me.

Of course I knew it wasn't appropriate for teenagers to vault on beds. They could have damaged something. But sometimes joy just outweighed common sense.

I took a breath and met Tom's eyes. He did most of the driving again, which meant he needed to decompress. Instead of arguing, I shrugged. And gave him a hug.

After washing up, we asked the lobby clerk for a good place to eat. He pointed directly across Highway 101 to a local seafood joint with green day-glo script on its window: Best Fish Fry Around. He also recommended the restaurant next door.

"Fish Fry looks good to me," enthused Aislínn. We all agreed and followed her out the door across the parking lot. She was about to step off the curb when Tom, 10 feet behind, shouted, *"Aislínn! WAIT!"*

Everyone stopped and looked back at him. Did he forget something?

"Aislínn," he continued sternly. "You *can't* cross the street like that!"

We regarded him curiously. My daughter, annoyed at losing her lead to her brothers, slammed her hand on her hip in perfect teen girl disgust. "Whaaaaat???"

With the concern and command of a scout leader warning his Webelos, Tom said, "You have your flip flops on. You can't cross the street in *flip flops.*"

In the seconds that no one said anything, giggles filled the rest of our cheeks like helium then burst into a collective spit of glee. For a full minute, we laughed so hard, we cried. I turned to Tom, my eyes damp. *"Really?"*

We knew he was obsessed with proper hiking footwear, but this was, well, ridiculous. And hilarious. He looked at each of us, face reddening. I knew it could go either way and I sucked in the sides of my cheeks to stop laughing.

"Tom…" I ventured quietly. "It's an empty street… not a mountain. She's fine. She wears her flip flops all the time around town at home. And she can make it safely across the street in them."

He looked around, wobbling closer to rage. Then we practically saw the light bulb go off. He palmed his brow and shook his head. "Man, I don't even know what I was thinking. I must be hungry."

That made us laugh even harder as we strolled across the street. After all that, the eatery was closed. So we retraced our steps, with the boys' teasing chorus, "Careful Aislínn!" "Watch your ankles!"

I tried not to smirk. Poor Tom. Long day of driving. Teenage bed acrobatics. The weight of being a control freak. Boy did he need a big meal and a good night's sleep.

For the rest of the trip, the flip flop faux pas soared as a sure-fire crack-up prompt. "On no, Aislínn, how are you going to handle the museum in those flip flops?" "Where's your boots, Bean? That's a dangerous sidewalk ahead."

Even now, the sight of any thonged footwear on the feet of my daughter,

> **LIGHTHOUSE ILLUMINATION**
>
> Battery Point, connected by isthmus to mainland Crescent City boasts one of the first lighthouses on the California coast. It initially was illuminated in December 1856 with a groundbreaking Fresnel lens that concentrated light into a narrow beam, said to be "the invention that saved a million ships."

who has since run a half marathon, trekked in Tibet and wandered all over Europe sans family, can bring back our Crescent City giggles.

Tricky tide

The next morning, well rested and again well fed, we set off (all in hiking boots) to the nearby Crescent City Lighthouse. Although automated, the 150-plus year-old historic landmark remained manned in case of emergency. A keeper and his family lived in the scenic beaconed homestead atop a tiny island known as Battery Point.

We couldn't understand why they called it an island, especially since we walked directly across rocky sand to explore the area, including its small museum. But when we were ready to head back, the 200-foot return path lay hidden under surf.

We had to slosh through incoming tide. It suddenly made sense why driftwood and stones haphazardly littered the dry ground on our way over: they were moved every 12 hours with the surge.

Thank goodness, really, that we had on boots to cross the rocky, fast-moving stream. Once on dry ground again, Tom noticed a sign we'd missed:

Only visit the Lighthouse at low tide.
Use extreme care and caution at any time, as waves may cover the crossing area and threaten visitors standing on or near the rocks and shore of Battery Point Island.

Fog rolling in over Mt. Tamalpais

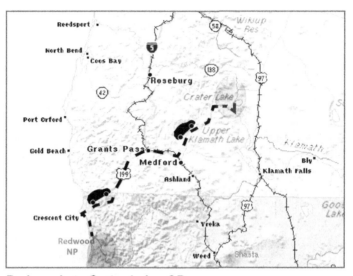

Redwoods to Crater Lake, OR
4 hours

AT-A-GLANCE:
CRATER LAKE NATIONAL PARK
Born of a violent volcanic past, Crater Lake is the deepest (and possibly most pristine) lake in the U.S. The breathtakingly blue body of water is surrounded by cliffs almost 2,000 feet high. Dramatic views abound in this unique park.

LOCATION: Crater Lake is in southern Oregon on the crest of the Cascade Mountain Range. It is 100 miles east of the Pacific Ocean, 110 miles from the California and halfway between Bend to the north and Klamath Falls to the to the south.

OPEN: Crater Lake is open all year but some roads and facilities are closed in the winter.

COST: $30 per vehicle, $25 per motorcycle and $15 per bicyclist, pedestrian; under 16 is free

INFO:https://www.nps.gov/crla/index.htm

Chapter 11
Full Moon Birthday

We strolled around in cool grayness on the municipal pier before bidding adieu to Crescent City. Just miles away, the weather altered dramatically. Fog evaporated like steam from a mirror as we emerged from the coastal shroud. In minutes, the thermometer rocketed from 56° to 85° under a blindingly blue sky with the first sun we'd seen in days. We gladly flung off our fleeces.

Tom had me pull his sleeve while he held the wheel. "Man. Must be tough living by the shore here."

"Says Crescent City has 182 sunny days with a high of 64 in July," announced Aislínn, reading from her guidebook.

Her older brother scoffed. "Just 182? That's not even half. I could *never* live there."

"Me neither," agreed Sean. "Sixty four's not even hot and I betcha they don't even get snow."

I laughed. "Well some people are just fine without the white stuff."

"Not me," said Ciarán. "Gimme snow over fog any day." Little could he guess he'd soon get his wish.

Jedediah Smith State Park allowed us one last ride through the royal redwoods before they gave way to pine forests near the Oregon border. The slender mountain lanes boasted lots of shops and eateries, yet it wasn't until I spied a huge roadside fountain gushing purple water in Kerby, OR, that I insisted we stop.

The cascading sculpture fronted an outdoor gallery that could have been an oasis for fairies and elves. My kids raced through maze-like paths from one discovery to another: three-story tree houses, astonishing furniture, clever fences, creative clocks and gorgeous collectibles – all crafted from burls.

WHAT CAUSES A BURL?

Viruses, fungi and bacteria can make a tree's cells go haywire, forcing abnormal growths. One common microscopic invader called the crown gall bacterium even infiltrates a tree's genetics. Its DNA slips in and links with the tree's DNA. The altered cells divide uncontrollably, creating a tumor-like swelling or "gall." Burls and galls don't necessarily harm a tree or cut its life short, since even contorted xylem still seems to do its job of transporting water and nutrients from roots to branches. However, cutting out burls for their aesthetic appeal can leave the trees with gaping wounds ripe for infection.

Blown away by the artisan creations, I climbed happily back into the passenger seat and looked at Tom. "Well I don't know about you, but I could definitely live around *here*."

Ideal campsite

Sunshine, mountain streams and happy kids made for a pleasant ride north. In the town before Crater Lake National Park, we resupplied at a supermarket. We'd become champs at inventorying our stock and quickly grabbing what we needed. But this time we wanted to add a cake to celebrate Ciarán's 16th birthday.

Since the element of surprise was impossible, we told him he could choose his favorite. Sadly, the area's talents didn't spill over to baking. Our young foodie groaned at the pickins: plain yellow cake with white frosting or plain chocolate cake with chocolate frosting. He opted for brown.

Arriving at the park in late afternoon, we stopped at the first overlook to check out its namesake Crater Lake. Aislínn rushed to the cliff's edge and her gasp said it all.

We knew the lake was the deepest in the U.S., but we never imagined it would be *that* blue. I'm not talking calm Caribbean turquoise or the stark midnight hue off Maine's coast. No, the water below us seemed a brilliant, ethereal sapphire with a windless, high-gloss sheen that reflected the rugged cliffs around it. We stared wordlessly.

The spell broke quicker for Ciarán, who plopped down on all fours, urged his sister to do the same and then instructed Sean to balance on them, pyramid style. That became our first official photo of Crater Lake.

A few miles down the road, we located our large secluded campsite in the park's Mazama Village. Encircled by towering pines, the boys and I set up our tent. Aislínn claimed the picnic table and whistled while she prepped her deluxe grilled cheese and soup specialty.

Grew, blew, fell and filled

After dinner, the kids and I headed to the amphitheater. We had no idea what was on the program, but I had come to enjoy these outdoor classrooms so much that I wanted to go regardless. I was delighted to have all three join me.

We lucked into another cool "ology" talk. Ranger Mike, a middle-aged science teacher, spent his summers weaving geology, biology and hydrology into a whopping tale about Crater Lake.

He said it all started hundreds of thousands of years ago with Mount

Mazama. More than a just a single mountain, Mazama contained a bunch of volcanoes stacked together.

"Hundreds to be exact. Every time one blew, the lava made the *whole* mountain higher until it was soaring above sea level. It became *huge*. More than 12,000 feet!"

Then, he explained, 7,700 years ago, around the same time the wheel was invented in the middle east, another type of furious whirling took place under Mazama. The bowels of its main chamber roiled into an eruption so violent that ash spewed thousands of miles, as far away as Greenland.

"It was *cataclysmic*! *Catastrophic*! The mountaintop *completely* disappeared," Mike dramatically sliced his hand across his neck, eliciting a few laughs.

"But...," he paused for effect. "Do you think Mount Mazama really blew its top off?"

Turning in a small circle he pointed at random attendees, who each nodded. When he got to us and singled out Ciarán, my eldest also agreed. The ranger jumped up and shouted, "WRONG!" Then he ran around the circle like he was playing *Duck, Duck, Goose*, tapping each respondee on the shoulder with a cheery, "wrong... wrong... wrong... wrong... wrong..."

The sing-song performance got us all chuckling. Ranger Mike seriously enjoyed his job. He returned to the center and said, "Really folks. This is crazy. But Mount Mazama did *not* blow its top."

He stood in silence. Finally, a dad across the circle took the bait. "So what happened?"

"Glad you asked." My three kids and I leaned in expectantly. "Nope, the mountain didn't blow *out*... it collapsed *in*."

He waited a moment for us to get it. "There was sooooo much magna flying out sooooo fast," he waved rapidly, "that it created this huge empty void *under* the mountain. Without any support for the massive dome, it caved *in* on itself!" He accompanied his arm movements with smashing, spitting mouth noises.

He wiped his forehead. "When all was said and done, it left a bowl-shaped depression we call a caldera. Kind of like a cauldron."

Aislínn nudged me and smiled. I looked around the circle and could tell she wasn't the only one remembering *The Black Cauldron*, an old Disney fave.

"I guess we could have called it Cauldron Lake," continued the ranger. "But craters aren't always from asteroids or meteors, they're from collapsing volcanoes, too, right? And Crater Lake has a nicer ring, don't you think?"

He ignored a few protests and asked. "Sooooo, after the big collapse, how long do you think it took to fill up this huge crater-cauldron, whatever you

SCIENCE of BLUE

What makes Crater Lake such a unique, intense cobalt blue? Three things: depth, clarity and the way our brains see. Sunlight is made up of a spectrum of colors – reds, oranges, yellows, greens, blues and violets – all visible in a rainbow. These hues each have different wavelengths, which determine whether they are absorbed or reflected from surfaces. We only "see" colors that are reflected back to us. A yellow t-shirt, for instance, appears yellow because the chemicals in the fabric dye are put together in a way that absorb all colors except yellow. The yellow wavelengths bounce back onto our retinas, so our brain registers "yellow." Because the water in Crater Lake is so pure (unlike other lakes, it is fed by precipitation, not streams) sunlight penetrates deeply. Plain water molecules (without salt, algae, pollution, sediments or other influencers) absorb all the colors in the light spectrum except blues, which are reflected. With 4.6 trillion gallons of water in the lake, that's a lot of pure blue bouncing back to our retinas!

prefer to call it? We're talking almost 2,000 feet deep in the middle!"

Guesses rang out. "Ten years." He lifted his thumb upwards. "A hundred years." The thumb went up again. "A thousand years." His thumb pointed down. "Five hundred." Thumb down.

"After the eruption settled and cooled, it took about 250 years for rain and snow to fill 'er up." He smiled. "And for the last five or six thousand years, the level has pretty much stayed the same, balanced by precipitation and evaporation."

"It's really pretty cool." He gushed as if talking about a prized pet. "Our Crater Lake is the clearest, the deepest, the bluest lake in the country. Most waterways are fed by rivers or streams. But our lake only gets what comes from the clouds."

The ranger pointed skyward then walked over to throw more wood on a fire he started before his talk. He stoked it a little then turned back to us. "So that's it folks. That's the history of Crater Lake in a nutshell. How Mount Mazama grew, blew, fell and filled."

His rhythmic synopsis drew smiles. "C'mon," he urged. "Say it with me." A dozen voices joined his chant. "Grew. Blew. Fell. And filled." After a few rounds, he opened a bag of marshmallows, pointed to a pile of sticks and was rushed by eager hands.

As we roasted our treats, Ranger Mike answered questions. Yes, Mount Mazama was still an active volcano, but geologists didn't expect activity any time soon. Yes, people could swim in a designated area, but the water only reached about 60 degrees in the summer, too cold for most. No, the lake didn't have any native fish. Rainbow Trout and Kokanee Salmon were introduced more than a century ago. Because these fish weren't indigenous, the park encouraged people to catch them as long as they used artificial bait so no other species were accidentally introduced.

When the questions petered out, I moved in to chat with Mike, who told me he'd been spending summers at the park with his wife and three kids for 17 years. He showed me a photo of their cabin, noting it had no indoor plumbing. I was still enticed by the thought of becoming a seasonal ranger… but a whole summer with a porta potty? Hmmmmmmm.

Unsweetened 16

"You could always walk to the restrooms, Mom," said Aislínn during our stroll back to camp. "They're really clean here."

Ciarán, ever the spontaneous poet, broke into a quick rendition, with his siblings joining in the chorus.

> *When you wanna be a ranger*
> *But you feel the stomach danger*
> *DI-A-RRHEA!*
> *DI-A-RRHEA!*

"Stop." I swatted at them. From science to silliness in 10 seconds flat.

> *Got a summer with no flusher*
> *And it's gonna be a gusher*
> *DI-A-RRHEA! (Cha Cha Cha)*
> *DI-A-RRHEA! (Cha Cha Cha)*

They were still laughing when we got to the site, where Tom had a great fire going. We circled our chairs and I retrieved the cake from our cooler. We didn't want to risk it getting smooshed or soggy by the next day, so we had a night-before celebration. After a rousing happy birthday refrain, I divided wedges onto paper plates.

I always got sentimental at birthdays for my kids, especially since I never thought I'd have any. After failed surgeries, failed hormone treatments and, ultimately, a failed first marriage, I gave up trying. In my new single life, traveling was my passion. I already planned to backpack through South

America when Tom and I fell in love. He assured me that the no-kid thing didn't matter and I left happily for my trip.

A month in, though, I found out my uncharacteristic queasiness was not altitude sickness after all, or an aversion to whole chicken claws popping out of soup. No, after 14 years of infertility, I walked into a rudimentary clinic in the Amazonian town of Iquitos and heard the resounding, "Es positivo." I was pregnant.

Our offspring knew most of this already. But with nowhere else to go and a gorgeous night around us, they got a kick out of Tom and I embellishing the tale. How a Peruvian shaman blessed me and my "niño milagro" – my miracle baby – in a midnight ceremony. How it took three weeks to get to Lima to call Tom on a pay phone. How every night for the rest of the journey I played a cassette tape he recorded and mailed to me at my next stop in Ecuador.

At that one, Tom broke out into the old Loggins and Messina lyrics, *People smile and tell me I'm the lucky one, And we've only just begun, Think I'm gonna have a son...*

I still treasured the song. But the boys, apparently, lost interest.

Next thing I knew, Sean leapt out of his canvas chair and punched Ciarán on the arm. "Happy birthday, *mir*-a-cle baby."

Ciarán moved fast, catching his fleeing brother in seconds, tripping him to the ground and pinning him. Sean flailed his legs in a giggle-scream. Every time he wiggled, Ciarán doubled down on the pressure.

Anyone could have predicted Tom's reaction. "*Knock it off, you two!*

Ciarán loosened his grip, stood up and extended a hand to his brother. As soon as Sean grabbed on and started to pull up, Ciarán let go. So much for the miracle baby. And for the attention span of teenage boys.

They settled in again and Sean challenged Aislínn to a game of thumbs, starting a family match. No one on earth could beat Tom, his big guitar hands squishing us all, although my birthday boy kept trying until he was weak with laughter.

I served up second helpings of cake as a full moon rose gorgeously above the tall pines at 10 p.m. Our fire roared under the storybook sky. I leaned back to bask in the glow.

Perfect reflections

Ranger Mike advised the best time to see Crater Lake was early morning from the east side. So we ate a quick breakfast and proceeded on the 33-mile Crater Lake Rim Loop until we were due east.

TRAVEL TIP: Phones, Fuel & Frost Warnings

Most areas in and around Crater Lake National Park have little or no cell service. Also, from November to May, no gasoline is for sale in the park. You have to travel 35 miles to fill up. Winter usually drops over 40 feet of snow, making it a haven for winter sports. But hiking trails don't usually melt open until mid-June; higher elevations like Mount Scott are still covered into July.

The wind shifted overnight, bringing some haze from forest fires in the south. That didn't matter. Post-dawn sunlight made the calm, deep lake even more stunning than the previous afternoon. Steep, snow-covered peaks duplicated flawlessly in the astoundingly blue water. The more we gazed, the more the mirror images became one. We couldn't tell where water ended and land began. I wished some giant would dip a finger into the stillness so I could see ripples on that hypnotizing reflection.

Sean must've been reading my mind. "Imagine if Sean Eagle dropped a rock into that water?" He meant the character that he made up when he was just five. For years, he would create Sean Eagle stories wherever we went, the supermarket, playground or even just walking to school. We even published an e-book starring his winged namesake with illustrations by both boys. For real, you could check it out on Amazon and probably be the fourth person to see it.

But Sean hadn't mentioned the eagle in a long time. The recollection added glue to our road-trip bond. I smiled. "Yep. That would be awesome." I could have kept staring at the optical illusion of mountains in water. But everyone else got antsy, especially Mr. Birthday Boy. He wanted to hike and it was his day, so onward we went. After stopping at the visitor center to purchase tickets for an afternoon boat tour, we drove a few miles east of Crater Lake to Mt. Scott, the tallest elevation in the area at more than 8,900 feet.

Seasonal mashup

Snow-covered peaks added to the dramatic aesthetics around Crater Lake. The park got 44 feet of the white stuff the past winter that, lucky for us, lasted well into July on the summit paths.

Grinning ear to ear, my teens strode across packed piles at the head of the 4.4-mile Mt. Scott trail. Months of warming sun compacted its surface making the snow impossible to play with, but lending a charming sheen to the entire landscape.

The 60-degree temps felt refreshing when we started, but a 1,300-foot ascent had us sweating and unzipping in no time. With the snowpack, I didn't expect wildflowers. Yet high alpine beauties bloomed in every nook and cranny along our hike. Red Indian paintbrush, yellow buttercups, purple penstemons and blue forget-me-nots rose like ornaments on the sparkling white ground.

Handsome trees added to the eye candy. Mountain hemlock. Whitebark pines. A few Shasta red firs. Singular conifers growing right out of cracks in the rocky ground simply amazed me.

One greeted us at the mountain top, arching starkly from a boulder. I studied its lone beauty as we sat on the steps of a 1926 fire lookout enjoying our lunch of pre-packed sandwiches. Long needles bunched like pom poms along spindly branches. Vibrant clusters of berries bounced in the breeze next to small, tight cones. How delicate and rugged all at once!

Although haze veiled some of the beautiful landscape, we still enjoyed a sweeping vista of lake and peaks. How bizarre to be surrounded in July by snow, flowers, berries and people swimming far below.

Top to bottom

We made our way down and drove to Cleetwood Cove Trail, which would bring us to Crater Lake for our "Volcano Boat Cruise." Although only a little more than a mile long, the trail dropped nearly 700 feet, definitely not for the faint of heart. In fact, signs warned those with health or mobility issues to stay off, especially since the way back up was even harder.

Personally, I found descents more difficult, probably from my free-range fear of tripping forward and cracking my head. Likewise, Tom worried about slipping on his back. The kids took off at a trot while the two of us dug our heels in and inched our way down.

At lake's edge, we kicked off our boots and dropped our tootsies into the crystal clear 58-degree water. Of course, at that temp, mine was only a quick dip. But the rest of the Brennans luxuriated in a cool, silky foot bath. The sun felt luscious as we stretched out on large rocks along the shore and rested until our cruise ship — an open deck 60-passenger pontoon — arrived.

Wizards and pirate ships

Our guide was none other than Ranger Mike, who high-fived the boys as they strode on deck. Not far from the launch, he slowed the vessel and pointed to cliff-side cracks that reminded me of a Jackson Pollack painting.

TRAVEL TIP: Crater Lake's Volcano Boat Cruises

Two types of boat tours are available for Crater Lake. A two-hour guided tour travels around the lake's perimeter. Or, visitors can choose a three- or six-hour drop-off on Wizard Island, a large volcanic landmass in the lake. Prices range from $37 to $47 per adult, with discounts for children. Tickets are available at kiosks in the park or online at:
www.nationalparkcentralreservations.com/activity/volcano-boat-cruises

"Imagine them as veins," he instructed in his animated enthusiasm. "Liquid rock used to flow through these like blood."

Then he steered us to the lake's eastern edge, where a stark red clay formation jutted out of the rocky cliff 1,300 feet above us, higher than a 120-story building. A boatload of heads peered upwards.

"That, my friends, is the famous Pumice Castle. Looks like it should be on the Arizona desert instead of the rim wall, right?"

He explained that the spikey natural sculpture formed when softer minerals around it eroded during eons of rainfall, leaving the tough, porous pumice rock that spewed from volcanic eruptions.

Aislínn elbowed me, whispering, "Just like the Mesa Verde cliff dwellings."

I smiled at my observant daughter.

We motored south toward the unmistakable Phantom Ship. The formation posed on the water, the cliff wall looming hundreds of feet behind it. Sean, sitting on a wooden bench in front of me, jumped up in astonishment.

From the top rim, the island appeared as tiny as an acorn cap floating in a bathtub. Up close, it towered over us. And it looked exactly like an old pirate vessel.

Enjoying everyone's reactions, Ranger Mike noted we were fortunate, that cloudy mist often obscured the "Ship," hence its "Phantom" moniker. He said the formation, almost as long as a football field, was just the tip of a huge ridge below. The volcanic rocks that formed it were the oldest on the lake, dating back nearly half a million years.

He steered to the western rim, directly into bright afternoon sunlight. The water seemed, incredibly, even more blue. As if on cue with my thoughts, Ranger Mike stopped the pontoon and reached for a weighted circular device about the size of a dinner plate decorated with alternate black and white quadrants.

The Secchi disk, he told us, measured water clarity. He slowly lowered it into the lake and all the Brennans leaned over the edge. Down. Down. Down it went. We could still see its stark markings for hundreds of feet.

"The lake is so clear, I could go even farther, but we'd be here forever." He retracted the disk, smiling like a proud parent. Then he steered us closer to cliffside to view Devils Backbone, a fault line of hardened magma that looked like triangular stegosaurus spikes or lethal dragon's teeth hanging right out of the western wall.

Tom laughed. "I'd hate to get caught on one of those."

Ciarán grinned. "Not me. That would be so fun to climb."

Finally, we sailed slowly past the lake's most famous geological landmark: Wizard Island. It really did look like an immense sorcerer's hat. From the rim, the lake dwarfed the tiny green speck. Now the tree-covered mass, almost a mile wide, dwarfed us. Ranger Mike noted we could only see its top quarter; the island stood in more than 2,400 feet of water.

"After Mt. Mazama collapsed, hot cinders spewed from the caldera floor, building up like gigantic pimples into these formations." His spewing, spitting sound effects drew gleeful chortles as they had the night before.

"What makes it even more interesting?" He pointed toward the conical top. "The island is crowned by its own crater. Yep. It's more than 300 feet wide and 90 feet deep! You could lay down the Statue of Liberty or Big Ben in that baby. Technically it's known as a steep conical hill built around a volcanic vent, but we just like to call it a cinder cone."

He stared adoringly. "Some scientists consider Wizard Island to be the most spectacular cinder cone in the world!"

How could we not appreciate geology shared with such gusto? All the passengers debarked with three cheers for Ranger Mike. But before we did, we got one last spectacular treat. As we docked, a bald eagle soared gracefully above the cliffside near its nesting eaglet, circling as if to keep an on eye on our boatload of intruders. I thought Sean would fly off the deck.

Another slump

They weren't kidding about the trek back up Cleetwood Cove trail. After an hour of huffing and puffing, we gladly flopped on the ground with ice cream from a topside kiosk. Since it was Ciarán's actual birthday, we scrapped plans for a chili dinner and pulled into Annie Creek Restaurant, one of the park's eateries near our campground.

The kids went to town ordering whatever they wanted then hightailed it into the game room for an electronic fix. We told them we were returning to the campsite to start a final fire; they should walk back together when they were done. I bristled inside that they opted for virtual reality, but I kept it to myself, figuring it would make my eldest's birthday happier.

Only it didn't work that way.

Absorbed by waltzing flames, totally relaxed after such a great day, I startled when Ciarán stormed over.

"I don't wanna do this anymore. I wanna go home."

Before I could even take it in, Aislínn marched next to him. "Me too." Sean followed with a gruff staccato, "Yeah. It's been good, but I had enough."

Tom, half snoozing in the camp chair next to me, straightened quickly. "Wha? What happened?"

"Nothin." Ciarán tightened his lips and narrowed his eyes. "We just wanna go home."

He kicked the pile of Tom's carefully stacked kindling, scattering it and getting the reaction he bargained for.

"*Hey!*" Anger smothered any concern he might have had.

"C'mon guys." I tried to swallow my own frustration. "It's been a long day… maybe we all just need to…"

"I DON'T CARE. IT'S *MY* BIRTHDAY AND I DIDN'T WANT TO SPEND IT *HERE*. I MISS MY FRIENDS. I MISS TV. I MISS MY VIDEO GAMES." Ciarán kicked the wood pile again, strewing the few remaining pieces.

I felt like he struck my solar plexus. Aislínn stood icily, hand on hip. Sean nodded, arms crossed defiantly on his chest. Guilt flooded every pore in my body. I was speechless.

I wish I could tell you that we calmly validated their feelings and offered sage words of wisdom. Something along the lines of how natural it was to be homesick, especially on a birthday. How living in tight quarters could be stressful. That our amazing experiences were worth it. That, at nearly half way through, we just tripped into a mid-game slump.

But once again, our maturity went missing. Even if I knew what to say, Ciarán's sucker punch into his brother's gut proved the last straw for Tom.

Through gritted teeth he shouted, "Get. In. The. Tent. And. Go. To. Bed. NOWWWW!"

I wilted, wallowing in a soup of remorse and anger. My mind whirled, trying to figure out a way to go home early. What would it cost to change our flights and cancel the rest of our reservations? How could we kick out the people watching our dog?

The voices in the tent stayed snotty, irritable, agitated.

"Get outta my way!"

"Shut your flashlight!"

"Don't touch my book!"

143

"Move over!"

Tom barked, "Go. To. Sleep."

Tears rolled down my cheeks as I watched the fire die down to embers. The dazzling full moon emerged above the swaying pines again. But this time, its magic passed me by. The squabbling ceased and we soon heard Sean's rhythmic snores. I grabbed my sleeping sweats and walked to the restrooms to wash up and brush my teeth. Tom was just as mad as the kids. I didn't know what to do.

The night haunted me after I crawled in my warm sleeping bag. Everyone else snoozed deeply. But my mental assault would not stop. *Bad mom. Bad idea. Bad trip. Bad kids. Ugh.*

Final view

I woke to an empty tent. I must have really passed out, because normally I'd never sleep through the commotion of my tribe finding clothes, walking across air mattresses and unzipping the door. I lay there rubbing the back of my neck to ease my unsurprising headache.

"Hey dad, you want more milk or should I put it away?" Ciarán seemed downright jovial.

"Nah, thanks. I'm done. We gotta start packing up. Grab the rest of the stuff and put it in the cooler, okay?" Tom, too, sounded perfectly calm.

I slowly got myself into my clothes, listening to footsteps, things being moved, the fire crackling. I stood bewildered. Was last night a bad dream? When I finally emerged, Tom said, "There she is! Want some tea?"

I saw Sean and Aislínn walking back from the restrooms, laughing.

"Hey, Ciarán," shouted Sean, throwing a rubber ball that he picked up the day before in the camp store. Ciarán ran toward the pass and returned it. I gingerly looked at Tom and gratefully took my warm cup while the boys continued their volley.

"Hey mom." Aislínn sat in the camp chair next to me. "You okay?"

"Yeah," I said tentatively, feeling like I fell in Alice's rabbit hole. "But I have a headache. Can you grab the Advil?"

She reached into The Couch for our medical kit and brought me the orange tablets. I swallowed them quickly, grabbed a yogurt for breakfast then retreated back into the dome to help Tom roll up the sleeping bags and mattresses. He and the boys packed the tent and ground cloth, while Aislínn and I gathered everything else.

When we were ready to go, Tom asked, "Want one more look at the lake?"

"Sure!" Ciarán nodded. The other two echoed agreement.

Did I hear enthusiasm? I sighed.

With the air clear and bright, devoid of remnant smoke, we wished we could have climbed Mt. Scott then. But viewing the magically blue water and the otherworldly formations we now knew by name provided a fitting end to our time at Crater Lake.

I never found out what happened between Thursday night and Friday morning. Tom stayed mum, so I was left to wonder if he talked to the kids or they simply got over their mood. No one apologized. No one spoke of it again. I kept my lingering guilt to myself.

Crater Lake reflections

 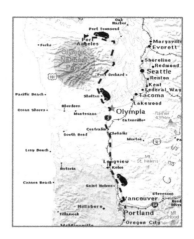

Crater Lake to Portland to Olympic, WA

5 hours + 5 hours

AT-A-GLANCE:

OLYMPIC NATIONAL PARK

Isolated on a peninsula, Olympic National Park encompasses nearly one million acres with distinctly different ecosystems. The internationally recognized wildness includes the majestic Olympic Mountains, a rugged pacific shoreline and one of the largest rainforests in the U.S. This diverse and beautiful land offers something for everyone.

LOCATION: Olympic National Park is on the Olympic Peninsula in Washington state. Its diverse areas can all be reached via Hwy 101.

OPEN: Olympic is open all year but some roads and facilities are closed in the winter.

COST: $30 per vehicle, $25 per motorcycle and $15 per bicyclist/ pedestrian; under 16 is free

INFO: https://www.nps.gov/olym/index.htm

Chapter 12
Olympic Enchantments

A cloudy sky made for perfect driving to Tiggard, OR, a Portland suburb half way to Olympic National Park. We booked a Howard Johnson's to show our teens the iconic 1960's hotel with angled orange rooftops. But it was no-go for HoJo.

In the months since we reserved, the place turned into a dull rectangular Quality Inn. So much for nostalgia. The pool was nice, though, and I lounged for a long time after the kids retreated to binge on TV and cell phones. Then they caught the latest Batman flick with their dad while I caught up on work.

Key blunder

A couple of hours into the next day's ride to Olympic, I had to fuel up. I barely pulled to the pumps when everyone piled out for leg-stretching and snacks. I returned the nozzle (yes, this Jersey girl did learn how) and hopped back in the driver's seat. But I changed my mind and decided to join them in the store. I opened my door, pressed the electronic lock and lobbed it shut.

Before the metal even clicked, my stomach clenched. In a blink of wishful thinking I hurriedly tapped my pocket. But no. I really did lock them in. The keys dangled from the ignition like a pompom.

AAA's roadside assistance eventually arrived and got us back on the road. To their credit, none of my family complained – much.

The ride up the eastern shore of Olympic Peninsula erased lingering grumbles. Puget Sound, with its forested shorelines framing the estuary's mix of salt and fresh water, seem to offer a peaceful balm that carried us into the park.

Of Olympic's 15 campgrounds, only two, Kalaloch and Sol Duc, accepted reservations. We planned to take our chances at Heart O' the Hills, a first-come, first-served site in the park's northeast. Our gamble quickly went bust.

TRAVEL TIP: Ease Car Hassles

Unless you're an expert, make sure you can beckon help if you have a flat tire, lock yourself out or have any other vehicle mishap. Along with AAA and other independent services, most new or rental cars offer their own roadside assistance programs. Check your options before you travel. Know what is covered by your own insurance, rental insurance and your emergency assistance service.

We crawled around the large campground loop behind two other cars also searching for a place to stay. Every one of the 105 sites was taken.

"If we got here *earlier*, like we were *supposed* to," griped Ciarán.

"Yeah, if you remembered the *keys*," snorted Sean.

"Leave your mother alone. That wasn't anyone's fault." Tom turned and glared at his sons.

"Yes it *was*." Ciarán slammed his elbow into his seat.

I gripped the wheel and continued a second time through the circuit. Anxiety tendrilled in my gut like peas on a trellis. The vehicles in front already ditched the quest. If we didn't find anything, we'd have to drive a long way to the next first-come area. Who knew what would happen there? The only sound louder than my pulse was the rumble of The Couch's tires on rough gravel.

I started around a third time, more out of indecision than hope. Near the turn-around curve, Aislínn tapped her window. "Wait, wait! Over there."

Sure enough, an empty site lay half hidden behind tangled overgrowth. Smoldering heat rising off its fire ring meant someone literally just left. We snagged the last available spot.

Glacial glimmer

After rapidly setting up camp, we took off for Hurricane Ridge, about 12 miles away. Aislínn insisted on staying behind, claiming a sore ankle. I would have argued but I had my fill of drama for the afternoon, so we left without her.

The Olympic Mountains rose before us in a stunning display unlike any we'd seen so far. The curving hillsides swelled in a patchwork of distinct greens, a verdant quilt capped white by massive, ancient glaciers.

We parked next to a vast alpine meadow singing with tall grasses and wildflowers. Three black-tail deer stood knee deep, nibbling on the beautiful buffet oblivious to our doors opening. Even as we inched closer, they kept eating. I didn't know who was cuter, them or Sean.

"Sooooo sweeeeeet," he kept mouthing, his eyes wider than the doe's.

When the buck finally sauntered toward the adjacent forest, his family followed. We watched them enter the woods then rotated in the direction of the majestic mountain range. A handsome lone blackbird eyed us from his perch on a stone wall. Behind him, early evening sunlight turned the peaks into a soiree of glistening white.

I did a slow 360, taking in the wild meadow, then shadowed forest, back to the glowing highlands. Streaks of pre-sunset pink painted the sky. Mr.

Blackbird remained a sentry. I knew that meant he, like the deer, grew so used to human intrusion that he didn't feel the need to flee. I was glad. His presence added to the magic. My cells tingled with gratitude for the remarkable gifts of time and place. I exhaled deeply and felt knots I hadn't even realized I harbored unfurl and release.

My reverie snapped quicker than a winter twig when the boys hollered for me from a trail on a nearby ridge. In contrast to the warm, dry meadow, the entire path stood blanketed in snow. Giggling, they scrambled hundreds of yards up the mountain to pose in sunglasses and shorts. Even their shadows, elongated in the slanting light, smiled.

Back at the site Aislínn had her own thrill in the form of another young deer who visited while she sat reading.

"You know that feeling, mom? When your head's down but you know someone's looking at you?" Her excitement was palpable, music to my ears. I nodded. "She stood there a looong time and we just stared at each other. It was the best."

Night sounds

Tom and Ciarán built another blazing fire while I made the chili we skipped two nights back. I had no takers for the ranger program, so I headed over alone. Just as well.

A quiet older ranger spent most of the time reading poems and prose. One stayed with me, about a tiny starling who carried a seed in its beak but dropped it to catch a moth. The seed grew into the biggest tree in the forest, providing oxygen in the air, shelter to countless creatures and beauty for all who passed. Then one day, with no heartwood left, the mighty timber crashed to the forest floor, dropping more seeds, one of which was grabbed by a tiny starling. The actual story was quite beautiful and fed my love for a good circle-of-life tale.

In my absence, the kids finger-painted in the dust and grime that built up on The Couch for weeks. I circled the SUV, admiring flowers, superheroes, peace signs and funny graffiti. When I got to the back, two words filled the large rear window: GREAT MOM!!!

Could have been Tom for all I knew, but I grinned from ear to ear.

We sprawled around the fire roasting marshmallows well past dark, which at that latitude was nearly 11 p.m., late by camping standards. Aislínn and I sat gabbing when Sean, ever the wildlife stalker, hushed us.

"SHHHHHHH! Hear that?"

We listened. A low, guttural noise emerged. Rhythmic yet grating, sharp against the wisps of crackling flames. "Hear it?" My youngest leaned to one side then the other. We all nodded, silently trying to place it beyond the trees and shrubs that secluded our small campsite.

"Over there...maybe it's a raccoon rooting for food," he whispered, practically shaking with glee. "Or even a bobcat or something!"

Sean tiptoed toward the brush, stopping every few feet to make sure "it" hadn't been scared away. He got right to the edge of the thicket, moved some branches and burst into giggles.

"What?" I raised my hands questioningly.

Ciarán loped over, looked and laughed out loud. "It's the guy in the tent next door. Snoring his head off."

Un-tree-lievable!

We should have known better from Crescent City, but were still surprised when we left camp in sunshine and drove into full-on fog near Rialto Beach on the park's 60-mile stretch of Pacific coast.

"Good thing we decided against staying in the campground here," said Tom as he pulled into a mostly deserted parking lot.

"Yeah, but we would'a found a site right away." Ciarán jabbed my arm.

Ugh, kids, I thought. But the sentiment vanished as soon as I stepped out in front of a huge patch of delicate Queen Anne's lace intertwined with bright sweet pea petals. This unexpected tangle of waist-high wildflowers, even more ethereal in the gray vapor, separated blacktop and beach. As if this border wasn't strange enough, beyond it we beheld the most bizarre landscape ever.

Downed trees layered the entire shore. Sitka spruce, western red cedars, Douglas firs – the same ones that practically reached the sky – were strewn on the sand like pick-up sticks.

Mist hovered eerily over branches, gargantuan root-balls and whole trunks on their sides. None had bark or greenery; they laid bleached and scoured as bare as bones in a giant's graveyard. For a full minute no one moved or said a word. Our brains had to process the view. I remained dumbstruck until I heard, "Oh. My. God! This is *awesome!*"

At that, the boys dashed off to enjoy the world's best playground. Leaping ninja-style from tree to sideways tree, they brandished smaller sticks to duel on the weather-polished conifers. Even when the fog swallowed their bodies, I could hear hoots of joy.

Once my psyche adjusted to the incredible detritus, I took in the rest of the rugged environment. Angry waves crashed on shore where millions of

---

RIALTO's DRAMATIC DRIFTWOOD

The downed trees on Rialto Beach tell a dual story of strong gales and mighty tides. Part of the pile comes from a thick grove of old growth evergreens found directly inland from the narrow beach. These giants can't put down deep roots in wet, sandy soil, so hundreds a year are toppled by the Pacific Northwest's driving windstorms and blown onto the beach. The rest of the collection is massive timber that travels north on the adjacent Hoh River. Some trunks come from quite a distance, floating in the water for years before landing ashore on powerful tides.

---

round granite stones glistened against dark sand. Dozens of rocky formations known as seastacks rose from the angry water like guardians.

I caught up with Aislínn and we climbed our way across a maze of wooden peaks and gullies to join Tom at ocean's edge. He paced next to one magnificent cedar which, by his footstep calculation, measured almost 200 feet long. My tall daughter couldn't reach the top of its horizontal trunk.

She climbed a twisted ladder of splayed branches to stand on the smooth surface. Tom and I followed. From that perch, the landscape seemed even more fantastical, an endless concourse of daredevil driftwood.

The brothers, specks in the distance, bounced and balanced on the surreal timber. Like them, we navigated from trunk to trunk, slid into sunken crannies and jumped beneath twisted branches to explore the undersides of these once-grand trees.

Eventually, breathless and elated, we all headed back to The Couch. What a surprising and joyful find! We indulged one more long look at the peculiar shore, our last view of the wild gray Pacific.

Tribal headquarters

In no time, we emerged back into bright sunshine and decided to stop at the small coastal reservation of the Quileute Indians in LaPush, WA.

In tribal lore, the Quileutes descended from wolves, a fact well-known by millions of teen girls, including my own, thanks to *Twilight*. Heartthrob Jacob, with powers to change into a wolf, was a member of the Quileute nation who fought for Bella's love in the four-part saga by Stephanie Meyer that helped launch a vampire craze around the world.

It also turned the poor, quiet towns of LaPush and neighboring Forks into instant tourist destinations. Needless to say, Aislínn was on cloud nine and ignored all teasing from her less impressed brothers.

Salmon cascade

I, too, didn't fawn over LaPush. I couldn't wait for our five-mile hike to Sol Duc Hot Springs, a perfect half-way stop on the two-hour drive back to camp from Rialto Beach. I'd never dipped into a natural hot spring and could almost feel the nirvana already.

I pulled up the map to check directions when Ciarán declared, "I'm tired. I don't feel like hiking."

In unison came "Me neither" and "me too."

I raised my eyes toward Tom.

"Well, Mer. We did get a lot of action on those trees. I'm kinda beat, too."

I folded my arms across myself, slumped lower into the passenger seat and looked out my window. I huffed loudly in case anyone missed my annoyance.

We drove for miles, paralleling the gorgeous aquamarine Sol Duc River. Tom rubbed my arm. "Tell you what. Let's stop for lunch and see how we feel after that."

At the pull-off, the water hummed from below. We followed a path dressed in ferns, moss and rich brown tree trunks, even more lush in contrast to that morning's ashen timber. Gnarled roots offered footsteps to the rushing whitewater.

I scrambled down and planted myself on a boulder, immediately soothed and mesmerized by bright afternoon light skipping on the churning tributary. I didn't notice Sean on an adjacent rock until he yelled over the river noise.

"Hey ma. This is a sammonron. D'ya know that?"

"What?"

"It's a sammonron." He pointed with one hand to the rushing river while he held his half-eaten peanut butter sandwich in the other.

I looked at the water and shrugged at him. "Huh?"

"SA-MON. You know. The *fish*?" He said it very slowly. "Who go upstream to spawn?"

"Ohhhhh.... *salmon* run!" I laughed. "Really?"

He nodded. We both stared at one particularly raging torrent. Sean swallowed a bite and shook his head. "Imagine having to swim up *that* just to have kids?"

I glanced at my youngest, burying the urge to say that I would have done anything to have him. Instead, I nibbled my own sandwich. In seconds he finished his and jumped up to explore the riverbank with his brother. I reclined, basking in the bliss of solar shine on my closed lids and the river's enchanting music.

Smelly belly flops

Our respite didn't change anyone's vote about the hot springs hike, so I had to let it go. But signs for Sol Duc Hot Springs *Resort*, boasting "three spring-fed mineral baths," stirred my yearning and didn't involve any trails.

Ciarán was gung ho to go. My two youngest thought the $15 per person entry fee was "a huge rip off" for the time left before closing. I normally blew a gasket about expenses, so their sudden fiscal concern tickled me. Tom, feeling inklings of an earache, said he'd pass either way.

I hemmed and hawed. It was a lot of money for just a couple of hours. But, boy, had I dreamed of jumping in those healing pools! Hot springs had been relieving pain, stress, skin woes and more for millenia. How could I pass up the chance?

I sprang for four adult tickets, fighting my temptation to save a few dollars by getting Sean a child's pass. I didn't want to ignite his spit-fire fury over the kid meals again, or risk any merciless "leeeetle" teasing from his brother. Plus, anyone whose everyday lexicon included salmon facts was worth the few extra bucks.

We hurried into the changing rooms but stopped in our tracks upon entering the pool area, gob-smacked by stench.

"What the..." Ciarán squeezed his face into a pucker.

"Ewwwwwww." Sean held his breath in chipmunk cheeks, which his brother quickly deflated with a two-handed clap.

Aislínn shrugged. "It's a *mineral* bath. What d'ya think they meant by minerals?"

Of course she was right. I just hadn't expected rotten eggs.

The boys took off in chase until warned by a lifeguard, then race-walked past everything else to happily cannonball into a large chlorinated pool at the far end of the property.

I stared sourly at three round basins before me. Except for fountains in their centers, they seemed like regular concrete pools painted aqua for water aesthetics. The deepest would barely cover my waist. Worst of all, people packed into them like sardines.

"You're kidding, mom." My daughter shook her head.

"But I imagined floating."

"Get over it."

She shook her head and squeezed past bathers into a tiny space in the largest pool. She sat down so the water rose to her chest. I inched next to her, waiting for the 103-degree mineral soup to do its magic. Within seconds, I grimaced again.

> ## HOT SPRINGS STINKY FACTS
>
> The "springs" come from rain and melting snow that seep underground, picking up all sorts of geologic minerals along the way. The "hot" happens when this moisture mingles far below the earth's surface with gases from steaming volcanic rocks. The water then rises to the surface along natural cracks and bubbles out as a "hot spring." Soaking in these bubbling pools is believed to convey a slew of health benefits, from improving circulation and metabolism to treating diabetes or gout. During its rocky travels, the water often attracts sulfide compounds. While we usually blame sulfur for the famous rotten egg smell at many hot springs, the nose-holding stench is actually caused by bacteria that feed off sulfur. These bacteria are anaerobic, meaning they only can live in the absence of oxygen. When they hit air, they die and dispel stinky hydrogen sulfide. So the hotter and smellier the hot spring, the deeper it came from in the earth and the faster the water pushed up to the surface, where millions of microscopic critters let out their gas all at once.

"What now?"

I leaned closer and whispered, "How can the water be clean with all these bodies in it?"

Aislínn motioned to a tiny sign noting the pools were emptied daily.

"Yeah, but probably first thing in the morning... It's late now."

"What d'ya think would be different in real hot springs?

"The water moves and filters all day."

She snorted. "You are *such* a germ-o-phobe. Just let it go."

To taunt me, she leaned back and dunked her head. It could have been straight out of that movie where the mature mom switched bodies with her whining teen. But I couldn't help it.

I really tried. I sat for at least another five minutes attempting to focus on the picturesque Olympic Peninsula trees surrounding us. I just couldn't shake my inner skeevies. I got out and joined the boys in the cold chlorinated pool. Barely anyone else was in it. Aislínn soon dove in too.

The four of us challenged each other to underwater handstands and flips, seeing who could hold our breath the longest (me). Then we swam across seeing who was fastest (me). My trio got even, though, when I became monkey in the middle as they tossed Sean's ever-present rubber ball.

Finally, Ciarán and Aislínn emerged victorious in chicken fights because every time my youngest climbed on my shoulders, he slid off in a giggling fit.

Tom wandered in after napping in the SUV. Although reluctant to pay, he didn't want to wait in the parking lot either. I lounged next to him on a chaise, diagonal sunrays a perfect antidote to the chilly pool.

Sure, I missed out on the benefits of steeping in those natural pools. And the whole place was a "rip off." But spending an afternoon playing in a forest-ringed swimming pool with my teens? Worth every penny!

Stark raven mad

Driving back to camp, snowy peaks shimmered in the distance.

"Man, can you believe it," observed Ciarán. "The beach… the forest… the mountains… all within a couple hours. It's like New Jersey!"

I laughed out loud. We actually could go from the Jersey Shore to hiking and skiing within an hour or so, but I don't think anyone ever compared New Jersey to the Olympic Peninsula.

Tom put the kibosh on our planned hot dog dinner, saying he'd rather stop somewhere. Of course, the chorus concurred. I put my foot down, reminding how much we spent for the pool. Instead, I suggested we pick up some extra snacks at a supermarket for around the campfire.

I had yet to learn that "some extra" translated to "free-for-all" in adolescent (and Tom's) brains. The kids took off in all directions and came back with armloads of sugar and crunch. My husband, unable to ignore the ready-made counter, ordered a huge bucket of fried chicken. While we waited our turn, our three adorable spawn scoffed soup, sandwich and pizza samples. I retreated to the car.

We spent another gorgeous night at the campfire, bolstered by munchies. But what goes around, comes around. After his third trip to the bathroom, Ciarán whipped up another verse.

When sitting at the fire
and you get a big desire,
DI-A-RRHEA!
DI-A-RRHEA!

Sean got a stomach ache from laughing and he, too, ran to the facilities. When the three siblings finally went in the tent to play cards, we heard them teasing, singing and cracking up for nearly an hour.

Then Tom and I called it a night, too, and we all fell fast asleep. In what seemed like minutes, although it was already 5 a.m., sharp screaming abruptly roused us.

Tom bolted up muttering "those jerky a-holes," thinking the noise was from rowdy campers we heard the previous night. He unzipped the door and strode outside. I followed. Another shriek punctuated the air. I lifted my head and smiled.

Ravens. Soaring, squealing and diving. One of the names for a flock is an "unkindness." Tom called them something else. Snoring the day before, now birds. We wondered what would have surprised us if we stayed in this tiny campsite another night.

Primeval paradise

After snoozing another couple of hours, Tom and I left the kids sleeping while we hiked a few miles on the Heart O' the Hills Trail adjacent to our campground. Unlike popular Hurricane Ridge with its mile-high vistas, this lowland wilderness remained devoid of crowds.

Yet it teemed with life. Lavish emerald moss and pale textured lichen bejeweled old-growth evergreens. Opulent fungi and thin draping vines upholstered gigantic stumps. I hadn't seen this kind of plush jungle since I was in South America's Amazon. How exhilarating to walk a rain forest in the state of Washington!

The wide trail soon narrowed into a dense winding path where, clearly, few humans tread. Sun barely reached the forest floor. What little did shone like spotlights on skunk cabbage, hemlock and dainty trillium. Delicate prehistoric ferns sparkled with diamond droplets, a gift from the canopy.

We grinned joyfully as we shimmied, squeezed and skulked our way through the primeval landscape. At one ravine, we hung onto a thick vine to limbo under fallen trunks suspended over the ground. Tom hooted his best Tarzan call, "AAH-EEH-AAAAAH-EEH-AAAAH,"

An acoustic ecologist once called this section of park, known as the Hoh Rain Forest, among the quietest places in the nation. I only partially agreed. True, from this ancient patch of woods, we couldn't hear cars or any sound of civilization. Yet when we were silent, our ears overflowed with the melodic calls of chickadees, wrens and scores of singing insects.

Not that our offspring asked, but our smiles told all as we sauntered back to camp. We pretty much had our vanishing act down to a science, until I snagged a tent pole on a nylon seam. Instead of gently massaging past the roadblock, I yanked. Everyone heard the snap. Thank god for duct tape.

We waved a sad goodbye to Olympic. It definitely topped our "revisit" list for the parks we'd seen so far. Two days were just not enough.

Rialto Beach driftwood

Olympic to Seattle, WA
3 hours

Chapter 13
Superb Surprises

We picked Seattle as a resting point en route to North Cascades National Park. Getting there meant crossing Puget Sound. First we figured The Couch should shed her mountain grime. I swallowed a tiny frog as car wash scrubbers erased the "GREAT MOM" from its dusty back window.

The SUV gleamed like a new penny as we lined up for the Kingston-Edmonds ferry, where they did a brisk business piling more than a hundred cars into the commuter boat's hull. Our wait took longer than the 20-minute ride across the Sound. Still, both were much shorter than the land route. Plus, standing on deck taking in the gorgeous panorama was lovely.

University finds

Rather than center city, we purposely booked a college neighborhood near the Universities of Washington and Seattle. The kids immediately rushed to the outdoor pool while Tom and I scouted the streets for a laundromat and pharmacy.

As I waited for the wash, Tom had a prescription for antibiotics called in from New Jersey for what seemed to be a worsening ear infection. He got them so often that his doc was fine with the long-distance Rx.

We feasted that evening at a Thai place we'd passed earlier. It wasn't quite the Chinatown gorge, but we sure had to loosen our pants again. Tom retreated to the hotel to lie down. The rest of us meandered through funky little shops, laughing and trying on goofy hats and hippie shoes. Ciarán fell in love with a zipped hoodie handwoven in Nepal. With no money as usual, he convinced me that I owed him another birthday present. He wore that bulky green striped sweater out of the store and almost every day for the rest of the trip.

We returned with Tom refreshed and raring to go. He didn't have to ask twice if our progeny wanted to hit the local theater to see *HellBoy*.

"*HellBoy*?" Really?" I bit my lip. My shopping joy slid off like rain on a windshield.

My older son started to laugh. "You just did it again."

I turned sharply toward him. "Did what?"

"Made the *face*." Now Sean and Aislínn sniggered.

"What are you talking about?"

Sean squeaked between his giggles, "You make it every time you're mad."

159

TRAVEL TIP: Scouting Out Souvenirs

Bringing home a few cherished mementos from your travels can be joyful and meaningful. National park visitor centers often have fine gift shops. We also found unique souvenirs from local artisans in small villages, roadside shops and city boutiques. But we learned the hard way: ship delicate items home rather than assume they are well bundled in a corner of your car or suitcase.

"You're doing it even more right now." Ciarán contorted his lips into an exaggerated fish mouth and widened his eyes. "It's the dumpsta-funk face."

They all erupted, scrunching their expressions, dancing around to, "*It's the dumpsta-funk...the dumpsta-funk*" that sounded suspiciously like the *Monster Mash*. I was not amused. At all.

Tom walked out of the bathroom, took one peek at me and tried to be serious. But at Aislínn's high-pitched hip hop harmony of "*ye-ah, the dum-sta-funk!*" he burst into hysterics. I glared.

He wagged a finger at his daughter." Now you..." but lost it when the boys chanted behind him. He tried again to firmly insist they apologize for that name, but exploded into guffaws before he finished pronouncing the word "dumpsta."

"Just. Get. Out." I slammed into the bathroom. I heard them choking all the way to the elevator. A long, hot shower rinsed away my mad. How odd yet comforting, I mused, to be living our normal drama during this magnificent adventure. If anything, the nonstop proximity and constant moving freed us to be even more ourselves, whether I liked it or not. And that definitely included my own fierce (and unrealistic) desire for everything to be perfect, or at least affable.

As I dried off, I flashed on Shawnodese, the Native American spirit keeper who I'd learned about. He encouraged us to be vulnerable, be in the moment and enjoy what is. If only I could always remember that.

Smiling, I made myself a cup of tea. Then I finished a little work and was watching the end of some smarmy movie on TV when they got back around midnight. Tom snuggled next to me. "It was great," he whispered. "You would have *hated* it."

Funky-tecture

So far, our hotels' "breakfast included" meant packaged pastries, a fruity cereal dispenser, plastic utensils and coffee in Styrofoam cups. We all did a double-take at the University Inn's complimentary buffet: linens, china, silverware and more hot and cold delights than on a diner menu. Needless to say, the Brennans beamed.

After second helpings, we took the hotel's free shuttle to Seattle Center. Originally built for the 1962 World's Fair, the huge campus centered around an International Fountain shooting dozens of water spouts in time to music from around the world. Alone, the multi-sensory sculpture would have captivated us. But it paled compared to the strange building next to it: the MoPOP Museum.

Its huge warped roof glistened in sections of metallic purple, silver and gold as if extraterrestrials dropped ginormous sheets of foil from space that crumpled and curled where they landed. The outsized exterior rippled and angled like a fun house mirror.

Aislínn grinned, stepping side to side. "C'mere ma. They change color when you move."

Tom nodded. "Talk about weird with a capital W."

At that moment, an elevated monorail drove straight into one of the glimmering metal walls and disappeared.

Sean hooted. "Holy crap. It's like *Harry Potter!*"

We continued to gawk. Was it cool or ugly? We couldn't decide. So we called it clugly and knew we had to go in.

ELECTRIFYING MoPOP

Microsoft billionaire Paul Allen created the Experience Music Project and Science Fiction Museum, originally known as EMP Museum. The name changed in 2016 to Museum of Pop Culture, or MoPOP, which is chock full of interactive exhibits, virtual music labs, video games, sci-fi/fantasy galleries and a 70-foot tall "Sky Church," a state-of-the-art concert hall that pays homage to Seattle-born rock star Jimi Hendrix. When first built in 2000, the shiny sheet-metal exterior drew a host of reactions for architect Frank O. Gehry, celebrated for the Guggenheim Museum Bilbao, Walt Disney Concert Hall and other world-famous designs. While *Architecture Week's* reviewer applauded the "shimmering purple haze," and *Fodor's Seattle* called it "a fitting backdrop for the world's largest collection of Jimi Hendrix memorabilia," one critic derided it as "something that crawled out of the sea, rolled over, and died." Others called it "a blob" and "hemorrhoids." Regardless of your aesthetic impressions, the museum is a must-see part of Seattle Center. (www.mopop.org)

Turned out the fusion of textures and hues – actually made from 21,000 individual metal shingles – was designed to convey the "energy and fluidity of music." In fact, the architect sliced up electric guitars to make some of the original tiles. That's all Tom needed to hear.

"Okay," he conceded. "It's definitely cool."

Rockin' out

He was even more starstruck when we entered and saw a guitar sculpture that blossomed out of the floor like a bouquet, filling the multi-level atrium.

"Telecaster! Stratocaster! Les Paul!" He shook Ciarán's shoulder. "Holy crap. Check *that* one out."

The spiraling guitar tornado, made of more than 500 instruments, actually played, too. Hundreds of strings, orchestrated by 30 computers, generated the tunes. The kids reached for earphones to amplify the sound. I thought Tom, circling the base, might kneel in worship.

I found the musical monument mind-boggling, especially its name, *If VI was IX*. But what did I know? My rock 'n roll IQ was so deficient that I had no idea Jimi Hendrix even hailed from Seattle, let alone that the strange title came from one of his songs.

I got the memo as soon as we entered the first of four huge galleries dedicated to the hometown legend. Tom and Ciarán air-strummed at interactive exhibits and tried to outdo each other in answering trivia about the rock star's electric legacy.

TRAVEL TIP: Memberships and Other Discounts

Whether you are traveling solo or in a large family, check out the membership price at museums, parks, zoos and other attractions you'd like to visit. Often, a membership more than pays for itself. For instance, it cost us $9 more for a family membership to Seattle's MoPOP Museum than it would buying separate tickets. But the membership included a coffee table rock 'n roll book, a t-shirt, free audio tours and 10% off lunch in the museum café – worth more than the extra $9. Plus we got a quarterly EMP magazine for the next year and used EMP's "reciprocal affiliate" benefit to get in free at a science museum in Montana. All told, we came home with memberships to MoPOP, Woodland Park Zoo, Grand Canyon Foundation and Crazy Horse Foundation. Also check for discounts that might not be listed on admission signs, like AAA, AARP, veteran's, trade or credit card discounts. Some companies offer employee discounts for arts, entertainment and other venues. As an artist with a valid website, I have received deeply discounted memberships at many art museums. If you plan to visit a number of attractions in a metropolitan area, a "City Pass" might be your best buy.

Because of the crowds, I thought we should stay together. That lasted less than 15 minutes. Aislínn liked pushing a few buttons, glimpsing at pictures and moving on. Tom wanted to read every tiny footnote on each display. After one room of power struggles, we decided the kids could go off on their own as long as they didn't leave the floor. My daughter happily raced away.

Tom OD'ed on the roots of northwest rock, then we all reconvened and headed upstairs where everyone got into the act. Literally. Sound studios lined the walls, each featuring keyboards, drums, guitars or microphones. The guys jumped into empty seats and grabbed instruments while Aislínn cuddled the mike. After a few good minutes of recording, Ciarán hopped off his drum stool and went into a mixing booth to amp up the "Brennan band."

Like a groupie at Madison Square Garden, I jumped and applauded, not only because my family sounded great, they were also having a blast!

One with the Force

The Science Fiction and Fantasy wing fueled their elation even more. If youth *Jeopardy* had a category for all things *Star Wars*, our kids could've won their college tuitions. They knew every alien, animal and starship from earth to Tatooine. Whenever a new movie came out, they'd binge the old ones before going with their dad to its midnight opening.

So imagine jaws dropping when Yoda greeted us from his cave. Well, of course, not the real Yoda, but the best wax figure we'd ever seen. Darth Vader leered outside the Death Star. Obi-Wan Kenobi and Chewbacca stood protectively by Han Solo, beads of sweat on his life-like forehead.

The Force definitely surrounded us.

Sean trotted to a cordoned Light Saber Arena, eyes glinting. In seconds, he and his siblings were jousting.

"*I* am the dark lord," growled Ciarán. He gestured his glowing laser saber at me. "Oh come, mo-ther."

Then he quickly lunged toward his sister, who deftly blocked the thrust.

I picked up an elongated weapon and swung it over my head.

"Nooooo." Sean laughed and pushed his bright blue tip into my back. "You're supposed to zap not swing it like a lasso."

"Leave her alone." Aislínn rushed to my side, plunging her weapon into her brother's thigh. "Take that."

When Tom charged into the fray, dodging and pirouetting like a ballerina, we all cracked up.

SPACE AGE WONDER

When built for the 1962 World's Fair, seven years before the Apollo 11 moon landing, the futuristic Space Needle symbolized man's Space Age aspirations. The original design for the 605-foot observation tower changed from a UFO to a tethered balloon and even a cocktail shaker before becoming the iconic flying saucer shape. Extravagant renovations begun in 2017 offer visitors even more thrills with The Oculus, a staircase connecting the upper level to The Loupe, the world's first rotating glass floor. (www.spaceneedle.org)

After our fill of galaxies far, far away, we moved into the next rooms with hundreds of displays on everything from *War of the Worlds* to *Men in Black*. By then, even my husband couldn't read one more word so we hustled out of MoPOP.

Cloudy heights

Despite gray skies, the fresh air cleansed our overloaded brains. We relaxed at the musical fountain, splitting sides about whether to go to Seattle Center's other iconic landmark, the Space Needle. It wasn't cheap. But clouds or no, we finally decided we wouldn't be back any time soon. So up we went.

Speeding to the top of what once was the tallest structure west of the Mississippi River, acrophobic Aislínn closed her eyes and hummed loudly. Tom white knuckled the elevator rail, swearing the tower swayed in the wind. Lucky for them, the lift whooshed us to the 520-foot observation deck in just 41 seconds.

Father and daughter quickly circled the glass-enclosed perimeter barely peeking out at the landscape. Then they hustled to the down elevator and disappeared with a quick wave. Ironically, both had argued for the attraction.

"They should 'a just stayed on the ground," snorted Ciarán, who initially voted no.

Sean smirked. "Would 'a saved us two tickets."

I shrugged. "At least they can say they went up the Needle."

We strolled the saucer-style deck for a quite a while, peering out in all directions. Even with the poor view, we made out Puget Sound and other shrouded highlights on the horizon. A man standing next to me on the southeast side remarked, "Guess we don't get any mountains today."

"True." I nodded, not so disappointed. We might not have spied the Cascades from our perch, but we soon would be seeing them up close and personal.

Triple play

After rocketing to ground level we met Tom and Aislínn in a one-way-out gift shop where I stopped to read a few placards about the 1962 World's Fair. I couldn't help but imagine attendees marveling at the first microwave ovens and touch tone phones. Ancient history for my kids but nostalgic for me, with parents who lived in those dark ages.

Sean, psyched to hop the Harry Potter monorail we'd seen earlier, hurried us out and sprinted to get the first car. The train, another Fair relic, actually did disappear right into MoPOP, but through a large tunnel. Not as magical but still entertaining.

Whizzing through the building and out into the city, we exited the tram at Westlake Center. From there it was a short walk to Pike Place Market, one of the oldest public farmer's markets in the country. We joined the masses of people mingling around aromatic food stalls and unique artisan booths.

On one busy curb, a street artist sprayed Krylon enamel onto white poster paper. With conductor-like strokes, he rapidly aimed colors. Over the next half-hour, he turned nondescript blobs into a gorgeous Seattle cityscape over Puget Sound. Spellbound, we watched him dab final touches of moonlight with his palette knife.

"Man, that's amazing,." Aislínn leaned in to get a closer look. Others around her nodded.

I couldn't believe he only wanted $20 for the artwork. I would have grabbed it in a blink. But it was too wet to carry and we had a game to get to.

Yes, Tom had Mariners tickets. We found the local bus to Safeco Field, where Ciarán and Aislínn grabbed their tickets and went ahead. Tom read his stub wrong, so Sean and I wound up following him up and down the same set of stairs three times until we finally checked our own tickets and located the gate. The other two were comfy in their seats munching hot dogs and fries by the time we puffed our way there.

We did our best to cheer on the ailing home team. The Red Sox kicked butt, 4-2. No help for the Yankees that year. By then, a steady drizzle had begun to fall. We didn't mind. Better to rain on a hotel than a tent.

As we took a public bus back to the University Inn, I grinned. What a day. Music, *Star Wars* and major league baseball. A Brennan trifecta!

Zootastic

Tom sat savoring his third cup of strong Seattle coffee when the rest of us finally joined him for breakfast. The kids over-indulged to the point where I wound up yelling at Sean to get out of the bathroom because we were supposed to have checked out already.

I griped to Tom as he packed The Couch. "Forget about gas costs, I'm gonna call this trip the Brennan Bathroom Blues. It's just not normal for kids to take that long on the toilet."

He eyeballed me and smirked. "I definitely wouldn't bring that up if I were you."

When we finally rolled away, a sickening scrape of metal stopped us. For some curious reason, huge stanchions dotted the hotel parking lot, making it a concrete obstacle course.

"*Shit!* I didn't even see it." Tom slammed out to inspect the damage. I joined him. A nice long abrasion decorated the rear passenger side.

Tom's jaw tightened; he huffed through his nose. He kicked the tire. "I can't f&#king believe it! God damn it!"

I grabbed his arm. "C'mon. Nothing we can do about it now. We'll deal when we return the rental. Let's just get going."

We moved slowly in city traffic. No one said anything until Sean spotted a roadside attraction sign. On vacation, those small brown placards with white letters stood out like beacons.

"Hey, ma, it's a zoo." His yearning was clear.

Tom, clenching the steering wheel, immediately shot down the idea.

"Pu-leeeeeeeze." Our youngest leaned forward into the front to cock his head up at his dad.

"I said *no*. I don't want to stop."

Sean hurtled back, grumbling.

Tom eyed him in the rearview. "We're in a neighborhood for god's sake. What kind of zoo can you have here?"

"I don't know," I ventured, my own zoo worship getting the better of me. "It *might* be good."

That unleashed triplicate pleading from the back. Tom grumpily caved with one final grouse. "We're gonna leave by two, or it'll be late when we're setting up our stuff."

NATURAL LEADER

Woodland Park Zoo pioneered a change in zoos worldwide with its natural habitat enclosures. Founded in 1899, it is home to some 1,100 animals representing nearly 300 species. The small sanctuary in the Phinney Ridge neighborhood of Seattle, WA, attracts more than a million people a year and remains a global conservation leader. A visit is well worth the price of admission! (www.zoo.org)

Sean lit up. "Thanks Dad! Two hours is plenty of time."

Within minutes of rushing through the entrance, we saw two gorilla brothers playing keep-away with a short branch.

I grinned. "Looks like you guys."

"Yeah and that looks like you and Bean." Sean nodded to the plexiglass in front of us. A sleeping mother lay just inches away with her infant curled in her arm. The baby wriggled, looked right at us then flopped comfortably down again.

My daughter pressed her face to the barrier and cooed. "Awwwwwww. She's soooooo cute!"

We had to force ourselves away. In no time, though, our attention landed on an orangutan hanging in a jangle of branches, all furry limbs and goofy face.

Aislínn snorted at her older brother. "Haha, talk about look-alikes."

Ciarán got as close as he could, lifted his arms to mimic the primate and tried to stare him down. The hairy fellow could not have cared less. But we all hooted.

The whole time, ear-piercing screeches filled the air. Sean tried to spy hidden tamarinds in the rich canopy above. He excitedly indicated a drape of low-hanging leaves. "Over there."

"Where?" Aislínn squinted.

"There. He's *there.*" He darted across the path, pointing. "I saw him."

"Sure Sean." She shrugged.

We chuckled. Though he probably did.

As we continued, large natural habitats with ideal viewing stations gave us intimate looks at the tenants. In the plains section, giraffes strode across fields while magnificent leopards posed atop rocky coves. From savannas to rainforests, Asia to the arctic, the entire world could be glimpsed in this tiny treasure of a zoo, known for groundbreaking conservation efforts. Even night animals became visible in a specially-designed nocturnal haven.

Our time flew by and we still had half the habitats left. Tom wouldn't budge. We had to leave.. Woodland Park Zoo became another come-back fave.

Missing device

Sally Satellite got us lost finding the highway north, so Tom remained on edge until we finally saw the silhouette of George Washington with a big number "5" in his profile. The kids and I decided we really liked the distinctive state road signs. We joked for a while about who would be the perfect image for New Jersey. Then Ciarán and Aislínn popped in their earbuds and I reached for my book.

I barely began to read when Tom growled into the mirror. "Heyyyy, what're you doing?"

I turned to see Sean reaching across his sister and frantically digging into her door compartments. He swung to the other side and did the same across Ciarán. Then he rifled through the net pockets on the back of my seat.

"I can't find my iPod." He unbuckled his belt and clambered over the back to look in his suitcase.

"Get in your seat," ordered Tom.

Sean ignored the command and furiously unzipped his bag. Tom pulled over. I waited for the outburst. Instead, he helped his son search. No luck.

We tried to reconstruct the last time he remembered having it. In the hotel bathroom…when I rushed him out. Ugh.

I called University Inn, gave them our room number and was told they'd check and let us know. My stomach sank. Sean glowered. Tom, sticking up for me, insisted it was the kids' responsibility to watch their own stuff.

So many peaks and valleys, even when we weren't on mountains. We never did see that iPod again. Good thing for Sirius and shared earbuds.

Woodland Park Zoo

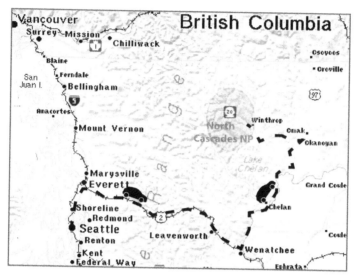

Seattle to North Cascades, WA
2.5 hours

AT-A-GLANCE:
NORTH CASCADES NATIONAL PARK
From moist greenery in the west to arid landscape in the east, the North Cascades are vast and varied. More than 300 glaciers crown jagged peaks while namesake cascades rush into lush valleys from conifer-clad mountains. Known as the "American Alps," the Cascades is home to a diverse ecosystem that includes grizzly bears and gray wolves.

LOCATION: Less than three hours from Seattle, the park crosses sections of Whatcom, Skagit and Chelan counties in Washington state. It consists of a northern and southern district bisected by Ross Lake National Recreation Area.

OPEN: North Cascades is open all year, although avalanches typically close North Cascades Highway in winter.

COST: The park is free to all visitors.

INFO: https://www.nps.gov/noca/index.htm

170

Chapter 14
Northern Exposure

Thick, dreary clouds accompanied us the couple of hours to Marblemount, WA, where we stopped to stock up at the Skagit General Store on the western edge of North Cascades National Park. After that, we barely saw another car on the skinny mountain road.

"Kinda creepy!" Aislínn verbalized what we each thought. The parks we visited so far had been packed. We should have been thrilled. Yet eerie mist swallowed our enthusiasm.

Miles down the lonely thoroughfare, we found Newhalen Campground, where not a single site seemed occupied. Sean giggled nervously. Again Aislínn echoed our anxiety. "You sure this is the right place?"

I glanced at Tom, who double-checked our assigned number against a marker sticking out of the ground. He pulled in and shut off The Couch.

"Yes. It'll be great. C'mon!" We waited for him to get out first.

Everyone set to work unpacking and setting up camp. I kept expecting Tom to jump from behind a big tree and smirk, *"Heeeeere's Johnny"* or for Ciarán to creepy crawl from under the deflated tent. But not a single Brennan dipped their toe in *Friday the 13th* or did anything to leverage the unnerving emptiness for laughs.

The boys didn't protest when their dad suggested they stay together to seach the woods for kindling. He rapidly built a fire while Aislínn and I prepared a pasta dinner. We were so far north that it was nearly 11 p.m. before the shroud that pretended to be daylight finally deepened into night. Without any stars, any visible light, or any neighbors, our temporary home was truly dark and isolated.

The blaze created a comforting dome around us in the vapor, at least until Ciarán grabbed our camera and started narrating ala *Blair Witch.* "The Brennans… alone… in the woods… surrounded by fog…" He circled the flames, his voice husky. "With only a fire for protection… who knows what lurks…"

My eldest was clearly over his heebie jeebies.

"Stooooooop," pleaded Sean amidst giggles.

"You are such a jerk." Aislínn, not at all entertained, swatted the lens away from her face. "Just leave me alone."

I quickly started talking about the zoo, asking everyone's favorite animal. It seemed to do the trick. We settled back into a quiet lull. Of course we knew the sounds of the night had to be, well, just sounds of the night. But still, for the first time in the trip, we walked to the facilities en masse to brush our teeth and get ready for bed.

Overruled

After that spooky dose of gloom, we woke to a completely different park. The sun bejeweled a cloudless blue sky. Huge evergreens danced around us in delightful adagio sways. The restroom path welcomed us with delicate ferns and tiny wildflowers that raised hairs on our legs the evening before.

Tom and I yearned for a leisurely long hike to Cascade Pass with reportedly magnificent views of glaciers and snow-capped peaks. The kids revolted in a thrash of protests.

"I don't feel like hiking." Aislínn retreated to the tent.

"Yeah." Ciarán plopped into a camp chair. "Especially all day."

"Me neither. I'm not going." Sean sat next to his brother, crossing his arms over his chest.

Tom just shook his head and poured another cup of coffee. Rather than argue, I took off down a nearby trail to the visitor center, enjoying early morning sunrays angling through old growth cedars. My sons decided to follow and caught up. When I asked about their unexpected objection, they shrugged.

"I dunno." Ciarán kicked a stone and sent it flying. "Just want to wander around, not take a big deal long hike."

"Yeah. What he said." Sean ran to soccer-punt his brother's rock, still in motion on the dirt, but missed when Ciarán shoved him off course. I let it go. Maybe it would be better to just hang close without having to prepare our packs, find the trail or listen to complaints.

The rustic visitor center brought immediate balm to my brain. I loved random factoids and collected them like some people accumulated stamps. As soon as I read it, I knew my favorite trivia from the Cascades would be:

MORE SCIENCE of BLUE

While depth and clarity create Crater Lake's royal blue, the dazzling turquoise of Skagit River's three manmade lakes comes from glacial dust. Mountain streams carry down millions of particles from the glacier-covered peaks that tower 8,000 feet over Gorge, Diablo and Ross lakes. This glacier rock dust is suspended in the water and reflects sunlight in a brilliant hue of greenish-blue.

the section where we stood got more rain in a single month than its arid east side received all year! That explained the vast contrast between the temperate rain forest in the west and the park's much dryer ponderosa pine ecosystem. What a difference water made!

On the walk back to camp, Ciarán kept bumping his brother. After the third time, Sean shoved back. Before I knew it, they were tussling on the ground until Ciarán yelled, "PIN!" He jumped up with a broad grin.

Sean clambered to his feet and wiped himself off, mumbling, "Jerk."

In a second, Ciarán had him in a bear hug. "What'd you say, punk?"

I exhaled noisily. "Cut it out, Ciarán. Go burn your energy somewhere else. Why can't you…" He blew me off and trotted away smiling. I tried to appease Sean, urging him to ignore his older brother.

"He's a real a-hole." He kicked his foot into the dirt path. "You just don't know."

I moved to hug him, but he peeled away.

"You don't, ma. He does so much crap you don't see. To me and Bean."

A deep sigh crawled up from my belly.

Electric turquoise

I brought a map back from the visitor center with a scenic driving loop and took my family's lukewarm response to be a yes. Back on the park's main road, we paralleled the Skagit River, its rushing water gleaming under a line of glacier-capped mountains. What a postcard perfect contrast to our arrival the day before.

Through closed car doors at the first overlook, we heard unmistakable rumbling from Gorge Creek Falls. The noise became thunderous as we got out and peered over a cliff edge to see the powerful cascade crash 300 feet below into a body of water so astonishingly turquoise that it rivaled Crater Lake for the most surreal hue of our trip.

Gorge Lake was one of three manmade lakes created by hydroelectric dams installed in the early 20th century to supply power to Seattle. But glaciers, not electricity, produced that magnificent aquamarine.

Aislínn and her dad stayed at the top while the boys followed me down a narrow trail that brought us closer to the dam and the lake. Around a sharp bend, we surprised a lone mottled bird.

"Wow." My youngest brought his index finger to lips to urge our quiet.

I lifted my hands in a silent "what is it?"

Sean barely whispered. "Ptarmigan."

"Hmmmmm?" It looked like a weird chicken to me.

Sean motioned us to stay back as he crept closer for a better look. The fowl stood frozen for a few seconds then waddled away.

"A what?"

"Ptarmigan."

"Tarmigan?"

"Yes, p-t-a-r-m-i-g-a-n. You don't pronounce the p."

We started walking again. "It's a really cool bird cause it changes color in different seasons to blend with the surroundings. You see his grayish brown?"

I nodded.

"Well in winter, it's pure white."

"Really?" I smiled at my son. "How do you *know* that?"

He shrugged. "*Animal Planet.*"

Even Ciarán was impressed.

At a wooden platform atop the dam, we could not only hear and see but also feel the hurling fury of water. I wasn't crazy about the power lines overhead, but it was definitely thrilling to see the Force being used for good.

Our next stop, Diablo Pass, looked just as riveting, with towering snowcaps above and shimmering Lake Diablo below. Tom and I stood reading placards with geological and historical tidbits when Aislínn yelled, "Stop it!"

I spun around in time to see my eldest quickly shove his hands into his pockets. I inhaled slowly.

Before Tom could say a word, our son proclaimed his innocence. We both gave him The Look. My husband issued a firm warning and Ciarán scuffed away, spraying up dirt that "accidentally" blew toward his sister. She elbowed him as he passed. He leaned in to knock her but she stepped out of the way.

Tom and I raised our eyebrows at each other, took deep breaths and went on to the next sign. But we both knew it was time to head back and have a conversation with number one son.

Sibling space

The squall continued to brew in the rear of The Couch. Sean, in the middle, muttered with Aislínn. Ciarán tried to annoy them both by man-spreading his legs and stretching his arms aggressively across the entire back seat. Sean tightened his thighs in defense, pushing back as hard as he could.

I gave them credit for keeping the muscle wars silent, since Tom would have blown a gasket. His hearing loss was a blessing sometimes. But I could feel the rippling energy. I often mused how it would have been to have four kids. Not that I wasn't thankful for three. Especially since I didn't think I'd have any. But would an even number have changed the dynamic? Could it have tempered the shifting allegiances of odd man out?

Back at camp, Aislínn, so fed up with Ciarán's increasing teasing and poking announced she was going into the tent to read and wanted TO BE LEFT ALONNNNE!

I followed her. "Bean?"

"I'm okay mom. I just want them out of here. Can't you all go somewhere for a while?"

"How 'bout we go for a walk. Just you and me?"

"No. My ankle's sore. Can't you just go with them?"

I wanted to push the ankle issue, but I just didn't have the energy. A part of me wanted to be left alone, too. "OK sweetie. You relax. We'll be back in a while."

I emerged and told Tom and the boys the four of us were going for a river loop hike that started near our campground and wove around the visitor center.

"We already went there," dismissed Ciarán.

"No, this is a different trail. It's supposed to be awesome down by the river. C'mon. It's not that long. Then we'll get ice cream at the VC."

The boys reluctantly agreed and all was quiet as we headed own the old forest path. Although we were in the wettest part of the park, the area got less rain than the temperate rainforest in Olympic, so the surroundings were not quite as Amazonian.

Still, ferns, lichens and sphagnum sprang from most tree stumps. Lime green moss hung like cotton candy from branches above. It wasn't Heart O' the Hills, but similarly strange and beautiful.

Ciarán retrieved a long fallen stick and marched ahead of us, swinging it like a bojutsu warrior with popping, spitting sound effects to each jab of his staff. Sean kept his distance. I proceeded stiffly, knowing it could go either way.

Soon we heard the burbling Skagit. By the hydroelectric dams, the river raged downstream like a bull through the streets of Pamplona. Yet at these southern banks, the water practically stood still. A dry winter left it unusually slow and low, exposing thousands of smooth stones on one large section of shoreline. Sized from dimes to doorknobs, their wet veneers sparkled.

Sean broke out into a broad grin. He ran across the wild rock garden, took off his boots and shrieked at the frigid laps on his toes. He selected an oval stone and landed four skips on his first toss.

In seconds, Ciarán jumped beside him with a high five. The two scooped up an artillery and burst into hoots as they tried to out-throw each other. Tom joined in the barefoot delight.

The knot in my stomach loosened at the sound of their laughter. I strolled alone along the fertile bank and gazed farther out to the deeper, greener moving waters. I sighed. Yes, I thought, during our journeys we all pick up sediment that colors us in so many ways.

Around a bend, I came upon a huge waist-high tree branch splayed over the water like a princess bed. I climbed up and laid on my back. Hot, windy sun warmed my face. The river's soothing symphony filled my ears. The glaciers smiled on my private moment of bliss.

How many others, I wondered, found solace, joy or rest here? What kind of eyes looked out from this exact angle at the dazzling landscape of mountains and stream? I spent a while deep in my reverie when I heard, "Hey, maaaaaa. Where y'at???"

I remained silent. The males quickly found me.

"Wow! Sweet tree." Ciarán started inching up. I moved off to give both boys a chance to appreciate its comfort. Thankfully, they shared instead of shoved.

Attack!

When we finally decided to move again, Tom strode ahead pumping his arms. Sean and I sauntered far behind. Ciarán, stick back in hands, stayed with us. He twirled the staff and started to hum, *"Asante sana squash banana... asante sana squash de banana..."*

I smiled. Rafiki from *Lion King*.

My youngest and I began our own little Pumbaa-Timón step-dance in time to the rhythm. Ciarán whirled around to march backwards, leading us like a drum major with Swahili swing. *"Asante sana squash banana... asante sana squash de banana..."*

We laughed out loud, causing him to ham it up even more. He pranced with high kicks, bouncing as he belted out the tune. We marched in full silly mode when an ear-splitting scream stopped us in our tracks. In seconds, we heard it again. "AAAAGGGGHHHHHHHH, HELLLLLLP."

It was Tom! We took off in a sprint. My husband had covered quite a distance while we fooled around. Breathless, we found him in the middle of the path bent over moaning. "SH#@! OWWWWWWW!"

Fear gripped my gut. "You okay? What happened?"

"It *bit* me. On-the-back-of-my-leg." His words ran together as he frantically tried to look, but couldn't twist enough to see his wound.

My alarm increased. Was it a snake? A rabid animal?

"What bit you?" I tried to remain calm while the boys and I squatted to inspect his lower leg.

"I don't know," he barked. "But it hurts."

We couldn't see any punctures. Perhaps it was a spider or stinging insect that didn't leave as big a mark. Tom continued to moan.

"Where," I asked quietly.

"Right there!" He jabbed the air toward his calf.

We peered up and down his entire left leg. Eagle eye Sean examined every inch.

"Do you know what it was?" probed Ciarán.

"No," Tom snapped. "I already told you. I don't know what it was. All I know is something bit me. And it hurts!"

"Where exactly?" Sean squinted a few inches from the skin. He pulled Tom's sock down and peered into the area around his ankle. Then he scrutinized his calf again.

I leaned in behind him. There still weren't any red marks, any scratches, any sign of anything.

"You sure?" I tried to gently rub my hand over the area. He yanked away.

"Yes, I'm god damn sure. And it still hurts." He limped around, testing his left leg.

The boys and I stood up and looked at each other. My husband circled angrily, wobbling to avoid putting too much weight on the injury.

"Sorry, we can't see anything…"

His glare cut me off.

Chain reaction

I don't know whether it was his fury (I've left out his choicer words) or disdain for our concern. And I'm not sure who started laughing first. But that initial giggle was a match in a puddle of fuel. We exploded into hysterics. I tried to bite the inside of my cheeks, especially after Tom hobbled off, steam rising from his head.

"Wait… Wait…" I swallowed hard. "They'll have first aid at the visitor center."

"*You. Are. All. IDIOTS!*" He glowered over his shoulder then limped ahead.

We rushed after him. He strode pretty quickly for someone in pain, which made the boys laugh even more. I attempted to regain my composure. No luck. Every time I caught their eyes, I erupted. Soon, I was crying. Each

---

TRAVEL TIP: Beware the Isolation Bubble

Families love, families laugh and families fight, no matter where they are. But when you share only each other's company for extended periods of time, small annoyances or passing moods can magnify. Without the distraction of school, work or even escaping to another room in your house, it's easy to lose sight of the normal ebb and flow of human emotion. If there were one thing I would have done differently on the road, I would have stepped back and given myself — and my family — much more metaphorical space. I would have embraced the fact that we each have our moments and that life is truly a cycle.

---

time I composed myself, Ciarán would mimic, "IT BIT ME! AAAAHHH! I NEED AN AMPUTATION!" and I'd lose it again.

In my defense, I was one of those people who giggled uncontrollably under stress, so maybe the day just overpowered me. And the boys were so used to Tom's dramatics that they found him funny, especially since no bite or sting was apparent. But, really, we had no excuse for our lack of empathy at my poor husband's pain.

We arrived at the visitor center shortly before closing. I shakily asked for some ice for Tom's wound. There still wasn't any swelling or redness or marks on his calf, but I had to at least act as if I was seeking first aid.

Hopefully the Ranger thought the tremulous spasms in my chest and shoulders were distress, not suppressed chuckles. I was so weak from laughing that I couldn't snap the instant cold pack. Tom snatched it and cracked the seal himself. This got the boys going again, so they scurried into another room of exhibits even though they'd already seen everything.

Despite his clear annoyance at me, I dragged Tom and his ice pack into a small theater. We sank into wooden seats, alone in the room. A large screen looped stunning nature slides overlayed with Buddhist quotes on peace and connection. A spa-like soundtrack enhanced it all. I doubt it helped Tom but was exactly what I needed to calm down and reground.

When the rangers announced they were locking up for the night, Ciarán, suddenly mature and serious, offered to help his dad. He walked him back to the campsite to find hydrocortisone. Sean and I followed, not in any hurry.

I eventually made chili and rice while the boys followed Tom's commands to build a fire. He was still clearly aggravated. Aislínn remained on tenuous terms with Ciarán as they slouched in their camp chairs.

Yes, a perfect setting for another round of my second guessing. I looked at all of them. We'd had almost a month of togetherness. Was it past everyone's limits? Did I make a horrible mistake?

I poked a kindling stick into the fire so the end would burn like incense as

I twirled it in front of me. No, I countered to myself. We were a regular old family, with regular old teenagers who got on each other's nerves. We'd seen so much great stuff.

But... maybe we just had enough and it was time to leave. Ugh. I had to force myself to stop. I definitely didn't want to get lost in that mental maze all night again.

I went into the tent and retrieved *The Alchemist* from Aislínn's suitcase, one of nearly a dozen books the kids brought for their summer reading assignments that kept us all in good literature for the trip.

Paul Coelho's mystical fable about a shepherd boy named Santiago turned out to be an ideal choice, a reminder that if we listened to our hearts, the universe conspired to help us on our journeys, despite pain and challenges along the way.

Yep, that was it. As long as I listened to my heart, we'd all be fine.

I read until the sun finally set, well after 10:30 p.m. The kids had already gone to lie down and mercifully seemed to be leaving each other alone. Or at least I didn't hear any grumblings.

Tom and I sat quietly gazing at the brilliant stars visible through a small clearing in our moss-covered campsite. I would have loved for him to grab my hand and tell me everything would be all right, or even grab my hand and not say a word. He was still too upset.

A long time passed before my husband saw the humor, but "something bit me" sent the rest of us into spasms for months. Yet that night, nothing was funny to me. I tossed and turned for hours in agitated half sleep. Sean and Tom snored on either side of me; across the tent the other two breathed deeply.

When I finally succumbed, I dreamt of standing with my family, admiring *Alchemist*-like views from a mountaintop. Out of nowhere, a hideous creature emerged growling thunderously at us. I turned to tell everyone to run. When I looked at Tom, in the crazy way of dreams, he was the creature, covered with oozing slime. He bellowed something I couldn't understand. I only knew we had to escape. The kids raced with me, but Ciarán stuck his leg out to trip his sister, who fell off the side of the cliff. I screamed in panic. Sean raced down to find her.

I woke drenched in sweat. Talk about Freud! I tried to count backwards. Cleanse my chakras. Breathe methodically. Anything else I could think of to avoid dissecting the grim patches in this nightmare. But I kept landing back in my mental ditch, thinking over and over, maybe I'm just too old, too tired and too done to listen to my heart any more.

My restless night and glum mood followed me into daylight. Tom seemed as if a switch flipped in his brain. He stood chipper, cheery and raring to go. Classic. Like a summer thunderstorm, my spouse's anger was quick, furious and done. Mine? I perfected the slow, long, grudge-laden burn that was more like monsoon season. Moody, muddy and stuck.

If I weren't so trapped in my own tangle, I would have laughed out loud when he asked if he did anything to annoy me since I looked so upset. I took a deep breath and tried to smile.

I really needed to get out of my own way so I could enjoy the next few weeks. The kids, like Tom, chatted amiably as we packed up and headed towards Republic, WA.

You think I would have figured on this by now.

Skipping rocks in North Cascades' Skagit River

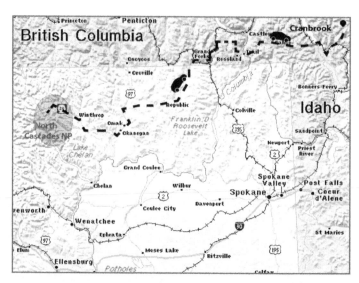

North Cascades to Republic, WA, to Cranbrook, BC
4.5 hours + 5 hours

Chapter 15
Eastward Ho

We kicked off our return leg to the east with a final look at the sparkling manmade waters of lakes Gorge, Diablo and Ross. They turned out to be just a preview for the visual treasures on North Cascades Highway (Washington Route 20) that traversed the park. Many called the 140-mile national scenic byway the most beautiful drive in Washington State.

Impossibly balanced rock spires, some in groups, some singular, pierced the blue sky like ancient idols. Lush forests and deep valleys provided rolling velvet carpets between these striking sculptures. The jagged white peaks of the North Cascades range reigned over everything.

"So beautiful!" Tom stole glances as he drove on the wide, empty road.

Aislínn looked up from a guidebook. "American Alps for sure! That's what they call them. And says here a lot of the higher peaks are volcanoes."

"Sweet! Imagine seeing one of 'em blow?" Ciarán kicked the back of my seat. "Ka'booooom!"

"Not this close," I said. "Waaaay too scary."

I could feel him roll his eyes at me.

Sean peered out his window searching for eagles. The Cascades provided the second largest home in the U.S. for our national avian. Only Alaska boasted more. While the beautiful birds of prey normally congregated in the winter months, it didn't hurt to hope. His disappointment at not seeing any vanished as the terrain took over.

Practically vertical at times, we cheered on The Couch like an America's Cup crew in ocean swells. Ears popped as we powered up Washington Pass, the route's highest elevation at nearly 5,500 feet. The 360-degree view, beautifully brilliant and clear, almost made us dizzy. Speeding downward, our stomachs dropped until it was time to head up again. What a blast!

The park's eastern side brought far fewer trees from lack of rainfall, but cliffs – and thrills – remained dramatically high. Finally, after hours of roller coaster delight, we descended to an unexpected bend that immediately opened upon a broad valley of farmland.

Small town Washington

Stopping miles outside the park in Winthrop, WA, the air was not only remarkably hotter and drier, it also seemed kinder. We had literally and emotionally scaled some very big humps.

Tom and the kids, as usual, wanted something to eat. They went for burgers and fries in an outdoor food court. I took the opportunity to wander around the former gold mining mecca, fully festooned with Western facades and the oldest legal saloon in Washington state.

I eventually found my family finishing a game of mini-golf. A few scoops of ice cream and many smiles later we returned to The Couch in jolly good spirits. In an hour, we entered our night's respite, Republic, WA, another throwback to old time America, only a little rustier around the edges.

Tom's earache, eased by antibiotics in Seattle, suddenly reared with a vengeance so he laid down. The boys unloaded and claimed the second bed to binge TV.

This time, Aislínn agreed to explore with me. While we browsed small shops and galleries, I once again wondered how the trip would have gone if it were just the two of us like we originally planned. I wanted to say something but couldn't find the right words.

Instead, I steered her into the Stonerose Interpretive Center and Eocene Fossil Site. We loved earth treasures and couldn't get enough of the geodes, limestone carvings and ancient artifacts on display.

"You gotta see this one, ma." Aislínn stared into a glass case at a tiny brown cluster of petals.

"What is it?"

"Flor-is-san-tia… quil-chen-en-sis." She giggled trying to pronounce the name on a plaque. "It's a famous prehistoric flower. It's been in *National Geographic!*"

"No kidding." I peered more closely at the ancient bloom. "Kinda like a miniature brown periwinkle. Sorta pretty."

"Yeah. Comes from an extinct cocoa tree. One of the store's former curators and a paleobotanist discovered it." She pointed at the Stonerose logo at the front of the store. "And they used it for their design."

"Oh. Thought that was a rose. You know? Stonerose?"

"Nope. It's the Flor-is-san-tia." She grinned.

That was my Bean, I thought, joyfully soaking up factoids like a sponge. I smiled back. "There's a crossword puzzle stumper for sure."

Although just window shopping, I kept circling back to a stunning mollusk fossil with golden snail spirals. Every time I picked it up, I quickly told myself it was too expensive.

Aislínn changed my mind. "Go ahead mom. You love it. It will bring you pleasure for a long, long time."

My wise daughter.

While we were gone, Tom's increasing pain compelled him to a nearby walk-in clinic. The doctor couldn't find anything brewing in his ear and advised him to double down on Advil for pain. A few tablets did the trick.

We found a tasty Mexican restaurant near our hotel then the kids lost themselves in more TV while I worked. Light years from my previous night's worry, sleep welcomed me like an old friend.

Oh, Canada

We could have bee-lined through Idaho to our next stop at Glacier National Park in Montana. But when we planned the adventure, Aislínn thought an arc through our northern neighbor would be fun. So bright and early the next morning we headed to British Columbia.

More than 30,000 vehicles a day passed through Washington's 13 official crossings into Canada, often resulting in hours of waiting. We got super lucky.

The drive to the border took less than 60 minutes. A tall, bearded officer had the occupants of the car before us get out while he opened each door, bent in and inspected their stuff. We expected the same. When we rolled up, he just looked at our passports, leaned in through Tom's window to say hi to the kids and waved us through.

No sooner had we landed on BC soil when Tom rounded his lips and asked, "What did one Canadian say to the other Canadian, *eh*?"

We groaned. From Maine to Mississippi, Ireland to Italy, Tom instantly adopted any geographic language inflection. Brogues, twangs, drawls, you name it, he could chat like a local. But Canada's "raising" – a lilting vowel shift on the words in a sentence, followed by the ever-present "eh" – was one of his favorites.

"Oh, you heard that one already, *eh*?" He smiled broadly.

"Dad!" The chorus responded instantly.

"Oh, c'mon, it's beautiful here, *eh*?"

I laughed. It was indeed.

If we thought the North Cascades views spectacular, the Purcell Mountains filled us with even greater awe. For as far as the eye could see, pines rippled in a lush green carpet. The horizon gleamed from snow-covered peaks under a perfect blue sky filled with cotton candy clouds.

Highway elevations made the Cascades seem like a kiddie ride. At one point our "oil warning" light came on, which normally would have sent Tom into a tizzy. But we knew even the rock-solid Couch felt the challenge. Up, up, up into heaven-nicking passes we went, then so far down into valleys that we barely glimpsed the top again. Climbing from the depths, we were momentarily blinded by bright sun rays shooting over the next silhouetted peak.

Each dip transformed the lighting and perspective so we never tired of looking out our windows. Even Tom, sometimes tense when driving through the unknown, relaxed and enjoyed the wide roadway, sparse traffic and magnificent surroundings.

Jokes on us

We pulled off in Creston, BC, for some eats and fuel. The roadside restaurant looked fine but as the saying went, you couldn't judge a book by its cover. The dreary interior bordered on dirty. The kids quickly derided my dumpsta-funk face. I didn't care.

"Look. They're gross." I pointed to the smeared tables and greasy menus then invoked the "nothing with mayo" decree my mother instilled in me, convinced that tuna, chicken salad or anything with mayonnaise might be sketchy.

Almost all the lunch choices involved mayo, so I went a step further and imposed a "let's have breakfast for lunch" mandate, squashing all protests. Who, after all, could mess up eggs? Apparently, the Creston restaurant. While probably safe, the meals were barely edible. Thank goodness for those snacks in The Couch.

We struck out again when we went to gas up. Well not exactly struck out, but we had egg on our faces instead of in our stomachs.

As mentioned, soaring petroleum prices led us to name our journey the *We-Don't-Care-What-Gas-Costs* adventure. We purposely avoided the math during our 7,000-mile trip, especially after paying more than $5 a gallon outside of San Francisco.

Imagine our delight when we pulled into a small station where the sign boasted an amazing $1.39. We knew the exchange rate was about even at the time so Canada must have been doing something right! I could have cartwheeled with glee. The food might have been crappy in Creston, but who cared when gas was so cheap?

Tom pumped the fuel, cheering our northern neighbors nonstop, replete with eh, eh's. Then he retrieved the receipt.

"What the...?"

He handed it in through my window. The total? $163.11!

I stared dumbfounded. Tom started to laugh. "Oh my god, we're idiots."

Yep, we were. The bargain price was per liter. With nearly 3.8 liters in a gallon, that actually meant paying $5.26 for each gallon, our highest cost yet. You think the light bulb would've gone off earlier after we saw a large 100 on the speed limit signs and thought Canadians embraced velocity. Then we noticed the tiny "kph." Aislínn looked it up and found 100 kilometers per hour was about 62 mph in our old Imperial measure.

We were just dumb Yankees after all. And poorer for our ignorance. Yet nothing diminished our wonderment as we climbed and dipped, this time with me at the wheel. What a difference from our Jersey Shore flatlands!

At 5,823 foot-high Kootenay Pass, we truly felt on top of the world. My glance in the rearview revealed each of my teens with mouths open wide in amazement. I could not have asked for a better view.

Oil and ear pains

After another hour of exquisite environs, we exited towards Cranbrook, BC, where we booked the Heritage Inn with swimming pool and free hot breakfast. Only, Sally Satellite navigated us to a paint-peeling, unkempt dump of a motel that didn't even have a sign near the road. A plaque on the building said *The Heritage*. Weeds sprang from cracks in the lot, where just a single car was parked.

"This can't be it. You sure you put in the right address?"

Tom pointed to our trip bible. "Yeah. I put in whatever you had."

We took less than a minute to decide to bail. Tom urged me to turn into the first hotel we saw, the Prestige Inn. The two of us went to check availability. I visibly tensed at the price, more than double what we planned.

"We should just keep looking," I whispered.

"Meh-rrrrrrrr," growled Tom, his angry code for 'don't argue with me.' We locked eyes in a stare down. The receptionist smiled politely and asked if we'd like a room.

"We shouldn't drive anymore with the light on," Tom hissed. The oil warning that we ignored during the mountain driving remained red at lower elevation. "And my ear is killing me again. Let's just stay here."

I exhaled loudly. Tom handed our credit card to the still-smiling clerk. "C'mon," he softened. "We'll order a cheap pizza for dinner and save on food." I gritted my teeth and signed the receipt.

The hotel clock read an hour ahead of the 4:26 p.m. on my watch. When I mentioned this, the receptionist, who certainly had enough of us, sweetly informed me Cranbrook was in Central time. Duh. We were not only metric-challenged, we were time-zone clueless, too.

Tom smiled at the woman then turned to me. "It's okay. We still have time to have The Couch checked out."

The kids lit up when they entered our large, gorgeous room and happily hung out while we went in search of the car fix. Tom found an auto repair place online that was supposed to be just a few miles away.

Less than two minutes down the road, I noticed something else. On the left stood a lovely hotel with a large bright sign: *Heritage Inn – Indoor Pool – Free Hot Breakfast!* I dumpsta-funked big time.

Tom frowned at me defensively. "Well the coordinates might have been a *little* off..." We drove in silence to the service center.

"Must be a slow afternoon," Tom mumbled as we pulled in to the empty lot.

"Yeah. Real slow." I pointed at the darkened interior with a sign on the door that read: CLOSED. Once again, the light bulb went off too late. It was Sunday. That's why so many of the places we passed stood empty. Used to New Jersey's commercial overload, we never considered that other places practiced a consumer day of rest.

Back at the hotel, Sean napped on one of the extravagantly comfortable beds. Tom took more Advil and joined him. Aislínn and Ciarán barely had to ask before I changed into my bathing suit for the indoor pool.

The only ones there, we played and swam for quite a while. Then I soaked in an adjacent hot tub, growing less tense with each jet of water on my back and neck. I wrapped in one of the hotel's thick white cushy towels, sank into a padded lounge and read.

Business brainstorm

Awake and upset he missed the pool, Sean perked up when I suggested we go down to the Kootenay Pass Hot Shots café off the lobby. The two of us gaped at the mouth-watering offerings written in colorful chalk on a blackboard menu: build-your-own wraps, designer shakes, paninis, gourmet greens.

"We should open one of these at home!" Sean gushed as he sipped his cookie nookie smoothie, leaning his elbows on our high-top black lacquer table.

I nodded enthusiastically, relishing my hand-crafted organic salad with artisan dressing. We pictured empty storefronts on our Main Street and brainstormed names.

"How 'bout Merrymom's Bistro?" I asked, tapping into my longtime email moniker.

"Nah. Has to be cool."

I ignored the insult and ventured a few others. "Moonlight Café? Luna Delight? Velespia Cuisine?"

TRAVEL TIP: It's Only Money

As a genetically programmed bargain hunter and exceptionally frugal traveler, this was a hard lesson to learn. But I've never once looked back years later and wished I had that extra $100 we splurged on a hotel or adventure. Not that you should carelessly spend beyond your means; budgets provide necessary guidelines for most of us. Just make sure you weigh the real costs and benefits of an indulgence. Does the extra fun you'll have in a hotel within walking distance from attractions outweigh the cost of a cheaper option miles away? Are unexpected fees or admission prices a reason to pass up on once-in-a-lifetime experiences? No one can answer for you. But this world-class penny pincher has come a long way in regard to the price of travel. I've learned memories are treasures, well worth some added cost.

"Absolutely not, mom. You want something to bring in kids and families, not airy-fairy ladies."

"Well what do you have?"

"I dunno. Maybe The Hat Trick. Or Home Run. Or Hoop Shack. Or even Hot Shots."

"Hahaha. Figures."

We finished our eats and perused games stacked on a fireside table. We opted for a serious game of War. Sean was happily clobbering me when Ciarán strolled in. His eyes widened at the menu selections.

As he waited for his first ever chicken-pesto-sundried tomato panini, Sean eagerly shared our business development plan. The brothers went to town on more names. Tom and Aislínn appeared a while later and also delighted at the food options.

Clearly we scrapped the idea of a cheap pizza for dinner. They ordered and pulled stools around the table, Sean again imparting our Belmar brainstorm. Ideas flew back and forth until we finally agreed, amid lots of laughter, that maybe someone else should open a place like this near us.

We played a few rousing rounds of poker with our nightcaps. I enjoyed a delicious cup of organic green-mint-ginger tea while the rest of my clan filled up on personalized smoothies. Each left smiling, but Sean, finishing his second of the day, was in heaven.

Back to the states

In the morning, the pain in Tom's ear intensified, radiating to his jaw. I advised we find a local doctor and stay an extra night if needed. He balked.

Trying a different tact, I said, "We could get The Couch checked out, too."

"Nah. I told you it'll be okay." He had found an online forum that noted

The GREAT DIVIDE

It's often referred to as the name of an old movie or a mondo hiking trail. But the Continental Divide (aka the Great Divide) is actually the main hydrological boundary in the American continent. That means it is the separation point for where rain and snowmelt flow. All waters west of the divide drain into the Pacific Ocean; waters on the east eventually drain into the Atlantic Ocean. Though there are other drainage divides in the Americas, the Continental Divide is by far the most prominent because it pretty much follows the line of high peaks along the Rockies and Andes mountain ranges.

we could drive thousands of miles with the oil light on.

"Well I don't think *you* should go anywhere without getting checked."

"I'll be fine, too. I'll take more Advil. You know how it is."

I did. He had a long history of earaches. But I worried. After a lot of back and forth, I agreed to leave so we'd have the full three nights planned in Glacier National Park. The family each ordered one last specialty drink-to-go from our favorite café and had our seat belts on by 9:30 a.m.

Our plan to stop at a nearby supermarket scuttled when we pulled in and saw it didn't open until 11 a.m. Boy, I mused, Canadians certainly had a great work-life balance. We'd just have to stock up closer to Glacier.

Driving into open countryside toward the Canadian Rockies, we admired the fluffy cumulus clouds once again sailing slowly across a gorgeous blue sky. As we passed from British Columbia to Alberta, Tom let out a spontaneous whoop, announcing our milestone of crossing the Continental Divide. Soon the landscape leveled out to high plains. Just north of the U.S. border, towering crags rose out of the flat sweeping horizon.

"Hey, we must be in the peace place." Aislínn squinted. "Yep. Look at the sign. Waterton-Glacier International Peace Park."

"Ohhhh," I cooed.

Along with the sheer aesthetic, I loved the concept of the cross-border partnership between Glacier National Park and Canada's Waterton Lakes National Park. Their overlap became a joint sanctuary dedicated to protection and peace for all living things. At the next pull-off, we got out to breathe in the philosophical and physical magnificence of the land.

Sitting on a roadside boulder next to Sean, I couldn't imagine a more exquisite world.

Canadian Rockies

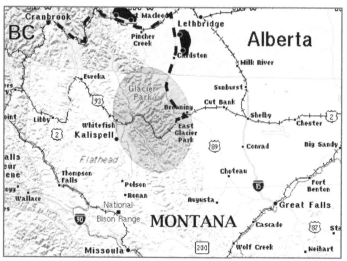

Cranbrook, BC, to Glacier, MT
4.5 hours

AT-A-GLANCE:

GLACIER NATIONAL PARK

A crown jewel of national and international biosphere preserves, Glacier National Park remains largely uncharted, much as it was a hundred years ago. But the 1.2 million-acre park boasts over 700 miles of trails, making it a paradise for adventurous visitors seeking wilderness and solitude. Those less bold will still find spectacular views of pristine forests, alpine meadows, rugged mountains and glacial lakes.

LOCATION: Glacier National Park is in the northwest corner of Montana along the spine of the Rocky Mountains. Vehicle access is through Highway 2 along the southern boundary or Highway 89 along the eastern boundary.

OPEN: Glacier is open all year, although some access is limited in winter.

COST: $35 per vehicle for 7 days; $30 per motorcycle, $20 per vehicle, bicyclist or pedestrian for single day.

NFO: https://www.nps.gov/glac/index.htm

Chapter 16
Glorious Glacier

On our long line crawling toward the Chief Mountain checkpoint between Alberta, Canada, and Babb, MT, Aislínn spotted the namesake monolith towering over the eastern side of Peace Park.

"Y' know." She looked up from her Montana guidebook. "Chief Mountain isn't the highest around here. But it's super sacred for Blackfeet tribes on both sides of the border. It's the first one of the Rockies you see from here, so they think of it kind 'a like a guardian for the rest of the range."

"That's pretty cool, Bean." Her elder sibling nodded.

"I know. Look at these pix. There's a ton of burial sites around the bottom."

"Sweet." Sean leaned over to scan the illustrations. "Ceremonial sites, too?"

"Um hmmm. That's cause they believe it's the oldest spirit of any mountain."

I studied the powerful peak. Throughout our trip I'd sensed extraordinary life force in trees, summits, water. Yet my connections were nebulous and momentary. Imagine living every day with such reverence? How different, I pondered, would our lives, and planet, be if we walked the earth in constant relationship with nature?

My daughter's joyful voice brought me back. "Ya gotta hear this one. Did you know Montana only has seven people per square mile? And there's three cows for every person?"

"Haha," chuckled Tom. "That must be pretty mooo-valous."

Ciarán groaned. "Bad one, dad."

Sean leaned forward. "How many are in Jersey?"

"Cows? Must be a lot. They don't call it the Garden State for nothing,"

"No, *people*. And I think it's the Garden State for its veggies not cows."

"Hmmm, maybe you're right." Tom got his phone. "Says here we have 1,185 people per square mile. And the census is old so there's probably more now."

"Yeah," I said. "We live in the most densely populated state in the country. Lucky us."

Ciarán shook his head. "Jeeze. Eleven hundred people per mile in Jersey versus seven here? What do they *do* out here?"

"Milk cows," quipped Tom.

"Duhhhh." Ciarán mock slapped his forehead.

"Listen to this." Aislínn broke in. "Montana's so big that it's like ten hours to drive across the state."

"Really?" I glanced at her in the rearview. Without traffic, we could shoot

---

GEOLOGICAL TOPSY-TURVY

Long considered a sacred site for local tribes in the U.S. and Canada, Chief Mountain is also revered scientifically. Why? Because the top of the mountain is actually millions of years *older* than the ground underneath. This contrary geological phenomenon is known as "overthrust." Normally layers get progressively younger toward the top. Scientists believe that when tectonic plates in the earth's crust collided and formed the Rocky Mountains some 170 million years ago, a huge rock slab, several miles thick and hundreds of miles long, got pushed or slid eastward. This slab, dubbed the Lewis Overthrust, eventually landed on top of softer rock more than 1,400 million years younger. After this big slide, the area around Chief Mountain eroded, leaving it as the stand-alone eastern marker of the Lewis Overthrust. The thrust itself, however, runs through much of Glacier Park and is studied by scientists worldwide. It provides insight into similar geologic processes happening in other parts of the world, like the Andes and Himalaya Mountains.

---

across the middle of tiny New Jersey in 45 minutes. Tip to tip took only a couple of hours.

"Yep. It's 600 to 800 miles, depending on where you cross."

"In ten hours, we could drive to Maine," I said.

"Yeah, or South Carolina," added Tom.

It gave new meaning to Big Sky Country!

Site gripes

Our reentry to the U.S. took a little longer than our exit; we did have to step out for an inspection. But the road crossed directly into Glacier so we figured finding our campground would be a snap.

With Tom back in the driver's seat, we hugged the east side of the vast park. Periodically the highway wove into the neighboring Blackfeet Reservation past weather-worn trailers on dusty brown yards. For the hundredth time, our teens pondered growing up in such a different place.

Spying the tell-tale teal of glacially fed water, we knew the lakeside St. Mary Campground couldn't be far. We rushed through lunch at a roadside restaurant and continued for miles, waiting for Sally Satellite to tell us to turn. I thought we'd gone too far, but my husband swore we were fine.

After almost an hour, I became more adamant.

194

"Tom, we passed it. I'm telling you it was way back. You know GPS is always spotty in the parks."

"Nah. Don't worry. We're still on a highway, not out of reach. Sally's good."

"Dad…" Ciarán popped his head between us.

"Don't start," warned Tom. "I said we're good."

I grabbed our travel notebook, which I should've done long before. Flipping to the right map, I clearly saw we had gone far past our turn-off.

Tom, hands squarely on the wheel, still wanted to trust the GPS. I gritted my teeth then shouted so he'd finally listen.

"PULL OVER!"

I showed him the mistake. After a u-turn and an hour of backtracking, we veered into the campground's long entryway just miles from where we'd eaten hours earlier. Four pairs of eyes glared at the driver. He shrugged.

Finally at the campsite, my mood flew further south. I had envisioned a peaceful prairie with a serene view of St. Mary Lake. The second we opened our doors, wind gusted through The Couch like an attack from an air gun. We had to lean in to stand straight.

Practically flattened by the bluster, tall grasses bordering our site offered little buffer. Grit layered the lone picnic table in the center of our ring. The lake was nowhere in sight.

I evenly suggested we find another campground since two others were in easy driving distance. Tom reacted as if I asked to push The Couch back to Canada.

"You *crazy*? NO WAY! The *only* place we're looking for now is somewhere to get food and supplies." He turned his back to open the liftgate.

I knew his lingering ear pain and GPS faux pas affected his patience, but I had a bad feeling about this site.

"Maybe we could…"

He cut me off. "I said this is *fine*." He barked at the boys to "get the stuff."

The unrolled ground cloth went soaring. Sean comically flopped forward, arms and legs wide to calm as much of the plastic as he could. Aislínn grabbed anything in sight to throw on its corners. Ciarán jumped on the percolating air bubbles. They were laughing. I was not.

"How can we even put up the tent? It'll lift off like a parachute. And we can't have a fire here." I furiously waved the cap that just flew off my head. "We can't even keep our friggin' hats on."

"It'll be okay." Tom faced me, speaking calmly and slowly now like I was one of his kindergartners. He assured me the wind would die down. "It's like the beach. You know, clouds and wind blow in for a couple of hours

---

TRAVEL TIP: Avoid Supply Shopping in the Parks

Market options vary greatly from state to state. But even in areas without "super-stores," you are still better off stocking outside a national park. Park retailers, for the most part, have limited options and can be much more expensive.

---

every afternoon, then it's done and everything's quiet."

I paced the site's circumference to calm down then grudgingly agreed go shopping with him. We left the kids and set off for St. Mary Grocery, which was so understocked and so expensive that we decided to continue to the next area with its own campground and store.

At Rising Sun Campground, we drove past beautiful, tree-covered sites where leaves barely moved in the light breeze. Even the store was bigger and better stocked (although still expensive.) Envy and agitation bombarded my brain. I doubled down on my pleas.

Tom refused to budge, claiming it too late to move. We finished shopping and returned to what I started calling the Bluster Hole. The wind didn't abate a single bit.

I stalked off and let him put up the tent with the kids, something he hadn't done in a while. He snarled directions, but they just ignored him and snapped together the poles in the same way they had at every campsite since we banned him from helping.

They laughingly wrestled the nylon to hook it in place, cracking up every time it wafted skyward. Once up, the tent become airborne until they threw in the sleeping bags. Even then, the dome continued to rustle and flap like a sail in a storm.

Leaving Tom to stake down our temporary abode, the rest of us walked to St. Mary Visitor Center. I continued to grumble internally when halfway down the path, it happened again: the magical, soothing infusion of being in nature with my children.

Sean shushed everyone and pointed at a huge, bulky nest atop a wooden pole in the swaying prairie grasses. "Baby ospreys."

TRAVEL TIP: Slay Comparison-itis! (It's ALL Good)

I made everyone miserable whenever I thought a different campsite, restaurant or activity would be better than what we chose. Sometimes we switched, sometimes we didn't. In retrospect, we all would have had more fun (and peace) if I behaved maturely and stopped comparing. In the end, it's about your time together and your shared experiences. Make them as good as possible, no matter what.

Sweet tiny chirps filled the air, making us smile. Soon two striking adults circled, hovered near the chicks, then took off. "Must be their parents," Sean's eyes tracked the pair as he spoke. "They mate for life and keep coming back to the same place. They probably got fish from the lake to feed the babies."

For the next twenty minutes, we watched the mesmerizing cycle repeat. Although we couldn't actually see them dropping goodies into open beaks, Sean conjured up a perfect play-by-play. My remaining traces of frustration evaporated like dew in morning sun.

Snow good

The wind never did die down enough for a campfire. In fact, the tent fluttered all night like sheets on a midwest clothesline. But we crawled into our sleeping bags early to be on the road at dawn for a hike near Logan's Pass on the Continental Divide.

We'd read warnings about crowds on Glacier's famous Going-to-the-Sun Road and especially at its popular Logan's Pass Visitor Center. So we were well on our way up winding blacktop before the sun even crested the army of peaks around us.

A cloud swallowed The Couch near Logan Pass, the road's 6,600-foot highest point. Tom gripped the wheel while the rest of us grinned inside

---

GOING-TO-THE-SUN MARVELS and METAPHORS

Glacier National Park's remarkable Going-to-the-Sun-Road treats visitors to some of the most spectacular sights in the Rocky Mountains. Spanning 52 miles across the park's interior, it straddles the Continental Divide at Logan Pass and offers incredible views of glaciers, waterfalls, lush valleys and high peaks. To build the engineering marvel, work crews, most of whom were not mountaineers, had to hang suspended from old hemp ropes to carve the shale cliffs that tower 1,000 feet over the road in some places. After 20 years of planning and construction (and loss of several lives), the landmark highway opened in 1933, named for the Going-to-the-Sun Mountain. One Native American legend attributes the term to a deity who traveled down the peak from the sun to teach hunting basics to the Blackfeet. Another local myth talks about the mountain's importance in vision quests, the Native American rite of passage that helps reveal a life's purpose. In describing these quests, the mountain's name was metaphorically translated into English as Going-to-the-Sun.

---

the surreal bubble of mist.

A full minute passed before we popped out and saw the visitor center exit. Ciarán hooted with glee after we parked in the near-empty lot and scooted through the building toward the trailhead. A blanket of white buried what should have been a grassy field. He happily lobbed a few snowballs, nailing his sister and paying the price with a fast one from his father. No sooner had I darted ahead on a boardwalk that led to Hidden Lake Trail than I felt a neat thwack on the back of my sweatshirt.

"Heyyyy. No fair, I'm going..." A barrage interrupted my whines. I ducked and ran to Aislínn, quickly packing more ammunition as she used her softball prowess to target Ciarán's new green sweater and Sean's orange sweatshirt. We urged Tom to join our ranks, but he stayed with the male contingent. Several shrieking volleys later, we surrendered.

Beaming, Ciarán led the way up the boardwalk to a wide snowy trail. We'd seen a few inches of the white stuff in Crater Lake and Olympic, but this was bona-fide snowpack. Sean stepped a foot off the path and sank giggling to his knees. Half a mile up, a bearded young ranger shoveled stairs in the snow.

"Is it usually like this in late July?" Tom asked.

The ranger shook his head. "Nope. We had a really blizzardy winter that lasted into spring and hasn't melted yet. Hence the summer wonderland."

"Lucky us!" Ciarán shouted as he bounded up the new steps.

Hidden treasure

We scrambled and slid higher and higher, warm sunshine gleaming off the snow. Sean was first to spot a handsome bighorn sheep ahead on the trail. We slowed, expecting him to bolt at our approach. The regal ram stood his ground, close enough for us to make out the ridged texture on his magnificent curved horns.

Having seen advisories, I remained wary about invading his territory. Tom went so far as to suggest we turn back. Our youngest, however, rationalized that the husky male seemed extremely tranquil and quite used to hikers.

Sean gently walked past, giving a wide berth. The ram remained still. I followed, trying not to stare into his beautiful almond eyes. I peeked back several times; the bighorn never budged.

Still enthusing about the majestic mammal, our animal lover almost cartwheeled when he noticed a marmot in the snowy bushes further up the trail.

"Awwww, how cute." Aislínn moved for a better look but her brother

---

KING of the RODENTS

If you're gonna be a rodent, you might as well be at the top of the line. Marmots are kings of the sciuridae family, which also includes squirrels, prairie dogs and lots of other small furry creatures. Champion excavators, marmots revolve their lives around burrowed communities, where neighborhoods of extended families thrive and hibernate. Ground-hogs and woodchucks are probably the most famous of the 15 types of marmots, but Glacier and Yellowstone National Parks are home to two adorable cousins. Hoary marmots live in the alpine areas of Glacier, burrowing among rocks and boulders. Unlikely as it sounds, the word "hoary" means grayish white, and refers to the silver-gray fur on the animal's shoulders and upper back. The yellow-bellied marmots of Yellowstone, named for the blonde fur on their undersection, usually burrow in open grassy communities but sometimes gravitate to the rocks.

---

yanked her back.

"You'll scare him off," he mouthed. "You gotta just watch him from here."

Good thing he didn't see us. Five Brennans would have been towering giants to the furry, spaniel-sized rodent. We admired silently until he scurried away.

While Sean's radar targeted fauna, I noticed the flora. Periodic bursts of yellow glacier lilies, magenta monkey flowers and bright orange poppies found their way through the snow, even more flamboyant against the white ground. But I was most smitten with tiny navy-colored pinecones that clustered amid short needles on bushy little evergreens.

I stopped to capture one. Zooming in, I said, "Can you believe they're blue? I've never seen that before!"

No one answered. My family had already turned a sharp bend in the trail where a stunning white mountain goat lounged on a rocky plateau like a queen on her throne. She practically smiled when I pointed my camera and didn't blink when we passed within feet of her folded legs. For sure, like the seagulls on our beach, these animals became accustomed to human visitors. But as we'd soon see, they were still plenty wild.

We rounded another curve to Hidden Lake Overlook. Our breaths drew in at once, making us giggle at the synchronized reaction. Then we just stared at the fantasy panorama before us.

In the valley far below, snow patches glistened on bright green pastures and rocky crags. Graceful lines of dark pines garlanded the dell. Bands of mountain goats seemed like tiny magical creatures roaming the land. Hidden

---

MAAAAAAD AWESOME MAMMALS

Mountain goats and Bighorn sheep have a lot in common. They thrive in an extreme environment too steep and rocky for their predators. They're about the same size and both have pliable hooves with soft rubbery pads that act like suction cups on craggy surfaces. They baaa, bleat, like the same eats (grasses and other plants) and usually live about 10 years. Unlike many other mammals, neither migrates nor hibernates to survive the winter, although they may head to lower altitudes for a while.

But along with similarities, the alpine goats and sheep have some obvious differences. For starters, the goats sport a coat of woolly white fur and are easy to spot from a distance. The males (billies) and females (nannies) both have "beards" and straight, black horns. (Fun fact: like rings of a tree or scales on a fish, the bands on a goat's horn tell us their age.) Their kids are called, well, kids. The other mountain marvel, bighorn sheep, are predominantly gray or tan, great for camouflage. The males (rams) have large, thick curving horns. The horns on females (ewes) are also curved, but much smaller. (Fun fact: every fall, rams compete for ewes in butting contests, charging each other at speeds more than 20 mph, foreheads crashing with a crack that can be heard more than a mile away.) Their offspring are called lambs. Another interesting difference? Rank. In the goat world, nannies are at the top of the herd and billies rank lowest of all, except during mating season. Not so for the sheep: all ewes are subordinate to even young rams with bigger horns.

Lake sparkled in their midst. The only thing missing was Hobbit huts.

Standing like sentries over this secluded gem were three dark, snow-marbled peaks: 8,684-foot Bearhat Mountain to the southwest, 8,760-foot Clements Mountain to the north, and 9,125-foot Reynolds Mountain to the east. Temperamental clouds hovered over and between them in eerie contrast to the fairy-tale scene below.

No wonder this was such a popular spot. We stood enchanted, alone on the wooden overlook. No one whined to move on. Each of us seemed to revel in the vast, yet intimate, surroundings. After quite a while a young couple arrived. I was pleased to see them. We barely had any photos with the five of us. The shot above Hidden Lake became one of my favorite family portraits ever.

Idiot alert

We could have ventured four-plus miles down to the shores of Hidden Lake. But with another hike in mind for the afternoon, we only walked a bit further then retraced our footsteps. So many people were headed up that we doubly appreciated our early start.

"Su-*per*-ior experience! You'll *love* it." Tom offered his thumbs up to all we passed, netting plenty of smiles and laughs in return. Near the bottom, Ciarán launched another sneak attack. This time Tom joined the females, rounding perfect artillery from snow warmed by the sun. We ran, dove and torpedoed until, out of breath, we finally declared a truce. The boys slid the rest of the way down on a path slick from foot traffic, hooting out loud.

Back near the visitor center, we joined a crowd admiring a lone ram grazing on grass where snow had melted. Everyone kept their distance. Parents lifted toddlers on their shoulders and we squeezed over to make room in the growing circle. Like others, I retrieved my camera and took several shots.

Then a middle age woman ordered loudly, "Hey, Joey, get a picture of me next to him." She moved toward the sheep. He reared his head. She kept going.

Sean poked me in alarm. "What is she *doing*?"

Numerous signs warned visitors to keep away from animals. One stood just feet from this tourist. Oblivious, she continued. Several people, including us, urged her to stop. She ignored all cautions. The ram breathed heavily, his head swinging back and forth.

"What a *rass*-role," Ciarán muttered. "He's gonna charge."

Fortunately, someone must have run into the visitor center because in the 30 seconds this took to unfold, a ranger appeared and commanded the woman to retreat. He cleared the crowd enough so the ram could escape up the mountain.

We'd seen the park's *Don't Be an Idiot* campaign with cartoons of ignorant tourists being clawed by bears or trampled by wild herds. But this was the first idiot we'd actually encountered.

We returned to an overflowing lot. Two minivans vied for our spot as we quickly escaped. How fabulous to have had empty trails and such spectacular sights – all before noon!

Nicer digs

If we bottled our good mood, we'd have had gallons as we drove down Going-to-the-Sun Road. Tom surprised me by pulling into Rising Sun

Campground and snagging an empty site for the next two nights. That added another gallon right there. No more Bluster Hole!

We ate at the campground restaurant then hightailed it to make our switch. The St. Mary breeze was still so brisk that we just threw everything in the SUV without formally packing. In less than an hour, we had it all set back up. I felt ecstatic. More trees, better views and no crazy wind.

All five of us went to browse in the Rising Sun store. Sean bought a t-shirt. Tom got what became one of his well-worn baseball caps. Aislínn splurged for a necklace. Ciarán, broke as usual, begged me to buy him some snacks. I laughed. But of course I tossed him a few bucks. We walked back to our Amazingly Awesome Site and spent the next few hours napping, reading and playing cards.

Around 6 p.m., we piled back into The Couch and headed up Going-to-the-Sun Road once more, this time to another well-known trailhead for St. Mary and Virginia Falls. While barely any parking spaces remained, we figured most people would be finishing their hikes as we got started.

Sure enough, after walking 30 minutes past dozens coming the other way, we had the trail to ourselves. It really paid to explore early and late, especially when days were 15 hours long.

Cover photo

Almost immediately, dense pine forest engulfed us on the gently sloped, family-friendly trail. A few openings in the canopy offered views of the triple peaks surrounding us: 8064-foot Dusty Star Mountain, 8922-foot Almost-a-Dog Mountain and 9541-foot Little Chief Mountain.

Before long, we came to St. Mary River. Slanted late-day light frolicked on its glacial aquamarine surface. We paralleled its banks, the din of crashing water growing more thunderous by the minute. At St. Mary Falls, three powerful tiers rushed down a narrow ravine.

"Wowwwww." The noise drowned Aislínn's voice but I could see her rounded exclamation.

"Swee-eeee-eeet!" Ciarán's shout barely carried.

They scuttled down rocks to a bridge that crossed the river just below the falls. Tom and Sean followed. I stayed put, taking it all in.

Roaring whitewater blasted over granite. Frisky sunlight pirouetted on the cascades. A gentle breeze brushed the air. Pure nirvana. I couldn't believe we were completely alone at this normally teeming treasure.

A booming "WOOOOOOOOO HOOOOOOOOOO" broke through my

reverie. Tom's resounding music-teacher chant filled the air. An immediate "woooooooooo hoooooooooooo" answered from the rocks.

"WEEEEEEEEEE HEEEEEEEEEEEEEEE," he shouted for a returning "weeeeeeeeeeee heeeeeeeeeeeee."

I laughed out loud.

"YA-HOOOOOOOOOOO." Aislínn joyfully joined in the echo fest and grinned at the responding "ya-hooooooo."

The boys scrambled up to the highest waterfall tier and yelled at the top of their lungs. For many minutes, the slender gorge ricocheted with resonance from above and below me. I could have bottled five more gallons of bliss.

When Sean's voice finally cracked, he got us all rolling with his infectious giggles. The boys came down to my spot and we headed to Tom and Aislínn, still on the bridge below. Spray drizzled from the lower falls.

"Didn't realize you were getting soaked here." I pulled on my sweatshirt hood.

"Feels great!" Tom extended his arms to gather more moisture.

Sean waved our attention at tiny birds diving in the froth.

"Looks like they're playing hide-and-seek," Aislínn mused.

"Probably are." Her brother explained that the American dippers, aka water ouzels, nested near the falls and were famous for their hilarious antics.

"Good you're here Mr. Animal Planet." Ciarán smiled without a trace of sarcasm. Sean bowed.

Angled beams shone on us like Broadway spotlights. The shafts shimmered with rainbow droplets, a fleeting, enchanting gift from the lowering sun. The water's symphony filled our ears. Silken vapor tickled our skin.

Our relationship with nature, I realized again, boiled down to a blend of environment, timing and light. In the rare wondrous moments when they converged perfectly, our spirits sang.

Those few minutes impacted me so much, I chose that backdrop for the cover of my young adult book about Peace Pilgrim, who gave up all her possessions and walked across the U.S. for 28 years with only the clothes on her back, touching tens of thousands of people with her message of peace. I superimposed the gray-haired wanderer in front of the glowing sunrays of St. Mary Falls.

But photos were only placeholders for experiences. Even the most beautiful could never really capture the full magic of a moment. That job was left to our hearts.

After the twinkling gleams faded, we continued on the trail to Virginia Creek. We didn't know before, but the path actually boasted five breathtaking waterfalls and gorges. In the space of half a mile, we passed two more impressive cascades, which should have been standout destinations on their own. Yet sandwiched between their famous cousins, St. Mary and Virginia, these unnamed orphans rarely got their due.

Arriving at Virginia Falls, we saw, and heard, why. The highest yet, this multi-tiered waterfall had a top drop of 50 feet. A secondary chute fed into a shorter torrent at the bottom, flowing over earthen red rocks that seemed like gemstones in the lowering sunlight.

Talk about velocity and power. The big-snow winter truly melted into potent surges. We chuckled as we tried to escape the blast of cool spray, much stronger than St. Mary's. Then we scooted to a bridge for a broad view of the mighty falls.

While still plenty light out, the sun inched behind the peaks, filling our return walk with interesting shadows. I could see why people hiked the same trails time after time; they always offered new surprises.

In million-dollar moods, we spied The Couch, the sole vehicle in the lot. At our Amazingly Awesome Site, draped in dusk, Ciarán and Aislínn built an excellent fire.

We roasted delicious wieners over open flames with huge cooking forks we bought earlier at the camp store. Then we switched to marshmallows and relived our glorious day. By 11 p.m., barely an hour after sunset, we were all fast asleep.

Dawn's early light

When I exited our tent, the center of our solar system greeted me with its daybreak extravaganza. Deep shade cloaked everything below the treetops. Beyond them, night still hung on the immense mountains. But their very peaks glowed almost neon from the waking sun. Striking hues of salmon and coral grew luminous in the brightening sky. I grabbed my Canon and ran to a clearing to witness the rest of the unveiling.

Darkness edged down the cliffsides like an outgoing tide. Massive gray swaths gave way to finely etched crags and razor-sharp ridges, all intensely pink. It took only minutes for the daily ritual to unfold. The dazzling canvas quickly settled into its normal tan and tawny palette.

Like the previous night's sunset at St. Mary Falls, this was a gift of time and place. I exhaled, not realizing I had been holding my breath. Some things were too stunning even for autonomic body functions.

Back at the campsite, however, no one cared about my spellbinding dawn. Tom grumped at Aislínn that her ramen noodles were taking too long. Ciarán yelled at Sean that he better find his water bottle. Through the tent's window netting, I saw my youngest digging through a pile on his air mattress.

"I got everyone up and no one's ready," grizzled Tom. "We gotta leave in fifteen minutes. The backpacks aren't packed, Aislínn didn't eat, no one washed up."

I sighed and checked my watch. He was right. We had booked a Hikers Express boat ride for 8:30 a.m. and the departure ramp was nearly an hour away. We had to skedaddle.

In my Monday-morning-quarterback fantasy, I took a deep breath, calmed everyone down, orchestrated a cooperative effort, and lovingly herded my clan into The Couch.

What really happened is I let the turmoil tackle my serenity and dove head first into the frenzy. I snatched the backpacks, ordered the boys to brush their teeth, rushed Aislínn's meal, grabbed a yogurt for myself and hastily made five sandwiches.

I wouldn't say any of it was done too kindly, either. In fact, I added to the vocal fray when I couldn't find my sunglasses. But we were on the road, happy or not, in 20 minutes.

Boating benefits

Tom grumbled, anxious about traffic, especially since we had to return to the highway and travel north through the Blackfeet reservation until the Many Glacier entrance. Many Glacier, often called the heart of the park, would certainly be teeming.

Once again, though, our early morning strategy paid off. The roadway was a breeze and parking plentiful at the Many Glacier Hotel on the shores of Swiftcurrent Lake, where we were catching our boat.

With time to spare, we went inside the five-story Swiss-chalet lodge, a National Historic Landmark dating back to 1915. Tom gestured excitedly out the lobby's floor-to-ceiling windows. Across the lake, postcard-perfect peaks posed upright on land and laid reflected horizontally in the crystal water.

"We're going *there*." He looked up from his trail map at one towering snow-covered summit. I squinted to find Grinnell Glacier, our ultimate destination, but everything just looked white. On our side of the lake, I noticed a crowd gathering at the dock.

"Hey, I think they're boarding." Before I got the words out, the kids raced

> ## GLACIER PARK BOAT CO.
>
> Since 1938, authorized concessionaire Glacier Park Boat Company has been taking visitors on its historic fleet of classic wooden vessels in gorgeous areas of Glacier National Park: St. Mary, Lake McDonald, Two Medicine and Many Glacier. We did the Many Glacier "Hiker's Express" tour ($16.75-$33.25 per person), which included boat rides across Swiftcurrent Lake, Lake Josephine and an optional free guided hike up to Grinnell Glacier. For info, visit http://glacierparkboats.com.

each other out the door to the first of two boat shuttles that cut five miles off the round-trip trek to the park's most famous glacier.

At the waterfront we loaded onto Chief Two Guns, a classic 49-passenger wooden launch that cruised across Swiftcurrent Lake in less than 10 minutes. About half way, Sean leaned over the rail peering at the distant shore.

"Could those be grizzlies?"

A park ranger, on board to lead a guided hike, rushed over and followed my son's outstretched finger. So did a dozen other passengers, some with binoculars. Two brown shapes definitely moved among the greenery.

"Sure are!" The ranger smiled at Sean. "Yesterday, a colleague encountered a mother and her baby foraging for huckleberries. May be the same ones."

Tom stiffened. "Is that the glacier trail from the hotel?"

"Yes, sir."

"Good thing we decided to take the boat!"

"Too bad," sighed Sean.

The ranger chuckled. "You know," he spoke louder so others could hear. "You're all on the first shuttle of the day. It's not uncommon to see grizzlies and black bears on Grinnell Glacier Trail this time of year, particularly in early morning. So if you're the first ones off, make a lot of noise. Before you head around any bends or blind corners, talk, clap and proceed cautiously."

"We're staying behind him," whispered Tom.

I laughed. We already planned to take the interpretive hike included in the Hiker's Express fee. I looked forward to soaking up facts and trivia about the beautiful landscape around us.

From the landing on the south side of Swiftcurrent Lake, we followed the ranger over a steep paved hill to Lake Josephine. We boarded Morning Eagle, another historic 45-footer made of cedar and oak. During the 15-minute ride, the kids kept their eyes peeled at the shoreline, but no more bears.

Apparently everyone aboard decided on the escorted tour since no one took off on their own. We all gathered round while Ranger Tim introduced himself and shared his "safe hiking" rules.

Going rogue

Near the back of the pack, my family followed on an incline toward the trailhead. When the climb got steep, my offspring sprang ahead of slowpokes. I went after them, trying to pull Tom with me but he shook off my hand. Soon, though, the snail's pace got to him and we both joined our trio, huffing from the exertion.

Below, participants stopped to rest, one woman barely beyond the bottom. The ranger's number one rule was that the group had to stay together, which meant waiting for stragglers at this crest. Many Glacier trail gained 1,600 feet in elevation; we hadn't even gone 200.

Ansty, the younger Brennans started in on their dad. As much as I would have enjoyed expert commentary, the tempo would have driven me crazy, too. We finally goaded Tom into ditching the guide, despite his bear fears.

The trail flattened enough to let Tom and me catch our breaths, rest our burning thighs and keep pace with the young'uns. When we came to the first switchback, though, we all stopped. No one would admit it but we each wanted someone else to go first.

"Hah!" Tom smirked at us one by one. Validated after all our teasing, he strode ahead breaking into a forceful, *"IS IT THE REAL LIFE?... IS THIS JUST FAN-TA-SY?"*

Rounding the sharp bend, we all belted our *Bohemian Rhapsody* best. If any bears had been nearby, they surely would have been dancing. The only creature we saw on the trail was another fat-bellied marmot.

After climbing about half a mile, still singing at every curve, we got our first peek at Grinnell Lake in the valley below. Its opaque turquoise shimmered amidst the velvet of vivid green pine trees. Grinnell Falls, like a silver ribbon at this distance, tumbled hundreds of feet down the mountain's headwall into the lake. Another fairytale setting.

I stared, grinning. "Oh my god. That's just gorgeous." But gorgeous was not nearly adjective enough.

Ciarán put his arm across my shoulder. "Jeez. How can one park have so many cool places?"

How, indeed.

The view grew more spectacular with each step on the red-sediment trail. We'd enjoyed lush alpine meadows in other parks. Yet nothing compared to the waves of lithe wildflowers that filled the rolling hillside all the way down to the aquamarine lake. Pink fireweed, fuzzy-headed western anemones, and other willowy purples, oranges and yellows fluttered in a smorgasbord of color and texture.

Looking up, we saw Mount Gould and glimpsed our destination, Grinnell Glacier, on its northern flank. I pointed with delight, although the bowl-like glacier seemed like a small saucer of frost from where we stood.

The distinctive peak also housed two other glaciers. Salamander lay 700 feet above Grinnell. At one time the two were connected through an ice apron, almost like a frozen waterfall. Tiny Gem Glacier, the smallest named glacier in the park, hung in a notch just below the mountain's 9,554-foot summit. Although active glaciers usually had to be at least 25 square acres, five-acre Gem remained on the list, but no one knew for how long.

Narrow nerves

A couple of miles and a few song-filled switchbacks later, we reached a stretch of narrow trail. Really narrow. But it wasn't the slender ledge under our feet that stopped us in our tracks. We'd already been on slim channels. Even the vertical cliff on our right wasn't too intimidating. What paralyzed us was the sheer drop-off on our left. No gentle slope. No soft grasses or pretty flowers. This section crossed sheer rock that plummeted straight down into the abyss.

Tom went into drill sergeant mode, insisting we proceed in single file, as if we had another choice. He warned the boys not to fool around.

Ciarán peered over the edge. "*Really* dad?"

Without delay, Miss Acrophobia rushed across, eyes forward. The boys bounded quickly, undaunted but without any jostling. Tom made his way next. Normally, I loved a good birds-eye view. But my balance had never been the best. I shuffled slowly hugging the cliff, my back to the void.

I laughed when the ridge widened. The boys applauded. It certainly put perspective into our perspective. Thirty-six inches seemed like a runway at sea-level, but waaaay skinnier a few thousand feet up.

Further on, moisture dripped down the cliff wall next to us, forming rivulets that made their long way to Grinnell Lake. We easily jumped these small streams, until we came to a spray spilling over the trail like a high-pressure shower.

Aislínn, as she'd done at every water crossing on the trip, yelled, "ADDDD-VEN-TURE!" and ran through, hands on head to deflect large drops. Ciarán whooped out loud, stalling under the fountain. Sean and Tom followed.

Last, I squealed. "Ahhhhh. It's freezing,"

"What d'ya expect ma. It's *snow* melt." We smiled ear to ear, quickly drying under the bright sun. Before Grinnell Glacier Overlook, we came to a small rest area with benches and a pit toilet. Of course, Sean had no qualms. Then the others took their turns. I passed.

I leaned back against a weathered wooden seat, breathing in air as clear as I could ever remember. Storybook clouds fluffed overhead while the enchanting valley below dazzled with color. Serenity filled my soul.

A series of steep switchbacks led us through a boulder-strewn moraine, a huge natural gravel pile compliments of shifting glaciers. Bare most of the way, the trail became snowier.

In the lead around one bend, Ciarán shouted, "Hey! How ya' doin'?" Our ranger friend from the day before again dug steps. We joked with him for a bit then proceeded up his custom stairway.

"Enjoy the view," he yelled after we disappeared around the rocks.

Barely past the turn, I stood motionless. Grinnell Lake twinkled, a precious jewel far below. I knew its color came from glacial particles swept away in the moisture traveling down the mountain. Yet at this elevation and vantage, the brilliant blue-green seemed a dreamy endowment from the heavens, which were surely within reach from where I stood.

Gleaming Lake Josephine dotted the distance. A rugged saw-toothed ridge known as the Garden Wall, formed by two eroding glaciers, stood starkly across from me. I stared and stared and stared, lost in the moment.

Aislínn broke through. "Hey mom? We're going…You okay?

I nodded. I had never been better.

Glacial exultation

Finally, after three-and-a-half miles, we reached Grinnell Glacier Overlook, more than 7,000 feet high!

Ancient ice on Salamander and Gem flashed from above while Grinnell shimmered before us in its bowl formation. A worn brown sign explained that George Bird Grinnell discovered the glacier in 1887. I could only imagine his awe at this remarkable sight. Little wonder he pushed so hard for the park's creation.

Tom read the sign's next line out loud: "GRINNELL COVERS APPX. 300 ACRES…Man, that's double what the ranger told us. Pretty grim."

One thing we'd heard him say before we went rogue was that Grinnell currently comprised 152 acres. The frozen area still appeared massive, yet the mental math on its demise gave us pause.

So did the written warning not to venture onto the glacier alone or too far. Thin layers of snow could hide deep, dangerous crevasses; one wrong step could spell disaster.

That did it for Tom. No amount of urging could inch him away from the overlook. But the kids and I itched to explore. We had been among the first to arrive but by then other people started moving onto the ice. We edged out slowly.

In minutes, we felt the Force. What else would explain the tingles that coursed through our stomachs as we stood on frost thousands of years old? Ciarán and I squatted, placing palms against the cool surface. Aislínn and Sean laid down completely, stretching arms and legs.

We stayed silent for many minutes, momentarily becoming part of the earth, living it, breathing it, letting the sun bake it into us. I couldn't know if my offspring were as conscious of this as I, but I knew this oneness would remain in their cells. We basked in the glacier's odd warmth, feeling huge and minuscule all at once.

Hoisting ourselves up, we shuffled a few dozen yards or so, studying the depth under our feet. In the shiniest places, we saw the fanciful sky in perfect reflection. Aislínn giggled as she tip-toed on the clouds.

The longer we gazed at the gray and white landscape, more colors emerged from its ancient layers. Muted azures, sediment reds, faded jades and understated ochers formed an ancestral rainbow encapsulated in eons of ice. Like the redwoods, the energy of the glaciers pulsed in our guts.

DISAPPEARING GLACIERS

When snow remains in one place long enough, it compresses into a thick mass laced with water, rock and sediment. Voila – a glacier! Over the centuries, these icy wonders have sculpted the land, slowly carving and grinding away mountain rock through cycles of snowfall and snowmelt. When founded in 1910, Glacier National Park had nearly 150 active known glaciers, thought to date back 7,000 years. Scientists believe they reached peak size in the mid-1800's, a period known as the "Little Ice Age," and have been retreating ever since. As of 2017, only 25 glaciers remained. Grinnell Glacier, the most studied in the park, lost 40% of its acreage between 1966 and 2005. A 10-acre chunk broke off in 2015, shattering into small icebergs in Upper Grinnell Lake. Sophisticated climate models predict current warming trends are speeding glacial demise. Some scientists warn the park's glaciers will be gone by 2030, others say it will take longer.

> **TRAVEL TIP: Just Stop!**
>
> *Nature speaks to us. When we are patient enough, quiet enough, able to pay attention enough, we can engage in cycles, eavesdrop on mysteries, even glimpse our own place in the world. Allow yourself to stop. Really stop. Smell. Touch. Listen. See. Savor. I promise: it will immerse you in a totally different – and remarkable – experience.*

Across the huge basin, snow and gravel interspersed with the ice. Herds of bighorn roamed the far rim. Rams stood majestically, daring mere humans to interfere. Dozens of ewes and half-grown lambs, less wary, wandered aimlessly nearer to the growing number of people on the glacier.

We kept our distance. But the babies, their tiny horn bumps on furry faces, crept curiously close before running away, their moms staring us down just in case.

Trail mix trauma

We returned to Tom, also infused by the primordial gift. Normally too loud, his volume was reverent whisper. "I can't believe how amazing this is!"

High in altitude and spirit, we backtracked to the rest area for PB&J sandwiches. Ranger Tim arrived, acknowledging us with a broad smile. From the looks of things, he'd be here quite a while waiting for his group.

"Just amazing," Tom repeated, both as a greeting to the ranger and as motivation for the few troopers reaching the plateau. "Really too spectacular for words."

"Yes!" The ranger looked around, lifting his sunglasses. "You sure picked a fantastic day!"

Tom nodded and sat on the bench next to me. He reached into my bag of trail mix and put a handful in his mouth.

"AHHHHHHHHHH! AHHHHHHHHHH!" His screams pierced the air. He launched up, leaned over and spit everything out. "Uhhhhhhhhhhh. Ahhhhhhhhhhhhhhh." He moaned, hands pressing his cheek.

The kids and I huddled around him. The ranger rushed over. Other hikers stared. We were used to his dramatic outbursts and regularly riffed him over his "something bit me" incident in the Cascades. But this was different.

I gently squeezed his hands. "Take a breath."

He rasped in short bursts. "It's. My. Tooooooooth,"

Ciarán reached for his arm. Tom pulled away and stood up, letting out a long whoosh of air. "It… it… it's better now…" He exhaled again. "Man… that was like a knife in my jaw."

Then he shot me a look that said *I gotta get down* and started walking quickly. His sons and daughter flanked him. I packed our lunch remains, thanked the ranger and followed. When I caught up, Tom informed me he was okay but his tooth throbbed.

"I thought it was your ear."

"Me too. Now I think my tooth is bad and just seemed like my ear." He rushed ahead. "The trail mix must've hit a nerve."

I tried to keep up while digging in my pack for Advil. Nothing like reality to bring us back to reality. We continued down, the kids speeding ahead.

The trail was truly as breathtaking in reverse. Yet running back through the falls and shimmying on the narrow ledge held little excitement this time around. Tom had no interest in gushing over the view. His sole focus was making the next return boat, which meant we had to hustle.

I lost sight of our trio until we rounded a switchback and saw them staring at trees along the path. I glimpsed velvety antlers for a split second before they disappeared farther into the brush.

"A baby elk!" Sean's eyes glowed. "He was right on the trail! We surprised him when we turned the bend."

Ciarán and Aislínn continued with Tom, who barely slowed down. I stayed with my youngest scanning the spot for a while, even though we knew the calf wouldn't reappear. Then we loitered, talking, admiring flowers and watching the valley grow nearer and nearer.

The surroundings returned my calm, until I checked my watch. We couldn't miss the launch; Tom would kill us. The next ride wasn't for hours.

We began to jog. But the lower portion was packed by then and we got stuck behind a mother cooing her toddler down rocky steps. By the time we hightailed around them, the scheduled departure had come and gone.

From our far view of Lake Josephine, I couldn't see the Morning Eagle. Had we missed it? My stomach tightened. I hoped they at least got on before it left.

"C'mon," yelled Sean. "I see it coming." We kicked into high gear and zoomed over more boulders and dirt, finally reaching the dock, gasping. The boat, delayed from an earlier run, had just pulled up. Tom offered us a special scowl.

Ciarán provided welcome distraction. "Hey look. He likes people." Everyone on line followed his gaze to another fat hoary marmot sitting on the pier near some bushes. Cute beady eyes gawked back at us. Nothing like an adorable rodent to break the tension.

We settled into our seats. I regarded the majestic peak and glistening glacier above us, musing over the "before" and "after" contrast. Although the same spectacular scenery I witnessed that morning, the vision totally transformed. My earlier boat ride burst with anticipation, adrenaline, mystery. Now, I beheld the exquisite, rugged terrain with an adoration and intimacy that I never could have imagined.

Medical detour

Back in the hotel lobby, Tom sank into a lounge chair. I felt the pangs of a migraine and prayed for them to recede. I'd had hormonal headaches for years. I usually ignored them until I couldn't, then crawled into a dark room, cold rags on my head. If all else failed, I gave in and took a pill. This was the first one on the trip that threatened to sideline me.

Please, please, please, not now, I silently begged. Tom sat massaging his jaw, eyes closed, moaning softly. I steeled myself and asked a hotel manager about local dentists or healthcare facilities. The closest was Blackfeet Community Hospital, 40 miles away in Browning, MT, the largest town on the reservation. Tom only half-heartedly argued when I told him we were going, so I knew he needed care.

With my skull steadily pounding, I drove us back to the campsite, gave the kids money for food and showers, popped one of my migraine meds and headed out of the park. Tom programmed Sally Satellite and reclined his seat.

I prayed again, this time for my pill to kick in quickly. The afternoon sunlight torched my brain. But I definitely couldn't complain or Tom would have tried to drive. What a pair!

I soon heard him snoring, and thankfully the edge lifted on my own misery. The dusty roadway had little traffic. I passed trailer homes, small pre-fabs and a few stray dogs, but no people. As usual, I mulled over what it was like to actually live here. To find a job. To go food shopping.

At first glance, the hospital looked like a touristy strip mall. Its parking lot boasted a sculpture of a warrior leading a buffalo, bear, moose, eagle and wolf. The sprawling one-story building, painted bright pink and white, had contrasting triangles on its roof line and a bright red door for the entrance.

Scanning the edifice, I noticed a smaller red door with the familiar white block letters: "EMERGENCY." The facility might have been a far cry from our modern high-rises, but some things remained the same no matter where we were. I shut off The Couch and woke Tom.

The ER receptionist didn't blink at our Jersey accents. She took Tom's information and pointed us to the waiting area. My husband quickly drowsed into another nap on one of the worn seats lining the wall.

I studied my surroundings and wondered if the ER lobby had been updated since the hospital opened in 1937. Drab green walls, bare of any decorations, blended in with floors scuffed too many times to ever appear clean. A single end table held magazines dated years earlier.

We were clearly the only outsiders seeking care. A beautiful Native American woman comforted a crying baby. An elderly couple bent over their forms. Another mother sat surrounded by four handsome, well-behaved children. The youngest snuck a look at me. I waved and smiled. She quickly hid her face, then peeked to see if I was still looking. I waved again. She giggled. We repeated this until her older sister, who seemed all of about eight, scolded her to sit straight.

A very pregnant woman stood against a wall by herself. One middle-aged man paced the floor, coughing into the air. This didn't help my germ-a-phobia, but I couldn't add that to my stress. So I stared toward the door trying to channel the magic of Grinnell Glacier. Had that only been just this morning?

Dramatic diagnosis

More than two hours passed before we were ushered into a small cubby and greeted by the doc on duty. The young physician sat behind his desk with us directly across as if we were taking out a bank loan or consulting a lawyer. Where were the examining rooms? Machines? Cots?

He proceeded to tell us about the hospital and his experience in larger trauma centers. Tom nodded. I wondered what he was doing. Was it a marketing pitch? A Doogie Howser-like assurance to us Easterners that he was a good physician? Finally, he asked about Tom's pain and had a nurse take my husband's temperature and blood pressure.

"I thought it was my ear at first." Tom explained his history of ear infections and hearing loss. "But it's really my tooth."

The doctor came around, pulled a penlight out of his pocket and looked into Tom's mouth and ears. Then he pressed areas on his face, taking extra time along the jawline. The physician went back to his seat and without pause announced, "I think this is one of two things. The first is trigeminal neuralgia."

I startled. I had no idea what that was, but it sounded serious.

"The trigeminal nerve carries sensation from your face to your brain." The young man leaned forward, elbows on desk. "Trigeminal neuralgia is a chronic condition that can trigger jolts of excruciating pain even with the mildest stimulation of your face, like brushing your teeth or shaving."

Tom shook his head. "But it only gets bad when I eat. I really think it's my tooth."

"Or," the doctor continued without acknowledging he heard anything, "it may be a bone infection that could spread to your brain if not treated."

"What?" I sat up straight. My neck tensed.

Tom's history of chronic ear infections made him a candidate for this possible diagnosis, the doctor explained. Either way, he recommended we drive the couple of hours to Kalispell, MT, for the nearest "good" hospital, or better yet, travel five hours to Bozeman, where a specialist could order a CT scan or MRI.

We were speechless. Then Tom sighed. "Do you think I could just finish our trip and get care at home?"

The reply was curt. "That's your choice, but I wouldn't risk it." The doctor, obviously done, wrote a script for strong pain meds and steered us into the hallway. "You can get this filled in the pharmacy down there"

We followed his direction. I immediately jumped into mental action. We could go back to the camp, pack everything up, drive to Bozeman, cancel the rest of our adventure… maybe I could fly the kids home if we had to remain there for any amount of time. I could call my sister-in-law to take care of them…

"I'm not going anywhere." Tom interrupted my preparations.

"What? You heard him! You can't take the chan…"

"No! It's my tooth. That made no sense at all. It doesn't hurt when I shave or do anything from the outside. It hurts when I bite down on it."

We arrived at the pharmacy window and Tom handed over the Rx. We leaned against the hallway wall.

"Well, what if it's the bone infection?"

"It's not."

"How do you know?"

"I just know. I was so focused on my ear that I didn't realize it's my tooth. But I'm telling you, it's definitely my tooth."

I wrestled with the choice. Yeah, it probably wasn't the bone thing. But who hadn't heard horror stories about weird life-threatening infections? The pounding in my head came back in spades.

"How can you be sure?"

Tom huffed. "Even if it is, nothing's gonna happen in 10 days. We'll be home then."

"What if it does?" Annoyance wove into my worry.

215

"So then I die."

"Not funny."

"Yeah, well I die in a really cool place like Yellowstone or Custer."

"*Really* not funny."

"Oh, c'mon. You'd do the same thing. You'd never leave if it was you."

We argued for many more minutes, oblivious to people passing. I turned away, unable to keep bickering. I wanted to put *him* on the plane and finish the trip with my kids.

"I'll be fine once I get the pain killers." He spun me around to look in my eyes. "As long as you're willing to drive, we'll be okay."

The last thing I wanted to think about at that moment was driving thousands of miles. I looked at my watch. Sure enough, my migraine med was fading fast. I exhaled loudly. "I'm stealing one of your pills when you get them."

"Nah, you can't...you're driving." He reached out to rub my temples. I leaned in against him.

Long day

The hour ride back gave us time to chew over that weird hospital visit. If the doctor suspected an infection, why didn't he do any blood work? How come there was no fever? Plus, shouldn't he have prescribed an antibiotic, just in case?

This made me feel a little bit better about our decision to keep going, with Tom's promise to let me know if he got even a centimeter worse. But it also made me angry. While I couldn't jump to conclusions, it certainly provided a glimpse into healthcare services for the Blackfeet Nation.

The evening sun blanketed the reservation with an eerie oblique light and, again, traffic stayed sparse until we neared the park. By then, my headache was tolerable once more and thanks to his pain pill, Tom felt great.

With the campsite empty, we strolled to the Rising Sun restaurant where we saw the kids at a window table picking at near-finished plates. Tom took the one unoccupied seat. He joked with the hostess about getting our own private table for two, but I pulled over an extra chair.

"Not much" and "hung out" seemed to be what they did in our absence. Filling them in about our afternoon, I recognized my own initial alarm on their faces. Tom tried to calm their concerns.

More stressed than I realized, I lashed out at the waitress when my meal was MIA for 25 minutes. My uncalled-for sarcasm mortified my kids. They lasered me with disgust and tried to offset my rudeness by piling their own plates and silverware to make them easier to clear. I apologized as soon as the woman finally brought my food.

I hadn't imbibed much on this trip, but when Tom asked if I wanted a bourbon, I couldn't get the yes out fast enough. Since we were obviously staying a while, the kids jumped on dessert.

"Oh, I forgot to tell you," Aislínn said in between spoonfuls of ice cream. "Remember how scared you were about fires in that windy campground? Guess what? There was a big fire there today."

Sean nodded. "Yeah, they were sayin' a bunch of people's stuff got burned."

I gasped. "St. Mary's? Holy crap! That's horrible!"

Tom asked the waitress and she confirmed the blaze but said rumors were "overblown."

"Excuse the pun." She reached for our neatly stacked dishes. "The wind's tough over there, but they put it out pretty quickly."

Still, I thanked our lucky stars we switched. Imagine if we had been at the hospital and the kids had to deal with a fire? Things, I reminded myself, could always be worse.

I sipped my Jack Daniels. What a day for the books, with spirits lifting and sinking more than the topsy turvy topography around us.

Spectacular stretch

In the middle of the night, I heard the tentative ti-ti-tip, ti-ti-tip of rain drops on the tent and issued another blast of gratitude for the spectacular sunshine we had during our Many Glacier Hike. The drizzle increased and I let the rhythm loll me back to sleep.

Extra diligent about packing up, the kids didn't let their dad lift anything. He smiled the whole time, feeling no pain. With me at the wheel, we left for our last ride up gorgeous Going-to-the-Sun Road.

Tom turned on our traveling tunes. "Was it only two days ago that we first drove up to Logan Pass? Time sure warps in the wilderness!"

Traffic and construction slowed our progress but couldn't diminish the marvel of the epic 50-mile drive. In fact, the congestion offered me a chance I otherwise wouldn't have had to glimpse the deep gorges, rushing waterfalls,

---

TRAVEL TIP: RV Bans

A major reason we opted for an SUV instead of an RV when planning our trip is because we wanted to drive the entire Going-to-the-Sun Road, which has seasonal and size restrictions for RV's. Check the park website if you're traveling in a large vehicle. (https:// www.nps.gov/glac/planyourvisit/gtsrinfo.htm)

---

glaciers and alpine meadows visible from the comfort of our car.

That didn't mean I could relax, though. Portions of the road hugged the cliffside with steep drop-offs. I felt like I only had inches of leeway before our tires would veer over the edge. Tom kept assuring me we had plenty of room.

I also feared rock overhangs would scalp The Couch. My husband pointed out three SUV's in front of us that made the clearance just fine. I still white knuckled the steering wheel, glad he didn't lord over me that he'd already maneuvered this section twice.

East of Logan Pass, where we hadn't yet gone, I cringed as The Couch entered a slender 400-foot long tunnel carved into the mountain. The kids snickered at me and wished, too loudly, that their father would drive.

Yet emerging from the rock-encompassed darkness, everyone startled. We took in the breadth... the depth... the dark clouds hovering between mountains, and were stunned by the visual drama of this unrivaled view.

Two hours and many wide eyes later, we came to Lake McDonald on the park's western edge. The rain stopped miles earlier, or more accurately, we drove out of it and watched the gray sky blue up like dye in a bowl of vinegar. The color spread until it was full-on cobalt, decorated with cumulus cotton candy clouds.

Lake McDonald, the largest in the park, wiggled with sunlight for all of its 10 miles. Grand peaks bordered three sides of the fjord-like body and we debated whether the Rising Sun and Many Glacier areas were more appealing than this gorgeous view. Either way, we vowed to come back to our favorite park so far.

Many Glacier hike

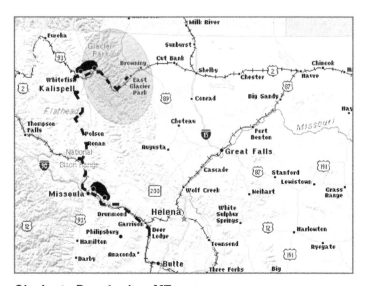

Glacier to Deer Lodge, MT
4.5 hours

Chapter 17
Prisons and MOR

The critiques on my driving magnified when I wound up behind a lumbering logging truck for the entire 90-mile stretch of Seeley-Swan Highway. What started as "c'mon, mom, you can do it" at the first passing lane, escalated into a chant of "GO…GO…GO….GO" at the next dotted line.

I actually tried venturing to the left, but the cedar-filled flatbed bounced slightly over the line into what I already thought was too skinny a lane. I chickened out and pulled back behind the timber lorry. A collective groan ensued from the rear.

"Can't dad drive for a little while?" Sean dramatically plopped his head forward on the front console. "Pul-leeeeeeze?"

"Yeah," moaned Aislínn.

"I'll drive," snapped Ciarán. "At least I can pass the guy."

"No way." I bit my tongue about winding up in the pine trees lining the route. "We're doing fine. He's not crawling."

"Yes, he *is*."

I checked the speedometer. "He's doing sixty."

"Speed limit's sixty-five and everyone else's going a lot faster than that. Two cars passed him already. " Ciarán kicked the seat in front of him. The jolt broke into Tom's haze.

"Knock it off." The pain pills definitely bumped his normal growl down a notch. "Leave your mother alone. The road's narrow, there's no shoulder and the truck's not going that slow."

I knew Tom wished I would zoom ahead too; I mouthed a sideways "thank you."

To my kids I just said, "Be quiet and enjoy the view. C'mon, Seely-Swan's a national scenic byway. Just check out those lush forests and pristine lakes."

They harrumphed. I sighed and continued to follow the freshly cut trunks stacked into a neat pyramid on the flatbed in front of me.

"Well then count the rings and see how old the trees were when they died," joked Tom.

"Ha ha. So funny I forgot to laugh." Ciarán slumped down and started manspreading to annoy his brother.

Only 70 more miles of this, I thought, and reached over to crank up the comedy channel. Thankfully it did the trick.

I expected them to break into cheers when I parted ways with the truck after a long hour-and-a-half. But it was old news by then. And when I came upon a second logging truck a while later, the road was wide enough for me to make a clean, quick pass without anyone noticing.

Prison break

Rather than drive all day to Yellowstone National Park, we planned to stop about half way in Deer Lodge, MT. A few miles out, Aislínn grabbed one of her guides.

"Guess what Deer Lodge is known for?"

"Cows?" quipped Tom.

"Nope."

"Logging," guessed Ciarán.

"Nope."

"Deer?" ventured Sean.

"Haha. No."

"Well, what then?" I glanced at her in the rearview.

"Prisons."

"Prisons? Like jail?" Sean perked up.

"Yep. There's a real penitentiary on the outskirts of town. It's Montana's main lock-up. But it says there's an old prison in the middle of town that turned into a museum. It's a national historic landmark."

Amusingly, the attraction's castle-like turrets and jail cell bars were visible from our Main Street hotel. Sean asked if I wanted to check it out. But the only solitary confinement that interested me had to do with hot water. As

---

BARS, CARS & GHOSTLY STARS

Twenty-two years after the Old Montana Territorial Prison opened in 1871, convicts were forced to build a citadel-like granite wall around the building, complete with watch towers. Eventually, the institution became so plagued with overcrowding, poor funding and outdated facilities that violence erupted in a deadly 1959 uprising. The notorious revolt was the turning point in Montana's corrections operations. The old prison is now a sprawling complex run by the Power County Museum and Arts Foundation (http://pc-maf.org). Along with the Old Montana Prison Museum, it features a Law Enforcement Museum, Desert John's Saloon, Montana Auto Museum and Yesterday's Playthings, a collection of childhood toys and memorabilia. Paranormal activity in the prison is also a big draw, attracting researchers and tourists looking for a good ghost tour.

---

soon as we got to our second story room in the classic Scharf's Motor Inn, I claimed the shower. Tom laid down and the kids swarmed the TV.

After gorging ourselves with dinner at the hotel's restaurant, I retreated to our old-fashioned balcony where I watched a brilliant tangerine sunset fill Montana's big, big sky.

Huge sky, little scrapes

The next morning, Tom swore he felt well enough to skip his pain pill and do some of the driving. I tried to argue but the kids cheered.

"Shot gun!" Ciarán jumped in the front.

"Not fair!" Sean moped outside the rear door, so I took the hump seat.

"Where does that even come from." Sean grumpily slid in next to me.

Not surprisingly, Tom knew. "The old west. Like right here. In the 1800's, stagecoach drivers needed a gun-toting friend to sit in the front with them to ward off thieves and plunderers."

The trivia made Sean smile. "Sweet."

From Deer Lodge, we immediately accessed I-90. I never thought I'd say it, but the interstate seemed marvelous after navigating so many mountain roads. No hairpin turns, no lagging loggers, no narrow squeezes. Just fast, through wide open spaces.

Expansive plains rolled out like an immense carpet. Mountain ranges loomed on the horizon. Yet the best mouth-wide-open view was above. Rich blue air and feathery white clouds cavorted as far as our eyes could see.

I leaned my head back to peer out the moon roof. "It's like a spectacular endless mural."

Sean did the same. "Or one of those looping video game screens."

I laughed, settling in with my laptop. I zoned out while working, so it wasn't until Aislínn nudged me that I noticed the tension.

"It's right *there* and we're gonna be right *here*." Ciarán pleaded with his dad.

Sean hung over the front seat squinting at a *Dinosaur Trail* map they picked up at the hotel. "Da-ad, it has one of the largest fossil collections in the world!"

Tom glanced sideways at his co-pilot, clearly annoyed.

"Give it to me." I reached for the glossy fold-out. Most of the stops on the Montana Dinosaur Trail were far north and east. But one dot appeared pretty close to our section of I-90. The Museum of the Rockies at Montana State University in Bozeman would only be a few miles out of our way.

"Pwease, pwease, pwease." Sean leaned into me with his palms in prayer. The goofy pose and baby whine always made me smile.

I thought of the hours my boys had drooled over dinosaurs. And not just the famous T. rex and diplodocus. No. They knew mouthfuls of prehistoric reptiles. Coelophysis. Carcharodontosaurus. Efraasia. Archaeopteryx (which, they taught me, was really a bird.) Books, video games, even Halloween costumes cashed in on this craze. In fact, until *Star Wars* edged into their obsession, I thought they both might grow up to become paleontologists.

I ventured. "Tommm?"

"*No!*" I saw him glaring at me in the mirror. "We can't. Then we'll get to Yellowstone too late."

I looked at my watch. Not even two o'clock. We only had a couple more hours driving. It would stay light until at least nine. Tom just hated being spontaneous. Maybe he should have taken his medicine after all, I thought.

I took a deep breath and blurted as quickly as I could. "Well, how about if we just go for a quick stop? It sounds really cool. Then I'll drive the rest of the way and I'll set everything up with the kids. You can just hang out."

The expected chorus filled The Couch. "Yeah." "C'mon, dad." "Please?"

He gruffly conceded. "All right. But just for an hour or so."

Prehistoric prize

In the parking lot, the kids raced out of The Couch. Tom dawdled grumpily until a couple of flying pterosaurs ignited even his gusto. Their enormous colorful wings arched across the glass entryway, a preview for what turned out to be the best dinosaur exhibits we'd ever seen.

We inched through astounding themed displays. First the Hall of Giants, then the Hall of Horns and Teeth and, after watching some researchers work in a glass-enclosed lab, we finally exalted in the Hall of Growth and Behavior.

Jurassic Park tapped a museum director for technical advice and he must have brought back the dramatic black walls and targeted lighting that made displays pop. Or maybe the movie learned from him? Either way we felt like we hit the jackpot.

We saw Big Al, one of the most complete Allosaurus ever discovered, and Oryctodromeus, a burrow-digging dino who cared for its young in dens. I fawned over the fossilized eggs and babies, although Sean claimed *adorable* didn't apply to dinosaurs. Everyone else preferred Rocky Rex, the museum's famous mascot.

A handful of museums in the world displayed a full fossilized skeleton of Tyrannosaurus rex, the "tyrant lizard king" that roamed the earth 65 million

---

MOR THAN WE IMAGINED

The Museum of the Rockies (MOR) in Bozeman, MT, is both a college-level division of Montana State University and an independent nonprofit institution. The museum, which includes a planetarium and children's discovery area, focuses on paleontology, Native American history, Montana history and changing exhibits from around the world. A signature feature is Rocky Rex, MOR's famous T. rex mascot, discovered in the Badlands of Eastern Montana. MOR is another gem well worth the admission ($14.50/adults; $9.50 kids). (https://museumoftherockies.org)

---

years ago. Experts considered MOR's Rocky, unearthed in the Badlands of eastern Montana, one of the most spectacular specimens ever discovered. At 12-feet tall and 40-feet long, he would have weighed almost seven tons.

Fascinating factoids, a Brennan favorite, added to the visual spectacle. My sons already knew a lot of geek-caliber paleontology, like the dinosaur-avian connection (apparently dinos never went extinct; they just evolved into birds). But their jaws dropped to read that the audacious T. rex wasn't a fierce hunter after all. The latest evidence showed him to be just another vulture-like scavenger.

Our two hours flew. The kids looked at me hopefully. I knew better than to push it. We added this to our list of places to visit again!

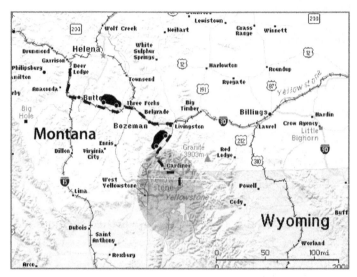

Deer Lodge to Yellowstone and Grand Teton, WY
4.5 hours

AT-A-GLANCE:
YELLOWSTONE NATIONAL PARK

Volcanos. Hot springs. Mudpots. Geysers. Yellowstone is all about underground drama. But the world's first national park also features rugged mountains, fertile forests, beautiful lakes and abundant wildlife.

LOCATION: Yellowstone Park covers nearly 3,500 square miles in the north-west corner of Wyoming; 3% is in Montana and 1% in Idaho.

OPEN: Yellowstone is open all year although some areas are inaccessible by car during the winter.

COST: $35 per vehicle, $30 per motorcycle and $20 per bicyclist/ pedestrian; under 16 is free (There is a discounted double pass for Yellowstone National Park and Grand Teton National Park.)

INFO: https://www.nps.gov/yell/index.htm

Chapter 18
Granddaddy of Parks

The Yellowstone River meandered next to us for miles and miles as we headed east into Gardiner, MT, home of the famous Roosevelt Arch. From quite a distance, we could see the block letters etched above its 50-foot high opening: FOR THE BENEFIT AND ENJOYMENT OF THE PEOPLE.

Neither ornate nor extravagant, the stone portico instead steeped with significance as entrance to the first national park in the world. Although founded in 1872, Yellowstone welcomed most visitors by horse-drawn carriages until the railway expanded to Gardiner in 1903. That year, President Teddy Roosevelt dedicated the newly constructed archway bearing his name.

While Tom usually vocalized, I was the one to let out a loud, "*Hooooo-eeeeee*," when we passed under the historic entry. The kids high-fived.

This northern access also brought us across state lines from Montana to Wyoming. While Montana and Idaho claimed tiny pieces of Yellowstone, the Equality State (so called because it was the first to grant women the right to vote) boasted most of the park's 3,500 square miles.

Just minutes through the arch, Sean practically jumped out of his seat. "Look, look! *Elk*! Everywhere!"

Sure enough, ungainly ungulates roamed both sides of the road. Even in bustling Mammoth Hot Springs Village, the visitor area closest to the north entry, they mulled around on a grassy median like poodles in a dog park. Bulls, cows and calves chewed grass and meandered, oblivious to cars and cameras.

Delight flooded The Couch, my youngest beyond ecstatic.

GLOBAL MODEL

On March 1, 1872, President Ulysses S. Grant signed the Yellowstone National Park Protection Act, giving birth to the world's first national park. During the next quarter century, as more national parks were established, it became clear these public lands would benefit from centralized management. The National Park Service Organic Act, signed by President Woodrow Wilson on Aug. 25, 1916, created the National Park Service, which celebrated its centennial in 2016. From its founding, Yellowstone has been a global inspiration. Today, more than 1,200 national parks or preserves can be found in over 100 countries.

> ## ELK ANTLER OR HORN?
>
> Bison, bighorns and mountain goats have horns that continue to grow throughout the animal's life. Not so with elk. Like other members of the deer family, males have antlers that grow and shed each year. A soft skin-like covering known as "velvet" provides nourishment for the antlers, which actually are an extension of the animal's skull. In other words, antlers are true bone, not the specialized follicles (like human fingernails) that make up the visible part of horns. Antlers are usually symmetrical, with the average healthy bull boasting six tines on each antler, aka a "six point." In autumn rutting season, bulls as large as 700 pounds use these six-by-sixes to win and protect their mates. As with bighorn battles, crashing elk antlers can be heard from great distances.

"I told you! Yellowstone's gonna be *the* Animal Sighting Capital of our trip," he beamed.

Not surprising for a gorgeous Friday evening, heavy traffic slowed us on our way toward Canyon Campground. Strange rock formations and eerie poofs of steam kept excitement high. We couldn't wait to explore.

True to our promise, the kids and I set up camp while Tom rested. We left him snoozing and walked to the Canyon visitor area, shocked by a complex that looked more like a suburban shopping plaza. Stores and snack stands buzzed with families. With the visitor center already closed, we sat at a round lobby table and wagered M&M's in a few rounds of blackjack before wandering back. My teens whipped up a just-right dinner then built a perfect fire. Tom offered nary a critique.

Lodgepole pines covered our site, providing such a wonderful dome that we barely noticed the night fall. But when I eventually stepped onto the open path en route to the restroom, my breath caught. Above, a ribbon of diamonds draped across the seamless sky. A new moon allowed the darkest backdrop yet for this Milky Way wonder.

I couldn't keep the gift to myself. "Hey guys, you gotta see this!"

Aislínn wandered into the opening. "Ho-ly!"

That beckoned her brothers and dad.

Sean cupped his hands around his eyes to ward off even the slightest light from our campfire. "The more you look, the more there are!"

"I know." With each passing second, the sparkles multiplied. I sighed adoringly. "Pure magic."

"Sure mom." Ciarán couldn't help himself. "Not your eyes adjusting to the dark at all."

I laughed, neck craned. Mystical or biological didn't matter. It was truly incredible: the celestial treat, standing there with my family, everything.

Tom pointed out a couple of constellations, impressing us with mythological tidbits. Then one by one the others sauntered back to the fire. I gazed until I couldn't wait any longer. Duty called.

At the loo I found another lovely surprise, although light-years more mundane. While my tolerance skyrocketed over the past month, I still gagged at certain facilities. Yellowstone's were exceptional. Actual soap dispensers. Paper towels. Electric outlets. Clean commodes. Strong, warm showers. Ahhhhh.

Iconic eruption

Rising at dawn to beat crowds, we discovered Sean whimpering in fetal position on his mattress. He'd already rushed out twice. I hadn't heard him or his sister, who apparently had the same thing in the middle of the night. Somehow they escaped the tent without waking us, quite a feat given the stuff strewn all around and a very defiant door zipper.

Poor kids! Trying to puzzle out what they ate that the rest of us didn't, I dug in our medical kit for anti-diarrhea tablets. Thankfully, those and bananas did the trick. Although an hour later than planned, we hit the road by 7 a.m., with Sean and Aislínn actually asking for breakfast. Ciarán bragged about the bacon and eggs he got at the cafeteria. I shushed him and gave them saltines.

Topping our day's to-do list? Buffalo! As in North America's largest mammal and our country's national animal. Officially called American Bison, they remained simply *buffalo* to the locals. Yellowstone reportedly had more than anywhere in the U.S. and we were determined to find some.

We rode north to Dunraven Pass, a popular wildlife area. No luck. Stunning alpine meadows greeted us, but no beautiful beasts. In a quick family pow-wow we decided before continuing our search we'd check out the park's celebrity fountain: Old Faithful.

We wound through Upper Geyser Basin, one of seven major areas in Yellowstone. Steam rose on either side of us, looking eerily similar to the simmering forest fires we'd seen. But rather than trees, the smoke emerged from patches of bare ground and dark puddles.

Ciarán pressed his face against his window. "Like another planet."

Aislínn did the same on her side. "No kidding."

Sean alternated leaning across each of them. Tom added sound effects in a ghostly sing-song. "Ooo-ooo-ooooooo. It's the creeeea-ture feeeeeea-ture…"

Though still early, the busy road cut our speed on the way to Old Faithful Inn and Visitor Education Center. Luckily the landscape trumped whines. We vowed to stop later at some pull-offs for a closer look at the fascinating mudpots and fumaroles. Barely any people wandered around them. Too bad we couldn't say the same for the world's most well-known geyser.

In contrast to the anonymous thermal areas along the road, sprawling

GEOTHERMAL THEATER

Yellowstone has more volcanic activity beneath the land than any other place on earth; in fact, some consider it to be one huge volcano. The drama starts when magma far below ground heats water beyond boiling. This hot water must find a way out, so it heads upward and releases in four main types of thermal features.

Hot springs: If the underground path is unobstructed, the boiling water simply gurgles up and flows into cold rivers, creating pockets of hot water.

Geysers: If the route is constricted or blocked, the boiling water and its resultant steam get stuck. They build up until they erupt in a periodic burst. Yellowstone includes seven major geyser basins: Upper, Midway, Lower, Norris, West Thumb, Shoshone and Heart Lake. Old Faithful remains the most famous geyser, but the park has about 500, more than 75% of the world's total. Some geyser steam has been measured at 350 degrees.

Mudpots: These do not contain much water. Instead, microorganisms convert underground steam into sulfuric acid that breaks down rock, turning it into muddy puddles bubbling with escaping gasses. These mudpots are so acidic, they can burn holes in clothing.

Fumaroles: Unlike the massive amounts of water gushing from a geyser, limited water boils into underground steam that escapes in loud hissing releases. These steam vents are the park's hottest hydrothermal features.

Yellowstone's geothermal footprint is always in flux thanks to never-ending seismic activity.

porches at Old Faithful Inn held stadium-like benches already filling up. Eyes peered toward a large grassy area where the eruption would take place.

The blast occurred about every 90 minutes. The last, we learned, had been 15 minutes earlier which meant we had more than an hour to kill. We automatically headed into the visitor center, but squeezing through throngs to peek at exhibits pushed our patience. So we quickly made our way out and started along a gray boardwalk curving in a half-mile loop around the main attraction.

Random fizzes and gurgles startled us until we got used to the thermal soundtrack. Steam tendrils willowed from dozens of holes in the ground. Aislínn squatted by one, darting her hand through the top vapors. "Man. Is that weird!"

Both boys reached into the mist, pirouetting their palms like magicians. Sean giggled. "Sweet!"

I extended my arm expecting a blast of heat. Instead, I felt tingly moisture like waterfall spray. "Haha. How cool!"

Ciarán dared to move his digits lower and quickly yelped. He blew on his fingers.

Tom shook his head. "What d'ya expect? The higher wisps get cooled by the air. But steam vents are boiling."

At the half-way mark with no other humans in sight, Tom gestured widely. "Only thing missing are dinosaurs."

Aislínn stood next to him. "Or aliens."

How true! Every park so far offered its own captivating charms. Yet this was the most other-worldly landscape of all.

After completing the circle, we found a lone bench far from the growing porch mob. My husband joined in the zombie-like stares at the empty knoll. Ciarán and Sean wrestled on the dry ground. Aislínn pulled a book from her backpack.

Twenty minutes later, Tom's loud voice rang out with others who spied tentative splashes. The kids rushed to sit on the bench, watching the hillside.

Small puffs, a baby dragon's breath, curled away into nothingness. Bubbles foamed and sputtered. Then all was still. Until another spurt frothed, this time a little taller, a little longer, a little louder. Two feet tall, then five. Again and again, in fits and starts like an uphill tractor trailer, the spout got stronger with each convulsion.

Finally, water and steam rocketed into the sky to boisterous cheers and applause. For the next five minutes, Old Faithful shot its fireworks 20 feet, 30 feet, 60 feet, higher and higher until the thunderous jet of liquid and

> ## HUGE BUT NOT FAITHFUL
>
> Old Faithful is the most famous and visited geyser, but Yellowstone National Park contains an even more spectacular natural wonder. Steamboat Geyser, the world's tallest active geyser, blasts water more than 300 feet into the air for up to 40 minutes, followed by powerful jets of steam. While Old Faithful reliably puts on its show for up to five minutes about 16 times every day, the lesser-known geothermal gem erupts erratically, with gaps lasting days or years. Since 2018, activity has been more frequent.

mist towered 150 feet against a pure blue sky. After stretching to its full pinnacle, the ballet of water, steam and air reversed until the curtain closed with tiny bubbles melting back into their hole in the hill.

I knew the geologic *CliffsNotes* behind the performance: water heated by the earth's magma searched for a way out. It boiled into steam 1,500 times the volume of liquid, bursting against its underground trap. Finally, the pressure cooker exploded like an overinflated balloon, shooting vapors and water out of the earth. Fully released, the cycle started again. Scientifically, it was like popping a pimple or expelling gas after eating beans.

I preferred to stay in the realm of wonder. And wondrous it was!

Not the tallest of Yellowstone's 500 geysers, Old Faithful earned its rep for being frequent and predictable or, well, faithful. Despite its touristy trappings, the gorgeous gusher was definitely worth seeing.

Buffalo or bust

In our brief push through the visitor center, Ciarán overheard that Antelope Flats in Grand Teton National Park was a sure-fire magnet for free-roaming bison. The two parks connected at Yellowstone's southern border. Anxious to escape the crowds anyway, we happily resumed our quest.

A caravan of crawling RVs doubled what would have been an hour ride. But the sight of the Grand Tetons erased all annoyance. Their silver-gray peaks punctured the sky and stood sentry over fields of sage and wildflowers that carpeted either side of the road like *Wizard of Oz* poppy fields.

When the line of motor homes turned into the first campground, I floored it from 25 to a whopping 50 mph. The peanut gallery applauded. We practically had the road to ourselves as we headed farther south with the mountains anchoring our horizon.

Unlike the strange, raw energy in Yellowstone, the Tetons seemed to exude tranquility. Serene lakes sparkled calmly. Split rail fences, straight out of cowboy westerns, bordered acres of lush meadows.

Eagle-eye Sean was first to spot the prize. He leaned across Aislínn and squinted out her window. "Wait. Wait. Over there!"

I pulled off and, sure enough, tiny brown humps moved in the distance. A herd. We could barely see them, but that didn't lessen our excitement.

"Real buffalo! C'mon." Sean hopped onto the bottom fence rail and lifted his leg over the top.

Tom grabbed his t-shirt. "What're ya doing?"

Sean pointed.

"You can't go all the way over there."

Aislínn followed her brother. "Yeah we can. It's a park, not private."

Ciarán sprang after them.

"We are *not* going over there." Tom's tone stopped them. "Look. They're dots. It's gotta be miles. "

The kids puppy-eyed me. I strained to see, then got binoculars from the console. I sighed. "Dad's right. Maybe not miles, but it would take a lot longer than it looks and we really don't know what's in that terrain. How 'bout we eat and keep searching?"

They reluctantly plopped their rears on the fence with sandwiches. A dejected Sean kept ogling through the field glasses.

I put an arm on his shoulder. "Bet you a bag of M&M's we find some a lot closer."

We drove many more miles south. Not a single buffalo. Eventually I turned around. Even double scoop ice cream at Colter Bay Visitor Center on gorgeous Jackson Lake barely soothed our disappointment.

AT-A-GLANCE:
GRAND TETON NATIONAL PARK
The Teton Range rises above a scene rich with extraordinary wildlife, pristine lakes and alpine terrain. Visitors can explore over 200 miles of trails, float the Snake River or just relax in this beautiful place.

LOCATION: Grand Teton Park is in northwestern Wyoming, north of Jackson and south of Yellowstone National Park.

OPEN: Grand Teton is open all year but in the winter some areas of the park are inaccessible by car.

COST: $35 per vehicle, $30 per motorcycle and $20 per bicyclist/ pedestrian; under 16 is free (There is a discounted double pass for Yellowstone National Park and Grand Teton National Park.)

INFO: https://www.nps.gov/yell/index.htm

Fire sense

We remained mostly silent until we were back in Yellowstone en route to our Canyon Village campsite. On either side of the road, charred pines hovered like dark skeletons over slender new trees sprouting from the ground. Life and death. Literally.

"Wow. So that's what they meant by the fire plan."

Intrigued by the wildfires we'd encountered since Yosemite, Tom had done some digging.

"The Park Service used to extinguish every blaze. Then they cut down the dead stuff and manually filled in by planting new trees," he told us. "Then they did a real 180. Started to just let the fires burn."

He gestured at the acres of tree carcasses and saplings. "Now they know healthy forests need fire. It clears the way for new growth. And it lets trees propagate naturally."

"Duuuhhhh." Sean leaned forward to roll his eyes and tsk. "We learned that on *Sesame Street* when I was like six, dad. Pine cones have some kind of waxy coating that only bursts open if it gets hot enough. Fires make the seeds drop. And the ash makes better soil."

"Well I'm glad you learned it from Big Bird, but it took the Park Service decades to find out. Forests need fire almost as much as sun and rain."

I smiled. "*Ohhhh... I've seen fire and I've seen rain.*" I couldn't help myself, the lyrics popped into my head. I sang so off key that the kids booed.

Tom shored up the tune on the next line. "*I've seen sunny days that I thought would never end.*"

"Uggghhh." Sean dropped back against his seat.

Tom returned to the lesson. "Y'know, they finally found out that if you let a fire burn the ground bare, it actually prevents new fires from spreading."

"Huh? How?" I didn't get that logic.

"Think about it. Take our campfire. If we put it out before everything burns, there's charcoal and small pieces of logs left that make it easier for the next fire to catch. It's the same in the woods. If they let *everything* burn, there's nothing left to catch fire. So it creates empty boundaries that new fires can't jump across. It actually helps contain future wildfires."

I wasn't convinced. "Maybe. But that blaze back in Yosemite looked pretty big. And there were tons of smokejumpers. I don't think they were just letting it burn."

He shrugged. We were still driving through acres of skinny green-needled pines that were knee high to their eerie burned ancestors. After a long pause, he continued.

FIERY CONFLICTS

Nowhere is the Man vs. Nature struggle more evident than in the growing debate about wildfires on public land. Ten percent of all blazes start naturally, set off by lava or lightening. The rest are caused by people. Whether arson or carelessness (as in unattended campfires, tossed cigarettes, smoldering debris), it seems six decades of urging by Smokey Bear were not enough. Wildfires in the U.S. are at an all-time high. The culprit? A dangerous combination of climate change and development. Severe drought, howling winds and other weather shifts are churning blazes into uncontrollable firestorms. Just three or four decades ago, a 20,000-acre blaze was rare. Now they are standard. In the same time period, more homes and communities have been built next to wilderness areas, upping the danger – and potential causes – of wild infernos. Fire might be good for the forest ecosystem, but with blazes bigger and people closer, the National Park Service can no longer simply let wildfires burn. They must juggle the competing challenges of ecology and development.

"I'm telling you. The burn thing really works. They proved it with this huge fire back in 1988. This was after they already adopted the let-it-burn thing in Yellowstone, so they were just trying to keep the fire contained until it died naturally. But this mother *never* burned itself out. They couldn't stop it. More than 25,000 firefighters. They even brought in the Marines and Army. It was waaaaay crazy."

In the rearview, I saw the kids leaning in to hear.

"Got so out of control, the fire burned almost half the park. More than a million acres. They had to evacuate everyone. It was the first time the park closed in almost 100 years. Took two months before the blaze was fully out. They called it the Summer of Fire."

I didn't know whether I was more impressed by the story itself or his factoid retention. But that was Tom for you.

"Everything was bare, a burned mess. They thought Yellowstone was doomed But then the forest started popping back up. Richer than ever. So now, unless people and private property are threatened, the fire plan is to try to let the forest burn and reseed naturally."

He gestured again out the windshield. "Can't have a better example than this. Look how many dead trees there are. These have been dead for years and new pines are growing all over."

The seared trunks continued for miles until a full, thriving forest made it clear where the old fire ended. Further down the road, however, we saw and smelled brand new smoldering.

"Hmmmm. Must be the fire that closed the bridge yesterday." Tom shook his head. "It's really tough now. The fires keep getting worse each year. It's harder and harder to just let them burn anymore."

Raging bull

Tom and I were still mulling mother nature's challenges when Sean bellowed, "UP AHEAD. LOOOOOOK!"

Buffalo! Huge hump-backed animals munched grass in the field. More than a dozen moseyed and chewed, oblivious to smoke mushrooming beyond the nearby hillside or to the handful of staring humans.

The Brennans lit up like laser beams. After driving all day, we found our bison just 10 minutes from our campground!

I joined a few cars angled off a sandy shoulder. The kids and I rushed out of The Couch. We took in the amazing bulk of these beautiful beings. Bulls ignored our attention while moms stayed close to their gamboling red-dogs, the nickname for their ginger-hued calves.

Sean practically lifted off. "I can't believe it. This is soooooooo awesome!"

He led us to a clearing across the road where a man was taking photos of two lone bulls lazily swishing their tails. Tom stayed at the SUV.

I put the telephoto to my eye, zooming in. I scanned one bull's curved horn, thick woolly cap and broad mounded shoulder before focusing on his large dark eye. The orb, clear and penetrating, stared right back at me. Startled, I stiffened. I had to remind myself I was looking through a lens, that the bison was hundreds of feet away. I read somewhere that a "bull's eye" is metaphor for seeing into someone's soul. Was he peering into mine?

"Give *me* the camera mom." Ciarán misread my momentary lack of snapping and took the Canon from my hands. He squatted down for an even more dramatic angle.

The bulls barely moved, except to bow their heads for more grass.

"This sure is once-in-a-lifetime," remarked the man, copying Ciarán's squatting pose.

"Sure is!" I couldn't help but think of the long-gone American frontier where, as the old song memorialized, millions of buffalo truly did roam.

Our concentration remained so focused on the calm magnificence around us, we barely registered Tom's scream until it was too late.

"WATCH OUTTTTT!"

We all turned to see a bull racing toward us from the opposite direction. Everyone froze. No sound came from my open mouth. A tsunami of panic crashed in my gut.

I could hear his pounding hooves and fiery breath. Or was that my heart? Dirt flew from under his moving bulk. As he charged past, maybe 30 feet from us, a shriek finally escaped from my chest.

He stormed across the street and stopped short. Panting heavily, he lowered his snout and nonchalantly began to munch. The other buffalo could not have cared less.

No one said a word. I tried to catch my own breath. Finally Sean giggled, a pitch higher than normal. We all joined in with shocked, relieved chuckles.

Ciarán exhaled slowly. "Man, wish I got a picture of *that!*"

Rotten eggs

It happened so fast that it took a while to fully grasp our close call. Tom ran over and ushered us back to The Couch. I got in and gripped the steering wheel to calm my shaking hands. I started the engine and slowly pulled away with one last look at the perpetrator, calmly swishing his tail.

"Holy shit." My husband put a hand on my leg. "He came out of nowhere. From the patch of trees to your right I think."

I still couldn't speak. In the back, the kids tripped over each other to rehash.

PUREBRED "BOEUF"-ALOS

Yellowstone's bison population numbers around 4,900 – the most on any public land in the U.S. The park is the one place in the country where these magnificent mammals have lived since prehistoric times, when millions roamed North America. That makes today's residents the only pure descendants, free of cattle genes. Although many people still call them buffalos (believed to come from the French boeuf for beef), the correct name is American bison. In a scientific giggle, it's really *"Bison bison bison"* (genus: Bison, species: bison, subspecies: bison.) Standing six-feet tall and weighing up to a ton, with trademark horns, scraggly beard and huge humpback, male bison are the largest mammals in the U.S. In 2016, the American bison joined the bald eagle as a symbol of our country when it became the national mammal of the United States. What an honor and a testament to conservation for an animal that almost became extinct in the late 1800s.

"He went like right by us," gushed Sean, still giggling. "I could smell him!" His sister and brother chimed in from both sides.

"Yeah, d'ya see that dirt? He was flyin'!"

"What about his eyes? What was he lookin' at?"

"That man."

"Yeah, that man. Haha. Poor old guy was crappin' a brick!"

"So were you." Aislínn poked her little brother. "Imagine if he nailed us?"

"I would'a jumped him." Ciarán rounded his arms.

"And I would'a grabbed his tail." Sean shot his arm out, squeezing his fist.

They were off to the races, excitedly embellishing the tale. Up front, I continued to shudder, caught in overwhelming mom-guilt of not protecting my kids. We were so careful to respect the wildlife. To maintain distance. What a freak thing!

I tried to tell myself I couldn't have done much. It happened in a blink. Yet...shouldn't I have instinctively pulled them to me? Stepped in the line of fire? Yelled? I kept my eyes on the road, inhaling deeply.

Somewhere after the boys had downed the buffalo and had him in a lock-hold, Aislínn leaned as far away as she could and exclaimed loudly, "Ewwwww. Sean! Did you let one out?"

In milliseconds we all noticed.

"Seaaaaaan!" Tom doubled down on the accusation.

"I didn't *do* anything."

"Sure Sean. Bull scare the crap out of you?" Ciarán opened his window.

Instead of dissipating, the stench increased. Tom and I instantly realized and simultaneously shouted, "*Close it* Ciarán!!"

Too late. We were nearing Yellowstone's Mud Volcano mecca.

If we thought geysers and steam vents were the be-all in the park's alien landscape, we hadn't yet witnessed the hissing, gurgling, eerie muck of the marvelous mud pots.

Sulfur, the villain behind intestinal gas and stinky eggs, also sculpted this other-worldly wonder. Like flesh-eating bacteria, it fed on the wet earth, breaking down rock into reeking cauldrons of simmering silica and clay.

The smell was ten times worse than Sol Duc Hot Springs, but by the time we parked and began a half-mile boardwalk loop through the sloshing and belching, we stopped grumbling about the odor and started ooohing over the scenery.

It definitely provided an antidote to my lingering anxiety.

Pots varied from thick pudding to soapy slop. The goopier the clay, the bigger the erupting blobs. We laughed and wowed our way along the sensory carnival of plopping, crackling sounds; rippling, fantastical shapes; wickedly foul scents and delightful surprises of color.

Who knew sludge didn't only come in gray and tan? Some mud pools swirled with bright pinks, reds and purples, courtesy of minerals like iron oxides. Others shimmered blue, green and gold like earthbound aurora borealis' thanks to acid in the mucky water.

The kids ran to the edge of Dragon's Mouth Spring, a small cave opening where boiling water rolled in and out like a flashing tongue. Sean retrieved a stick from his pocket, tossed it in and watched it enter and exit beneath them. Rhythmic hiccups of steam added to the mystique.

Ciarán raised both arms toward the mist, inclined his neck forward and in his best Voldemort voice snakily snarled, "No essssscape onccccce you're trapped in thissss." His siblings cracked up.

We continued to hydrothermal features with fun names like Cooking Hillside and Grizzly Fumarole. My favorite, though, had to be Black Dragon's Cauldron, a large, sizzling lake.

In the mid-1900's it exploded into existence through a crack in the earth with a fury that blew trees out of the ground and blanketed the area in mud. Decades later, the dark pot still churned so feverishly that it indeed looked like a fire-breathing creature could burst out any second.

Tom preferred the area's namesake Mud Volcano. Hundreds of years ago, the once 30-foot high cone violently erupted and eventually settled into a huge, bubbling crater that greeted us at the bottom of a boardwalk descent.

He leaned in closer. "Who would've thought mud could be so cool?"

Apparently buffalo liked the glop too. It deterred biting flies and helped them shed fur. Three beasts lay scattered around mud pots, wallowing not far from our path.

Ciarán pushed his sister off the foot-high boardwalk toward one dusty snoozer.

"You *kidding* me?!?" I quickly pulled her back.

My eldest shrugged. "Whaaat? He's not even awake."

I glared at him and stomped away, prompting laughter from all three.

Sure bet

What an amazing eight hours on the road! Geysers, steam vents, mud pots and more. Not to mention buffalo. We'd searched all the way to the end of the Grand Tetons and now saw them everywhere, including two more herds on the few minutes back to our campsite.

With plenty of daylight left, we ventured to Canyon Visitor Education

Center where I learned my most mind-blowing geology yet: Yellowstone was thought to be one gigantic volcano, perhaps the world's largest!

Unlike traditional cones rising from the earth with vertical cavities, this caldera tunneled underground in 60 miles of subterranean channels filled with roiling gas and water. If the whole thing blew at once, scientists predicted ash would smother most of the United States. Instead, trapped contents leaked out every day in more than 10,000 mud pots, boiling rivers and geysers.

I stared at the 3-D map, wonderstruck. Imagine if the buried monster didn't have these natural release valves? What fantastical secrets our earth held! Humongous networks of redwood roots. Mysterious multi-layered caves. Buried rivers. And now this, a huge hidden volcano!

The kids interrupted my musings. They'd finished their visual sweep of exhibits and wanted to hang in the lounge. Tom and I continued to indulge ourselves, reading every display.

I joined my trio just as they were finishing a round of blackjack. From the pile of peanuts in front of Sean, it looked like he was raking it in.

"What, no M&Ms today?" I scooped out a handful from the open Planters' can. "Deal me in."

"Hey, you can't bet all of those," scolded Aislínn at the same time Ciarán asked, "Where's dad?"

"He went back to start dinner. What's the bank, 20?" I counted them out onto the table and cupped the rest into my mouth. I sank deeper into the cushioned seat, watching my eldest shuffle. "What a great day, huh?"

Aislínn nodded. "Can't believe we almost got gored!"

Sean giggled. "Did ya see the stuff about bison in there? Said they can run like 35 miles per hour. He had to be doing at least 25."

"More than that." Ciarán put the deck down and motioned for his sister to cut it. "He must a gone from zero to 30 in a flash. Wish we saw him start. That dust was insane."

Sean leaned in. "Did any of you see his tail?"

"Who could notice a tail?" Ciarán dealt a card down to each of us. "Only thing I saw was that big angry snout."

I chuckled. "Oh, I read that, too, Sean. Said they usually swish back and forth but if the tail's standing straight up, watch out!"

"Bet it was up like a switchblade." Ciarán laughed and placed our face-up cards.

Mine showed a queen. I peeked at my hidden card and smiled broadly. "Yes!"

"She's bluffin' again." Sean smirked at his siblings.

"How do you know?" I pushed five peanuts to the center.

Aislínn, with a seven on top, folded immediately. Sean had a ten. Ciarán showed a two. "Meet you and raise you five." He tapped the nuts forward. "You in Sean?"

Sean lifted his lower card again.

"C'mon." Ciarán egged him on. You know she's bluffin'. You got a mountain there."

"Yeah." I pushed his shoulder. "You should go big on this one, Sean. Ten whole peanuts."

He dipped into his pile and thrust his bet into the pot. "Hit me."

Ciarán flipped over a five and placed it neatly. Sean waved his hand to pass on any more. I did the same. Ciarán opted for two cards, so he had a two, four and six showing.

I fingered five more peanuts to the center.

Sean moved them back. "You can't bet again."

"Why not?"

"It's the rules."

"Oh, like we're in Vegas or something?"

"Let her go, she's still bluffing." Ciarán slid the last four of his peanuts to the middle and grabbed one from his sister.

"Heyyyyy."

"I'll give it back in a minute."

"I'm out." Sean slapped his ten face down.

"Wimp." Ciarán eyeballed me. "What d'ya got?"

I turned over my card to reveal a ten next to my queen. "Twenty."

"WHAT?" Sean threw his cards up. A ten and a king. "Not fair! I thought you had 21."

Ciarán chuckled. "Ahhh man, we're both idiots. I really thought she was scammin' us." He showed his last card, another ten. "Twenty-two."

"Maybe you need to shuffle better." I pulled in my winnings.

He took half of my peanuts so he could stay in the game, tossing one to Aislínn. He handed me the deck and shrugged.

"I can usually tell when you're lying. See it in your eyes. Guess you're getting better at it."

I laughed. "Speaking of eyes, did you see that thing about their eyes?"

Sean perked up. "What about 'em?"

"They have awful vision." I started mixing the cards. "Great smell and hearing. But they're really nearsighted. Wish I knew that when I was looking through the telephoto. I felt like he was searing into me. Now I know he

241

was just seeing a blue blob."

Aislínn raised her brows. "Nearsighted? How do they know that? They have a buffalo eye chart or something?"

"Yeah." Sean giggled. "For buffalo bifocals."

Ciarán jumped in, "Maybe the raging bull thought that guy's big bent over butt was a hot cow lady or something."

Sean choked. "He *was* pretty big. I bet he crapped a huge one afterwards."

"Okay. E-nough. You're not starting that again." I dealt the hands. As the boys still laughed, I sighed. "Thank god we're here to joke about it."

We played a few more rounds before heading back to camp, where Tom had spaghetti and sauce ready. By 7:30 p.m., we cleaned up and relaxed around a blazing fire. My eyelids slid closed. The only constellations I witnessed that night were in my dreams.

Purely petrified

What a treat to sleep until 8:30 a.m. and wake to Tom's bacon and eggs. Two for two on cooking duty! He took the back-to-back chore to thank the kids for helping when he couldn't do anything. I was just glad he felt better. After breakfast, I strolled to the Canyon strip mall to mail a slew of postcards to family and friends. Then we gathered our gear.

Whitewater had been high on our bucket list so we booked an afternoon rafting trip with an outfitter in Gardiner. First, though, we wanted to explore the northern part of Yellowstone starting with Tower Falls, the second most popular cascade in the park.

A short walk from the parking lot brought us to an overlook. I leaned against its wooden fence and tracked the water's 132-foot torrential plunge into Tower Creek, hypnotized by the velocity and power of its crash. Tiny water molecules gathered such collective fury, then like waves in the ocean just mellowed back into their gentle floating. All part of the same whole.

I was trying to discern some meaning in that observation when Aislínn tapped my shoulder. "Hey, ma. Check those out."

I followed her finger to rock pillars atop the falls, jagged and stark against the azure sky.

"Jeez. They look like guards."

Ciarán shook his head. "Nah, more like ghouls."

"Yeah. Bet they move around at night, patrolling the hillside like rock cousins to the Ents." Tom pulled from another father-teen favorite, *Lord of the Rings* and illustrated with a stiff-legged, Frankenstein-like gait, as if he were a walking tree Ent. The kids loved it.

> ## TOWERING CUSTODIANS
>
> Tower Falls gets its name (and nickname "Devil's Den") from a brood of rock formations that hover 50 to 100 feet above the cascade. These angular volcanic pinnacles or breccia, as they are known, formed millions of years ago when lava cracked and dried. Over time, several of the eerie columns have crumbled and fallen, their debris sometimes changing the course of Tower Creek. The latest collapse was in the early 2000's.

Erosion ruined what used to be a trail to the bottom of the falls. We opted instead for a three-quarter mile path to see where Tower Creek flowed into the larger Yellowstone River. On the way, we passed a returning family.

One young son, wide-eyed, asked, "Did you see the bear?"

Sean lit up. "Bear? Where? Where is he?"

The father told us they spotted a small black bear right off the trail, just a few hundred yards back.

My youngest took off in a trot, his siblings on his tail. I offered the family a quick thanks and followed.

"Shhhhhhhhhhhhhh." Sean slowed and implored silence when he thought we had gone far enough. He tiptoed, looking left and right into the brush. He treaded softly, shushing us for at least another eighth mile before giving up.

Frowning, he kicked the path. "We missed him."

"Don't worry, we'll see one soon." What else could a mother say?

"It's okay. No need to bother the bears." A jovial Tom caught up after purposely lagging behind.

"Not funny, dad."

We arrived at the merging waterways, a gift for ears and eyes. Tower Creek bubbled over its rocky bed, one of many tributaries feeding Yellowstone River on its long journey to the even mightier Missouri River.

Staring at the frothy, mesmerizing union below, I again flashed on the unshakable connectedness of things. These graceful capillaries, like our own, fed and fueled life itself. Yet, as the Greek philosopher Heraclitus said, 'No man ever steps in the same river twice, for it's not the same river and he's not the same man.'

I had no idea where my random ponderings were going, but once more an excited offspring shifted my attention. Ciarán spotted an osprey soaring above the river. Sean, moping with head down, cheered up at the graceful bird of prey. He grabbed binoculars from my backpack and tailed the river hawk until it was a dot on the horizon.

A massive male elk, complete with a stunning antler six-pack, elevated my son's mood even more when we drove by the lone bull chomping away near Blacktail Deer Plateau, another beautiful area of the park.

Before exiting Yellowstone we made one last stop at Specimen Ridge, home to the famous Petrified Forest. Tom gestured toward a hillside dotted with broken tree trunks of varying heights.

"Watch out, they're really scared."

"Yeah, the rock Ents probably come terrorize them after dark." Ciarán cracked up at his own joke.

Aislínn mock-slapped her forehead. "Ha ha. You're both so hilarious."

But we all chuckled. To be honest, if they didn't have metal fences around them for protection we never would have guessed the dead "trees" were 50 million year-old fossils. They looked like regular trunks that snapped off in some random lighting strike. Moss and lichen covered many, making them seem even more a part of the living landscape.

Climbing closer to the first specimen revealed a few nubs that appeared more stone-like than wooden. Tom leaned down. "Okay. Maybe these can pass for ancient remains."

Ciarán shook his head. "Nah. Still could be any old tree that lost its branches. Pretty lame."

I circled the petrified trunk. "Well, they might not look as impressive as we expected, but they're still pretty mind-boggling."

FOSSIL FASCINATION

Yellowstone is said to have more fossils (or, as scientists call them, "paleontological resources") than any other national park. Worms, animals, plants, you name it – either actual body parts or trace remains (imprints, burrows, dung) – have been preserved for millions or years. Among the best known in Yellowstone are fossil forests. Hundreds stand on a steep hillside in the northern part of the park known as Specimen Ridge. Some believe the petrified trunks, up to eight feet across and 20 feet tall, may have been uprooted by a volcano 50 million years ago, carried in rapidly flowing lava and deposited at their current elevation. Others think the hill contains layers of trees that became fossilized during different volcanic eruptions over the eons and are regularly unearthed through erosion. Either way, mineral-rich groundwater halted their decomposition. More specifically, silica built up in the tree cells over thousands of years, so they literally sculpted in place and formed a perfect stone replica of what once was wood.

"True," conceded my son. "Hard to believe these run-of-the-mill stumps are almost as old as the dinosaurs."

Paddle-antics

With an hour to kill in Gardener, Tom and Ciarán hung out on a sunny patio outside Yellowstone Raft Company while I ambled around town with the other two.

One trading post featured toys and novelties made from animal parts. Polished buffalo horns and shiny bone spearheads hung from crowded walls. Claws, paws, antlers, teeth, hides and skulls filled dozens of shelves. I thought Sean would go crazy for the authentic sling shots, arrows and rattlers. He did, just not in the way I anticipated.

Minutes after we entered, he found me admiring painted pottery. "Let's get out of here."

"Why?" I didn't turn from the shelf.

"Mom," he urged through clenched teeth. I twisted my torso and saw his red face and tight jaw. I thought he might cry.

I quickly turned toward Aislínn eyeing beaded bracelets in a center case. "Hey, Bean, we'll be outside."

She took one look at her brother and joined us. "You okay?"

He shook his head. "I can't believe they do that stuff… I get the antlers that fall off every year. Maybe even teeth they find. But they killed a lot of animals for that stupid shit. It's not pioneer times where they needed and used everything for survival. It's money time when they do it for greed."

"You're right." His sister nodded.

I glanced at him with newfound appreciation and gave him a quick side hug.

When we returned to the rafting outfitter, Tom stood filling out disclaimers. Ciarán, sitting on the steps, darted up and punched his brother in the arm. "What's smatter, bro?"

I shot him a scowl. "Leave him alone."

Sean shook him off and found a far seat on the store's wooden deck. A few minutes later, we were called inside to get fitted for vests and paddles. We met a couple and their son from London, who would round out our crew.

Gear in hand, the eight of us stepped back on the deck to be greeted by Keith, our cheery young guide in his third summer of leading newbies through whitewater.

"Hi everyone. Just want to assure you. I haven't lost anybody yet."

Too corny for my kids, but Tom and I chuckled along with the Brits. We boarded an old bus for the mile ride to Yellowstone River, where the boys happily helped Keith unload an inflated raft. Then the group circled him for instructions.

"I know you all signed the forms, but I'm required to say out loud that whitewater rafting has inherent risks and hazards. It can cause severe bodily injury or death."

Tom braced beside me.

"Make sure you listen to me when we're on the river. If you lean the wrong way or we hit a crazy patch, something might happen that's beyond my control as your guide."

"What?" Tom rose to high alert.

"Don't worry, dad." Ciarán sounded more embarrassed than reassuring.

Keith ignored them both, continuing what was clearly a rote speech. "We'll go over the commands when we're in the boat. If the crew listens and works together, we can prevent the raft from wrapping on a rock or flipping over."

Tom practically shouted. "Flipping *over*?"

Sean cringed. "Da-ad, it'll be oka-ay."

Keith had been scanning the group as he spoke. Now he and everyone looked directly at my husband. He smiled. "Don't worry. We just have to let you know in the off, off, *off* chance that something might happen. We'll be fine. These rafts are super stable."

This didn't appease Tom. "I don't know..." He looked back at the bus, ready to bail.

Aislínn put her hands on her hips, but spoke kindly. "Oh, c'mon dad... It'll be *awesome*."

The boys chimed in. "Yeah dad." I just looked at him, pleading silently.

"You'll be fine!" Keith lifted his faded baseball cap and ran his hand over his thick brown hair. "I've been out here every day this week and the water's not too rough or too calm. We're gonna have a great time. And I'll keep you in the back. It's the most stable spot."

Tom took a slow breath and exhaled. "All right, I guess."

I felt a tug of sympathy for him. Normally strong and capable, Tom was not a comfortable swimmer and other than a kayak, he didn't like any man-powered water vessel.

"Okay, then!" Keith returned his attention to the rest of us as if there had been no interruption. "You can lose your stuff really easily. So don't bring anything you don't absolutely need. We have a photographer half way through who will get plenty of pix so unless it's waterproof leave it on the bus."

As the guide shared a few more precautions and showed us how to hold our paddles, I side-eyed Tom. He remained stoic. At least Sean was back in an excited mood.

We put on our vests and each grabbed a webbed handle to carry the raft down to the shoreline. Keith kicked the inflated oval until it fully floated, then assigned our positions, explaining that the weight had to be balanced.

A thrilled Ciarán jumped onto the lead seat, with Aislínn, Sean and Tom behind him on the right bumper. I settled in on the left side, sandwiched between the English couple, their son in the back across from Tom. Keith took his place on the aft rim.

After a quick lesson on commands, he used his oar to push us into the middle of the river and told us to start paddling. In the bobbing calm we chatted, learning our guide hailed from Boston. This immediately ignited an animated Yankees vs. Red Sox debate between him and the rest of my family, thankfully distracting Tom. On my side of the boat, the Brits and I quietly pulled our blades through the water, enjoying the bright sunshine.

Soon enough Keith shouted. "Here it comes. Listen for my commands... PADDLE!"

In seconds, churling water hurtled over our rising bow, soaking us as we sailed skyward. I screamed and grabbed a loop to keep from landing in the lap of the English mom. We quickly crashed down and I flopped forward, steeling my legs against the rubber floor. Up front, Ciarán absorbed the brunt of the hit, bouncing so high I thought he would tumble out. We yelped and shrieked and laughed with abandon. Even Tom yee-hawed at the top of his lungs.

"PADDLE FRONT. PADDLE FRONT." Keith yelled over the next series of roaring waves, getting us into sync and using his oar to rudder through the mayhem. We dug in rhythm, pulling, pulling, pulling until we were out of the white foaming rapid.

Again on calm water, I peered across the raft at my family, each grinning in delight. For the next two hours we swirled, rolled, bumped and hooted through exhilarating rapids with names like *Pumphouse, Maneater, Rock Garden, Queen of the Waters, Sleeping Giant, Wake Up* and *Last Chance*.

Between rides, Keith shared area trivia. Pointing out the most prominent pinnacle in the northwest corner of Yellowstone, he said geologists climbed the 11,000-foot summit in 1872. They heard an intense crackling followed by such a jolt of electricity that they hightailed it down and named the mountain Electric Peak. Nearby Mount Sepulcher got its moniker for the strange tomb-like formations on top. How splendid it must have been, I mused, for early explorers to christen landmarks with labels that have lasted for centuries.

Floating past layers of sandstones and shale made it easy to see how the river became Yellowstone. These sedimentary remnants formed more than 70 million years ago when an inland sea covered the entire area. After eons of sulfur staining, the rocks practically glowed in shades of mustard, flax, dandelion and butterscotch.

At *Swimmer's Rapids*, Keith invited us to enjoy the slightly swirling pool. Ciarán, Aislínn and Sean, the only takers, cannon-balled into the chilly water then quickly clambered back on the raft. But at *LaDuke Hot Springs*, a primitive geothermal pool, we all enjoyed the delicious warmth. Floating on our backs, Sean and I spied a pair of ospreys gliding above the river as the afternoon sun glistened on the water. Sublime!

Near the end of our eight-mile paddle, Ciarán stood on the inflated bow like Captain Ahab in *Moby Dick*. Keith furiously swirled his oar off the rear until we spun in a 360.

"GO… GO… GO… GO…" We chanted and chortled at my bronco son until he finally belly flopped into the river with an ear-splitting holler. Even the quiet Londoners joined in. They didn't seem to mind the loud Yankee Brennans.

Soaked with water and joy, we helped load the raft and sloshed back onto

WATERPARK EXTRAORDINAIRE

A U.S. Army lieutenant invented the first rubber raft in the 1840's to survey rivers in the Great Plains and Rocky Mountains. About half a century later, commercial rafting trips began, thrilling paddlers across the country. Rapids need a river bed with a steep grade; the slope increases water velocity and turbulence, trapping air that then rises into bubbly froth. Classified on a scale of 1 to 6, rapids range from barely moving flat water to life-threatening perils. In addition to rapids, whitewater rafters may encounter challenges like eddies, caused by boulders that make the water swirl and flow in the opposite direction from the rest of the river. We enjoyed an eight-mile adventure on class 2-4 waters with the Yellowstone Raft Company (http://www.yellowstoneraft.com). They are the only outfitter fully permitted by the National Park Service to run trips on the Yellowstone River. Half-day trips are $42 for adults and $32 for children aged 6-12.

the bus. At the Yellowstone Raft office, we changed into dry clothes and headed back into the park where we were going to check out a couple of Keith's touristy recommendations.

Boiling turmoil

Midpoint between the equator and north pole, an imaginary line circles the globe, passing through Minneapolis, Ottawa, Bordeaux, Venice, Belgrade and northern Japan. It also happens to cross through Yellowstone. In fact, the park's marker, slightly north of the Montana-Wyoming border, is reputed to be the most photographed of all such destinations in the world.

We joined the trend by posing around a rustic wooden sign, engraved "45th PARALLEL of LATITUDE. HALFWAY BETWEEN EQUATOR and NORTH POLE"

"How do they know it's really the right place? That *this* is exactly the 45th parallel," pondered Aislínn, echoing her Four Corners query.

"They probably don't," said Ciarán, hamming it up for the camera by pretending to hurdle the sign.

Actually they did. Or more accurately, they knew it was *not* the correct location. For years, the sign stood near the Boiling River parking area. But mobs of people and cars turned the popular photo-op into a safety hazard. So in 2008, park officials moved the marker nearly a mile north to a small lot situated, ironically, closer to the actual 45th parallel. While they couldn't place the sign on the precise latitudinal locale, the new destination was only about 400 yards away.

With the iconic pic under our belts, we were eager for the celebrated Boiling River hot springs thanks to Keith's five-star review. Yellowstone boasted more than 10,000 wet, hot geological areas. The springs, where cold water from the Gardiner River mixed with the literally Boiling River, counted among the park's few safe and legal thermal soaking areas.

We hurried down a quarter-mile path from the packed parking lot to river's edge. Tom, although sure his tooth was the problem, remained reluctant to get his ear wet. He leaned against a split rail fence. After hemming and hawing, Sean decided to wait with him.

The rest of us waded knee deep in the cold stream to the first of many stone wall alcoves along its banks. I melted into the deliciously warm pool, apologizing when my elbow bumped the person next to me.

More people squeezed in by the minute. Ciarán and I shimmied over to make room and learned the hard way that boiling water really did enter at the edge of the cove.

"Ouch!" My son bounded up. I tried to squish back, but the circle was just too crowded. A few people smiled, the rest ignored our plight.

"Let's go there." Aislínn grabbed my hand to pull me out into the main channel and nodded at an emptier recess about 30 yards downstream.

We started walking. The river got deeper and quicker. Before we knew it, we were chest deep. Slipping on the rocky bottom, our water shoes couldn't get traction. We fought to remain erect in the rushing river.

That's when Ciarán lifted his legs and sailed past us. "Sweeeeeeeet!"

"Waaaaait." Aislínn copied her brother. I followed suit. Like sea turtles in *Finding Nemo*, we let the current propel us.

In 30 seconds, we reached the second nook. We scrambled sideways to escape, half running, half swimming out of the stream until we could grab onto the stone wall that protected the pool. Laughing, we found the right mix of hot and cold, then settled into the scrumptious natural tub.

Laying back with eyes closed, I heard Ciarán announce that his brother had headed in after all. I rose and watched the force push my youngest from waist to neck deep in a blink. He struggled to stand up but lost his footing and slapped the water with his arms. He immediately giggled, which made us laugh. Then his head went under mid-chuckle and he came up coughing. Floundering, he came flying toward our alcove. I rushed out and stood as close to the current as I could, both arms outstretched to grab him.

"Kick, Seanie Bee! Pump those leeeeettle legs." Ciarán stood by me offering another arm.

The words made Sean snicker again. He swallowed more water, flailing his arms. I launched forward and grasped his fingers.

"HOLD ON." It was like gripping butter. He slid out of my hand and rushed past us.

"SEANNNNN!" I dove into the current after him and caught up to his dragging toes. I was trying to catch my breath and grab his legs when out of nowhere, a tall man in a cowboy hat lifted my son. The fellow, soaking with friends in a cove another 50 yards down, apparently heard our commotion and came out to stop the straying body.

"Here ya go, ma'am." He handed the bounty off like a sack of onions. Of course Sean, pink from fatigue and embarrassment, giggled.

I thanked the man and, without letting go, got behind to guide my son back. The river had other ideas. While my kicks and one-handed strokes kept him from slipping further away, forging upstream was like crawling through sludge. Cowboy hat saw my predicament and helped me get Sean to an alcove about halfway between our two. I thrust my son into the pool. He shrieked. "It's *tooooo* hot."

"I don't care." I forced him back and followed.

"Shit!" I grimaced and quickly lurched him out. The cranny, a key ingress for the Boiling River, *was* scorching. No wonder it remained empty.

I started kicking as hard as I could, determined to get him to shore. Ciarán and Aislínn floated towards us to help. It was at that point we heard the unmistakable furious screaming. "I DON'T BELIEVE THIS! HOLD ON!"

Tom strode into the river. His heft mostly kept him afoot in the current, but he slipped twice, dunking his head – and ear. He met us, glaring, as we slowly steered Sean. He grabbed our youngest under the armpits.

Ciarán started to laugh.

"DON'T YOU DARE!"

"We had him. You didn't have to…" I started.

"Yeah, right..." He looked at me hard. "C'mon Sean."

He launched our son toward shore and pushed until he could stand on his own. Ciarán and Aislínn went back into our alcove. I joined them. For the second time in two days, guilt mummified my psyche. What the heck just happened? How? Why? What should I have done? Five minutes earlier I had been blissfully soaking with my son and daughter, and now my other kid was a wreck, his dad was enraged and I was quivering.

I looked around to see if people were staring at us. They weren't. Cowboy hat had his back to us. I shook my head and exhaled like I was blowing out a candle.

Ciarán snickered. "He's fine, mom."

"Yeah, what a drama queen. How lame." Aislínn leaned into me.

"Right? He can handle strong tides in junior lifeguards but he gets stuck in a leeetle current with his leeetle legs?" Ciarán flopped around feigning distress. They both cracked up.

"Stop. You don't know. It's really scary if you feel out of control in the water."

"Mom. He can swim. He can tread water. He can ride ocean waves. Look, there are 8-year-olds doing fine out here." Ciarán eyed youngsters not far from us.

"Yeah," agreed Aislínn. "If he didn't waste his energy giggling he would'a been great."

"Or if he didn't have *leeetle* legs." That sent them into another round.

I leaned back against the rocks. "Well, I'm just glad that cowboy hat was there."

"Man, did you see his pecs?" Ciarán pumped his own biceps.

Aislínn slapped the muscle. "His hat wasn't even wet. He walked all the way without even slipping."

"That's cause he was like 12 feet tall."

I shook my head again, sank lower into the hot spring and closed my lids against the late day light.

We marinated in the soothing warmth for a long time. A pair of crows circled above, cawing like bellyaching brats. American dippers, kin to the tiny rock-nesting birds we saw in Glacier, flitted around as the sun slid in the western sky.

Bear redemption

Fully pruned and much more peaceful, we finally forced ourselves out of the pool around 6:30. Tom and Sean stood tight-lipped. They had a lot of time to fester over the Boiling River welcome sign because my husband deepened his scowl and exaggerated his finger at the words, *"currents can be deceivingly fast."*

"Oh c'mon, it wasn't that bad." Ciarán bear-hugged Sean, eliciting a laugh.

"Yeah, Sean, you were being pretty dramatic. *You* should go out for next year's lead." Aislínn referred to the school drama club's annual production, in which she had many starring roles. She stepped in next to him on the way to the parking lot.

"Stop." Sean giggled then added in a baby voice, "It was ve-wee, ve-wee sca-wee. I thought I was gonna dwown."

Four of us laughed. Tom did not.

"Cut it out," he snapped.

I could tell he was hurting again and needed his medicine. I felt awful that his ear got wet and even worse for my youngest son. I hoped the last

---

TRAVEL TIP: Heed Cautions

Looking back, Sean's river scare is far more alarming than it seemed at the time. During those few minutes, I was automatically consumed with helping him, but didn't fully register the danger. If I swam out earlier, when my son first appeared to flail, I could have guided him into our alcove or gotten him back to shore. Instead I subconsciously took for granted that he was a good swimmer. While millions of people safely enjoy our national parks each year, tragedy does strike. Even if members of your traveling party are gold-medal freestylers, backpacking hikers, exceptional paddlers or whatever, make sure you read and heed all caution signs and act quickly on any potential problems.

hour didn't overshadow our whitewater fun.

Back in The Couch, I took a deep breath and used my old after-school mom trick again. "What was your favorite part of the raft trip, guys? I think mine had to be that first big wave. What a hoot!"

"Nah." Aislínn leaned forward. "I loved that humongous rapid when we were going backwards. Remember? We bounced up and down for like five minutes and couldn't see what was coming."

"Yeah, that was super sweet! But how about me standing on the bow?" Ciarán half rose in the back seat. "I coulda done it so much longer if you guys didn't make me laugh."

"No way. You were toast." Sean pulled his brother down. After a pause he smiled. "The whole thing was really awesome. But the funnest part? Hearing dad. You know how loud he screams at football? That's nothing compared to him in the boat."

Aislínn grinned. "Hahaha. You're right. He was soooo loud!"

"Those Brits were probably horrified." Ciarán widened his eyes and bared his clenched teeth.

"Yeah, well I was right in front of him." Sean snorted. "All I heard the whole time was AAAAAAAAAAAAHHHH. AAAAAAAAAAHHHH."

I burst out laughing and stole a glance at Tom. Even he was smiling.

A few minutes later, Ciarán knocked on his window. "Hey, check it out." The road paralleled the river and a young elk stood in a few inches of gently flowing stream. "Wow, Sean. He would 'a stopped you."

Sean elbowed him hard. "Jerk."

Aislínn put her arm across his shoulders. "Y'know Sean. We just passed a bunch of places you could've gotten out if you floated further. It was no big deal. And it's so shallow here you would've scraped your belly."

My husband twisted his head and glowered at her. "Don't start."

Ciarán shrugged. "It's not like we ever would've let anything happen to him, Dad."

"Leave it alone." I half-pleaded, half-ordered, then clicked on the radio. The kids settled in with their iPods, Ciarán sharing an earbud with his brother. Tom closed his eyes.

Stuck behind a slow RV, I could look around more than usual. After turning away from the water, we passed brushy forest where something dark caught my eye. The RV saw it too. We both stopped and backed up.

Now alert, Tom and Aislínn opened their windows. Near and clear, a large brown bear sauntered into the woods. Sean scrambled across his sister's lap and stuck his head out. The sighting improved his mood immeasurably.

Back at our campsite, we rock-paper-scissored to see who had to cook the hot dog dinner. Tom lost and immediately announced we were eating at the strip mall café. Ice cream sundaes and a few rounds of poker later, we snuggled in the tent, too tired for a fire. I was glad nature called in the middle of the night or I would have missed the best show of all: a million twinkling stars.

Where the wild things are

No place in the Lower 48 laid claim to more abundant wildlife than Yellowstone National Park. We'd heard Lamar Valley, in the northeast section, was the place to search. The earlier the better.

So at 5:15 a.m., bundled in sweatshirts over pj's and woolen socks under sandals, the boys and I took off. The Couch thermometer read 38 degrees. Fully recovered from any residue of trauma, Sean jangled excitedly in copilot position, binocs ready as we made our way in the pre-dawn emptiness.

"So glad Dad and the Bean didn't come." Ciarán spread out in the back. Tom had wanted to rest; Aislínn opted to sleep in.

Barely into Lamar three-quarters of an hour later, our headlights stunned a large dog-like figure that darted into the road. He stopped for several seconds and seemed to squint into our windshield before racing up a hill.

"Yes! A Coyote!" Sean shouted as if witnessing a game-winning goal. He twisted to his brother. "D'ya see that! Get the camera ready!"

I eased forward, grinning as much at his joy as at the unexpected sighting.

Sean sighed happily. "Y'know, coyotes are cool at finding their meals. They kill mice, squirrels and small mammals on their own. But they also get together and gang up on large prey like elk. Plus, they even scavenge, which really pisses off the wolves."

"Haha. Just like me, they'll do anything for food." Ciarán poked his head forward. "Hey ma, d'ya bring any snacks?"

I laughed. So began the opening act of an unforgettable three-hour show, both inside and outside our SUV.

Rounding a curve minutes later, we came face-to-face with a female elk and her sweet calf, frozen in our beams. I turned off the headlamps. They hardly twitched. We had quite the staring contest until, prompted by some unknown catalyst, the duo suddenly darted across an adjacent field. We watched until they were specks on the horizon.

With the apricot sky still on the cusp of daylight and the landscape bathed in gray, I drove slowly down the lonely road. Sean, on high alert, scanned the surroundings like a military guard. Ciarán peered between us.

"Up there!" He directed us to a rise ahead on our left. Three dark figures stood silhouetted on top in the cresting sun.

"More elk?" I braked gently until parallel with the slender animals.

Sean shaded his eyes. "No... I think... I think... yes! They're pronghorn!"

"Wow." I took in the buck's namesake horns, the doe's graceful curving back and the fawn's spindly legs. It still wasn't light enough to make out details, but their profiles against the salmon sky enchanted me.

"Looks like something out of a Disney fairytale."

"Yep." Sean nodded. "Did you know they're the fastest mammals on the planet?"

"No way." Ciarán feverishly clicked out the back window. "Gotta be cheetah, dude. Everyone knows it's the cheetah."

"Nope, you're wrong." Sean didn't take his eyes off the hilltop. "That's what people think. But pronghorns kick ass when they're running. The cheetas only win in a sprint. They can go a few hundred yards then bag out. Pronghorns take off at like 60 miles an hour and can keep running for 20 miles or more. Maybe not that quick the whole way, but no one can keep up with a pronghorn."

Luckily the speedsters had no urge to bolt that morning. We didn't move for many minutes and neither did they. As the day brightened, I could make out white fur on their bellies and butts, vivid against the caramel outline of their head, back and legs. White strokes seemed brushed on like necklaces below their long, delicate snouts.

"So gorgeous!" I barely said it aloud.

Sean lowered the field glasses. "You know what else? Most people think they're in the antelope family cause they're called American Antelopes. But they're not. Their closest relative is the giraffe."

"What?" Ciarán snorted. "Get outa here."

"Really? I was just thinking how much they look like fancified deer."

"Nope. Not even close. I'm telling you, it's the giraffe."

I took the binoculars and peered at the mom's face, now in more sunlight. Sure enough, the erect curled ears did have a giraffey kind of look to them.

"Hmmm. Never would've known. What else smarty pants?" I put the binocs back in his outstretched hand.

Sean lifted them to his eyes and adjusted. "See the dad's horns?"

"Yep." Ciarán had switched to the telephoto. "Like a mini-antler."

"Yeah. I'm trying to remember. I think it falls off every year like an antler but it's made of horn stuff? I don't know, something like that." He leaned the lenses over to me so I could peek through again.

> ## PUZZLING PRONGHORNS
>
> Despite deer-like bodies, pronghorn are most closely related to giraffes and central African okapi. These beautiful mammals, the single remaining member of the Antilocapridae family, are only found in the American plains where, like bison, they have been wandering for hundreds of thousands of years. Pronghorns are the only animals in the world with forked horns that shed each year. The sleek ungulates get their name from the forward facing prongs on a buck's head, similar to antlers. But true antlers are made of bone and fall off each year, while true horns consist of keratin and never drop. Pronghorns have hybrids. The sheath is made of keratin but the horns shed annually. Boy, does nature love to fool us!

"Oh! You know what else? Their eyes."

"What about 'em?" I moved my focus to the doe's face.

"In proportion to their body, they have the largest eyes of any hooved mammal in the country."

"Well that explains why they're so darn cute. Disney for sure!"

The sun fully afloat, the buck finally turned and disappeared behind the hill. His family followed.

I smiled. "That was amazing. Wonder if they even saw us."

"Oh, they did," guaranteed Sean. "They notice everything. That's how they survive. Their eyesight is great... not like buffalo."

I chuckled and began to drive. Ironically, our next encounter involved the humpbacked beasts. We came upon a large herd, beards lowered as they grazed in a grassy field next to the road. I pulled off on the opposite side so Ciarán could lean out and get a good shot. The flash fired and a spooked bull took a mini-second to start snorting.

"Holy shit, Ciarán, get in!" I floored the gas, with the boys hooting.

"Why'd you do that?"

"It was an accident. I didn't know the flash was on." Ciarán continued to snicker.

"Well, I think I've had my fill of bison."

We drove further into the stunning river valley, its palette of greens now fully lit on the panoramic prairies and hills. Dark pine clusters broke up miles of softly undulating landscape. Marine blue waters of the Lamar River ran easily beside us. Another gorgeous day had blossomed before our eyes.

As we proceeding slowly on the empty road, Sean squinted across the narrow stream. "Pull over mom."

I stopped and he scanned the far riverbank. Seconds later he joyfully leapt out of his seat. "BLACK BEAR!"

I almost jumped out of mine. There she was in distinct view across the narrow stream. Her large paw held down the branch on a bush while she bit berries from a hanging clump. We could see the matting on her brunette fur. Binoculars brought her muzzle within inches, letting us admire her small black eyes and rounded ears.

No one said anything. We just watched her determined search. She bent, leaned into the brambles and dug out more sweet fruit. Then she stood, shuffled to another section of shrubs and repeated the routine.

"Different than I thought," I murmured after my turn with the magnification. "I figured she'd be slobbering all over. Almost looks like she's plucking those berries one by one. Something delicate about it."

"Now that you say it, I remember that bears only eat ripe berries. They keep coming back to the same spot for the next rounds. It's like they can bite the good ones and leave the others."

Ciarán laughed. "Nimble lips."

I grinned. Did it get any better than this?

After a long while I turned to my oldest. "She kind'a looks like a real life Brown Bear." Ciarán's well-worn companion still had an honored place on his teenage bed.

"Yep. The best." He zoomed in for more shots. Over the next 20 minutes, we remained enthralled. Then our Ursus americanus stood tall, seemingly stretching, before lumbering away from the river.

DUMPSTER DIVING

In its early years Yellowstone National Park featured "shows" where garbage was purposely dumped in open-pit arenas to attract grizzlies. The feeding frenzy wowed crowds of visitors, who also tried to get good photos by tempting bears with food from their vehicles while driving through the park. The result? Bears that loved human treats, lots of maulings, major car damage and, sadly, killing of these "problem" predators. In the 1960's, the park leaders finally launched efforts to reduce bear-related injuries and property issues. Yellowstone kicked off a huge education program, installed bear-proof garbage cans, prohibited all bear feeding and worked to wean the bears back to their natural diet. Today, the goal remains to keep bear-human interactions to a minimum.

Sean kept his head out the window until the bear wandered out of sight. "I can't believe how lucky we are! Coyote, pronghorn, buffalo, bear. All we're missing are wolves and moose!"

He scanned the hillsides as we moved on. "Wolves are gonna be tough cause they sleep during the day. But who cares, we already hit the jackpot!"

During the next hour, we passed several more buffalo herds and barely braked. How fickle our yearnings had become. When Ciarán asked me to stop near a few dozen lying in a field, I didn't get it.

"Right now ma! WOLVES! Up there! On the hill! I swear!"

I slammed to a halt. Sean and I scanned the distance beyond the resting herd. I spotted the white wolf first, just visible against the dark green shadowy knoll. "I see it!"

"Me too!" Sean scrambled to adjust the field glasses while he balanced out the window. "There's a whole pack!"

"There are?" I squinted. Then slowly, several outlines registered. In all, we saw seven. Six reds and browns and the one white. Just small figures heading even further away, their strong canine bodies, pointed ears and signature tails still crystal clear.

"Wooooooow." Sean exhaled in awe.

The vision captivated me, too. I knew wolves had been reintroduced into Yellowstone and renewed the entire ecosystem. What a gift to glimpse the powerful Canis lupus in their wild home!

"I guess they weren't hungry." Ciarán chuckled. "Lots of bison burgers just lying there."

Sean giggled. "Nah. They prefer elk."

We only had a short way to go before turning around and heading back to camp. Basking in pure elation, we rode silently. Lost in my thoughts, I startled when Sean yelled.

"Ciarán, d'ya see that?"

"Yeah! Mom. Stop! Stop!"

I pulled off the pavement and followed their gaze. Under a constellation of pines on a hillock stood a huge, hulking moose.

I widened my eyes to make sure I wasn't mis-seeing. "Oh. My. God."

"He ran across the field." Sean gasped. "You saw it, right, Ciarán?"

"I definitely saw it. Totally sweet!"

He was too far away to study with the naked eye, but when Sean finally relinquished the binoculars, I took in the enormous antlers soaring like paddles on either side of his long face. His bell, a flappy muzzle of skin, swayed beneath a muscular neck.

HOWLING INTO ECO BALANCE

By 1926, the wolves in Yellowstone were gone, killed by humans for threatening nearby livestock. Their absence wreaked havoc on the park. With no natural predators, elk herds swelled beyond control. They ate the willow, aspen and vegetation that scores of other animals needed to survive. Eventually the valleys were bare and riverbeds eroded. It took some 70 years and the declaration of the gray wolf as endangered for Yellowstone management to rethink its philosophy. In 1995, park leaders relocated 31 gray wolves from western Canada. Two years later, they transferred another 10 from northern Montana. The return dramatically changed the ecosystem and geography. With elk kept in check, trees sprang back to stabilize stream banks. Other animals, from songbirds to beavers and rabbits to reptiles, returned and thrived. For the past two decades, wolves have been on and off the endangered list and the government continues to monitor their recovery. But this proves the scientific principle of "trophic cascade," that the top of the food chain affects everything below. And it makes very clear: Canis lupis are invaluable stewards that keep the land in balance.

Sean glowed. "Those antlers alone weigh like 40 pounds!"

"I believe it," I said. "He's huuuge!"

"Yep. Moose are the largest and heaviest members of the deer family."

Ciarán, unable to get any shots, leaned forward. "That's pretty funny. Pronghorn, who look like deer, aren't related. But moose who look nothing like deer, are. Go figure."

Again we sat engrossed until the magnificent mammal waddled away. I thought Sean would float through the moon roof.

Although Ciarán couldn't capture every animal – some were too far, some too fast – the morning would be forever imprinted in our memories.

Soaring ospreys circled a ravine on our way back, icing on the sweet morning. We also spotted more pronghorn, elk and far too many bison. The beasts loved hanging near the pavement, chewing, pawing and grunting. The growing traffic actually eased my nerves when we came upon a herd blocking the road. I was glad to let someone else weave through them first.

Windy wonderland

After a glorious five hours on the road, the boys and I rehashed every single

---

WILDLIFE JACKPOT

Yellowstone's Lamar Valley, in the northeast section of the park, boasts more wildlife than anywhere in the continental U.S. On our early morning drive, we spotted:

1. Coyote	4. Black bear	7. Bison
2. Elk	5. Wolf pack	8. Osprey
3. Pronghorn	6. Moose	9. White tail deer

---

sighting over omelets at the lodge. Then Ciarán rushed off to the restroom.

Sean and I took our time walking back to camp. Deep in conversation, we passed a kiosk when something hurtled from the corner, landing inches from us with a blasting "RAAAAAAAUGH."

We jumped back, gasping hard in that instant before recognition.

"You friggin' dimwit." Sean punched his brother, doubled over in laughter. "Got you good. You should'a seen your faces."

My heart pounded. "That wasn't funny Ciarán." I stomped away, of course cracking them both up.

Thankfully when he arrived at our site with his brother, his pent up energy had dissipated. Both boys sat down and animatedly detailed our adventure for their father and sister. Then we climbed into the tent and took naps to rest up for our next one.

We'd covered a lot of Yellowstone in The Couch yet were itching to get out on foot, too. I had read if you only had time for one good hike, make it Mount Washburn Trail. In mid-afternoon, four of us drove to Dunraven Pass in the northeast section of the park and found the trailhead.

Aislínn once again begged off blaming her ankle. This time I argued.

"No. You're coming. You already missed our great morning."

She shook her head, lips tight. "I just want to stay here and read. If I get bored, I'll go over to the lounge."

"Aislínn..."

She cut me off. "Mom. It's a hard hike. I don't want to hurt it more."

Even the boys tried.

Sean clasped his hands in a begging pose. "C'mon Bean. It'll be fun."

Ciarán wrapped his arm around her shoulder. "Yeah. You can lean on me if your ankle hurts."

She wriggled away and stood firm.

I let out a long breath. Reproach ambushed me. This was supposed to have been *our* trip. Was there something else going on? I wanted to sit with her, but doubted she would have let me at that moment. And the others were waiting. I gave her a quick hug and got into the driver's seat.

I drove in silence and forced a smile as we started the six-mile hike. But 15 minutes in, nature pushed away my pensiveness. The first switchback brought views of the magnificent Grand Canyon of the Yellowstone and the lush Hayden Valley. If not for smoky residue, we could have seen all the way to the Grand Tetons.

By the second turn we spied our destination: a fire tower perched atop the summit. We huffed up the wide trail, traversing a mix of forests, rocky outcrops and meadows. My spirit sailed at the canvas of pink monkey flowers, lemon balsamroots, blue lupines, red paintbrush, purple shooting stars, yellow violets and other wildflowers I couldn't even name as they swayed on the hillsides like dainty showgirls.

Further along, big horn sheep grazed on the path. Two ewes stood center trail, eyes on their lambs.

"Wait!" Tom spread his arms to halt us.

Ciarán walked by him, past the mellow moms. We followed, Tom between Sean and me. The kids, predictably, found their father's caution amusing.

Sean patted Tom's arm. "You think you'd be used to it by now, dad."

Winds escalated the higher we climbed on our 1,400-foot ascent. Ciarán lifted his sweatshirt until it billowed behind him like a sail.

"Watch this." Sean hocked up a loogie and spit full force ahead. The gob landed smack back on his shoulder.

"Ewwww." I grimaced. "Gross. Why?"

He giggled. "Don't know. Didn't think it'd do *that*."

Tom rolled his eyes. Ciarán shot out in between laughs, "Idiot. I wish it landed on your face."

We barreled forward, heads down. When we finally reached the summit, gusts blew our hats while the panorama blew our minds. At 10,243 feet, Mount Washburn became our highest peak yet. On a clearer day, we could've seen up to 50 miles in all directions.

To escape the bluster, we scurried into the weathered cement and glass building on the mountain's bald top, one of three lookout stations in the park staffed by firefighters who spent summers living alone watching for danger. A chalkboard informed us that 2,500 acres burned the day before in the southeastern blaze. Even without written confirmation, the smoky remnants were obvious from our vantage.

We tried to venture out on a second-story observation deck for photos, but blasts forced us back without a single click. Instead, we took advantage of 360-degree views through large windows. Waist-high murals provided a terrific cheat sheet to the peaks and attractions in every direction.

Filled with incredible vistas, we headed down. Sean, ever alert, spotted two yellow-bellied marmots, smaller cousins of the hoary marmots we saw in Glacier. Stunning late day light angled over the mountain, bestowing us with ten-foot shadows by the time we neared the bottom.

Ranger redux

After a dinner of mac 'n cheese and fire-cooked hot dogs, we relived our thrills by looking at that day's photos on Tom's laptop. Then the kids and I strolled to the campground amphitheater. We hadn't been at a ranger talk in a while and I was thrilled to skip the crowded poker lounge.

Ranger Charles, a stout older man from Wyoming, began with a gorgeous slide of a grey wolf. Sean elbowed me.

"These guys," he exclaimed, "make all the difference."

He went on to explain what happened in Yellowstone when all the wolves were killed in the 1920's. "We thought we were helping people, doing the right thing by shooting these dangerous predators. Boy, was that joke on us!"

A close-up of a bull elk appeared on the outdoor screen. "You know what happens to these guys when there's no one to keep them in check?"

The small group remained silent.

"Well, they multiplied like crazy. Before we knew it, elk were everywhere. Eating up vegetation. Wrecking marshes. Basically destroying everything needed to support the park's web of wildlife."

The ranger displayed a stunning series of images. Moose. Beavers. Birds. Insects. "Many had to leave to survive. The ones that stayed suffered greatly. But if we want to get sentimental, *these* black beauties probably missed the wolves the most."

Charles played us along. We all figured he had to be talking about bears. Instead, after a calculated pause, the screen filled with the shining feathers of a raven. The open theater wasn't crowded, but those present laughed.

The ranger smiled and quickly shifted to pictures of a bear and an eagle. "Oh, I know. You're right. These guys used to feast on carcasses left by the packs. So with the wolves gone, they were in trouble, too."

"However these wolf-birds, as we call them, missed their long-tailed friends the most." He clicked to beady eyes and a gray-white beak.

"Any of you ever hear about the strange relationship between ravens and wolves?"

Sean leaned forward eagerly, elbows on knees.

Charles tapped the raven close-up with a thin stick. "From earliest times, there's records of this odd duo. Seems ravens have been hanging with wolves for many millennium. Diving at them, pecking until their Canis lupus comrades chase them..."

He forwarded to a photo of three birds hovering over a bright-eyed cub. "Even pulling pups' tails to get them to play."

My trio grinned broadly beside me.

"Scientists have known for some time that ravens heed the howls issued by wolves before a hunt. They fly behind their four-legged friends and grab the leftovers."

He clicked onto a vivid shot of a wolf kill with half a dozen ravens standing by in wait.

"It's no secret that wolves can take down most meals by themselves. But some observers think they hunt in packs just to keep the ravens from diving in sooner."

"These birds're in the same family as crows but a little bigger." He flicked through more slides, snickering at a mass of ravens in flight. "Know what a group of these birds is called?"

Aislínn beat her brother. "An unkindness!"

"Right! Haha. Guess whoever came up with that name didn't care for ravens. But the funny thing?" He again showed the raven close-up. "Some people who study the weird relationship believe it's symbiotic. They figure the ravens have super senses and serve as a kind of lookout when the wolves take down their kill. And when ravens come upon an injured elk or other animal, they have been known to use their raucous caws to get the attention of the local pack."

Charles looked around our semi-circle. "So what do you think? How many of you believe they really are friends?"

Most of us, including my captivated teens, nodded.

He shrugged. "Who knows. Another scientific mystery waiting to be solved."

He returned to his original magnificent wolf image.

"Either way, the reintroduction of wolves in 1995 returned our mother nature to her balance. Trees and bushes grew, marshes reestablished, the birds and animals came back."

Charles tipped his ranger hat, as if in reverence to the slide. Then he spoke slowly.

"In fact, it turned Yellowstone into one of the largest unmanaged natural wilderness areas in the world. Like an American Serengeti."

The words swirled around me like incense. I wasn't the only one clearly moved by such a declaration. It stayed with me long after I crawled into my sleeping bag. Imagine, I thought. Not Australia. Not Asia. Not the Amazon jungle. Right there in Yellowstone. We had one of the biggest untamed ecosystems on the planet!

Sure, most people came for Old Faithful or the park's Grand Canyon. But Yellowstone's real power, its full magnificence and palpable energy surged through the collective and connected wild web of life above and below the earth.

Although hard to discern at the manicured visitor center or in bumper-to-bumper traffic, this force, this spirit surely surrounded all of us. In Lamar Valley, atop Mount Washburn and under millions of miles of blinking stars, it pulsed through some ancient part of our brains and took hold of our souls.

Double rainbow

Along with my vivid ponderings, two things marked that night. First, temperatures dipped into triple-sock digits. Our coldest yet. We just snuggled further into our bags, recalling and laughing about the freeze that caught us off guard the previous month in Yosemite. How long ago that seemed!

Next, more bitter-sweet, we'd booked a cabin for our final park stay. So it was the last time in our trusty, well-worn tent.

Standing in the unzipped doorway shortly after dawn Tom snarked, "What a lovely sight. Teenagers cocooned like larva...Think they'll miss it?"

"Will you?" I crawled out to the fire he already had blazing.

"Ask me when I'm not so cold." He chuckled and handed me a steaming cup of tea.

We let the tribe sleep while we relaxed in the early morning stillness. I closed my eyes and allowed sounds to tiptoe into the silence. Leaves gently rustled. Birds greeted the daylight. Like eyes adjusting to darkness, my ears slowly opened up to the symphony around me. Sparks crackled in the fire. Water trickled. Feet skittered across the campsite. Something yowled in the distance. I smiled contentedly.

We took a walk along well-worn trails by the campground, enjoying the peace of the hour. When we returned and finally heard stirring inside, we started pancakes and eggs. Then mid-morning, we rolled up our nylon house for the final time. I sighed. We'd gotten so good at the whole camping thing, cooking, cleaning, packing the car.

As she tossed the sack to her dad, Aislínn shouted, "AD-I-OS tent!"

The boys applauded. I panged inside. It'd been a while since any of them threatened mutiny or even mentioned missing their friends. But I knew they were ready to go. One more week.

Fully loaded, we shoved off for a front-line view of the famous Grand Canyon of Yellowstone. Erosion over thousands of years created 24 miles of twisting, sheer cliffs up to 1,200 feet deep, with the Yellowstone River coursing through the bottom.

Like its Colorado namesake, Yellowstone's Grand Canyon boasted a north and south rim, in places 4,000 feet apart, each with spectacular views. We opted for the most celebrated site: two thundering waterfalls aptly named Upper Falls and Lower Falls.

Starting on the South Rim Trail, we headed north along the river. We happily recognized lofty Mount Washburn and its iconic fire tower in the distance. Sean pointed out the rolling slopes and deep grassy meadows of Hayden Valley to the south. The familiarity felt like a prized accomplishment, a badge of honor.

We strolled about a half mile on a wide, mostly paved path for our first good peek at Upper Falls. No matter how many cascades we'd seen over the summer, the joy never got old. The rhythmic force and endless roar were as spellbinding as a hypnotist's pendulum. At least for me.

My teens bounced ahead, stopping about 20 minutes later at an old brown sign. Ciarán tapped the words. "Hey look, dad. It's yours."

Sure enough, white letters on a worn wooden rectangle declared: UNCLE TOM'S TRAIL. At the turn of the 1900's, "Uncle" Tom Richardson enjoyed bringing adventurous visitors down into the canyon through a combination of 528 steps and rope ladders. Since then the half-mile trail to the lip of

---

FREE FLOWING YELLOWSTONE

The 692-mile Yellowstone River, the force that sculpted the park's Grand Canyon, has no dams, making it the only free-flowing river in the continental U.S. From headwaters in Wyoming, the river courses through the park, dropping 422 feet into the Canyon in two spectacular waterfalls. Then the river flows to Gardiner, MT, moving eastward into North Dakota and eventually emptying into the Missouri River. Native Americans knew it as the Elk River, but on his return voyage of the Lewis and Clark Expedition to the Pacific Northwest, Lt. William Clark described it using the English translation of "Yellow Stone."

Lower Falls had been upgraded to *only* 328 grated metal steps.

Sean peered down. "You wanna go?"

My husband read the "extremely difficult" caution and shrugged. "Only if everyone else wants to."

I looked at Aislínn. She nodded.

"YAY!" The boys yelled and scampered off. The rest of us took our time on the steep, intimidating staircase. Between her ankle and her acrophobia, I gave Aislínn a lot of credit for making her way down.

Worth every bend of our knees, the descent provided an incredible up-close look at the massive wall of water plummeting hundreds of feet to the canyon bottom.

Sean pulled me to the edge of the viewpoint. "I bet you'd die if you got pounded with that."

His sister snorted. "Duh. Ya think?"

Right then, the sun eased out from a cloud, producing not one but two rainbows. We squinted at the slight, ghostly tints. Before our eyes, like Easter eggs marinating in dye, the misty arcs slowly brightened into perfect lanes of vibrant color. They glowed translucently against the multi-toned backdrop of canyon walls.

No one said a word. Not even other families on the platform. Forget the science of reflection, refraction and dispersion of sun in water droplets. We could have been experts on the light spectrum. It didn't matter. Witnessing the birth of a double rainbow, being close enough to practically touch the brilliant vapor, seemed nothing short of magical.

JUST RUSTING AWAY

Even with all the gurgles and geysers that garner camera clicks in Yellowstone, more photos are taken at its Grand Canyon than anywhere else in the park. The most popular shots? Two waterfalls, 109-foot Upper Falls and 308-foot Lower Falls, which have more than double the drop of Niagara. Along with the captivating cascades, photographers also capture the stunning yellows, reds, white and pinks on the canyon walls. Seeming like brush strokes from an unseen giant, the other-worldly pigments actually derive from thousands of years of upwardly percolating fluids erupting in hot springs and steam vents. The boiling liquids alter the chemistry in the rock's iron content. In essence, the canyon's colors come from oxidation, more commonly known as rusting. Perhaps the giant artist is more appealing.

We gazed until the last twinkles of hue faded into waterfall. Then we slogged back up all those steps. I laughed as Aislínn kept count.

"What, do you think," I asked. "They lied about the number?"

"Nah." She exhaled and sucked in more air. "I figured it's a good way to distract myself."

Even the boys had to take breaks on the way up. But they were ready to go by the time we reached them at the top.

"Not fair," accused Aislínn. "You need to wait."

"Give us a minute." I huffed and sat down. We shared a few oranges, entertained by the looks, and curses, of others scaling the last step. We walked another mile up a sharp switchback and through lovely woods until we reached Artist Point. While Uncle Tom's Trail brought us face-to-face with Lower Falls, this popular lookout offered broader views of the canyon's powerful cascade.

After a few minutes of appreciative observation, we headed back. We came to four teens excitedly peered into a section of the woods.

One of them whispered, nodding toward leafy branches. "Grizzly!"

In bear-thrill redux, Sean leapt closer, eagerness oozing out of his pores. Tom stiffened and inched away.

"There he is!" My youngest aimed his index finger at a small clearing about 20 feet away. A furry lump laid on the ground. Aislínn and I leaned in. Ciarán already had the camera pointed.

"Yeah." The teen spoke softly. "We saw it walking toward us and turned to run 'cause we thought it was gonna come after us. But instead, it went in there."

The huge mammal, as if he knew dozens of eyes were on him, lifted his head for a few seconds and seemed to blink at us. Then he plopped back down.

"Did you get that?" Sean practically begged his brother.

"No, dude. Sorry. Too fast."

We watched expectantly for a while longer, but he didn't move again. After the other teens left, I realized we should have told them never to run in bear encounters.

"Would'a served them right," grumped Sean.

"What are you pissy about? You just saw a grizzly!" I was glad Aislínn said it before I did.

"Yeah, but they got to see him standing up. We just saw a blurry ball of fur."

"Oh, get over it." Clearly relieved, Tom gave Sean a friendly shove.

Fiery farewell

Our exit from the park's eastern perimeter took us past stunning hills and meadows, as well as gorgeous Yellowstone Lake. But billowing smoke riveted our attention. Fire blazed in the valley across from where we drove. Rubberneckers, including us, slowed traffic to a crawl.

"Holy crap!" Tom leaned over me to point out my driver's side window at the inferno. "Did you see *that*?"

Bursts of flames shot above tree tops, hissing in the air. Thank goodness they weren't close.

Once out of Yellowstone, though, cars still backed up. We inched through dank, gray air, assuming the awful fire behind us caused lingering acrid visibility. Yet the smoke grew even thicker and we realized we were headed toward another blaze.

After nearly an hour of stop and go, we rolled to a barricade. The sheriff and firefighters were only allowing one lane of traffic. When we finally got the signal to move, we rolled past gooey tarred areas of road. Sweat-laden, ash-covered men and women in bright yellow helmets, jackets and olive-green pants clustered near the smoldering hillside.

"You know what?" Tom smacked his leg. "These smokejumpers *just* got this fire under control. I bet they had orders to get the highway open ASAP."

One lone road ran from Yellowstone's east entrance to our destination in Cody, WY. No easy alternate routes existed. These brave, hard-working hot shots saved us, and countless others, at least six hours of detours.

For the second time in as many days, we traveled through horrifying, incredible scenes of active firefighting. The fear and drama unfortunately eclipsed Wyoming's beauty, where carved cliff-tops rivaled Arizona's Monument Valley. Too distracted and amazed by the heroic firefighters, we didn't take a single photo of our surroundings.

American Bison

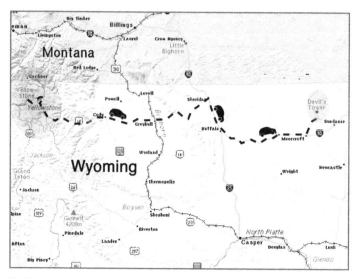

Yellowstone to Cody to Sheridan to Devil's Tower, WY
2.5 hours + 2.5 hours + 3 hours

AT-A-GLANCE:
DEVILS TOWER NATIONAL MONUMENT
Designated by President Theodore Roosevelt in 1906 as the first National Monument, Devils Tower looms like a sentinel above the northeastern Wyoming landscape. The ancient 1200-foot tall monolith has been a sacred site to more than 20 Native tribes and attracted daredevil climbers since the late 1800's.
LOCATION: Devils Tower is in the Black Hills of Wyoming, easily accessible on Route 24.
OPEN: Devils Tower is open 24 hours a day, year-round.
COST: $20 per vehicle; $15 per motorcycle; $10 per individual
INFO: https://www.nps.gov/deto/index.htm

Chapter 19
Cowboys & Chrome

Nowhere did our Jersey Shore ignorance stand out more than at the legendary Night Rodeo in Cody, WY, the country's longest-running Wild West extravaganza. The closest we'd come to cowboy hats and chaps was the Halloween costume I made for Aislínn when she was five.

After checking into our hotel, we found the iconic Cody Stampede Rodeo stadium, ripe with hay, manure and concession stand BBQ. Settling into five open seats on aluminum bleachers, I studied the sea of plaid, yokes, snaps and fringe around us. I'd never seen so many ten-gallon hats in one place. Leather, felt, straw, one even looked like snakeskin. Despite the sweaty heat, denim and pointy boots filled the stands. At the dirt floor show ring, a line of cowboys leaned against a rail.

"Quit staring, ma." Ciarán elbowed me, whispering through clenched teeth. "We're the ones who look like dorky camping nerds."

"I'm not staring."

"Yeah, sure." Aislínn opened her eyes wide, leaned forward and rotated in a slow, exaggerated survey of the crowd.

"I'm just curious. I like people watching."

Tom snorted and put an arm around my shoulders. "So discreet, dear."

I shook him off. "I wasn't..."

A loudspeaker cut me off, broadcasting a request to bow our heads. The gathering quieted and thousands of necks inclined. I lifted my forehead enough to peek around the venue during a resonant Christian blessing. A unified *amen* signaled the start of a slow, regal parade of equestrians waving American flags to boisterous applause.

The cheers continued when a rodeo clown and several spur-clad pals ran out spinning lassos into fierce circles.

I smiled. "Cool. I want to try that next time we're by the campfire." I'd been practicing my bowline and other sailing knots, so why not attempt some lariat action?

"Haha. I can just see it." Ciarán lifted his fist, circled his wrist overhead, then jerked his neck back as if the imaginary rope had caught. "You'll choke yourself in no time."

My family laughed.

A booming voice introduced the first Bronc Rider. I had no idea what that meant. One of the young cowboys I'd been watching earlier climbed over the rail onto the back of a horse in a gated chute. The steed seemed pretty calm. Then the gate opened. The stallion burst out like a raging tornado, twisting, bucking and kicking. I gasped. The kids shushed me.

One by one, tough competitors jerked and lunged on fired-up horses until they either fell off or a buzzer sounded. Every time I saw a young man's neck whiplash in the saddle, I shrieked. My trio kept hissing that I embarrassed them. I couldn't help it. When one flailing rider crashed to the ground I screamed "OH MY GOD" so loudly that they asked me to move. I promised I'd be quiet.

But then came the bulls. I could barely watch, yet I couldn't turn away. They reared so fiercely that each eight-second ride seemed an eternity. How could a body withstand such wrenching? I loved adventure, I appreciated the rush of extreme sports, but this seemed crazy. Every boom of powerful hooves, each unnatural rag-doll lurch of a rider, made me cringe.

I bit my bottom lip to keep from making noise and flooded with relief when the rodeo clown came back on. That was until he almost got gored and had to be carried off in a stretcher. The crowds cheered the curly-wigged jester, who managed a lame wave before the EMTs whisked him through the arena gate. I sat horrified, glad to see him at least able to move.

Calf Roping calmed me a bit. At least it didn't seem fatal, plus I did admire those lasso skills. But when the first mounted rider yanked his prey into the air by her neck and slammed the calf to the ground, Sean joined in my revulsion with his own yelp.

At last, the life-threatening exploits decelerated into the mere amazing

REALITY RODEO

William Frederick "Buffalo Bill" Cody became a rider for the Pony Express at age 15, then received a Medal of Honor after serving in the Civil and Indian Wars. His soldiering and bison-hunting fame began to spread when he was only 23, after which he started performing in shows about the frontier and Indian Wars. He founded Buffalo Bill's Wild West in 1883, taking his large company on tours across the U.S. Since 1938, Buffalo Bill's spirit has been channeled into performances and competitions at the Cody Night Rodeo in Wyoming. Cowboys, bull-fighters and rodeo clowns offer a taste of Americana with two hours of western entertainment every summer night. Tickets are $20 for adults and $10 for kids aged 7-12. The Stampede Rodeo, Extreme Bulls Event and Wrangler Championships are also popular events. (www.codystampederodeo.com).

ROPES, REIGNS & RAWHIDE

Here are a few things I learned about the rodeo world:

• **Judging**: A professional bull ride, or PBR as the locals call it (no relation to Pabst), is a contest of strength, balance and endurance between a bull and rider. The rider must hold on for 8 seconds with one hand in the bull rope and one in the air in order to earn a score. This is the same with Bronc Riding on horses.

• **Mad bull**: The bull immediately starts trying to get the lump of weight (cowboy) off his back by kicking, bucking and jumping. A "flank strap" tightened around his rear torso near his privates eggs him on.

• **Scoring**: The rider and bull (or horse in Bronc Riding) are each awarded points (0-50) by two judges, so each ride can get up to 100 points. The clock starts when the bull's shoulder or flank leaves the gate. It ends when the rider touches the ground, his hand leaves the rope or his free arm touches the bull.

• **Big bucks**: Most PBR bulls are worth at least $10,000, some fetch more than half a million. While major cowboy stars in the bull-riding circuit make up to $4 million a year, rookies pull in about $30,000 on average. Rodeo clowns, though, can earn more than 50 grand a year

• **Riding**: In case you want to give it a try, here's a how-to from *Texas Monthly*. "Slip your palm under the handle, pull the rope tight, and wrap the loose tail once around your hand. Scooch your body toward the bull's shoulders until the handle is between your upper thighs. Grip the body of the bull with your spurs, making sure your feet are in front of the rope." Sounds like a breeze, right?

dexterity and speed of Barrel Racing. It took us a while to decipher their cloverleaf pattern as Americana-clad cowgirls galloped in circles around barrels, kicking up dust and ovations. We joined in the hearty applause.

I left the stadium slightly dazed by the unfamiliar entertainment. It must have been how rural farmers felt in mid-town Manhattan. For the millionth time in a month, my teens deliberated about growing up differently. They excitedly imagined riding horses, roping cattle, wearing Stetsons.

I pondered too. Yes, kids were kids were kids no matter what. Yet if we had settled in an old west town, my three most certainly would have had altered outlooks, dreams and personalities. Or, maybe they wouldn't. Who knew? They certainly left the rodeo with tons of energy.

On the way back to the hotel, we stopped at Dairy Queen, apparently the après-show place to go. Entire families in cowboy hats packed the place. Trying to be a friendly Benny, I made small talk with a woman behind me in line. Tom found a table and we enjoyed our blizzards, careful not to review the rodeo in mixed company. We exited single file. Aislínn led the way with Ciarán and Sean behind her.

"*Race you for the front seat!*" Ciarán twisted quickly to shout the dare at his brother, then pushed his sister out of the way with a rough shove.

She automatically stuck her leg out to snag him. He hopped over it. But Sean, thrusting into speed, tripped and thudded all fours onto the blacktop. He lifted up, stunned, his palms raw like chop meat. Blood spurted from his knees.

Yet again, I'd like to say I responded maturely. That I calmly walked my youngest to The Couch and cleansed his wounds. But let's just leave it that I put on a nice Yankee show for the locals. Even Tom, the serial screamer, tried to convince me it was just a jerky kid thing. But I went ballistic, railing at my older two, hurling "*stupid*," "*sick of this*," "*ruin it all*" and other loving words. They could have called me the mad bull.

Ditching the dump

The next morning everyone else had shed the night's fiasco. Of course. But I, no surprise, wore my mood like chainmail and retreated to a tiny balcony outside our room.

I sank into one of two wooden rocking chairs that filled the deck. The parking lot shenanigans *were* stupid kid stuff and I overreacted. My family was fine, even happy. So why did I feel an anchor pulling me down? I frowned at the cloudless sky. Then it hit me like a bucket of ice water on my head. I was jousting with melancholy. Only six more days on the road. I *always* got sad anticipating endings.

The last five weeks had seemed endless. Now they were a blink. Despite exasperations, I wanted to do this forever. Wander to wonderful places. Remain in my family bubble. Never go home.

I rocked gently thinking back to Mesa Verde, Olympic, the Grand Canyon, Yosemite. I absently moved my gaze to the flowers bordering the hotel property, trying to recall each adventure. Why did it have to end?

A loud knock on the sliding door disrupted my reverie. I jolted. Tom pantomimed eating and waved me in. Seeing the kids through the glass, I flashed back to Sean's bloody legs. To Aislínn and Ciarán each insisting it was the other's fault as I volleyed my venom at them.

Who needed more exhausting kid crap? Or exasperating quarrels? Or vagabond laundry? And zero privacy? Not to mention iffy toilets! Then I smiled because bathroom humor always did that for me.

I stood up. Whenever my offspring whined on the trip about something that already happened or might happen, I chided them: *Get your heads out of the past or future; enjoy where we are NOW.* Boy, I thought, I really needed to follow my own advice!

I took a deep breath and walked back in. Everyone had finished packing. We went to a small café for eggs and pancakes then hit the road again for another one of those travel days. We planned only short drives for the end of our journey, figuring we'd be pretty sick of being in a vehicle. We weren't wrong.

With clear roadways in what we thought was wide open Big Plains country, we estimated the ride from Cody to Sheridan, WY, should take less than an hour-and-a-half. Sally Satellite, however, predicted almost double that. What, we wondered, could possibly add that much extra time? Then we entered the Bighorn Mountains.

Maneuvering through Wyoming's version of painted hills, we gawked. Slopes worn by eons of erosion flaunted show-stopping layers of red, pink and amber, colors reminiscent of a mid-summer sunset or peak fall foliage.

The farther we got from residual fire haze, the more the hues popped against a sky so cobalt and so cloudless that it seemed computer generated. Even the winding, sometimes hairpin, lanes beneath us were brick red as if paved with cayenne pepper.

Early afternoon sun peeked above magnificent buttes, enveloping The Couch in reflective rays. As I drove, the sheer, unadulterated splendor of our country again infused me like strong, delicious tea. I definitely began steeping in the "now."

My mood carried when we arrived in Sheridan and discovered an awful hotel. The sign showed the correct address and name, minus a few letters. But no one wanted to go in. Scraps of faded siding hung haphazardly over still-visible holes. Grime layered the windows. Only two cars parked in the lot. Without a second thought, or a mention of money, I pulled away.

Not counting the mistaken identity in Canada, this was the only time we ditched a booking. Just down the main drag, we found a Best Western for only $15 more, a steal because it included breakfast.

While waiting for our room, we walked to a little organic eatery. I knew the other Brennans preferred grease and salt, but at that moment, probably still mindful of my morning blahs, they let me call the food shots.

To the kid's unbridled glee, the hotel's accommodations formed a rectangle around a large indoor pool and spa. Our door opened onto its glass-ceilinged deck with patio tables and chairs. In less than five minutes, they jumped into the deep end. I, on the other hand, jumped at the opportunity to wander around Sheridan alone.

Bustling with small shops and galleries, the town also boasted many buildings on the National Registry of Historic Places. I most enjoyed the public art: murals, sculptures, art deco façades. I could see why they called themselves Wyoming's Jewel. Against the Bighorn Mountain backdrop, Sheridan offered a fun mix of old west charm and hip culture.

The boys teased Aislínn and me every time we raved about special towns along our journey. In sarcastic high-pitched tones, they'd crack each other up, squeaking, "Oh, what a *cu-ute* town!" I couldn't wait to tell them that Sheridan definitely made my list of "cute" towns to visit again.

Back at the Best Western, I sank into the hot tub, letting bubbly jets massage my shoulders. The kids rallied me out with a few rounds of poolside poker before we grabbed dinner.

I noticed a couple of trendy restaurants during my stroll but the vetoes were vociferous. Instead, we lined up for fast-food take-out, which we ate poolside while gambling our fries. A pre-midnight dip capped off the night. Like a family of woozie Gumbies, we melted into our beds.

Close encounters

Bright and early, we proceeded across Wyoming's wide prairie. Tom offered to drive since his pain had eased enough to forego medication, but I thought it better to stick to our plan.

Easy and relaxing, the broad open highway took us over magnificent passes with breathtaking switchback views. Red-tinged pavement gave way to endless ranch land.

After miles in our individual lulls, I broke the quiet. "What is that?"

A ginormous piece of equipment hulked mid-field like a comic book Transformer with arms dangling. I'd seen two others in the last 20 miles. Definitely not a tractor and too tall to be one of the sculpturesque watering systems I admired. No, this seemed like some metallic apparition.

Tom looked up from his book. "Oil rig."

"What?"

"Oil rig. Like in extracting oil from the ground."

"But why? It's a farm."

"Actually it's a ranch."

"Okay. But, still, why?"

"Moolah."

I pursed my lips, puzzled.

"Totally about survival. These small ranchers and farmers have had the land for generations. Now they can't make it anymore. Can't compete."

"But these properties are *huge*." Aislínn piped up from the back. "Look at all those cows."

Tom shook his head. "Anything's huge to us. Our yard's a postage stamp. But these are small compared to industrial conglomerates. The ranchers lease part of their land to oil companies for the extra cash."

"Hmmmmm. Pretty sad. Guess it's like Taylor Hardware and Home Depot," I said, referring to the century-old hardware store in our town. "At least Taylor can win on service and community loyalty. These ranchers..."

Right then, two Harleys roared past so loudly that I jerked, forgetting my train of thought.

"SWEE-EEE-EEET!" Sean leaned forward from his middle back seat to follow them in the windshield. "They must be doing 90!"

Ciarán squeezed sideways to peer over his brother's head. "Nah. At least 100. Mom's doing 80... It'd be sooooo dope flying down the road on one of those. I'm gonna get me a Harley."

I snorted. "Let's just make sure you're okay in a car first."

He shot me a look I couldn't miss in the rearview. Thanks to me, he'd done exactly zero driving in weeks. For a split second I thought about pulling over and letting him get behind the wheel. But a dropkick of anxiety quickly brought me to my senses. I kept moving toward South Dakota.

Over the next hour, dozens of motorcycles raced past. It got to the point where the kids made up a spot-the-bike game. "There's a Yamaha... Honda... Kawasaki... Suzuki..."

"HAR-ley, HAR-ley, HAR-ley!" The backseat chorus pumped their fists every time the clear favorites zoomed by. They thought it was a blast. Not me. I gripped the wheel at each ear-splitting assault. I couldn't wait to get to Devils Tower.

We were spending our next three nights in South Dakota's Custer State Park. On the way, we wanted to visit the distinctive monolith that became the country's first National Monument, not to mention an alien landing pad in the 1970's movie, *Close Encounters of the Third Kind*.

Still miles away, we rounded one long curve in the highway. Aislínn squealed. "There it is!"

Sure enough, the strange stone stood tall in the sky-blue air. First a thimble on a mound of fabric, then an upside-down cup atop a bowl, finally a rugged silo on a hill, it grew larger and larger as we sped nearer.

"That's so bizarre... all by itself there." Ciarán leaned across his siblings to get a better view out his sister's window.

Rather than rebel, she pushed against her seat to give him room. "I know, right?"

I would have reveled, too, but the increasing number of speeding two-wheelers frazzled my nerves. I grimaced. "You know what's bizarre? These bikes all riding around I-90 the same day we are."

Tom shrugged. "Must be a popular road."

Things didn't get better after we exited. Instead of rocketing by on the four-lane interstate, the bikers hot-dogged around us on narrow, snaking back roads. I really wanted to just be at Devils Tower.

At the entrance, however, I stopped short. Literally. Motorcycles seemed to be *every*where. Two-wheelers lined the regular parking lot like rows of corn. They were backed against fences. Angled like spokes around trees. Crammed single file along dirt paths. Overlapped in random pockets of space. Blinding daggers of sunlight leapt from the ocean of chrome.

"What the heck?" Tom shaded his eyes with his palm. We wouldn't have been more surprised if we actually did encounter extraterrestrials.

A ranger walked over to my side and pointed at a distant gravel area. "All cars there, ma'am." I tensed. What was it about uniformed men and their "ma'am's?"

Tom bent over to my side and asked, "Why all the bikes?"

The ranger looked at us as if we were idiots, or maybe aliens ourselves. "Sturgis." Then he waved us on to deal with the next vehicle.

I slowly pulled forward. "Sturgeon? The fish?"

"No. Stur-gis. Heard of it. Some big biker thing."

TRAVEL TIP: Know Before You Go

We thought we dotted all i's and crossed all t's before our trip. We learned a huge lesson in South Dakota. Check your itinerary for any big events happening at the same time. A quick search might convince you to reroute or switch dates. Even if you keep the schedule as is, at least you won't be taken by surprise.

SACRED MONOLITH

Scientists theorize that molten rock cooled into the isolated formation known as Devils Tower. But Native legend credits the Great Spirit with sculpting what they called Mato Tipila, meaning Bear Lodge. (The current moniker came in 1875 when the native name was misinterpreted to mean "Bad God's tower.") One myth tells of girls chased by hungry bears. The youngsters ran atop a small rock and prayed for help. The rock rose toward the heavens, too steep for the bears to climb, although their attempts left deep claw marks. Different tribes have variations, but bears are always to blame for the trademark vertical indents on the remarkable geologic formation. The site of rituals for thousands of years, Devils Tower still attracts modern ceremonies like sweat lodges and sun dances. Visitors often leave colorful cloths or prayer bundles along the trails. The sacred monolith also helped make *Close Encounters of the Third Kind* among the highest grossing science fiction movies of all time when the character played by actor Richard Dreyfus became one of the "chosen" drawn toward the flat mountaintop where aliens were going to make first contact. The actual first contact with the top of the strange mountain – declared by a geologist in 1875 as "inaccessible to anything without wings" – came less than 20 years later when local ranchers built a 350-foot wooden ladder and attached it with wooden stakes to one of the vertical cracks. Their Fourth of July climb thrilled thousands of awe-struck spectators. Today, rock climbers use modern equipment to scale Devils Tower's challenging walls.

"Really? Ya think?" I harrumphed.

Tom truly was a *Jeopardy* whiz, but sometimes he pretended to know stuff he really didn't, so I questioned if he actually *had* heard of it. Turned out, he did. And not just the place called Sturgis, a city north of the Black Hills Forest in South Dakota. Tom was also familiar with the event. In fact, as soon as the light bulb went off, he realized we landed smack dab in the throes of the most famous biker gathering in the world.

Every August, a half-million "outlaws, renegades and wannabees" flocked to the Sturgis Motorcycle Rally and zipped around the Black Hills region like ants on a dropped lollipop. Sturgis' normal population of 6,700 exploded to 500,000.

This explained a lot, especially why gazillions of them were sight-seeing at Devils Tower, more than 80 miles from Sturgis. We had hoped to walk right up to the astounding natural wonder, check its visitor center, then hike a trail that wound around its hill-top base through grassland and ponderosa pines.

But we weren't up for close encounters of the deafening kind. While most bikes remained quietly parked, the ground shook every few seconds with explosive throttle thrusts. Plus the paths to the monument teemed with black t-shirts and leather vests.

It's not that we disliked motorcycles. Some of our good friends were bikers. We just didn't want thousands invading our experience. We would have felt the same about horses if cavalries came stampeding.

Even the kids preferred admiring the surreal rock from the gravel parking lot. We leaned against The Couch observing its jagged surface. Hundreds of long vertical cracks, almost like pleats, made it seem more an enormous tree stump than something that erupted from inner earth's magma. Either way, the flat-topped monument joined our growing list of mind-boggling natural marvels.

I thought Aislínn and Sean had started squealing in agreement about the unique monolith. But they sighted something far more charming. On the opposite side of the gravel, where the pebbles met the steppe, dozens of furry brown faces popped out of the ground like periscopes. Prairie dogs!

PURE PRAIRIE LEAGUE

They may seem like poster children for the word "adorable," but prairie dogs are tough, family-oriented, keystone animals who impact more than 125 other species through their activities and abodes. They live in large colonies under the grasslands of central and western North America. Complex tunnel networks lead to special rooms for sleeping, rearing their young, storing food and even eliminating waste (yes, private bathrooms.) Close-knit groups, called coteries, live together in wards. Several wards make up a colony or "dog town." Although standing on their raised burrows makes them look taller, these *Scuiridale* (same family as squirrels and marmots) are only about a foot high and weigh three pounds or less. Yet their communication is more advanced than almost any other studied animal language. Researchers found the squeaky calls (or barks, as those who first named them 'prairie dogs' assumed), send very descriptive messages about different kinds of enemies. Mainly, though, these burrowing brown cuties focus on family, sharing food, grooming each other and nuzzling nose to nose.

For as far as our eyes could see, tall grasses semi-camouflaged mound after dirt mound. As soon as another adorable caramel-colored pup sprang up, one of us yelled, "Over there... over there!" And we laughed in delight. Definitely an I spy of cuteness.

Devils Tower bikers

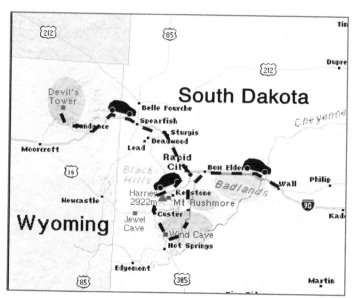

Devils Tower to Custer, SD (including Mt. Rushmore, Crazy Horse, Wind Cave and Badlands)
3 hours +

AT-A-GLANCE:

CUSTER STATE PARK

Originally established as a game preserve in 1913, Custer State Park was the brainchild of then-Gov. Peter Norbeck, who wanted a sanctuary in the Black Hills to reintroduce much of the wildlife eliminated by early gold seekers. Today it remains one of the nation's largest state parks, featuring scenic views, trails, resorts, cabins and camping. Its 71,000 acres are home to more than 1,300 bison, elk, big horn sheep, mountain goats, pronghorn antelope, mule deer, prairie dogs, eagles, hawks, wild turkeys and much more.

LOCATION: The park is 15 miles from the city of Custer, on US 16A.
OPEN: The park is open 24 hours a day, year round.
COST: Park entrance is free.
INFO: https://gfp.sd.gov/state-parks/directory/custer/

Chapter 20
Our Last Stand

Lunch in downtown Custer seemed like a good idea. That is, until I turned onto the main drag. Motorcycles paraded in both directions like beauty contestants, revving to each other every few seconds. Parked bikes tucked into the tiniest openings and leaned against every building in sight.

The Couch, a Gulliver among Lilliputians, would've snagged some chrome if I did anything but crawl behind the rider in front of us. The universe must've taken pity, because we lucked into a parking spot where a delivery truck happened to be pulling away.

"You think it's legal?" I asked Tom, my voice fraying.

Tom snorted. "Like the cops are gonna bother with us? I don't think so."

A long-haired black-vested dude in mirrored sunglasses stood by his Harley a few feet away. "You're good." He cheerily raised a red plastic cup.

I offered him a weak smile. "Thanks."

We exited our vehicle and peered around. Custer appeared to be another "cute" town, but I couldn't really tell through the throngs of leather and denim filling the sidewalks and weaving around the slow moving traffic. We joined the mob and headed toward the first eatery we spotted.

Clearly prepped for the onslaught, Cattleman's Restaurant only had a 10-minute wait, plenty of time for me to scrutinize the diners. Funny, I mused, beyond the boots and leather the bikers were as varied as visitors to our hometown beach. They could've been grandparents, tradesmen, teachers or techies.

Tom read my mind. "Looks kinda like amateur hour, don't you think?"

I laughed. "Definitely."

Huge, delicious plates eased our tension, really *my* tension, but the whole family appreciated not having to deal with my neuroses. We crept out of Custer as slowly as we entered and soon escaped into the gorgeous, pine-forested mountains of the Black Hills. Although our last wilderness stay wasn't in a national locale, we chose Custer State Park as a perfect jumping off point to other federal highlights.

When I finally pulled into Blue Bell Campground, though, my shoulders slumped. You think I would have expected two-wheelers, yet somehow the sight of dozens at different campsites surprised me. Instead of articulating, or even realizing, my bike bigotry, I lashed out about our cabin.

Others we passed had much better views, I griped. The bungalow across the path had a porch while we had dirt. Our fire ring laid too close to the picnic table. As the only accommodation Tom selected and booked himself without my input, of course everything was his fault.

One thing about spending so much intimate time together, my family had no problem ignoring me. Sean grabbed his book and bee-lined for a fancy outdoor privy. Tom and the other two unloaded The Couch. They unrolled our sleeping bags on the cabin's two double bunks.

Initially, their flagrant disregard fueled my anger. I ranted while they set up our portable stove on the picnic table and carried groceries inside. In 10 minutes, I ran out of steam. I looked around and admitted that the cabin was "nice." Sigh.

I strolled to the campground's deluxe restroom/laundry facility and took a long hot shower. Any residual tension washed down the drain. I grabbed everyone's dirty clothes and read my book while I did two loads in the comfortable complex. I even clicked with a biker chick.

In tight jeans and black lace camisole, she stood rinsing cowboy boots in a utility sink.

"These shit kickers get so dirty on the Harley," she announced in a soft drawl to no one in particular.

I, on the other side of the room in my khaki shorts, Tevas and baggy *Go Green* t-shirt, realized she was talking to me. "I bet."

"Been on the road two days." She bent over and twisted her long blonde curly hair into a bun. Then she stood up and splashed water onto her chest and neck. I think she purposely avoided her face to keep her eyeliner and mascara from running. "Whew! Glad to finally be here."

"I bet," I responded again, then hurried to say something else lest she thought that was the extent of my vocabulary. "Where 'r you from?"

"Down near Houston... How 'bout y'all?"

"Oh, we're from Jersey. Been on the road almost six weeks."

"Really? How awesome!

And just like that, we began chatting away. Theresa got an earful of the Brennan adventure and then told me all about the motorcycle rally. Every year for the past decade, she took two weeks off her job as a veterinary assistant and rode up with her husband. They loved the concerts in Sturgis, but it got too crazy so they preferred camping miles away in Blue Bell.

"I bet." The words were out before I could stop them. We laughed.

By the time she left, we felt, well, not exactly like old friends, but I definitely lightened up on my biker bluster.

By dusk, all the Brennans amazingly remained full from lunch. We decided to just munch on snacks instead of making dinner. Tom built a blazing fire and we relaxed as the night sky swallowed the last remnants of daylight. The heavenly ballet began; the Milky Way emitted stars like fairy dust and the constellations took their places on stage. It never grew old.

Subterranean treasure

A terrific tidbit about bikers: they liked to sleep in. Perhaps a generalization, but nary a metallic roar greeted us on the road when we got up early and headed down to Wind Cave National Park.

In fact, quiet permeated the morning so much that a dozen bison grazed in the woods surrounding our campground. A few miles later we were treated to a herd of prong-horned antelope foraging along the roadside. While these sightings didn't send Sean into elation anymore, they still gave all of us a magnificent pause.

At the national park, stunning long grasses danced in the breeze amid wild lilies and coneflowers. We sniffed the faintest scent of vanilla in the clusters of ponderosa pine, known for that wonderful aroma.

AT-A-GLANCE:
WIND CAVE NATIONAL PARK
Above ground, the South Dakota gem includes the largest remaining natural prairie in the U.S., teeming with bison, elk, antelope and, of course, prairie dogs. But far below the surface sits one of the longest and most complex underground mazes in the world. Named for the barometric breezes at its original entrance, the vast passages contain chambers like the Post Office and Elks Room. Many of its walls are rich in the rare and unique formation known as boxwork, a honeycomb calcite formation. Wind Cave became the eighth national park in 1903 and the first to protect a cave.

LOCATION: Wind Cave is in southwest South Dakota, about 22 miles south of Custer on US Highway 385. All tours begin at the visitor center, about a half-mile west of the highway.

OPEN: Cave tour schedules vary throughout the year, but the park is open 24 hours a day, year-round.

COST: Park entrance is free. There are a variety of cave tours priced from $10 to $30, with discounts for children and seniors.

NOTES: The park has limited food and beverage service. Bring lunch or prepare to eat in the nearby towns of Custer or Hot Springs. Also, wear closed toe walking shoes and bring a jacket for the tours; cave temps are always around 53 degrees Fahrenheit.

INFO: https://www.nps.gov/wica/index.htm

But the real thrill laid beneath us. Covered by just a square mile on the surface, the cave itself, the sixth longest in the world, snaked more than 143 miles stacked in layers, some hundreds of feet deep.

At the visitor center, we debated tour options, ranging from the easy Garden of Eden Tour (automatically nixed by my clan) to the four-hour Wild Cave Expedition. Aislínn and I coveted that taste of spelunking, but the male contingent had no interest in crawling through dark, hip-wide spaces. So, we opted for the hour-and-a-half Fairgrounds Tour, billed as the next most strenuous, with 450 stairs and loads of geologic formations.

Arriving early came with perks. We not only had our selection of tours, our group was small enough to seem like a private show. Our guide, Ranger Todd, told us late morning would bring lines of people and lots of sold-out time slots.

He led us to a window and pointed towards what had been the cave's natural entrance. He said the Lakotas passed down stories for centuries about the "hole that blew air," although no evidence showed they ever went in.

"But after white settlers streamed in during the Gold Rush, it was only a matter of time before they discovered the 10-by-12-inch opening. Legend has it that two brothers riding by in 1881 heard screeching wind and searched for its source. When one peered into the hole, a gust blew his hat off."

The ranger whooshed his own Stetson off his head.

"But when they returned later to show friends the trick, unbeknownst to them the wind had changed direction." He rushed his hat forward. "This time, it sucked the man's hat *into* the hole."

"Haha. Sweet." Ciarán chuckled.

"Certainly is." Ranger Todd smiled. "They've recorded 75 mile-per-hour gusts in that opening! Today we know the air stream is related to different atmospheric pressures between the cave and surface. This is actually one of the most complex barometric caves in the world and people come from all over to study it. But back then? That hat trick was one big mystery."

We all laughed.

"But we're not going in that way. You can take the Natural Entrance Tour or check it out on your own." He brought us outside and motioned in the opposite direction at a tall sandstone structure. "We're taking the elevator."

"Bummer," whispered Aislínn.

"Don't worry." The ranger winked. "I promise. This brings you a *lot* deeper into the cave, past *way* more interesting formations."

We followed him to the elevator building, built in the 1930's by the Civilian Conservation Corps, President Franklin D. Roosevelt's New Deal program that employed out-of-work men from low-income families. "You wouldn't

286

believe how much the CCC did in so many places," enthused the ranger. "They really helped make our national parks what they are today!"

He pushed a button to open the elevator doors. One man asked anxiously, "So this is over 80 years old?"

"No," assured Todd. "The building's pretty much the same, but the elevator's been replaced a couple of times and fully inspected."

He herded us into the metal carrier. In seconds we landed 204 feet below ground. We exited into a dark, chilly world of rock, the only illumination from the lamp in Todd's hand.

"Those brothers with the hats?" He spoke while he guided us along a narrow passage toward the first of many chambers with names like *Temple Room, Monte Cristo's Palace* and *Bachelor's Quarters*. "They never went in the cave. But later that year, curious locals ventured through the small opening and explored with torches and kerosene lanterns. Each time they went a little further on the craggy drops and ledges."

"Jeez," I murmured. We walked comfortably on fairly level pathways with safety rails. Although still dim, periodic bulbs let us glimpse the deep, ragged caverns on either side that greeted these original adventurers. "How the heck did they climb in with torches? What happened if they tripped?"

The ranger turned and shrugged. "That's all they had. Good thing rocks don't easily catch fire. Probably the scariest part was when they ran out of fuel and got lost in pitch blackness."

He moved forward again. "But it had to be more dangerous for the gals, tripping over long dresses and all."

Aislínn, watching her steps, looked up. "No kidding? Women came in here, too? Cool!"

"Sure did. In their bonnets and skirts. I've seen plenty of old pictures."

Though thrilled to hear females partook in the exploration, I couldn't imagine clambering hundreds of feet underground into mysterious dark tunnels with a prairie dress and measly lantern. It certainly made me want to shout out for those audacious pioneer women.

In our first "room," the ranger proudly pointed to boxwork, a geologic formation abundant in Wind Cave but rarely seen elsewhere. Looking like a web woven by cyborg arachnids, it hung in delicate clusters from the ceiling and walls. Its intersecting strands seemed so fragile that a wrong touch might break them, but Todd assured us they were hard as, well, rock. Calcite to be specific.

He explained most cave formations, scientifically known as "speleothems," stemmed from dripping water. "But boxwork origins remained a puzzle.

Theories abound, but no one knows for sure how it got here and why it's found almost exclusively in Wind Cave."

"Bet it was Spiderman!" Sean flicked his hand to shoot imaginary projectiles from his fingertips. "Wffffffffffttt…pshhhhhhhhaw…drrrrrrrrrrup…"

"Yeah, right!" agreed his siblings. Everyone in our small group chuckled.

As we continued, Todd told us that in 1897, local newspapers reported the cave to be three miles long. "Today, we've surveyed another 140, and we're still discovering more!"

I had no idea how he kept track of where we were in the multi-layered cave system. At one point we climbed 89 steps to the upper level, where delightful popcorn and frostwork formations decorated cave walls. Then

POPCORN, FROST & OTHER TREATS

The inner life of Wind Cave is as diverse as its above-ground prairies. Its maze of passages teem with wonders. They mainly consist of calcite, the most common rock-forming mineral in the world (it's a main ingredient in marble and limestone.) While other caves are famous for stalactites (hanging from the ceiling) and stalagmites (growing from the ground), these common formations are not found in Wind Cave. Instead, here are a few of the wonderful "speleothems" or formations seen in the 143-miles of cave:

Boxwork – thin blades of honeycomb-shaped calcite cross one another at various angles, creating 3-D "boxes" that project from the walls and ceilings. Rare in other caves, boxwork is abundant in Wind Cave's mid and lower levels.

Popcorn – small knobby growths of calcite on cave walls.

Helictite bushes – large growths of calcite that branch and twist like gnarled trees from the cave floor.

Frostwork – delicate needle-like growths of calcite or its cousin, aragonite. It seems to flourish in higher airflow, so evaporation may play a role in its formation.

Calcite rafts – thin sheets of calcite that float on the surface of Calcite Lake in the deepest part of the cave.

Gypsum crystals, flowers and cotton – In the cave's dryer areas, gypsum (containing calcium and sulfur) is found in anemone-like clusters on the floor. There are also curved and coiled "flower" crystals and "cotton" puffs of gypsum.

we descended again and followed our guide through a labyrinth of paths.

After the deepest descent Todd had us stop and cover our closed eyes. "Ready? Now open them."

I couldn't see at all. Our gasps and giggles magnified the visual void. I flailed my arm until I felt Tom next to me. Seconds later, the ranger's lamp clicked on. "Now you know what total darkness *really* looks like."

Sean grinned. "That was totally cool."

Aislínn shook her head. "Yeah, as long as you know the light's coming back on. Imagine when those kerosene lamps blew out?"

In all, we walked two-thirds of a mile, went hundreds of feet down and left with a whole new wonderful ecosphere in our heads.

Before parting, Ranger Todd mentioned that Wind Cave had been used for commercial mining prior to becoming a national park in 1903. Once again, I offered deep gratitude for the American leaders who had the vision to protect our natural treasures.

"Ow. Ow. Ow," joked Tom, shading his eyes when we emerged from the elevator into startling sunlight. The rays did feel fabulous after all that dark.

With the kids animatedly recapping their underground excitement, we wandered past the visitor center and found the natural cave entrance. Tom laughed. "I've seen groundhog holes bigger than this."

As we got closer, an unmistakable breeze wafted up from inside. Sean and I took turns snuggling backwards into the tiny opening, but only went down to our waists. My admiration grew even more for those frontier women!

On pins and needles

Early that morning, our trusty Coleman stove broke, failing to light for Tom's coffee. He figured out the culprit and looked up where we could get a replacement part. We left Wind Cave for a shop in Hill City about 30 miles north.

Rather than follow a direct route, we opted to take Needles Highway, known for spectacular roadside granite spires and one-lane tunnels. By then, the bikers were up and moving, so I again jimmied for position, a whale in the procession of minnows.

Just before the first scenic switchback, a downed Suzuki blocked the road. Wavy skid marks stopped at its horizontal rear tire, where the back fender hovered at a strange angle. Two black leather jackets tried to lift the cycle. A couple of other bikers stopped to help. I inched behind the traffic skirting the scene.

"Holy shit." Tom rubbernecked out his window. "Good thing no one's hurt."

Not even a quarter mile later, one of a pair of small Hondas in front of us slid sideways and clattered to the pavement. The driver landed hard on his shoulder. Although keeping distance behind them, I still had to slam on my brakes.

"What the…?" Tom blurted. Incredulous, we had no idea what caused the accident. He leaned out and yelled, "Hey, man, you okay?"

Other cyclists purred by on our right to assist. Soon, half a dozen arrived at the crash. "We should go," Tom suggested. "I think we're just in the way here."

I crawled slowly around. The kids knelt to look out the rear window. Aislínn announced, "He's up! Walking around."

"Thank god." I took a breath, unnerved. We heard a siren in the distance. "I wonder if that's for the first accident or this one. Sheesh!"

Tom nodded. "Like I said, amateur hour. Some of these guys never ride up these kinds of hills and switchbacks. Hate to see their tow-truck bill!"

I grew increasingly annoyed that we couldn't stop and admire the famous Cathedral Spires. Bikes crowded every pull-out. At least we made it to the first tunnel without another calamity.

Cycles lined up in twos and threes waiting their turn for the single-lane hole in the mountain. As if their engines weren't loud enough, we wound up behind a tricked out Harley blasting ZZ Top so loudly that it shook The Couch, and that was *before* we entered the opening.

Once inside, my neck muscles turned into high-tension wires. The revving and rock 'n roll exploded against the tunnel. I thought my eardrums would blow out. Or the rock walls would avalanche around us.

"WHAT. AN. A-HOLE!" My scream was barely audible. I gripped the steering wheel so hard the veins in my wrists surfaced.

The kids laughed. Tom, much more noise-tolerant and also a ZZ Top fan, smiled. "TRY TO RELAAAAAX."

A jam of motorcycles made it nearly impossible for us to squeeze out the other end. Like a sea of worms, they wriggled aside until I could finally press through.

PINNACLE PATHWAY

Former South Dakota Gov. Peter Norback personally marked the entire 14 miles of Needles Highway on foot and horseback. The spectacular hour-long drive, which opened in 1922, winds through pine and spruce forests as well as meadows ringed by birch and aspen. Highlights include rugged granite formations and two one-lane stone tunnels that are about eight feet wide and twelve feet high.

At the second tunnel, a retiree with his spouse in a sidecar somehow lost control and banged into the stone wall.

"This is effin crazy." Ciarán shook his head.

Sean giggled. "Old people bumper cars."

This time we did stop. They were fine. I couldn't say the same for me. The offspring chalked it off as entertainment. I remained shaken. So much for a peaceful connection with the stunning geography around Needles Highway.

Gems and gravel

We made our way to the hardware store and Tom picked up the stove part. On the ride back to camp, I spontaneously pulled into a rock and mineral shop, the second we'd seen along the pleasantly sparse highway. The peanut gallery moaned. Tom gave them a look in the rearview.

"Maaaa, let's just…" Aislínn started.

"You can wait here," I cut her off. "I'm going in."

They all followed, glad they did. Next to the burl magic in Oregon, this became my favorite store of the trip. So many Black Hills treasures crammed the deceptively small wooden shack. Dusty nooks and crannies hid all kinds of stones, fossils and raw hunks of gems. Geode chimes and delicate quartz hung from the rafters. Everyone found something they loved. I still adore my fist-sized chunk of mint green calcite crystal.

Nearly back at Blue Bell campground, Tom spotted a small sign by a narrow gravel road: Mount Coolidge Lookout and Fire Tower. I slowed to a stop.

"Bet there's not a lot of bikers up there. Definitely off the beaten path."

"Noooooooo," Ciarán whined. "Let's just go back."

I turned in. After the first blind curve my eldest stopped tapping my headrest and started admiring the scenery. For 1.7 winding, stony miles, we snaked to the top of Mount Coolidge. Tom called it. Only a few motorcycles parked at the summit, not surprising given the road's freaky steep drop-offs and lack of guardrails. If a biker spun out, they'd be a goner.

We relaxed against a stone wall surrounding the three-story fire tower. I closed my eyes against the healing balm of sunshine. Tom walked over to an interpretive display and announced. "Hey, we're at the highest point in Custer State Park… 6,023 feet."

I spun slowly to take in the magnificent view. "Look!" I grinned. "The Cathedral Spires!" It might not have been the roadside perspective we originally intended, but I swelled with appreciation at Mother Nature's masterpieces steepling into the brilliant blue sky. No wonder the sculptural pillars earned National Landmark registry.

Ciarán, peering east, spied another highlight. "Must be the Badlands. We should go there!"

"Too far," dismissed Tom at the exact moment I said, "Maybe."

Badlands National Park, 60 miles away, wasn't on our list. But with bikers swarming around Custer, it could be a great diversion. I raised my eyebrows, about to say something.

Tom disregarded me and quickly read another sign. "This was one of the last projects by the Civilian Conservation Corps in the late 1930's. The rangers still use it today to spot fires and send dispatches."

Aislínn, scanning the west, ignored him. "Is that Crazy Horse?"

Sean squinted. "Yep. I think I see him."

I joined them but couldn't make out a thing in the distant cliff. "Where?"

Both pointed; I still just saw a bare peak. "Forget it mom, you're so blind."

The day before, en route to the campsite, I'd pulled into the parking lot at Crazy Horse Memorial, where a likeness of the Indian chief was being carved into a Black Hills mountainside. Still in shock from Devils Tower and our Custer lunch, I took one pass through the ocean of chrome and hurried away. At least my kids could enjoy the figure from this passive perch.

We relaxed atop Mount Coolidge for quite a while, enjoying our birds-eye view of the dense, dark forests that native Lakota called "paha sapa" or "hills that are black."

Back at camp, it seemed too early for dinner but we hadn't had lunch.

"It's time for linner!" sing-songed Aislínn, rifling through the cooler.

"Nah, it's dunch," giggled her younger brother, shoving her away. He piled the contents on the picnic table.

We only had a couple more meals to make, so I urged them to use our supplies. Within minutes, Ciarán began sautéing our last peppers and onions next to a few hot dogs. He opened a can of beans. Sean chopped chicken breasts and threw them in the pan. Aislínn grabbed tortillas, cheese, peanut butter and bread.

When they placed the buffet on the table, I laughed out loud.

"It's *everything* burritos." Sean bowed. "Help yourself ma'am."

I nodded, but remained a purist, layering a few pieces of chicken, lettuce, cheddar and beans on my taco. The others tried the works.

"You're putting bread on your burrito?" I mocked Sean.

"It's not bread. It's gently toasted cubes," he said with the lilted staccato of a five-star maître 'd. Then he snickered. "You told us to use stuff up."

The cabin across from ours had a motorcycle and old pickup out front. Right then, a lean young man emerged onto his porch in jeans, boots and a black t-shirt. He nodded hello with a quick head tilt.

We all greeted him back. I asked if he wanted something to eat. He smiled and declined, then hopped onto his Harley and revved off.

"Ha ha," Ciarán lifted his wrap. "You see him eying my PB and dog burrito?"

"Probably thinks we're nuts." Tom chuckled and reached for another tortilla to load. "That's okay. More for us."

Wild and crazy

We lazed around as the afternoon tiptoed into evening. After returning from the restroom, Tom asked if we wanted to try Crazy Horse again. He'd just seen a flyer about a laser light show every night after dark.

Our response was soggier than the left-over tacos. The kids wanted more down time; I wanted nothing that would bring me close to motorcycles.

"C'mon. It'll be fun," he urged. "There won't be that many bikers now."

Still no takers. He persisted. "You'll be sorry! It's our last chance."

For me, the warning served as a gut punch about our trip's end. To the kids, it probably meant happy code for "almost home." Either way, it got us moving. We piled back into The Couch for the half-hour ride.

We'd barely taken off when Sean eyed a flock of wild turkeys in a field, at least 40 of them. I pulled over. They scurried around in the grass, long necks flouncing and darting into the ground for food. Then one flapped furiously and flew to a nearby tree.

"Going beddy-bye for the night," observed my youngest.

"What?" I asked.

"Yeah, wha?" echoed Aislínn.

"Turkeys hang on the ground during the day, but sleep in trees. You know, so predators can't get them?"

I snorted. "I didn't even know they could fly."

"Me neither," agreed Tom. "Thought they were like ostriches."

"Nah. Thanksgiving turkeys are probably too fat. But these wild turkeys buzz up at dusk to roost and come back down at dawn. They can't soar around like hawks or seagulls. But they definitely get from one place to the other."

"I can see that," I snickered. Dozens of birds flailed in various stages of airborne action. Everyone cracked up at the awkward wrangling of wings. Our eyes followed a few of them into the trees, but shadows made it too hard to discern their resting spots. "Not exactly the picture of grace."

"Yeah, they're never winning *Dancing With the Stars*," quipped Tom.

"But it's sooooo sweet." Sean leaned out his window until all the birds had disappeared into the branches.

Lucky for us, the avian display turned out to be just the first treat of the night. Crazy Horse wound up being crazy good!

From a distance, the mountaintop seemed flat, like a mesa, yet the cliff had a large hole straight through it and the front dropped off in angles too level to be nature's handiwork. The nearer we got, the smooth profile of the Oglala Sioux legend grew clearer.

Once in the parking lot, devoid of many motorcycles, we regarded the deep-set eyes, sharp nose and proud chin carved into the 6,532-foot peak. By night's end, we'd be blown away by what that face in the granite represented.

At first, sculptor Korczak Ziolkowski was just determined to create the world's largest statue. That became his initial mission when Lakota elders asked the renowned artist in 1939 to memorialize the mythic warrior on a monument in their sacred Black Hills. The sculptor spent years making a life-sized model of Crazy Horse riding a stallion, hair flying in the wind, arm outstretched over his ancestral lands.

But by the first blast in 1948 into what Ziolkowski ceremoniously named Mount Thunderhead, his purpose had exploded as well. After immersing himself in Indian history and culture for so many years, the Polish-American artist vowed to preserve, protect and champion everything Native American. Hence the sprawling campus we were at, boasting its impressive welcome center, museum and Native American educational-cultural complex.

With these other buildings competing for his attention, it took Ziolkowski

AT-A-GLANCE:
CRAZY HORSE MEMORIAL

In 1939, Lakota chiefs invited Boston sculptor Korczak Ziolkowski to carve a likeness of the great warrior Crazy Horse into the sacred Black Hills. The work continues under the direction of the late artist's children, grandchildren and supporters. The Crazy Horse campus includes an extensive Welcome Center, the Indian Museum of North America, and the Native American Education and Cultural Center, featuring more than 12,000 historic and contemporary items. Summer visitors can watch evening laser light shows. Two special night blasts are held each year.

LOCATION: Located in the Black Hills of South Dakota on Crazy Horse Memorial Highway (Us Hwy 16/385), the campus is nine miles south of Hill City and four miles north of Custer, SD. It is about a half-hour southwest of Mount Rushmore.

OPEN: Crazy Horse Memorial is open year round. Hours vary for attractions.

COST: $12-$30 per vehicle depending on occupancy; $7 per motorcycle or bicycle. Bus rides to the bottom of the mountain are $4 per person.

INFO: https://crazyhorsememorial.org

TOWERING OVER PRESIDENTS

Crazy Horse's face, finished in 1998, is nearly 90 feet tall. (For comparison, the heads on Mount Rushmore are 60 feet.) When complete, the horse's head alone will as tall as a 20-story skyscraper. The massive Crazy Horse Memorial is designed to be the largest in the world, at more than 640 feet long and 560 feet high. It honors the Lakota Chief killed in captivity in 1877 after fighting removal of his people to a reservation. He was 37 years old.

---

50 years just for Crazy Horse's face. Sadly, the sculptor didn't live to see its completion. His vision, however, thrived through many of his 10 children and 23 grandchildren.

Along with the mountain memorial, they embraced his dream of one day building a Native American University and a medical training center on the Crazy Horse campus. Like their patriarch, Ziolkowski's descendants refused federal funding, relying on donations from the million plus visitors who passed through each year.

We watched this amazing story in a Welcome Center movie, Tom and I whispering to each other. How had we never heard of this place?

Moved by the art, artifacts and anguished history, we wandered out to a viewing veranda with Ziolkowski's Crazy Horse prototype. Arresting in its own right, the white marble statue paled in comparison to the actual carving lined up in the distance. Although only the face was visible, we could really "see" the stallion and its rider's pointing arm in the leveled blocks of mountainside.

As dusk descended, two teen-aged brothers in Oglala Lakota dress drew our attention to a large outdoor platform. The white of their long calf-skin jackets glowed against the violet and rose-streaked sky. The older one, a college elementary education major, talked about his dream of teaching on the nearby reservation and giving local children greater opportunities for success. The younger brother began playing beautiful flute music and the pair entertained us with traditional song and dance until darkness fell.

Then bright purple and green beams leapt onto Mount Thunderhead, illuminating the cliffs. Music and audio effects swirled in the night air as laser animations dramatized the heritage and contributions of Native Americans. Immersed in sound and light, we gave ourselves fully to this unusual outdoor theater.

We had no idea what to expect when we pulled into the parking lot hours

---

ELECTRONIC EXTRAVAGANZA

The nightly *Legends in Light* at Crazy Horse Memorial turns Mount Thunderhead into a 500-foot screen. The show is produced with the industry's biggest lasers, 8,800 watts of stereo sound, and three of the world's largest slide projectors. A closed-loop ice-making system cools the lasers without drawing on water resources. When first launched, Ruth Ziolkowski, the late wife of late sculptor Korczak Ziolkowski explained, "This is laser-light storytelling to illuminate our cultural diversity, celebrate our similarities, and encourage better understanding and harmony among races and nations."

---

earlier. But Crazy Horse Memorial turned out to be another surprise gem in our journey. On our way back to camp, Aislínn summed it up over Dairy Queen sundaes. "Man, I wish I had a million dollars to give them to finish that carving!"

Pronghorn and presidents

Ciarán, Sean and I rose before sunrise for our final Great Animal Search. Like seasoned explorers, we jumped into The Couch, snacks on board. Sean took his lookout in the front while Ciarán readied the camera in the rear. We headed towards Custer State Park's 18-mile Wildlife Loop.

Twists and turns through the prairies and pine hills claimed most of my attention. But a dull edge gnawed at my focus. I recognized it immediately: the slinky stinky blues again. Today was our last real outing.

The boys weren't 100 percent, either. When we came upon a grazing bison herd, we barely mustered appreciation, took some photos and continued on. Was the joy-factor nil because we'd already seen hundreds? Or were we each just preoccupied?

The miles wore on. Then Sean spied a family of pronghorns, maybe the same ones we'd seen the day before. This time I rolled to a stop just yards away. The mother lifted her head, doe-eyed and graceful. Her fawn glanced from behind her legs, retreated in a circle, then looked again. We giggled at the adorable peekaboo.

Ciarán leaned out with his lens. The mom and babe practically posed. A tingly thrill pulsed through my veins. The energy in The Couch amped up in an instant, perhaps from the magic of nature, perhaps from just being present. Who cared? Suddenly it was game on again.

As dawn brightened into day, we struck gold with more amazing close-ups:

DAWDLING DONKEYS

Burros were brought to the Black Hills decades ago to haul visitors to the mountaintop. When the rides discontinued, the pack animals were set free. Today their charismatic descendants roam around the meadows and pine savannas. A relative of the horse, these amusing equines boast long ears and muzzle, bright eyes and, when you are at the correct angle, a goofy kind of smile.

---

a large herd of elk with their calves, dozens of mule and white-tailed deer, big horn sheep, prairie dogs, more turkeys, and of course, many of the park's 1,300 free-roaming buffalo.

Our highlight, though, was a lone wild burro. He stared at us with huge dark eyes ringed by beige circles that matched his long muzzle. His lower body stood hidden in a field of tall grasses so golden that they glowed against his rich brown coat. It seemed he was grinning at us. We couldn't stop smiling in return.

We saw no motorcycles, or any vehicles for that matter. Only wildlife. Once again, early did the trick. It might not have been Yellowstone's Lamar Valley, but the park loop was a great kick-off for our final day of adventure. When we returned to camp, Tom and Aislínn waited ready for our next stop: Mount Rushmore.

Commanding gaze

The morning's twisting route seemed downright monotonous compared to the motorway that took us to the sculpted presidents. Besides passing through some of the most beautiful scenery in the region, Iron Mountain Road, with its hundreds of extreme curves, also represented an amazing example of 1930s technology and environmental artistry.

Wooden "pigtail bridges," designed to navigate steep Black Hills' elevations and drops, spiraled like roller coaster coils. An architectural feat when built in the 1930s by the Civilian Conservation Corps, these looping spans remained pretty remarkable to the Brennans all these decades later.

We were still the only ones on the road, except for a dozen bison lolling on the pavement with their young. "Wouldn't want to be a biker caught on one side of this buffalo jam. It's freaky enough in an SUV," snarked Tom as I inched through the mob. "And I hope no bulls are in *there*!"

He pointed toward a darkened one-lane tunnel looming ahead. I smiled. "Nope. Looks okay."

> ## THE IMPOSSIBLE ROAD
>
> Although the speed limit is 35, you shouldn't go more than 20 mph on the impressive Iron Mountain Road (SD-16A), constructed in the 1930s to connect Custer State Park and Mount Rushmore National Memorial. In fact, according to its champion, former Gov. Peter Norbeck, (aka the father of the state park), to really do the 17-mile journey justice "you should get out and walk." The road that engineers once warned couldn't be built has: 314 curves, 14 switchbacks, 3 tunnels and 3 pigtails (unique spiraling wooden bridges), not to mention 4 stone presidents visible through the landscape. Some say it is the most captivating thoroughfare in America!

As I crept into the entrance, we all inhaled with wonder. Like a museum masterpiece, Mount Rushmore stood clearly framed in the light at the end of the passageway. The white granite monument and brilliant blue sky popped against the tunnel's dark interior. I rolled to a stop and Ciarán leaned out his window for some spectacular shots.

Further on, we drove through two more square openings cut through granite mountainside, each perfectly aligned to border the four presidents. These portholes made us appreciate even more the imagination of the highways' original advocate.

A few hairpin switchbacks and stomach-turning bends later, we arrived at Mt. Rushmore's empty parking lot. Stanchions and cones blocked off huge swaths of blacktop for the hordes of bikers sure to come.

In the Information Center, floor-to-ceiling windows offered a five-star view of the memorial. Too bad its cafeteria served only a one-star breakfast. It did the job, though, curbing everyone's hunger whines.

We filed out to the Avenue of Flags, the monument's official entryway. Emblems from 56 U.S. states and territories waved from tall pillars on either side of the walkway, a symphony of color against the brilliant sky.

It took Aislínn about three seconds to realize the flags were mounted in alphabetical order. She jogged to the center of the long line-up and signaled. "There it is. New Jersey!"

"Good eye, Bean." Ciarán loped to the pole, nodding appreciatively. We all gazed up and admired our coat of arms on its butterscotch yellow background.

The avenue led us to Grandview Terrace, the park's main viewing area, where we stopped for quick balcony views of the presidents. Next, a short *"Mount Rushmore: The Shrine"* film in Lincoln Borglum Visitor Center gave us a brief low-down about the site, the sculptor and his achievement.

Yet it wasn't until we studied the museum exhibits and artist's studio that we glimpsed the real drama behind the carving: money woes, cultural clashes and personal struggles aplenty, all with an Oscar-worthy cast of characters.

First came the South Dakota historian who wanted to promote visitation to the region and suggested a mountainside sculpture. He pictured western heroes like Buffalo Bill Cody.

Sculptor Gutzon Borglum scoffed at that triteness. He had a loftier vision, including none less that the U.S. presidents. He selected George Washington as the father of our country, Thomas Jefferson as author of the Declaration of Independence, Teddy Roosevelt for opening the waters of the east and west by completing the Panama Canal, and Abraham Lincoln for preserving the Union in one of America's darkest periods.

A maelstroms of artistic, political and media debate followed. Everyone had an opinion about the project. Finally, support, and federal funding, came through for Borglum and he started blasting in 1927.

"Says here the workers had to climb 506 steps every day to get to those faces," noted Tom. "I'd be too tired to work once I got there."

"Better than the roads at Glacier," piped in Ciarán. "Remember? They had to dangle hundreds of feet on rope swings!"

I elbowed Tom and smiled. See, they *were* listening.

We examined Borglum's life-sized model of what he originally planned: the presidents from head to waist in dress attire with expressive hands. Then we looked past the marble prototype out a large glass window to the

AT-A-GLANCE:
MOUNT RUSHMORE NATIONAL MEMORIAL
The massive sculpture carved into 5,725-foot high Mount Rushmore brings American history to life with 60-foot-high faces of U.S. Presidents George Washington, Thomas Jefferson, Theodore Roosevelt and Abraham Lincoln. It was created from 1927-1941 under the direction of sculptor Gutzon Borglum and his son, Lincoln. The 1.2-million-acre memorial park features the sculptor's studio, a museum with interactive exhibits and several trails.

LOCATION: Located in the Black Hills of South Dakota, the Memorial is off Route 244 in Keystone, SD. From the north, take US Highway 16 to Keystone; from the south, follow Highway 385.

OPEN: The Memorial is open year-round (buildings are closed on Dec. 25.)

COST: The Memorial is free, but parking fees apply: $11/per vehicle; $5 for seniors.

INFO: https://www.nps.gov/moru/index.htm

THE OTHER MT. RUSHMORE HISTORY

It might often be hailed as the "Shrine of Democracy," but for many Native Americans, Mt. Rushmore symbolizes betrayal and desecration. The 1868 Fort Laramie Treaty gave the Sioux nation their sacred Black Hills in perpetuity, only to have the land violently taken away again after gold was discovered there just seven years later. Conflicts escalated between federal troops and the Sioux until the U.S. "won" in a final clash in 1890: the massacre at Wounded Knee. Nearly four decades later, sculptor Gutzon Borglum, a known Ku Klux Klan member, designed a monument celebrating white leaders who Native Americans still hold responsible for killing their ancestors and stealing their land.

real thing. Except for the beginning of Washington's lapels, only rugged rock showed below the four chins. Financial hurdles, compounded by the sculptor's death in 1941, forced construction to end with just the heads. Unlike at Crazy Horse, no champions remained to finish the work.

It didn't matter. The immense, albeit incomplete, likenesses pumped up tourism beyond expectations. When opened in 1941, the memorial attracted nearly 400,000 visitors. By 2018, that annual number swelled to 2.3 million.

Hundreds must have arrived while we explored the museum. The half-mile Presidential Trail teemed as we strolled to the mountain's base. There were so many angles from which to capture the famous faces that we finally put our camera away and just walked until the growing growls of motorcycles from the parking lot kicked us into escape mode.

Not so Scenic

Exiting under the fluttering flags, Ciarán linked his arm into mine. "Soooo, beautiful, fun, adventurous mother..."

I stopped, pulled away and eyeballed him.

"Remember yesterday when you said maybe we could hit the Badlands?"

"Ohhhh, yeah!" Aislínn and Sean double teamed. "We should *go!*"

Tom scowled. "It's a least 90 minutes away. A lot more once we're in the park." He flicked his chin in my direction. "But it's up to you. You're driving."

I looked at my watch and shrugged. "It's 11:30. Think we'll still have time for the hike later?"

"Yesss!" The teen chorus rang out.

Our plan had been to take naps then try Cathedral Spires again on foot, where we'd avoid bikers and get in one last good trail. But a spontaneous adventure? Suggested by my offspring? My heart swelled.

Heading east across the rectangle that is South Dakota, the rich Black Hills greenery changed abruptly. Suddenly we found ourselves cruising through a dry, eerie landscape.

"Ho-ly," I whispered, dividing my focus between the two-lane road and the otherworldly vista around us. "It's amazing!"

Buttes and spires rose on the horizon like the Manhattan skyline. Only instead of steel and glass, this metropolis consisted of colorful striated rock. At first, the pinks and yellows appeared as sun glare until we realized they were encrusted in the formations like layers on a cake.

"Baaaaaa-dy-lands! It's the Baaaaaa-dy-lands!" rapped Ciarán, drumming on the seat. The other two joined in, circle dancing their torsos.

"Gonna be cool to see them up close," said Tom, surprisingly relaxed with the change of plans.

A few minutes of gorgeous gazing later, Ciarán said, "Hey, ya think there's a bathroom there?"

I eyed him in the mirror. "Why?"

"Why d'ya think?"

"Duh. But how urgent?"

"Pretty."

I sighed. We couldn't escape the Brennan refrain. Mind-boggling beauty one minute; intestinal intrusions the next. We had no idea where a visitor center might be once we got to the park, so I exited the highway at the next sign: Scenic, S.D.

The town might have been at one time. Scenic that is, like in the days of traders, trappers and traveling missionaries. But not when we rolled down the dirt main street. Crust and cobwebs covered storefront windows. Rust dimpled many doorways. An empty old train depot stood amidst fraying buildings.

We had unknowingly stumbled upon a bona fide ghost town. This might have been exciting, except nature still called.

Our choices were limited. I parked in front of the Longhorn Saloon where cattle skulls hung from wooden posts attached to the roof. A faded sign revealed its year of establishment: 1906.

"Looks like a Hollywood set," declared Tom. "Think it's open?"

I shrugged and got out with Ciarán.

He tried the well-worn wooden door. It creaked opened. We hesitated a few seconds, waiting for the other to go first. I chuckled nervously. Then we sort of edged in together. Sawdust blanketed the floor, broken up by scuffled footprints here and there. But we didn't see a soul.

Strange ceiling markings caught our attention: fraternity-style initials, weird names and odd designs. We squinted to figure them out.

After a few moments, Ciarán motioned upward. "Brands."

"What?"

"Brands."

I searched again, immediately thinking Nike, Coke, Apple, Ford. I looked at him perplexed.

"You know? What ranchers put on their cows?"

I nodded. "Ohhhhhh, yeah. You're right."

Shafts of light sloped through dirty windows onto a long wooden bar. Ciarán hopped onto one of the stools, made of a tractor seat atop an oil barrel. A large faded sign hung on the wall, "NO INDIANS ALLOWED," with a big X over the "NO." We could imagine the room filled with poker games and gunslingers.

Curiously, all interior doors were locked and we still needed a restroom so we left and found an old dusty General Store down the block.

The elderly woman behind the counter kindly let Ciarán use her facilities. While I waited, she shared the scoop on Scenic. In its Wild West heyday, the bustling railroad town boasted a hotel, school, bank, two restaurants, three gas stations, several churches and a huge dance hall. Plus, of course, the landmark saloon.

The Great Depression jump-started its downfall. In an attempt to save the burg, a local rodeo legend, Twila Merrill, purchased parcels little by little until she owned most of Scenic.

"She's the one who X'ed out that "NO" on the Indian sign in the bar," the woman explained. But in 2011, Twila sold the entire struggling town for less than $800,000 to the Iglesia ni Cristo Church.

I hmmmm-ed and nodded while the shop owner embellished. She told me that through it all, Scenic retained its U.S. Post Office, which had the area's only federal employee. "She's been there for decades!"

A ghost town with a working zip code? I couldn't help but smile.

"Do you get many people stopping by?"

"Sure do." She grinned. "People love to take a look-see. Believe it or not, some days we can get dozens and dozens a' cars come through here."

I didn't want to leave without spending money, so I bought a bunch of chips. But back in The Couch, I did the math. If she got even ten bucks from half the tourists who passed through, she made quite a living in Scenic!

Oh sooooo bad!

Before we even reached the highway again, Ciarán had everyone howling with his descriptions of the saloon. In no time, the kids had turned the saloon into a horror flick. Loose floorboards hid skeletons. Bloody finger-prints smeared the dust on the bar.

"Yeah! With deep gouges from fingernails," declared Aislínn.

Sean slowly scratched the back of my seat. "Heeeeellllllllllp meeeeeee!"

I smiled. Not just at their story. But at their unabashed enthusiasm; at what bubbled up when we were all stuck together with nothing else to do. For miles and miles they laughed out loud, trying to outdo each other.

When we entered Badlands National Park, though, everyone grew quiet. The close-up view around us seemed unlike anywhere else on earth.

"Those layers..." I stared in astonishment, unable to come up with the right adjective.

"Yeah," said Aislínn. "Kinda looks like ginormous versions of the sand art we used to make in arts and crafts."

"Haha. I remember those. You're right." Sean leaned across his sister to get a better look out her window. "Like a giant poured them."

We slowly rolled onto the 31-mile Badlands Loop Scenic Byway (SD 240) and got out at the first overlook. Endless plateaus stretched in front of us, separated by a maze of deep gorges seemingly too perilous for mere humans.

In fact, when early French-Canadian fur trappers encountered little water and extreme temperatures as they tried to cross these crevices, they called the place *les mauvais terres pour traverse* or "bad lands to travel through." Early Lakota had already labeled it *mako sica* or "land bad."

AT-A-GLANCE:
BADLANDS NATIONAL PARK

The Badlands consist of 244,000 acres of colorful buttes, pinnacles, and spires along with the largest protected mixed-grass prairie in the U.S. The park also features the world's greatest animal fossil beds from the Oligocene Epoch.

LOCATION: Located in the southwestern section of South Dakota, the park is 75 miles east of Rapid City, SD. I-90 is directly north of the park and provides access to the Hwy 240 Badlands Loop Road.

OPEN: The park is open year round. (The visitor center is closed on certain federal holidays.)

COST: $25/per vehicle; $15 for motorcycles, bikes; $12 individuals

INFO: https://www.nps.gov/badl/index.htm

FIERCE REMAINS

Saber-toothed cats. Huge rhino-like ancestors. Ancient camels. Three-toed horses. These are just some of the skeletons in the fossil beds in Badlands National Park – the world's greatest collection of mammal remains from the Oligocene Epoch over 30 million years ago. Prehistoric bones are still being discovered today.

But I could picture a giant easily hopscotching across the flattened peaks, perhaps to the immense castle pinnacles on the horizon with turrets striped in red, white and orange.

At another pull-off, we wandered along the edge of the roadside butte. Isolated clusters of stunning yellow coneflowers reached towards the blazing sun, their green stems and leaves moistly rich above the arid earth.

Ciarán laid down on the dirt to capture a close-up of the flowers with the layered mountains in the background, a photography trick he'd been honing the whole trip. "Man, that ground is hard." He hopped up and wiped his shirt. "How in the world do they grow here?"

How indeed. The power and destiny of seeds seemed as remarkable as the chiseled, unforgiving land from which they sprang.

Back on the loop, Aislínn read that the Badlands provided a home to many of the animals we'd seen in other parks: prairie dogs, mule deer, pronghorn, bison, coyotes and bighorn sheep. But its most famous residents were long gone. "Says here the Badlands are a hotbed of prehistoric fossils."

"Oh, yeah! This is where they found that Rocky Rex," enthused Sean, recalling the T. rex from the Museum of the Rockies. "Sweet!"

We could imagine a whole set of ancient creatures wandering this harsh, desolate landscape.

Looking at the map, Tom suggested hiking the popular Pinnacles Overlook that promised, unimaginably, even better views. But we never found out. At

HARSH GEOLOGY

Wind and water ravaged Badlands National Park for millions of years. Early travelers named the area for its challenging terrain and extreme weather. Modern geologists, however, have taken the human drama out of it and define badlands as "an environment in a dry climate created by extensive erosion of soft sedimentary rock." The picturesque colors are actually layers revealed by this erosion: volcanic ash (white), iron oxides (red, pink and orange), sand/gravel (tan and gray) and shale (purple and yellow).

the trailhead parking lot, rangers had cleared the pavement for a helicopter to land. One guard furiously waved his hand for vehicles to keep going. Even if we wanted to ask, we never would have heard anything in the deafening noise from the hovering chopper.

We snaked past and saw a biker splayed on the blacktop, horribly contorted.

The kids stared until the stream of traffic blocked their view. I shook my head and sighed. "It must have been one awful skid."

A-mazing tourist trap

Tom barely got involved in planning our route all those months ago, happily leaving it to Aislínn and me. Just once he looked at her list of South Dakota possibilities and weighed in.

"There's no way I'm going to Wall Drug," he had announced. "It's a huge tourist trap."

We forgot about it until I headed north out of Badlands National Park and a billboard teased: *How Far to Wall Drug? 8 miles!*

Tom mumbled in the front seat. But the peanut gallery geared up. By the third taunting sign, they hit full throttle.

"C'mon dad," urged Aislínn. "We pass it anyway."

"Nope, it's a rip-off. Not going there."

"We always do what *you* want," grumbled Ciarán

"Yeah," said Sean. "Not fair."

"Please dad. It's still so early," added Aislínn.

After the hundredth backseat plea, Tom growled, "Stop if you want. I'll stay in the car."

He didn't. After all that roadside hype, I wouldn't let him pass up at least a quick walk through the weird, wacky attraction that started in the 1930's as a tiny drugstore giving away free ice-water to weary travelers.

A Wild West façade united the tangle of connected buildings, clearly patch-worked over the decades. Inside, the jumble held a surprising cacophony of appeal. Western art museum? Check. Shooting gallery? Check. Ice cream

WALL DRUGOPOLIS

More than a million visitors a year wander through Wall Drug's sprawling cowboy-themed complex that occupies most of downtown Wall, S.D., and employs almost a third of its population. Located off exit 110 on I-90 at 510 Main St., Wall, SD, it's open daily from 6:30 am – 8 pm (call to verify: 605-279-2175). http://www.walldrug.com

MASTERFUL MARKETING

Ted and Dorothy Hustead turned their failing Wall Drug into a bustling enterprise through signs promising free ice water to parched travelers on their way to the newly opened Mount Rushmore Monument. Everyone who stopped to quench their thirsts usually spent a little on something else. The success of their homegrown publicity sent Ted into a billboard frenzy. He had thousands of wooden signs painted with catchy phrases like *"Wall I'll Be Drugged,"* and *"Wall Drug or Bust,"* and had them placed on roads in every state of the union. To this day, hundreds of billboards offering five cent coffee and free ice water still line Interstate 90. The drugstore walls are papered with snapshots of *"How Many Miles to Wall Drug?"* placards and bumper stickers taken all over the world, from France to the Taj Mahal. Even when I-90 bypassed Wall in the late 1960s, the Husteads tapped into their marketing creativity. They erected a 50-ton, 80-foot dinosaur with lighted eyes next to the freeway to remind travelers that Wall Drug was still open.

parlor? Taxidermied wildlife? Traveler's Chapel modeled on an 1850s Trappist monastery? Check, check and check. And the small pharmacy that started it all? Still there, the only operational drugstore for 50 miles around.

Eye candy crammed the knotty pine interior: totem poles, statues, stuffed animal heads and penny machines. A roaring life-sized T. rex and other mechanical thing-a-ma-jigs performed at every turn. It was clutter extraordinaire, almost too much to take in. Voices around us echoed our astonished, "Look at that one... Hey, check this out!"

The Apothecary Shoppe Museum, a replica of the original Wall Drug, stood across from a cafeteria where coffee remained five cents a cup. When Tom saw counters piled high with homemade fudge and donuts, he finally stopped grousing. He bought enough to ensure a sugar high for the rest of the day.

The famous free ice water remained available from a backyard patio well that pumped thousands of gallons a day cooled by 1.5 tons of man-made ice. The courtyard also offered corny photo ops, like a furry six-foot rabbit on wheels, a mini-Mount Rushmore and a giant fiberglass jackalope. What a hoot!

While my family sat on a bench relishing their sweets, I wandered through some of the quaint shops, impressed with their variety and uniqueness. Cars still piled in as we left Wall, marveling about where they could have possibly gotten all that stuff. Garage sales? Hollywood leftovers? Old amusement parks? Who knew? But they must've had a blast!

Was Wall Drug a tourist trap? Certainly. Was it worth the stop? Definitely!

Unbearable

The sugar did its trick, making everyone giggly silly on our way back to Custer. After passing an IHOP pancake restaurant in a Rapid City strip mall, Tom broke into spontaneous song.

"IHOP the eye cop, checks your eyes on a traffic stop."

"I'm down with brown, true with blue, but green's the one that gets me through," he improvised, poking my side on the word "green," my eye color.

We all laughed. After a few more forgettable verses, Ciarán asked, "Hey IHOP, what color are my eyes?"

Tom answered immediately. "Blue."

Sean followed suit. "What about me, eye cop?"

Tom smiled, with a little 'you kidding me' snort. "Blue."

"Okay, dad," chimed in Aislínn. "How about me?"

For effect, he dragged out his reply. "Blu-ue."

We all went quiet. The jolly chuckles stopped.

"What?" Aislínn and I reacted in unison. I gave Tom a sideways glance. The boys giggled.

Tom tried to turn in his seat, but Aislínn covered her face. "What color are my eyes, Dad?"

"They're not blue?"

"NO!"

I shook my head. The boys chuckled and yelled, "They're brown, dad. BROW-N!"

I didn't know whether I felt worse for Aislínn or Tom. But, with or without Van Morrison, he'd never again forget he had a lovely brown-eyed girl.

Aislínn got him back when conversation turned to state capitals. He insisted the place we were driving through, Rapid City, was the governing seat of South Dakota.

His daughter corrected him. "No, Dad. It's Pierre."

"No way. If it's not Rapid City, then it has to be Sioux Falls."

"Bet?"

The boys and I grinned. We knew we could always count on Aislínn for two things. Geography. And winning wagers. During those fifth-grade quizzes, she used to parade around the house chanting the names of the states and their capitals like lyrics to a pop hit. Plus, she rarely gambled unless it was a sure thing. We tried to warn Tom, but not too much. After all, he couldn't even identify her irises properly.

He ignored us anyway. "Bet!"

In less than a minute, he handed her $25 (yes, steep) and the rest of us cracked up. Shortly after, Sean spotted a huge roadside sign for Bear Country U.S.A: *Family fun adventure! A Unique Drive-Through Wildlife Park.*

Those darn billboards. They really worked. The kids again poured it on, begging to go since this was our last day to explore. As usual, Tom resisted; I gave in. I paid and we drove through what turned out to be a dreadful, sparse safari. We felt horrible for the few animals we observed and worried about their daily lives.

The only redeeming moments came in an area reserved for the wildlife babies. We had to park and walk its quarter-mile trail. This time Tom did stay in the car. The rest of us cooed over the antics of porcupines, foxes and other young 'uns segregated in pens. Adorable wrestling bear cubs held our attention for a while, but not one of us was sorry to leave.

Last (outdoor) supper

At 5:30 p.m., nearly 12 hours after we left that morning, we rolled back to our cabin. Too late for a hike, but that was okay. While I took a nice hot shower, Aislínn and Ciarán prepared the last of our food. Eating at the picnic table, we recounted our chock-full day of spontaneous sightseeing.

I washed and packed everything while the rest of the crew gathered wood for one more fire. With practiced ease, they started the blaze. I sank deeply into the canvas chair we purchased more than six weeks before. The kids had saved a half a bag of marshmallows and grahams. Sean splurged some of his stashed cash on chocolate bars from the camp store.

As they went to town on the s'mores, I stretched my legs and leaned as far back as I could. Flickers danced all over the darkening sky. I breathed out fully. We did it! We had our adventure. Days of not knowing the time. Not caring about dirty fingernails. Not tied to our screens.

I closed my eyes and savored the memories. We explored ruins. Climbed mountains. Soaked in hot springs. Threw snowballs. Ran rapids. Walked in caves. And, of course, overate.

Through the peaks and valleys – literal and emotional – I was truly blessed to have kids who were smart, funny and really good sports; to witness their charming moments of childlike relish and impressive displays of maturity.

Yes, how fortunate I was to have this remarkable journey that helped me better know my family, my country and even myself.

A sharp poke in my extended belly interrupted my thoughts. It came with the giggle I'd recognize anywhere. I opened my eyes to see Sean extending a stick with a perfectly browned crispy-gooey marshmallow.

"Last one, ma. It's for you."

Silly me, I almost cried.

Badlands

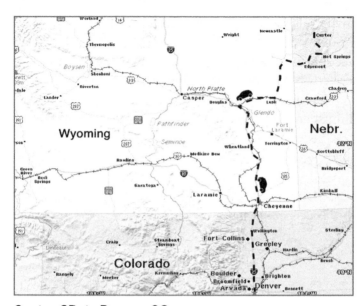

Custer, SD, to Denver, CO
6 hours

Chapter 21
Prairie Dog Farewell

After Tom loaded The Couch, I offered our newly arrived neighbors our camp chairs. They were thrilled. Although glad to keep them out of the trash, handing them over seemed like some kind of last rite to me.

We were just about to roll away when the biker across the path rushed to Tom's window.

"Hey y'all!" He offered a mini salute. "Sorry to bother ya, but I gotta head home. Thing is, my buddies were supposed to meet me here to help me get this big boy back on my truck." He snickered. "Guess 'n they overslept."

I could only imagine. He continued to chat as Tom and the boys opened their doors and walked toward his Harley.

"Lotsa folks like me tow their bikes, 'specially if you're driving far," he drawled, explaining he was from Tennessee. "We got Daytona Biker Week in Florida, but it ain't nothin' like Sturgis! This here's the best bikers in the world."

I rolled my eyes. Aislínn snorted from the back seat, catching me in the rearview. We both laughed. The males heaved the huge hunk of metal up the ramp onto his pick-up. I never realized how heavy they were. Thank goodness it didn't roll back.

"Man, I need another shower," announced Tom, dripping with sweat as he collapsed onto the front seat. The boys, stoked by their good deed, pumped fists as we once more headed south past Wind Cave National Park.

"Hey!" Aislínn rolled down her window. "Another prairie dog town!"

Sure enough, furry heads dotted the plain, an endearing view of cuteness! Good thing, too. Because after the adorable sighting, there wasn't much else of note. Eastern Wyoming is flat wide-open grassland. Aside from periodic trains passing on Union Pacific Railroad tracks, we saw miles and miles of nothing.

Clearly, we had started our sensory retreat. Weeks ago, we would have marveled at the big sky, the endless earth in these Great Plains and any little sign of enchantment. Unconsciously we were shifting, shrinking, preparing, processing. We were really going home.

Anti-climax

Cheyenne was probably another terrific town. Named for a Native American tribe, it sprang up during the construction of the railroad in the 1860s and became known as the "Magic City of the Plains." It still boasted one of the largest rodeos in the world.

But for us it was just a stopover. We arrived late and took off at the crack of dawn, so early in fact that we needed to kill time when we arrived in Denver before we could check into our motel – the same place we stayed at the beginning of our adventure.

On autopilot, we sought out the Denver Museum of Nature & Science. We found it smack dab in City Park near the Denver Zoo. A museum, park and zoo? What a thrilling prospect! Only no one could muster enthusiasm.

Instead of pretending, we opted for an IMAX show. Tom promptly started snoring behind his 3D glasses. The rest of us stayed at least semi-absorbed by the whales, dolphins and other pulsating creatures in *Wild Oceans*.

With hours still to wait and zero interest in the crowded museum, we ducked over to a second-story sitting area. City Park sprawled beyond floor-to-ceiling windows. Denver's downtown skyline stood at attention in the distance. We sat lost in our own thoughts, which for Sean circled on one thing.

"Can we eat?"

Ciarán and Aislínn seconded the idea.

I looked at my watch. Eleven thirty. "Sure."

We filled trays in the T-Rex Café for our final vacation lunch. On our way back to The Couch, I noticed a huge leaf moth on the sidewalk, which revved our attention for a few minutes. The poor bug was one of four photos we took all day. Definitely a far cry from the hundreds we'd been snapping daily.

I wanted to be the peppy, happy mom who made every minute count. Who rah-rahhed the troops into enjoying our last hours. But I couldn't.

Finally in our hotel room, the kids commandeered the remote. Their dad dove into super-intense packing mode. He got our cardboard boxes (kindly held in storage) ready for shipping and took them to a Pac 'n Post. Then he started working on our checked luggage.

After a long, hot shower, I planted myself in the room's only chair and tried to read. My eyes kept drifting to my children. Ciarán and Sean laid supine on one bed, heads lifted on stacks of pillows. Aislínn lounged stomach down on the other, propped up on her elbows. Sponge Bob had them grinning ear to ear. Every once in a while, Tom broke his laser focus, glanced up at the TV and guffawed so loudly that he drowned out Patrick Star and Squidward. That made the kids howl even more.

Eventually, I heated water in the room's old coffee maker and poured myself a cup of tea. Then I started seriously packing too. After weeks of living out of the back of an SUV, I had to consolidate for the plane.

I dumped a black garbage bag of laundry onto the floor and sighed. A huge part of me wanted to keep traveling, but maybe I wouldn't mind my own mattress, and washing machine, after all. I rolled dirty t-shirts into neat, packable piles.

I held up Ciarán's fraying shorts and smiled. Each piece of clothing carried the stories and stains of our adventure. We'd driven 7,000 miles. Hiked dozens more. Seen hundreds of wild animals. Breathed in some of the most beautiful landscapes on earth. We pondered ordinary lifestyles wherever we went and also had a front-row seat to mortal courage through the centuries, right up to the gritty sweat of smoke jumpers.

Beyond the sights and people, though, were the marvel and mystery absent in our everyday lives. Awe became an alarm clock that awakened intensely personal connections. The magnificence of Grand Canyon, the brilliance of Yellowstone Falls, the power of the Redwoods, the wonder of the night sky – they mingled with our souls.

I looked at my kids, still glued to the small hotel screen. By the end of the week they'd disappear into their normal routines. But this energy, this innate knowing, now steeped in their bones and would follow them into their adult lives.

Leaf moth in Denver

> *"* *Rejoice with your family in the*
> *beautiful land of life! "*
> Albert Einstein

Yellowstone hot springs

Epilogue: Sweet Return

After a nondescript dinner in the hotel restaurant, an early wake-up call and a moody drive to the airport, we boarded our flight. Back in Newark, NJ, our wonderful neighbor, Ol' Davy Taylor, chauffeured us home. Tom bantered with Davy up front while the rest of us slumped in zombie mode. No one even pushed or jabbed.

Only the sight of our big goofy lab sparked us to life. He wagged so violently, he almost gyrated off our porch. We cracked up and scrambled out of the van. I waited for him to come bounding toward me. But he didn't budge, just stood there wiggling. Aislínn and I exchanged curious glances.

"Good boy Scout. Stay." It was the soft, quiet voice of our house-sitter.

Cathy turned out to be not only a wonderful caretaker of our home, but also a dog whisperer. Somehow, she tamed our rambunctious hound. Sure, he still broke into the refrigerator regularly, but our canine was forever calmer.

I hugged and petted him, leaned my cheek against his wriggling bulk. He wrenched his neck to slobber me with his wide pink tongue. The boys gave quick pats, ran into the house and, having already reached out to friends, left within minutes. Aislínn retreated to her room.

Tom and I bid farewell to our summer tenants then my husband began unloading our gear. Plopping into a wicker porch chair, I grinned at Scout, still shimmying at my side. "Guess it's just me and you, bud. Back to normal now."

That would have been that. Except the next morning I announced I missed the ocean and was going for a swim before sorting through our suitcases. Tom, still in pain from what soon got treated as a tooth in need of a root canal (thankfully not some scary bone mass), declined.

But my offspring asked me to wait for them. I tried not to show surprise. They scrambled into their suits and we all bicycled over together. As usual, we went to the "locals" section of our touristy beach, where a lot of their pals were already hanging. I expected my three to rush off. Ordinarily they only stuck around if they wanted sunscreen, snacks or money.

Instead, they all pitched in, carrying stuff from our beach locker, setting up the blanket and opening the chairs. When I jogged to the water and dove into the surf, they were right behind me. As soon as my head popped up, Sean lobbed his rubber ball to me, starting a giggling game of keep-away. Then we grabbed our body boards and rode the waves, laughing out loud.

For nearly three hours, we played, joked and laid in the sun together like we were still at the shores of that beautiful lake in Yosemite, or the pool at Olympic, as if we didn't know anyone else.

It never happened again. The next day they were gone with gusto.

Our summer adventure held so many extraordinary moments. Yet, for me, floating in the Atlantic Ocean that day with my three teens, having fun in our family bubble on our home turf, was one this mom will never forget.

Afterword: The Science of Wow

Long after we settled back into busy lives, our road trip permeated my psyche. Out of nowhere, recollections would swirl like foamed milk on a cappuccino.

As Sean dribbled the soccer ball during a tournament, I suddenly saw him flying past his big brother to kick a winning goal over our Yosemite picnic table. Walks with Scout around our local pond brought flashes of the spectacular reflections in Crater Lake. Sunrises on my beach transported me to Grand Canyon's post-dawn show.

I couldn't help but laugh every time Aislínn crossed a street in flip-flops, hearing Tom's bizarre warnings in Crescent City, CA. I even smiled at Ciarán's smug gloating as he became a decent driver in spite of my freak-out at his first high-speed attempt in Arizona. And, god forbid, if I just happened to pass a tiny bit of wind in front of my offspring, they'd howl in recall of my historic Petroglyph Trail fart.

The more the memories marinated, the more my curiosity grew. We had tremendous fun, shared a thousand "wows" and spent an unusual amount of time together. I felt enormously grateful that we were able to see beautiful parts of our diverse country. I could imagine that decades later my kids would still embellish and giggle about The Couch and our road trip escapades.

Digging for data

At a deep level, I believed our adventure left an indelible mark on all of us. As a research nerd, I wondered if science would bear out what I sensed. Were there quantifiable benefits from a trip like ours?

The answer is a resounding "yes!" Even more so than I anticipated. My treasure trove of findings left me with three vital learnings:

- **A positive relationship with our teens and 'tweens is crucial to their health and well-being.**
- **Time in nature can make us all healthier, happier and more creative.**
- **We must help our adolescents develop a love affair with the wild, not only for their own benefit but for the future of these irreplaceable spaces.**

Each insight is highlighted in the following sections. Our journey fell at the intersection of these and I was thrilled to see that research proved what I already knew in my heart.

317

> " *When your children are teenagers, it's important to have a dog so that someone in the house is happy to see you.* "
>
> Nora Ephron

Glacier hike

Crucial Parent-Teen Connections

We poke fun at their insolence, mock their silences and imitate their eye rolls. The barbs have been around forever. But living with teens is often no joke.

If you want to throw up your arms in frustration as your not-so-little kid kicks up constant barriers, you're not alone. With 25 million adolescents age 12 to 17 in the country, you can bet there are a lot of us who find it easier to keep our distance, especially when we have our own distractions and challenges.

Yet taking time to compassionately lean in – no matter the pushback – can dramatically influence your teen's happiness and well-being.

Multiple scientific studies found that adolescents do better in school, make positive choices, and avoid risky behaviors when parents are involved in their lives.

Specifically, that means teens who spend regular time with their moms, dads or other important caregivers are less likely to drink, smoke, engage in early sexual activity, use drugs, turn to violence or attempt suicide.

These findings are particularly striking given that by 12th grade, surveys done by the American Pediatric Association, the Centers for Disease Control and Prevention (CDC), the Partnership for a Drug-Free America and others reveal that half of students reported using marijuana, two-thirds said they tried alcohol, about four in ten gave cigarettes a go, and nearly two in ten reported taking prescription medicine without a prescription.

The numbers are similarly surprising for adolescents who engage in sexual activity, with age of initial encounters growing younger.

Although drug overdose fatalities among young adults is relatively low overall, the rate of such casualties in that age group is increasing. And for every teen who dies from drugs, the CDC estimates at least a 100 others are treated in emergency rooms.

Even more concerning, young adult suicide has also been rising at alarming rates. By 2017, suicide had become the second-leading cause of death for people aged 15 to 24.

Many factors play into our children's ability to thrive. Some are out of our control. But the onus is on us to be available, regardless of slammed doors or brooding moods. Multiple analyses conclude that despite their contrary signals, our teens actually crave and value parental interest and advice.

Bio-social tsunami

When you're caught in the throes of a special dose of adolescent arrogance or sarcasm, it may help to take a step back and remember that your 'tween or teen is experiencing physical and emotional transformations rivaled only by their early years of life.

Brain research has shown that our limbic system (the emotional processing center that perceives rewards from risks) kicks into high gear in the early teens. But the brain's frontal lobes, which control impulses and recognize cause and effect, don't mature until later.

Puberty floods our teenagers with estrogen and testosterone that set off a biological chain of events. Among them is the increase of a hormone that triggers strong awareness of self, to the point that an adolescent may believe they are the focus of everyone's attention, hence their extreme (and often annoying) combination of self-centeredness and self-consciousness.

On top of this tidal wave of hormones, or because of them, our adolescents seek (even demand) increased independence to navigate all kinds of social interactions without our guidance, and sometimes without our knowledge.

They do hear you

It's true that friends have increasing influence on your middle and high schooler. It's also true that parent-teen conflict is normal.

Yet adolescents still need the important adults in their lives to provide emotional support and set boundaries. More and more research confirms that parents hold greater sway than peers on numerous behaviors, including smoking, drinking, using drugs or having sex.

In fact, the relationship between children and their parents or caregivers is so critical that the World Health Organization (WHO) named "family connectedness" as one of the top five protective factors linked with youth well-being.

A road trip with your teens takes this concept to the max, of course. But the good news is the quality of our connections matters more than the quantity. So anything that helps your young adult feel heard, even for a short time, is valuable. A regular family dinner, weekly game night, or activity of their choice fits the bill. Parents who don't live with their teens can embrace video chats and texting.

Don't let their attitudes and snubs deter you. Every attempt to positively connect with your teen lets them know you love them and gives them the foundation they need to blossom into their best selves.

SOURCES

1. *A social neuroscience perspective on adolescent risk-taking.* Steinberg, L. (2008) Developmental Review (https://www.ncbi.nlm.nih.gov/pmc/articles/PMC2396566/)
2. *Kids Count Data Center,* The Annie E. Casey Foundation (https://datacenter.kidscount.org/data/tables/101-child-population-by-age-group#detailed/1/any/false/870,573,869,36,868/62,63,64,6,4693/419,420)
3. *Parent-Teen Relationships and Interactions: Far More Positive Than Not,* Child Trends Research Brief (https://www.childtrends.org/wp-content/uploads/2009/11/Child_Trends-2004_12_01_RB_ParentTeen.pdf)
4. *Prevalence of Adolescent Opioid Misuse,* US Department of Health and Human Services, updated May 2013 (https://www.hhs.gov/ash/oah/adolescent-development/substance-use/drugs/opioids/index.html#prevalence)
5. *Suicide Rates Among Adolescents and Young Adults in the United States, 2000-2017,* Journal of the American Medical Association (JAMA), June 2019 (https://jamanetwork.com/journals/jama/article-abstract/2735809)
6. *Teen Substance Use & Risks,* Centers for Disease Control and Prevention, updated Feb. 2020 (https://www.cdc.gov/ncbddd/fasd/features/teen-substance-use.html)
7. *Teens and Their Parents in the 21st Century: An Examination of Trends in Teen Behavior and the Role of Parental Involvement,* National Inst. Of Child Health & Human Development/Council of Economic Advisers (https://eric.ed.gov/?id=ED443529)

" *Nature itself is the best physician.*
Hippocrates **"**

Grand Tetons

Natural Rx

It's old news that a walk in the woods is great exercise and can improve your cardiovascular health, weight, strength, balance and bone mass. But did you know exposure to nature might also help fight a cold? Reduce stress? Foster ingenuity? Help kids with attention deficit hyperactivity disorder (ADHD)? Diminish the risk of nearsightedness? And maybe even prevent certain kinds of cancer?

A growing body of research from around the world is demonstrating that exposure to natural surroundings confers a wide array of benefits. Indeed, science is proving that the great outdoors can make us happier, healthier and more creative. Here are some of the latest findings:

● Improved Mood

Anyone who has stood by a beautiful stream, viewed the world from a mountaintop, or strolled through a field of wildflowers has certainly felt a sense of peace and well-being. Now we have biological evidence to back up that perception. Digging your toes in the sand, walking in a forest or rafting on a river truly does rev up your "feel-good" serotonin levels and douse the stress hormone cortisol. In numerous experiments, outdoor experiences lit up parts of the brain keyed to love and empathy while reducing blood flow to the area associated with negative thoughts. Being in nature quieted the area of the prefrontal cortex that can obsessively brood over problems, leading to depression and anxiety. In the studies, the alfresco cure often worked as well or better than prescription meds. In addition, the research confirmed even short amounts of time in "green" spaces may boost energy levels and improve sleep, two factors that directly affect mood.

● Enhanced Focus

Fresh air pursuits also enhance memory, creativity and the ability to focus. Researchers found that engaging in outside activities increased concentration and problem solving skills in adults and children. In one study, after just 20 minutes in a park, kids did better in reading and math. Similarly, students with ADHD showed significant increases in their ability to control impulses and pay attention, possibly because the prefrontal cortex is also involved in ADHD. Research continues on the use of natural environments as a treatment for attention disorders. In urban environments, youngsters who have access to even a small patch of trees or garden have shown better social, emotional and academic skills. In other interesting experiments, adults reported enhanced memory, problem-solving, and creativity after time in nature.

☙ Healthier Body

We've long known about the exercise benefits of hiking, which can burn up to 700 calories an hour; is easier on the joints than running; and is good for our heart, muscle mass and bones. But newer research shows you don't have to exert yourself to get physical advantages from nature. Studies found just sitting looking at trees reduces blood pressure. Similarly, hospital patients with "green" views recovered from surgery faster and took fewer painkillers than those without sight-lines of nature. Even more exciting, early investigations indicate that time in nature may boost immunity, aid vision and even stimulate production of proteins that help prevent the development of cancer. Plants and trees give off phytoncides to protect themselves from insects and disease. Scientists found when study participants walked in the woods, automatically breathing in these chemicals, they produced more of a type of white blood cell that kills tumors and viruses in humans. Although the research is young, studies continue to explore whether forest exposure will prevent certain kinds of cancer.

Best side effects

Nearly 40 years ago, Japanese researchers coined the term *shinrin-yoku* for "forest bathing." Since then, medical professionals have regularly prescribed strolls in the woods for myriad maladies. In Norway, consistently ranked one of the happiest places on the planet, people have long embraced the outdoor philosophy of *friluftsliv*, pronounced free-loofts-liv and translated to "free air life."

In the decades since Japan's early groundbreaking findings, studies around the globe have concluded that even with socioeconomic and other variables factored in, a person is at greater risk for disease and death the less "green" their environment is.

For those without exposure to natural places, diverse research has linked a startling number of health perils, including increased chance of anxiety, depression, diabetes, ADHD, infectious diseases, cancer, surgical healing problems, obesity, birth issues, heart disease, musculo-skeletal concerns, migraines and respiratory disease.

Given the wealth of knowledge and ongoing research, shouldn't we ensure *all* children have access to green spaces? And doesn't it make sense for each of us to spend even small amounts of time in nature and tap into what the Happiness Research Institute in Copenhagen calls "outdoorphins?" This remedy has no negative side effects and is a wonderful way to improve health and well-being!

SOURCES

A collection of research can be found at *The Forest Library* (https://www.theforestlibrary.com/forest-bathing-online-articles)

Here are other specific articles:

1. *A forest bathing trip increases human natural killer activity*, NIH National Center for Biotechnology Information (https://www.ncbi.nlm.nih.gov/pubmed/18394317)
2. *Creativity in the Wild*, PLOS ONE (http://journals.plos.org/plosone/article?id=10.1371/journal.pone.0051474)
3. *Friluftsliv: The Norwegian Love of the Outdoors*, Life in Norway (https://www.lifeinnorway.net/friluftsliv-outdoors/)
4. *How Just 15 Minutes in Nature Can Make You Happier*, Time (http://time.com/4662650/nature-happiness-stress/)
5. *How might contact with nature promote human health? Promising mechanisms and a possible central pathway*, Frontiers in Psychology (https://www.ncbi.nlm.nih.gov/pmc/articles/PMC4548093/)
6. *How Nature Can Make You Kinder, Happier and More Creative*, Greater Good Magazine (https://greatergood.berkeley.edu/article/item/how_nature_makes_you_kinder_happier_more_creative)
7. *Improving Creative Reasoning through Immersion in Natural Settings*, PLOS ONE (http://journals.plos.org/plosone/article?id=10.1371/journal.pone.0051474)
8. *Nature experience reduces rumination and subgenual prefrontal cortex activation*, Proceedings of the National Academy of Sciences USA (https://www.ncbi.nlm.nih.gov/pmc/articles/PMC4507237/)
9. *Stanford researchers find mental health prescription: Nature*, Stanford News (https://news.stanford.edu/2015/06/30/hiking-mental-health-063015/)
10. *Therapeutic Effects of Forests*, Environmental Health and Preventive Medicine (https://www.ncbi.nlm.nih.gov/pmc/articles/PMC2793347/)

"
Our challenge isn't so much to teach children about the natural world, but to find ways to sustain the instinctive connections they already carry.
"

Terry Krautwurst

Glacier

Parks & Teens:
Entwining futures

There are two things we now know for sure:
- Teens and 'tweens do better when they spend quality time with their parents.
- We all do better when we spend quality time in nature.

It's a no-brainer that our national parks should be swarming with moms, dads and their adolescents, right? Wrong.

Despite recent record-breaking attendance at the parks, the majority of visitors are closer to retirement age. Although more than a third of all Americans are under age 18, most park visitors are old enough to be their grandparents.

A Junior Ranger program and the *Every Kid in a Park Pass,* which offers free visitation to all 4th graders in the U.S. and their families, have helped a little. So have park efforts to improve technology and connectivity. But the sad fact remains that wrinkles far outnumber young faces.

One former Yosemite ranger told CNN that the kids today seem "too 'plugged-in' to be drawn to the 'unpluggedness' of the great outdoors."

Retired NPS Director Jonathan Jarvis agreed. In a *National Geographic* feature he said, "Young people are more separated from the natural world than perhaps any generation before them."

Our American birthright

In 1968, Senegalese poet and naturalist Baba Dioum shared this statement with an international conservation gathering: *"In the end we will conserve only what we love, we will love only what we understand, and we will understand only what we are taught."*

Half a century later, his often quoted words are more crucial than ever. We must help our teens develop a love affair with the wild – not only for their own well-being, but for the future of these irreplaceable spaces.

The national parks, the monuments, the state reserves, they are *our* land. As climate change and politics threaten these natural wonders, we can't forget they belong to us, our children, our grandchildren and all the generations that follow.

When glaciers melt, acreage is sold or development encroaches, we lose our American birthright. Once a treasure is gone, it is gone forever.

Young adults have certainly grown up with greater awareness of climate change, and with more exposure to the effects of global warming than their parents. Not surprisingly, surveys over the past few years showed that a majority of teens in the U.S. are more concerned about the environment than older adults. But most adolescents don't know how to turn that worry into meaningful action.

When it comes to protecting our wild places, let's teach them, show them. Take a walk in the woods together. Giggle in a hot spring. Watch a canyon sunset. Practice reverence. What better way to build a relationship with each other and our remarkable county?

And as their natural connection and comfort grows, they will be able to passionately speak about and protect these precious lands from a deep place of love.

SOURCES

1. *Do younger generations care more about global warming?* Yale Program on Climate Change Communication, June 2019 (https://climatecommunication.yale.edu/publications/do-younger-generations-care-more-about-global-warming/)

2. *Does the National Park Service Have a Youth Problem?*, CNN, March 19, 2015, https://www.cnn.com/2015/03/19/us/im-national-parks-older-visitors-morgan-spurlock/index.html

3. *Kids Count Data Center,* The Annie E. Casey Foundation (https://bit.ly/2HMImwX)

4. *Unplugging the Selfie Generation,* National Geographic, October 2016 (https://on.natgeo.com/2wIh97E)

APPENDICES

❝ *Never measure the height of a mountain until you have reached the top. Then you will see how low it was.* ❞

Dag Hammarskjold

Northern Cascades

Appendix I
TIPS, LISTS & OTHER FUN STUFF

1. Planning Advice & Resources

Dreaming about a National Park trip can be tremendous fun. Making it a reality? Not always. Tips are sprinkled throughout the book, but here are our top recommendations to ease the stress:

YOU CAN'T MAKE A WRONG CHOICE — ALL THE PARKS ARE AMAZING
Aislínn and I dove into the black hole of internet and travel books, so we kept coming up with gem after enticing gem. But even if we did a quarter of the research and used a Ouija board to pick our stops, the trip would have been fabulous. Don't make yourself crazy with too much information.

START WITH SOME BASIC PARAMETERS
Since ours was a fantasy trip at first, we had no limits. This, I guarantee, is overwhelming. Figure out the basics first: How long do you have for your trip? Do you want to immerse and spend more time getting to know one park or enjoy brief highlights of several? What are your transportation options? Are you going to do major hiking or mostly drive/walk to popular attractions? Would you prefer to camp, live in luxury or something in between? Nailing down these decisions will help you focus your research.

YOU ARE NOT BOUND TO THE HOME FRONT
Most of us have jobs, pets or other commitments that need to be addressed before we can traipse on trails hundreds or thousands of miles from home. In fact, the most frequent question I am still asked is how we managed to travel for the summer when we had a dog, work, bills to pay and kids in Little League, Junior Lifeguards and soccer. Plus, I was a councilwoman on our borough's governing body, which meant I attended several meetings a week. My answer? If you want to travel, there are ways to make it happen. Ask your boss and co-workers (or fellow councilmen), call the kid's coaches, check web-sites for home rentals and pet sitters. And more than anything else, put it out there. Verbally spread the word about your trip. I can't tell

you how it works, but I've seen it happen again and again: when you express your dreams and needs, solutions often present themselves.

Reserve Well in Advance

Even the lesser known parks have increasing visitation numbers, so book your stay as early as possible for all forms of lodging. If you are just passing through for the day, no reservations are necessary. (You may have to pay park entrance fees.) Some parks also have diverse eating options; nicer restaurants often are booked in advanced. Again, do your homework and reserve what you can. But also remember #1: there are no bad choices and even if you are too late for a certain lodge or dinner, you'll still have terrific options.

Take Advantage of Resources

Type "National Parks" in a search engine and you'll find thousands of listings. A good place to start is the National Park Service site (https://www.nps.gov/index.htm.) It has a wealth of information as well as links to all the parks. But these links can swallow you for hours, leading you on a pleasant but often unfulfilling quest as far as trip planning. That's why I recommend guidebooks and directories specifically designed to help you plan a park vacation. Fodor's (http://www.fodors.com/trip-ideas/national-parks/) and Frommer's (http://www.frommers.com/destinations/us-national-parks) are the royalty of travel books, so check out their websites and maybe even order a guidebook or two. Did I need to read three books cover to cover, including one on "family" vacations in the parks? No. I think you realize by now that I'm an obsessive sleuth. Each offered a few valuable bits, but if you are not into perusing guidebooks for pleasure, then limit yourself. The point is that there are many resources out there. We also took advantage of AAA's TripTik and Travel Planner (www.aaa.com).

NOTE ON APPS: There are an abundance of trip planning apps. A good one is TripIt (https://www.tripit.com), which organizes your master itinerary and puts all the information you need at your fingertips. The many national park apps differ in quality and usefulness. Only a few parks have apps actually produced by the National Parks Service (https://www.nps.gov/subjects/digital/nps-apps.htm).

Don't Overschedule!

Reservations are often a must. Unless you are up for roughing it (which has its own unique perks) wandering aimlessly is difficult. That said, don't totally lock yourself in. We had a fairly planned itinerary, with reservations for accommodations every night. In retrospect, I'd still book a place to sleep but I'd be more willing to let a reservation go so we could explore a few of the unexpected gems we stumbled across while driving. We purposely didn't pre-schedule group hikes, tours, excursions or any of the many park offerings. This allowed us to relax and enjoy at our own pace once we set up camp. You can usually book programs once you are in the park, especially if you check visitor centers early.

The caveat: if you want a particular tour or time, like spelunking in caves or catching a limited boat shuttle, DO book in advance.

2. Lessons Learned

Here are a dozen other take-aways from our time on the road.

- LIVE A LITTLE DIRTY. Sure, there are laundry facilities in many parks and most towns. It's even fun the first few times playing M&M poker while waiting. But, believe me, it's worth easing your standards so you're not constantly sidelined. We made a rule that except for underwear and totally rank t-shirts, everything else had to be worn at least three times before washing.

- HAVE BACKUP MAPS. Don't expect to get accurate directions from your GPS or to be able to use your devices in some parks. Service is improving; just don't count on it. If you stop and ask for directions, follow the advice. Don't just plug the new info into the GPS that got you lost in the first place.

- DO DAWN AND DUSK. Definitely get out at sunrise. Second best is dusk. There's fabulous lighting for photos, fewer people and far more chance to actually see what you came looking for, especially wildlife.

- VALUE IS MORE IMPORTANT THAN PRICE. Don't pick your motels, excursions and activities based solely on cost. Free continental breakfast, knowledgeable guides, or a hot springs splurge can be worth their weight in fun.

- **But be smart about stocking supplies.** Stop at a supermarkets in larger towns for the best prices/choices on groceries. Supplies are much more limited and costly in park stores.

- **Trips are filled with peaks and valleys.** You will have plenty of ups and downs, visually, physically and emotionally. Breathe and embrace them all.

- **Allow yourself to really see.** As writer Anais Nin said, *"we don't see things as they are, we see them as we are."* Your mood, your presence, your openness all impact your experience.

- **Buffalo are cool.** You can drive through a herd standing in the road – just go slowly and don't honk your horn.

- **Canada uses Imperial gallons.** Duh.

- **Avoid Sturgis, SD, in August.** Unless you're on your Harley.

- **America does not run on Dunkin.** At least west of the Mississippi.

- **Squeegees are crucial.** It's the only way to get those bugs off the windshield.

3. Hiking Essentials

Whether you're walking a well-worn path for an hour or climbing a craggy summit all day, it's smart to bring a day-pack or carry a bag with the following 10 essentials.

- » **Water** (in bottle or hydration system), energy drinks/mixes for strenuous hikes
- » **Weather protection** (sunscreen, SPF lip balm, hat, sunglasses, rain poncho, gloves/hat if cold)
- » **Bug protection** (insect repellent; net face coverings if warranted)
- » **Binoculars and cameras**
- » **First aid kit** (there are a variety out there, you can make your own with a waterproof bag or container. Include antibiotic ointment,

anti-inflammatory medication, electrolyte tablets and an insect sting remedy, along with band-aids, bandages, gauze, tweezers and alcohol wipes.)

» **Food/snacks** (energy bars, trail mix, chews)
» **Whistle or bells** (in bear territory)
» **Duct tape and/or paracord** (these can fix broken hiking boots, shore up packs, secure splints in an emergency and so many other things. To save space, wrap a long strip of duct tape around itself.)
» **Multi-use tool** (like a Swiss army knife)
» **Lighter, matches** (in a waterproof container)

4. Leave No Trace

It's up to each of us to ensure our parks remain national treasures for generations to come. The Seven Principles of "Leave No Trace" are good reminders.

1. **Plan ahead and prepare**: know where you are going, check weather and environmental conditions, inform others of your whereabouts. Figure you'll cover about two miles an hour on a moderate hike (slower with small children or on challenging trails), so leave enough time to get back before dark.
2. **Travel/camp on durable surfaces**: stay off sensitive or hazardous areas.
3. **Dispose of waste properly**: put trash in proper receptacles or, if required, pack-in/out. Learn trail etiquette for your bathroom needs.
4. **Minimize campfire impacts**: use designated fire rings and grills.
5. **Leave what you find**: imagine if tens of thousands of visitors each took "just one" piece of ancient Puebloan pottery or gigantic Kings Canyon pine cone? It is illegal to remove natural materials from national parks. As the saying goes, "Take nothing but pictures, leave nothing but footprints."
6. **Respect wildlife**: you are visiting their home; do not feed or venture near animals, even "friendly" squirrels and birds. It can be dangerous and is also illegal to disturb or come too close to some wildlife.
7. **Be considerate of others**: use common social courtesy when hiking, camping or enjoying a popular view.

5. And the Winner Is...

On our last night around the Custer campfire, we debated bests, worsts and whatever else we could list. In no particular order, here they are:

BEST NIGHT SKY: Mesa Verde National Park (NP)

HOT AS H*LL: 115° in Las Vegas

FREEEEEEEZING: 36° without wind chill at Glacier NP

HIGHEST CLIMB: 10,423 feet, Mt. Washburn, Yellowstone NP

DEEPEST DESCENT: 2,200 feet, Grand Canyon NP

MOST WILDLIFE SIGHTINGS: Lamar Valley, Yellowstone NP

BLUEST WATER: Crater Lake NP

SCARIEST MOMENT: Buffalo charge in Yellowstone NP, although climbing the 30' ladder at Mesa Verde was a tie for Tom and Aislínn.

WANT TO GO BACK: Redwoods NP, Glacier NP, Olympic NP and Yellowstone NP

FAVORITE PARK: Glacier NP with Yellowstone NP a close second

NICEST CAMPGROUND: Rising Sun Campground, Glacier NP; Canyon Campground, Yellowstone NP; Newhalem Creek Campground, North Cascades NP and Mazama Campground, Crater Lake NP

BEST UNEXPECTED GEMS: Crazy Horse Monument, SD, and the Museum of the Rockies, WY

FAVORITE CITY: Seattle, WA

STUPIDEST COMMENT: "You can't cross the street like that. You have your flip-flops on!" (from Tom Brennan in Crescent City, CA)

MOST GRIPED-ABOUT STOP: Hoover Dam National Monument, NV

MOST WHITE-KNUCKLE BARF-BAG DRIVE: On CA-120 from Yosemite NP to San Francisco

BEST HIKE: Logan Pass to Hidden Lake and Grinnell Glacier, both Glacier NP

BEST RESTAURANT MEAL: Chinatown, San Francisco, CA

BEST CAMP MEAL: Chili burritos

BEST CAMP FACILITIES: Blue Bell Campground, Custer State Park (hot water, free showers!) and Canyon Campground, Yellowstone

CUTEST TOWN: Sheridan, WY (Ciarán refused to vote, calling all cute towns "stupid.")

MOST OBNOXIOUS: Motorcycles on Needles Highway, SD, and slow RVs that didn't move over

MOST HILARIOUS ACTIVITY: Teasing each other and whitewater rafting

FAVORITE STORES: SEAN: The Rock Store, Custer; AISLÍNN: Borders Books, San Francisco; CIARÁN: Ghirardelli's Chocolates, San Francisco; MERRY: It's A Burl Furniture, Kerby, OR; TOM: grocery store in Rockport, WA

BEST HOTELS: Hampton Inn, Kayenta, AZ; University Inn, Seattle, WA; Lighthouse Inn, Crescent City, CA; and Prestige Rocky Mt. Hotel, Cranbrook, BC

Appendix II
US NATIONAL PARK SYSTEM

> ❝ *I have always considered that the prime objectives of the National Parks were to provide inspiration, self-discovery of spirit in the wild places and appropriate recreation. The principal parks and monuments are set aside and protected for such human benefits – not for economic purposes. They are, in effect, vast areas devoted to the development of the spirit and for recreation in the true sense of the term. This concept places the National Parks at the highest level of an advanced civilization.* ❞
>
> Ansel Adams

HAPPY CENTENNIAL!

On August 25, 1916, President Woodrow Wilson signed the "Organic Act," creating the National Park Service (NPS) to protect and conserve the nation's natural and cultural heritage. Yellowstone, the granddaddy of U.S. parks, had actually been established 44 years earlier followed by a few other protected spaces. By 2016, when the NPS celebrated its 100th birthday, the vast system included 419 national treasures in every state, the District of Columbia, American Samoa, Guam, Puerto Rico and the Virgin Islands.

To see the full color map of the National Park System shown on the next pages, scan the QR code on the left.
To link to the NPS' extensive offering of other maps, scan the QR code on the right.

National Park Services...

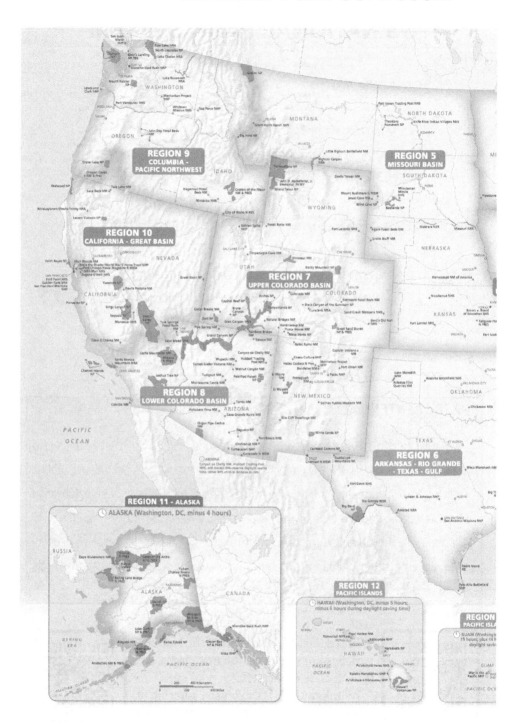

protecting our public lands

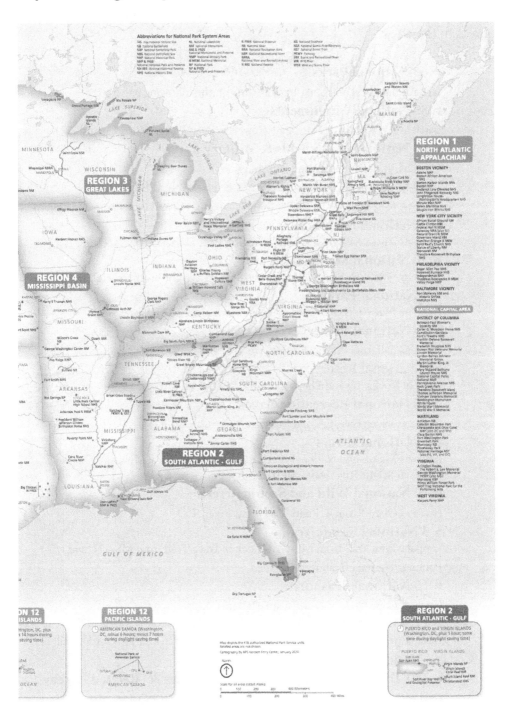

1. NPS Sites

As of January 2021, the National Park Service managed more than 400 areas in the US:

> ▷ **63 National Parks**
> (see Alphabetical and State-by-State lists on the following pages)
> ▷ **83 National Monuments**
> (such as Aztec Ruins, NM; Devils Tower, WY; and Organ Pipe Cactus, AZ)
> ▷ **25 National Battlefields & Military Parks**
> (such as Antietam, MD and Gettysburg, PA)
> ▷ **134 National Historical Parks & Historical Sites**
> (such as New Orleans Jazz, LA; Thomas Edison, NJ; and Fort Laramie, WY)
> ▷ **3 National Lakeshores**
> (such as Apostle Islands, WI and Sleeping Bear Dunes, MI)
> ▷ **30 National Memorials**
> (such as Flight 93, PA; Mt. Rushmore, SD and Wright Brothers, NC)
> ▷ **4 National Parkways**
> (such as Blue Ridge Parkway, NC and Natchez Trace Parkway, MS)
> ▷ **19 National Preserves**
> (such as Tallgrass Prairie, KS; Mojave, CA; and Great Sand Dunes, CO)
> ▷ **2 National Reserves**
> (City of Rocks, ID and Ebey's Landing, WA)
> ▷ **18 National Recreation Areas**
> (such as Golden Gate, CA, and Delaware Water Gap, PA-NJ)
> ▷ **5 National Rivers**
> (such as Mississippi National River and Recreation Area, MN;, and Ozark National Scenic Riverways, MO)
> ▷ **10 National Wild and Scenic Rivers**
> (such as Obed River, TN and Rio Grand River, TX)
> ▷ **3 National Scenic Trails**
> (Appalachian Trail from ME-GA; Natchez Trace Trail from MS-TN, and Potamac Heritage Trail from VA-PA)
> ▷ **10 National Seashores**
> (such as Cape Cod, MA, and Cape Hatteras, NC)
> ▷ **11 "Other" Designations**
> (such as the National Mall, the White House, and Constitution Gardens, all in Washington DC)
> ▷ **170 Trail Systems, Commemorative Sites & "Related" Areas**
> (such as Niagara Falls, NY and Merced River, CA, where NPS helps with oversight.)

National Park Trivia

MOST VISITED PARK: *Great Smokey Mountains National Park, North Carolina/Tennessee (12.5 million visitors in 2019; Grand Canyon National Park, Colorado, was second with 6 million visitors)*

LARGEST: *Wrangell-St. Elias National Park, Alaska (13,000 square miles)*

LARGEST IN LOWER 48: *Death Valley National Park, California/ Nevada (5,300 square miles)*

SMALLEST: *Hot Springs National Park, Arkansas (less than 10 square miles)*

HIGHEST POINT: *Mount McKinley (Alaska Range) in Denali National Park, Alaska (20,320 feet high)*

HIGHEST POINT IN LOWER 48: *Mount Whitney (Sierra Nevada Mountains) in Sequoia National Park, California (14,505 feet high)*

LOWEST POINT IN WESTERN HEMISPHERE: *Badwater Basin at 282 feet below sea level in Death Valley National Park, California/Nevada.*

LONGEST CAVE SYSTEM IN THE WORLD: *Mammoth Cave National Park, Kentucky (more than 400 mapped miles)*

DEEPEST LAKE IN THE U.S.: *Crater Lake in Crater Lake National Park, Oregon (1,932 ft. deep)*

WORLD'S LARGEST AND TALLEST TREES: *Giant Sequoias and Redwoods in Sequoia National Park and Redwood National Park, California*

WORLD'S LARGEST CARNIVORE: *Alaskan brown bear (Alaska National Parks)*

YELLOWSTONE COLOR POLLUTION: *The geothermal Morning Glory Pool in Yellowstone National Park changed color not because of sulfur but because of trash! Coins, bottles and other debris obstructed hot water circulations from the pool's vents, creating hues from dull green to turquoise.*

NPS LOGO: *The arrowhead logo contains images of a Sequoia tree, bison, mountains and water, symbolizing the major facets of the Park System.*

---

2. NPS Protection

A key NPS mission is to conserve wildlife along with natural or historic objects. Their work protects:

- 600 species of endangered or threatened plants and animals.
- 75,000 archeological sites.
- 27,000 historic/prehistoric structures.
- 167 million museum items (like George Washington's inaugural coat.)

3. National Park Passes

Of the 400-plus sites in the National Park System, about 300 are free. The rest (including the most popular National Parks) charge entrance fees. There is a range of prices, so check each park individually. If you plan to make repeated visits to the same park or visit multiple parks, it may be worthwhile to purchase a pass:

ANNUAL PARK VISITORS
1920: 1 million
1940: 17 million
1960: 79 million
1980: 198 million
2000: 286 million
2015: 307.2 million
2017 : 331 million
2019: 328 million
For other interesting stats, visit the National Park's Visitor Use Statistics Portal (https://irma.nps.gov/Stats/)

America the Beautiful – National Parks and Federal Recreational Lands Pass

$80 for an annual pass. Purchase directly at parks with entrance fees or online at: https://store.usgs.gov/pass

America the Beautiful – Senior Pass

U.S. citizens 62 years and older can get an *annual* pass for $20. A Lifetime Senior Pass is $80. Lifetime passes purchased before the 2017 price increase will still be honored. For details see: https://store.usgs.gov/pass

Every Kid In A Park Pass – for U.S. 4th Graders

To encourage park visits, the National Parks Foundation offers free passes to 4th graders, their teachers and parents. Vouchers are available from the Every Kid In A Park website: https://www.everykidinapark.gov

America the Beautiful – National Parks and Federal Recreational Lands ACCESS Pass

A free lifetime pass is available to U.S. citizens or permanent residents of the US who have been medically determined to have a permanent disability. You must submit a paper application and documentation. For details see https://store.usgs.gov/access-pass

America the Beautiful – Military Pass

Annual passes are free for current U.S. military members and dependents in the Army, Navy, Air Force, Marines, and Coast Guard, as well as Reserve and National Guard members. For details see: https://store.usgs.gov/pass

4. U.S. National Parks: Alphabetical List

Acadia National Park, ME

American Samoa National Park, American Samoa Territory

Arches National Park, UT

Badlands National Park, SD

Big Bend National Park, TX

Biscayne National Park, FL

Black Canyon of the Gunnison National Park, CO

Bryce Canyon National Park, UT

Canyonlands National Park, UT

Capitol Reef National Park UT

Carlsbad Caverns National Park, NM

Channel Islands National Park, CA

Congaree National Park, SC

Crater Lake National Park, OR

Cuyahoga Valley National Park, OH

Death Valley National Park, CA and NV

Denali National Park, AK

Dry Tortugas National Park, FL

Everglades National Park, FL

Gates of the Arctic National Park, AK

Gateway Arch National Park, MO

Glacier National Park, MT

Glacier Bay National Park, AK

Grand Canyon National Park, AZ

Grand Teton National Park, WY

Great Basin National Park, NV

Great Sand Dunes National Park, CO

Great Smoky Mountains National Park, NC and TN

Guadalupe Mountains National Park, TX

Haleakala National Park, HI

Hawaii Volcanoes National Park, HI

Hot Springs National Park, AR

Indiana Dunes National Park, IN

Isle Royale National Park, MI

Joshua Tree National Park, CA

Katmai National Park, AK

Kenai Fjords National Park, AK

Kings Canyon National Park, CA

Kobuk Valley National Park, AK
Lake Clark National Park, AK
Lassen Volcanic National Park, CA
Mammoth Cave National Park, KY
Mesa Verde National Park, CO
Mount Rainier National Park, WA
National Park of American Samoa, AS
New River Gorge National Park, W. VA
North Cascades National Park, WA
Olympic National Park, WA
Petrified Forest National Park, AZ
Pinnacles National Park, CA
Redwood National Park, CA
Rocky Mountain National Park, CO
Saguaro National Park, AZ
Sequoia National Park, CA
Shenandoah National Park, VA
Theodore Roosevelt National Park, ND
Virgin Islands National Park, US Virgin Islands
Voyageurs National Park, MN
White Sands National Park, NM
Wind Cave National Park, SD
Wrangell-St. Elias National Park, AK
Yellowstone National Park, WY, MT and ID
Yosemite National Park, CA
Zion National Park, UT

Spectacular Vernal Fall in Yosemite

5. U.S. National Parks: State-by-State List

Alaska
Denali National Park
Gates of the Arctic National Park
Glacier Bay National Park
Katmai National Park
Kenai Fjords National Park
Kobuk Valley National Park
Lake Clark National Park
Wrangell-St. Elias National Park

Arizona
Grand Canyon National Park
Petrified Forest National Park
Saguaro National Park

Arkansas
Hot Springs National Park

California
Channel Islands National Park
Death Valley National Park (also located in Nevada)
Joshua Tree National Park
Kings Canyon National Park
Lassen Volcanic Park
Pinnacles National Park
Redwood National Park
Sequoia National Park
Yosemite National Park

Colorado
Black Canyon of the Gunnison National Park
Great Sand Dunes National Park
Mesa Verde National Park
Rocky Mountain National Park

Florida
Biscayne National Park
Dry Tortugas National Park
Everglades National Park

Hawaii
Haleakala National Park
Hawaii Volcanoes National Park

Indiana
Indiana Dunes National Park

Kentucky
Mammoth Cave National Park

Maine
Acadia National Park

Michigan
Isle Royale National Park

Minnesota
Voyageurs National Park

Missouri
Gateway Arch National Park (also located in Illinois)

Montana
Glacier National Park
Yellowstone National Park (also located in Wyoming and Idaho)

Nevada
Death Valley National Park (also located in California)
Great Basin National Park

New Mexico
Carlsbad Caverns National Park
White Sands National Park

North Carolina
Great Smoky Mountains National Park (also located in Tennessee)

North Dakota
Theodore Roosevelt National Park

Ohio
Cuyahoga Valley National Park

Oregon
Crater Lake National Park

South Carolina
Congaree National Park

South Dakota
Badlands National Park
Wind Cave National Park

Tennessee
Great Smoky Mountains National Park (also located in North Carolina)

Texas
Big Bend National Park
Guadalupe Mountains National Park

Virginia
Shenandoah National Park

Utah
Arches National Park
Bryce Canyon National Park
Canyonlands National Park
Capitol Reef National Park
Zion National Park

Washington
Mount Rainier National Park
North Cascades National Park
Olympic National Park

West Virginia
New River Gorge National Park

Wyoming
Grand Teton National Park
Yellowstone National Park (also located in Montana and Idaho)

US Territories
American Samoa Territory: American Samoa National Park
US Virgin Islands : Virgin Islands National Park

Mesa Verde

" *Every good thing you do, every good thing you say, every good thought you think, vibrates on and on and never ceases.* "

Peace Pilgrim

Glacier mountain goat

Appendix III
OUR ADVENTURE: Day by day

Across 7,000 miles we visited 14 national parks; five national monuments; a dozen national waterways, scenic byways and forests; several great cities and towns; two major league baseball games and, sigh, one hospital.

Day 1: Belmar, NJ, to Denver, CO
Rockies Baseball Game

Day 2: Denver to Gunnison, CO

Day 3: Gunnison to Mesa Verde NP, CO
Blue Mesa Recreation Ara, Black Canyon of the Gunnison NP, Las Platas Mountains, San Juan National Forest, Morehead Campground

Day 4: Mesa Verde NP
Cliff Palace, Petroglyph Point Trail, Balcony House

Day 5: Mesa Verde NP to Kayenta, AZ
Point Lookout Trail, Anasazi Heritage Museum, Canyon of the Ancients, Lowry Pueblo, Four Corners, Monument Valley)

Day 6: Kayenta to Grand Canyon NP, AZ
Monument Valley, Painted Desert, Mohave Point Lookout, Yavapai Lodge

Day 7: Grand Canyon NP
Bright Angel Trail, Rim Drive, Desert View Overlook, Watchtower

Day 8: Grand Canyon NP
South Kaibab Trail, Rim Trail, Yavapai Point

Day 9: Grand Canyon NP to Las Vegas, NV
Mojave Desert, Route 66, Hoover Dam

Day 10: Las Vegas to Yosemite NP, CA
Mojave Desert, Sierra Mountains, White Wolf Campground, Lake Luken

Day 11: Yosemite NP
Vernal Falls Trail, Muir Trail, Lake Tenaya

Day 12: Yosemite NP to San Francisco, CA
Scenic CA 120, Fisherman's Wharf, Chinatown

Day 13: San Francisco
Cable Cars, Lombard Street, Union Square, Alcatraz

Day 14: San Francisco to Garberville, CA
Muir Woods, Mount Tamalpais Trail

Day 15: Garberville to Crescent City, CA
Avenue of the Ancients, Redwood NP, Coastal Drive

Day 16: Crescent City to Crater Lake NP, OR
Crescent City Lighthouse, Jedediah Smith State Park, Mazama Campgound

Day 17: Crater Lake NP
Rim Drive, Mount Scott Trail, Cleetwood Cove Trail, Crater Lake Boat Cruise

Day 18: Crater Lake NP to Tigard, OR

Day 19: Tigard to Olympic NP, WA
Heart O' the Hills Campground, Hurricane Ridge

Day 20: Olympic NP
Rialto Beach, Sol Duc River, Sol Duc Hot Springs

Day 21: Olympic NP to Seattle, WA
Heart O' the Hills Trail, Kingston-Edmonds Ferry, Puget Sound, University District

Day 22: Seattle, WA
EMP Museum, Space Needle, Pike Place Market, Mariners Baseball Game

Day 23: Seattle to North Cascades NP, WA
Woodland Park Zoo, Marblemount, Newhalen Campground

Day 24: North Cascades NP
Hydroelectric Dams, Skagit River Trail

Day 25: North Cascades to Republic, WA
Scenic WA 20; Winthrop, WA

Day 26: Republic, WA to Cranbrook, BC
Canadian Rockies

Day 27: Cranbrook, BC to Glacier NP, MT
    Waterton-Glacier International Peace Park, St. Mary's Campground
Day 28: Glacier NP
    Going to the Sun Road, Logan Pass, Hidden Lake Trail, Rising Sun
    Campground, St. Mary & Virginia Falls Trail
Day 29: Glacier NP
    Going to the Sun Road, Swiftcurrent Lake, Lake Josephine, Many
    Glacier/Grinnell Glacier Trail, Blackfeet Community Hospital
Day 30: Glacier to Deer Lodge, MT
    Going to the Sun Road, Lake MacDonald
Day 31: Deer Lodge to Yellowstone NP, WY
    Museum of the Rockies, Canyon Campground
Day 32: Yellowstone NP
    Dunraven Pass, Norris Geyser, Old Faithful, Grand Tetons Nation
    Park, Hayden Valley, Mud Volcano
Day 33: Yellowstone NP
    Tower Falls, Petrified Tree, Gardiner, Yellowstone River Rafting,
    Boiling Springs
Day 34: Yellowstone NP
    Lamar Valley, Mt. Washburn Trail
Day 35: Yellowstone NP to Cody, WY
    Uncle Tom's Point, Artist's Point, Cody Night Rodeo
Day 36: Cody to Sheridan WY
    Painted Hills, Bighorn National Forest
Day 37: Sheridan, WY, to Custer State Park, SD
    Devil's Tower, the Black Hills, Custer, Bluebell Campground
Day 38: Custer State Park
    Wind Cave NP, Needles Highway, Cathedral Spires, Mt. Coolidge
    Overlook, Crazy Horse Monument
Day 39: Custer State Park
    Wildlife Loop, Iron Mountain Road, Mt. Rushmore NM, Badlands
    NP, Wall Drug
Day 40: Custer State Park to Cheyenne, WY
    Wind Cave NP, Prairie Dog town, Eastern Wyoming
Day 41: Cheyenne, WY to Denver, CO
Day 42: Denver, CO to Belmar, NJ

Appendix IV
A FEW MORE PHOTOS

Many Glacier hike

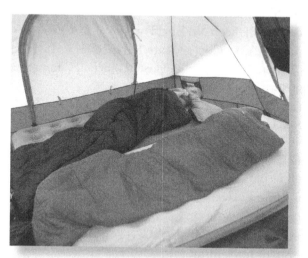

Sleeping late

Monument Valley Hoodoos

Mesa Verde campfire

Olympic river respite

Yosemite's Lukens Lake

Cody Night Rodeo

Dawn breaking over the mountains

Firefighting hero

Sneaking tech at Grand Canyon

Glacier ram

Redwoods reach

Yellowstone's Grand Canyon

Crazy Horse performers

Mesa Verde petroglyphs

Snow good in Glacier

Crater Lake

" *"Life is not measured by the number of breaths we take, but by the moments that take our breath away."* **"**

Maya Angelou

ABOUT THE AUTHOR: BEING MERRY

As a kid, Merry Brennan dreamed of a grown-up life writing books and making art. Then she got sidetracked – as a journalist, activist, columnist, naturalist, communications consultant, adjunct professor, and elected official. But she finally returned to her story-telling roots and couldn't be Merrier! Along with *Eye Rolls and Awe: A National Park Road Trip with Teens*, she authored the middle-grade biographical novel, *Peace Pilgrim: walking her talk against hate*. Her photographic and digital creations have been featured in many shows, shops, and publications. You can see her artwork at www. EarthwaysArt.com. The long-time Jersey Shore resident is always up for a good hike, sail or paddle; never turns down time with family; and looks forward to full moon meditations. She and her musician husband, Tom, have three terrific children, Ciarán, Aislínn and Sean.

30000000021090

Made in the USA
Middletown, DE
14 January 2021

978.

31542515R00205